The
Gardener's
Companion

The
Gardener's
Companion

Christopher Brickell

•

in Association with
The Royal Horticultural Society

American Editor: *John Elsley*

CROWN PUBLISHERS, INC.
NEW YORK

The Gardener's Companion
Christopher Brickell

Originally published in Great Britain in 1995
A DBP book, created and designed
by Duncan Baird Publishers
Sixth Floor, Castle House
75/76 Wells Street, London W1P 3RE

Published by Crown Publishers, Inc., 201 East 50th Street, New
York, New York 10022.
Member of the Crown Publishing Group

Random House, Inc. New York, Toronto, London, Sydney, Auckland

CROWN is a trademark of Crown Publishers, Inc.

Library of Congress Cataloging-in-Publication Data

Brickell, Christopher.
[Christopher Brickell's garden plants]
The gardener's companion/Christopher Brickell.—1st American ed.
p. cm.
Originally published: Christopher Brickell's garden plants. London
Duncan Baird Publishers, 1995.
Includes bibliographical references (p.) and index.
I. plants, Ornamental. 2. Plants, Ornamental—Pictorial works
I. Title
SB407.B675 1995
635.9—dc20
94-7892
CIP

ISBN 0-517-59934-1

10 9 8 7 6 5 4 3 2 1
First American Edition
Printed in China

CONTENTS

INTRODUCING THIS BOOK 6

THE PLANT SELECTOR

TREES 10

SHRUBS 30

INTRODUCING THIS BOOK

PREFACE BY THE AMERICAN EDITOR

Christopher Brickell is undoubtedly one of the most respected personalities in today's world of ornamental horticulture. His professional achievements are legendary; and an encyclopedic knowledge of plants from both a botanical and a horticultural standpoint has resulted in a worldwide demand for his services as a consultant and a lecturer. This new book, the first since his official retirement from The Royal Horticultural Society, is uniquely personal in nature – a book written "from the heart."

It has been my privilege to have known Chris since my appointment, under his Directorship, as Botanist to The RHS at the Society's garden in Wisley, some 30 years ago. His lifelong involvement with plants, combined with his extensive travels and his connections with gardeners worldwide, help to make this a book of wide appeal and lasting value.

Chris' numerous visits to North America have given him first-hand knowledge of both the unique opportunities and the limitations that govern the range of plants we can successfully grow in our gardens, in our widely differing climate zones. His selection in this book includes many established favorites with American gardeners (and many widely available North American native species), while at the same time we are challenged to expand our gardening repertoire with a diverse range of less familiar and recently introduced subjects. I fully endorse his championship of such plants as *Rosa* 'Graham Thomas', clones of *Mahonia x media*, *Scabiosa* 'Butterfly Blue' and *Crocus goulimyi*, subjects all worthy of becoming future "classics" in North American gardens.

It is an honor and a privilege for me to be associated with this highly informative, enjoyable and inspiring publication – a work I can enthusiastically recommend to all North American gardeners who profess a love and appreciation of the finest in ornamental plants.

John Elsley, *Vice-President, Wayside Gardens, Greenwood, South Carolina*
(Note: climate zones are specified in the plant entries where appropriate: see page 223.)

INTRODUCTION BY THE AUTHOR

Although I have spent a lifetime studying and growing plants, their fascination is endless, since there is always something new to learn or discover. Plant-hunters have combed the globe, and novelties are still being brought from the wild, but it is not always necessary to seek the unusual in remote parts of the world. Chance seedlings can crop up anywhere, and the keen-eyed gardener is always on the look-out for exciting new forms, while skilled amateur and professional plant breeders are continually striving to produce desirable new selections with which we can enhance our gardens.

Of course, such new input is partly offset by losses. There is a continual but significant loss of plants from our individual gardens: my own "dead label" collection bears testament to this! But most of such losses are replaceable and, although sad, are not tragic. It is the complete disappearance of horticulturally valuable plants that is tragic, and it is this that has prompted the emergence of the conservation bodies, whose activities I fully endorse. Indiscriminate collecting has threatened some wild plants, and we must all be on our guard against this. In some cases, however, our responsibility is to be the guardians of rare species until such time as they can be re-introduced into the wild. The Mexican *Cosmos atrosanguineus* is a good example, regarded as extinct in the wild but, as a result of concern and skilled propagation, now relatively widespread in gardens. Some plants, especially named garden selections, are lost because of confusion over identity and nomenclature, and a considerable part of my career has been taken up with such important matters. The trials at The Royal Horticultural Society's garden at Wisley in Surrey are not only concerned with the assessment of the garden value (the Award of Garden Merit) of a wide range of subjects, but also play a great part in trying to "sort out" the all too frequently tangled webs of cultivar names. Without a system of nomenclature we could not communicate about the plants we love.

I have been fortunate in my life among plants to have met many great gardeners. Some of them, or their gardens, are mentioned in the following pages, and in some instances have provided a strong motive for the choice of subject. Besides the intrinsic beauty of any plant, there is great delight in the associations it may evoke, sometimes of a personal, nostalgic nature. Botanical and gardening books are another love of mine, and the sight of some plants recaptures for me the lyrical descriptions of great plant-hunters such as Reginald Farrer and Ernest Henry Wilson.

Some of us, like these intrepid explorers, have felt the call of the wild to see plants in their native habitats, so their presence in our gardens also conjures up evocative memories. The sight of erythroniums in our Sussex garden, one of them named after my wife Jeanette, leads to thoughts of Californian woodlands where I saw some of the wild species many years ago. A summer display of *Convolvulus althaeoides,* sprawling over a sunny bank, reminds me of plant-hunting expeditions to Greece, where this delightful bindweed swathes the classical ruins. But fondness for a particular plant is sometimes inspired by scenes nearer home. A pot of *Cyrtanthus elatus* is likely to remind me of the windowsill of the Botany Department at Wisley, crammed with samples sent in for identification.

To select a list of favorites from the vast array of garden plants is extremely difficult, and if this book had been five times as long there would still have been painful omissions. Inevitably, then, this is a cross-section, chosen for a variety of reasons: some are plants of exceptional quality that are special favorites, others are plants which I would like to see promoted and made more readily available. There is nothing like a little exposure in a book to encourage nurserymen to obtain and propagate a plant! The main entries are given a fairly lengthy treatment, but in order to squeeze in a few more favourites I have mentioned others briefly at the ends of sections. The entries are categorized firstly into broad groups (trees, shrubs, and so on), and then according to flowering season within each group. Of course, all these categories are more fluid than they appear and must not be taken as clear-cut. The locality of any particular garden, and indeed even the microclimates within that garden, will affect the flowering time and perhaps the hardiness of some plants. But this is the fun of gardening: there are few hard-and-fast rules and one is always learning!

Christopher Brickell, November 1994

Blue-grey *Hosta sieboldii* 'Elegans' in a mixed border: a classic foliage plant (see page 129)

THE PLANT SELECTOR

TREES

Trees are like heirlooms: most gardeners inherit them, and value their maturity, as well as their contribution of a permanent framework to the garden, and often a great deal of privacy. However, even gardeners with a number of well-established trees should not be deterred from planting some new ones if there is a positive reason for doing so, coupled with sufficient space.

The scale of most gardens rules out many of the true forest trees, but there is often plenty of scope for smaller trees, and in many cases it will be best to opt for branched-head standards, because it is easier to plant around them. In the chapter that follows I have shamelessly selected some trees that require more space that many suburban gardens will allow, but plenty of medium and small trees are recommended here as well.

When planting new trees it is important to be aware of the dangers of positioning them too close to buildings. A tree can bring unwanted shade, or can undermine foundations, or can suck up moisture from beneath the house and cause a subsidence problem: willows have an almost uncanny ability to divine water, and are notorious for infiltrating drains.

If space is limited, trees that have some decorative value all year round – or at least in more than one season – are often the best choice. Evergreens might seem to be the most obvious candidates, and there are three evergreen conifers that I recommend under "Two or more seasons", but in the pages that follow I cannot disguise my greater attachment to deciduous trees, for their variety, their beauty and their seasonal rhythms.

SPRING

For some it is the bright greens of budding leaves that truly mark the arrival of spring, but others, myself among them, delight more in the promise that early blossom brings.

The magnolias' almost sculptural white or pink flowers make such a dramatic start to the new season that the relative insignificance of their later performance is easily forgiven. *Embothrium coccineum* 'Norquinco Valley' makes a fine show with its scarlet blooms, and the extraordinary graft hybrid +*Laburnocytisus adamii* is worth considering as a specimen tree for its three different types and colors of flower, all on the one plant.

For foliage, my selection is the splendid *Acer pseudoplatanus* 'Brilliantissimum,' with pink-orange leaves that turn through yellowish white to green.

FLOWERS OR FOLIAGE

Embothrium coccineum 'Norquinco Valley' (Proteaceae) (9A–10B*)

The evergreen Chilean Fire Bush, or Chilean Fire Tree, is one of the most spectacular spring-flowering trees that can be grown in certain West Coast areas, although it is an extremely variable species, and only the semievergreen, narrow-leaved form known as var. *lanceolatum* can withstand the worst winters.

'Norquinco Valley' is a selection of this variety raised from seed collected in Argentina in 1926 at a relatively high altitude and in drier, cooler conditions than its Chilean counterparts, which often inhabit the somewhat milder climatic areas of the Pacific coast. This clone is a magnificent plant when in full bloom, its branches wreathed in light scarlet pincushions made up of the individual tubular blooms, each with four reflexed segments and protruding styles, and differs from other cultivated forms in the extraordinary density of the flower clusters along the branches as well as its semievergreen habit.

Embothrium coccineum in all its forms requires a lime-free soil, moist but sharply drained, and well enriched with leafmold. It should preferably be grown in thin woodland, where it receives ample light and shelter from the wind. Once happily established, *E. coccineum* will sucker freely and develops into large thickets of upright stems, clothed in dark green, glossy leaves that reach 30ft (10m) or more in mild climates. In sheltered gardens in the San Francisco bay region, it is an unforgettable sight when at its brilliant best in late spring, the floral fireworks lasting for several weeks before fading to produce the woody fruits with their winged seeds. Seed (not always freely produced in cultivation), suckers (best potted up to establish prior to replanting), and occasionally root cuttings are the best methods of propagation.

Although the broader-leaved forms are less reliably hardy than 'Norquinco Valley,' any variation of this species is well worth growing where conditions allow.

+*Laburnocytisus adamii* (Leguminosae) (5B–7B)

This unusual graft hybrid (the plus sign indicating its derivation) is regarded by gardeners either as an odd but interesting freak, or as an ornamental notable for its ability to develop three different flower types. I fall into the latter category and enjoy the typical blooms of the yellow *Laburnum anagyroides* and the purple of the low-growing *Cytisus purpureus* as well as the intermediate, coppery pink and yellow clusters of blooms derived from the fused chimeral tissues, all on the same plant.

Inadvertently raised in 1825 by a French nurseryman who grafted the *Cytisus* on to the *Laburnum* and obtained a plant with coppery pink and yellow flowers, it was later found to produce flowering shoots of both parents. A cross-section of the stem of +*Laburnocytisus adamii* shows that there is an outer core of tissue of one parent and an inner core of the other, with fused tissue in between that provides the third flower type.

Similar to *L. anagyroides* in general character, this graft hybrid blooms in late spring and is a fascinating small tree of some 25ft (8m) in height that will thrive in any well-drained soil and provides a most unusual lawn specimen or focal point at the back of a shrub border. The three flower types are not produced together regularly or in any particular part of the tree each year, but when they do it is, to my eyes at least, a most attractive sight, with the pendent racemes of the laburnum contrasting with the rather stiff, congested flower clusters of the broom, and the dense 6in (15cm) racemes of the intermediate graft hybrid.

Propagation true to type is achieved by grafting scions taken from the graft hybrid onto a laburnum stock, making certain, of course, that suckers from the stock do not overwhelm the young grafted specimen.

Magnolia x *loebneri* 'Merrill' (Magnoliaceae)
(4A–8B)

I would venture to suggest that most magnolia fanciers regard this hybrid of *Magnolia kobus* and *M. stellata* as among the best of the smaller, deciduous, tree magnolias, with its compact but erect, densely branched habit, eventually reaching a height of 25 to 30ft (8–10m).

It flowers before the foliage develops, in midspring, when even young plants are covered in the upright, pure white blooms, subglobular, like an electric light bulb in bud and opening to reveal the thick petals surrounding peachy pink stamens and green central carpels. Each petal (strictly a tepal or perianth segment) is obovate in shape, about 2½ to 3in (6–8cm) long, and each of the freely borne blooms measures up to 4 or 5in (10–12cm) across when fully expanded. In character, it is like a vastly improved *M. stellata*, taller, with less congested growths, and with a lesser number, up to fifteen, of beautiful glistening petals of the utmost purity. Although inevitably damaged by severe frosts, the petals are remarkably resistant to cold weather and remain in reasonable condition even if midspring is unkind. The neat, matt green, obovate leaves are pleasant but undistinguished, and make excellent hosts for light-foliaged hybrids of *Clematis texensis* and *C. viticella* that are pruned to ground level each spring.

'Merrill' is widely available, being readily propagated from soft or semiripe cuttings of new growth rather than by grafting or chip-budding, techniques used for species and hybrids that do not root readily or grow well from cuttings. Many clones of this outstanding hybrid are well worth growing if room is available because they will flourish in a wide range of soil types,

FLOWERING AGE OF MAGNOLIAS

A young tree magnolia may not flower for twenty years or more. Careful selection of species or cultivars is essential if gardeners want to avoid this long wait to see their magnolia in bloom.

If flower production of similar grandeur to the splendid *Magnolia campbellii* (shown below) is the main requirement, one of its relatives or offspring, such as ssp. *mollicomata* or the hybrid 'Charles Raffill,' should bloom in about twelve years. A grafted or cutting-raised specimen of 'Star Wars' (*M. campbellii* x *M. liliiflora*) normally reaches flowering age in five or six years. Even *M. campbellii* may flower within ten years if grown in containers, root-bound and with a high potassium balanced diet.

acidic or alkaline, light or heavy, but are intolerant of wet, ill-drained conditions. If I could choose only one other clone of *M.* x *loebneri* parentage, it would be 'Leonard Messel,' which usually has ten to twelve narrower petals of lesser substance but with a soft lilac-pink color, the deeper-colored buds recurving like pink stars as they open.

Related plants The magnificent Himalayan *Magnolia campbellii* (7B–9B) must rank as one of the most beautiful of all deciduous trees, reaching over 100ft (30m) in the wild but more normally seen in gardens at between 40 and 70ft (12–21m) high. It blooms in late winter and early spring in many mild gardens on the West Coast and elsewhere, its deep purple-crimson, pink or white gobletlike flowers at least 9 or 10in (23–25cm) across covering every branch in a good season.

Although *M. campbellii* is unlikely to bloom at an early age, specimens of the slightly later-flowering subsp. *mollicomata* are often quicker to come into flower from seed. Because they can be rather variable in flower color, it is always better to empty your pockets and purchase a grafted, named clone such as 'Lanarth,'

Magnolia x *loebneri* 'Merrill'

'Kew's Surprise,' or 'Princess Margaret,' and patiently admire the handsome leaves until the first blooms open, frost-willing, when you will forget all about the foliage.

Magnolia 'Norman Gould' (4A–8A), named after my predecessor as botanist at Wisley, occurred among a number of seedlings of colchicine-treated seed raised at the garden. It was selected by Frank Knight, then Director, and myself as the best of the batch because it bore from an early age masses of snow-white flowers 4 to 6in (10–15cm) across with broad petals of fine substance that have a tendency to recurve near the apex. Unusually it was considered for an award at Wisley and received a First Class Certificate in April 1967. Readily raised from cuttings, 'Norman Gould' is a slow-growing, small tree reaching some 20ft (6m) after fifteen years, although flowering profusely from an early age.

Magnolia wilsonii (6A–9A) is distinguished by its superb, pendent, white, cup-shaped, fragrant flowers over 4in (10cm) across with a delightful purple-red boss of stamens, borne in early summer and sometimes providing a lesser second crop in late summer. A deciduous small tree or large shrub of some 20ft (6m) or more, *M. wilsonii* also has an attractive, spreading habit and fine foliage. It is readily raised from seed and grows in any well-drained soil that is not markedly alkaline, yet it is surprisingly uncommon in gardens. It occurs wild in Sichuan and Yunnan in China.

OTHER PLANTS

Acer pseudoplatanus 'Brilliantissimum' (Aceraceae) (5A–7A)

The common sycamore, *Acer pseudoplatanus*, although a magnificent deciduous tree valuable for exposed sites, is often regarded as a weed species because it spreads its seedlings to the eventual detriment of other plants. Some of its cultivars, however, are of outstanding garden value, and among these is the beautiful 'Brilliantissimum,' a foliage plant of great attraction in spring and early summer. Slow growing and very rarely more than 20 or 25ft (6–8m) high when mature, it produces shrimp-pink, orange-suffused young foliage in spring that gradually turns to pale yellowish-white and then to pale green as the season advances. The similar 'Prinz Handjery' (which often produces seedlings with very similarly colored foliage) is more robust, with the reverse of the leaves purple. A fine tree for small gardens, 'Brilliantissimum' is an excellent specimen tree or may be grown at the back of the shrub border, where, once its six to eight week display is over, it will fade into the background until the following spring. Some shade is required in American gardens.

SUMMER

After the blossoms and leaf buds of spring, summer trees take on their mature canopy of foliage, which can often be a positive joy in itself, rather than merely a restful backdrop to better and brighter things. The selection here is a personal miscellany of fine ornamental trees whose striking beauty would make any garden distinctive. My choice of willow, *Salix alba* var. *sericea*, is outstanding as a specimen tree, but is not for the small garden. For those with restricted space but plenty of sun, who are looking for a beautiful, easy-going tree, I would suggest *Genista aetnensis*, the Mount Etna Broom, for its sweet-scented, bright-yellow flowers and elegantly trailing branches. The variegated clone of *Quercus cerris* (the Turkey Oak) and *Cercis canadensis* 'Forest Pansy' also have excellent foliage.

FLOWERS

Genista aetnensis (Leguminosae) (6B–9B)

The Mount Etna Broom, *Genista aetnensis*, is surprisingly hardy in view of its Sicilian and Sardinian origin, and has been grown very successfully in many areas of Britain and the less humid areas of the West Coast, withstanding 5°F (–15°C). It is a plant of great beauty when mature and in full bloom during midsummer, its weeping, rushlike branches beset with numerous small, pealike flowers of bright yellow. Add to this the delicate, honeyed perfume of the flowers and the overall effect at other times of year of its slender, long, weeping trails of bright green branches, uncluttered with foliage apart from a very few narrow leaves, and you have one of the most attractive trees available for small gardens. The fine structure of its branchlets contrasts markedly with that of the vast majority of other trees and shrubs we are able to grow, and *G. aetnensis*, given sharp drainage and an open sunny site, will provide year-round pleasure with very little trouble.

It is best to select a single stem at a very early stage and train this to a strong cane to encourage its naturally upright habit in its youth and to ensure that a stout, central leader is developed. Removal of any shoot competing with the leader is important at this stage, but once its dominance has been established the natural growth habit should be allowed to develop more or less unchecked, apart from very minor pruning to balance the framework or to remove dead twigs or damaged shoots. The initially spreading branchlets gradually become pendent as the main stem gains height, eventually providing the year-round waterfall of light green and summer gold that makes *G. aetnensis* such a conspicuous and beautiful plant. Evergreen cuttings of the young shoots taken in summer or more mature material taken in autumn will root well and provide a ready means of increasing, as does seed, this most deserving recipient of the Royal Horticultural Society Award of Garden Merit.

Genista aetnensis

FOLIAGE

Cercis canadensis 'Forest Pansy' (Leguminosae) (4A–9B)

Although a much-treasured and very beautiful ornamental in the eastern and central United States where it occurs naturally, often in woodlands, the small tree or large shrub commonly and aptly known as the Redbud seldom blooms well in Britain. This is a pity, because many fine clones have been selected, none of which, apart from the recently introduced 'Forest Pansy,' impinges much on the European gardening scene.

I first saw this striking clone of *Cercis canadensis* some fifteen years ago, with the sun behind adding a translucency to the deep purple-red foliage that made the whole plant glow. At the time, it was only at the propagation stage, so plants were not available and relatively untried in Britain, although the specimen at the Arboretum was in robust health and was one of the finest foliage plants I had seen. Now that it has been growing happily in my own garden for four years and is over 5ft (1.5m) tall and as much across, I have had no cause to change my mind because each season its performance gets better and better. I suspect if it did bloom I would find the rosy-red pea-flowers a disagreeable contrast with the foliage, but that judgment may have to wait some years.

The broadly heart-shaped leaves, eventually 3 to 5in (8–12cm) long, are initially slightly shiny and dark rosy-purple on their upper surfaces, gradually losing

Cercis canadensis 'Forest Pansy'

the purple coloration along the veins above, but usually remaining purple-bronze otherwise. The undersurface retains its rosy-purple coloring, as do the leaf stalks and darker young twigs. A noticeable feature is the set of the leaf blades, which are horizontally disposed in relation to the leaf stalks, rather like a hand bent back from the forearm.

Because *C. canadensis* may eventually reach 30 to 40ft (10–12m) in height, it is possible that 'Forest Pansy' – its uninspiring name being the only drawback – may achieve a similar size. Even if it does not, it has established its credentials as one of the finest foliage plants introduced in recent years, and is not difficult to grow in reasonably fertile, moisture-retentive but well-drained soil in an open location – shade will result in a loss of leaf color by midsummer.

Quercus cerris 'Argenteovariegata' (Fagaceae) (6A–7B)

Among many oaks of great ornamental value, this variegated form of the Turkey oak, a deciduous species widespread in southern and central Europe and European Turkey, and well adapted to eastern and midwestern regions, makes a most effective specimen tree with its lobed foliage variably, but very noticeably, bordered creamy white. A handsome, spreading, broad-crowned tree when mature, *Quercus cerris* is distinguished by the long, whiskery, grayish stipules on the winter buds and the mossy-cupped small acorns. The foliage is rather similar to that of the common English Oak but harder-textured and dark, shining green, with the tips of the angular leaf lobes often somewhat sharper. This variegated clone (sometimes listed as 'Variegata') has been growing at Wisley for well over 100 years, planted before the garden came to The Royal Horticultural Society in 1903. It flourishes still in the dry, sandy soil, although no more than 30ft (10m) high, its head a spreading mushroom of dark green and creamy white for more than six months of the year.

Propagated only by grafting, preferably onto *Q. cerris* stock, there is always the possibility of some reversion to the green-leaved form. Once or twice a year, the effort then has to be made to cut out all the green-leaved, reverted shoots, which are stronger than their colored counterparts. The tree would soon return to its verdant state if this was not carried out regularly, but the effort is certainly worth it to maintain this fine tree that lightens the landscape with its cool and attractive leaf coloring and patterns.

Salix alba var. *sericea* (Salicaceae) (3B–8B)

In Britain the White Willow, *Salix alba*, is one of the most familiar of native trees, erect in growth and graceful in habit with the branches frequently pendulous at the tips, in leaf a shimmering silvered-green that makes it strikingly conspicuous in the landscape. A very variable deciduous tree, which can reach a height of 80ft (25m) or more when fully developed, *S. alba* has obligingly produced a hybrid to satisfy the British passion for cricket. This is the slender-crowned 'Caerulea,' sometimes called the Blue Willow, but more frequently known as the Cricket-bat Willow, in its own right a most ornamental foliage plant with silky leaves, blue-gray beneath, and much valued for making cricket bats.

Undoubtedly the finest variant of *S. alba*, however, is var. *sericea* (also known aptly as forma *argentea*), pyramidal in habit to 50ft (15m) in height, and from a distance appearing as a slender dome of silvered-white,

Salix alba var. *sericea*

the narrow silver-haired leaves shining with an intensity that makes them appear almost white even on relatively dull days.

Scarcely a tree for the small garden, *S. alba* var. *sericea* nonetheless makes a marvelous, relatively slow-growing specimen plant, and from the spring emergence of its fine foliage remains a constant pleasure until the leaves, that remain silver throughout, gradually turn to yellow as they fall in late autumn. Even then the silhouette and graceful structure of its bare branches remain attractive until submerged in new silver clothes as spring returns.

All forms of *S. alba* may be used not only as ornamentals but also for windbreaks in large sites and, because they root readily from hardwood cuttings and flourish in moist as well as well-drained sites, they are among the most adaptable as well as the most beautiful of trees, with var. *sericea* outstanding, in my view, in a very high-quality field.

AUTUMN

It is the variety of foliage color, in fiery shades of red, yellow, orange, and even purple, that makes the brilliant display of deciduous trees in autumn so welcome. The precise permutation of hues, and the timing of their appearance, are never quite predictable, as they depend on numerous complex factors (see p.20). Moreover, leaf colors vary not only from species to species, but sometimes between individuals of a species. This has allowed horticulturists to select individual clones that may be relied upon to give consistent autumn color each season provided that the climatic conditions are favorable.

The reliability of *Acer rubrum*'s long-lasting autumn coloring is one of its most valuable attributes, and I favor 'October Glory' above all others; the species also has attractive flowers in spring. My other recommendations in this section include *Nyssa sylvatica* and *Cercidiphyllum japonicum*.

FOLIAGE

Acer rubrum 'October Glory'

Acer rubrum 'October Glory' (Aceraceae) (3B–9A)

Cultivated in Britain since 1656, *Acer rubrum*, the eastern North American Red Maple, has long been valued as one of the most reliable of autumn coloring trees, producing a magnificent display of bright scarlet, orange or yellow foliage in midautumn or sometimes later. An open-crowned, fairly upright tree, it will eventually reach more than 70ft (21m) in height in European gardens and arboreta, but often achieves well over 100ft (30m) in the wild.

Acer rubrum is also attractive in early and mid-spring, before the opposite pairs of dark green, three- to five-lobed leaves with glaucous undersurfaces appear, and when the red clusters of flowers are produced on the previous year's wood. They create a red haze along the branches for two or three weeks before the reddish, upright-winged fruits develop in early summer. In America, all forms of *A. rubrum* appreciate moist, slightly acidic soils. They will grow, albeit slowly, on drier, more alkaline soils, but seldom color as well.

Well over forty clones of the red maple have been selected for their horticultural characteristics, but none, to my mind, has surpassed 'October Glory,' its foliage turning in midautumn from rich crimson to a glowing orange-red and remaining in beauty for some three or four weeks unless blasted by severe gales.

Relatively upright and vigorous, it is likely to achieve 50ft (15m) or more, but will take some years to do so. Somewhat less vigorous and with similar attributes are 'Red Sunset;' the older 'Schlesingeri,' with autumn color of bright, deep red; and the columnar 'Scanlon,' which turns to an upright pillar of red purple and orange-red, an ideal tree for smaller gardens by virtue of its limited ultimate width of 6 to 8ft (2–2.5m).

Acer saccharinum (Aceraceae) (3B–9A)

One of the most graceful of all trees, *Acer saccharinum*, the Silver Maple (not to be confused with the Sugar Maple, *A. saccharum*), has been one of my favorite trees since I saw it for the first time at Wisley forty years ago. Two magnificent trees, well over 60ft (20m) tall, open-habited with graceful, pendulous branches and opposite pairs of deeply lobed leaves, exhibiting their silver undersides in the slightest breeze, were then growing in the Wisley pinetum. Sadly one was lost in the 1987 storms, but the memory of their elegance, movement, and autumn color remains.

Its eventual size precludes *A. saccharinum* from wide garden cultivation in Europe, while in the United States it is the fastest-growing maple, but is often unappreciated as a cultivated plant because its somewhat brittle branchlets and extensive, fibrous root system make it unsuitable as a street tree. It is, however, one of the best trees for poor soil.

Cercidiphyllum japonicum (Cercidiphyllaceae) (5A–8B)

Sniff the smell of burnt sugar or toffee in a garden on a damp autumn day and you must be in the vicinity of *Cercidiphyllum japonicum*, one of the most beautiful of eastern Asian trees and found wild in Japan and China.

Easily grown in any reasonably fertile soil, but preferring humus-rich, moist conditions, *C. japonicum* is a quick-growing species that often forms a multi-stemmed specimen 50ft (15m) tall or more. It may also be encouraged to develop a single main stem from which the long, initially upright, later arching and pendulous branches develop to form an elegant tree of broadly conical shape. The matt, sea-green leaves, glaucous below, are borne in opposite pairs, well spaced

Cercidiphyllum japonicum

along the branches on their long, pinkish-red petioles. The emerging foliage is an attractive coppery-pink and, although in some seasons it may be frosted, after a week or two fresh foliage appears and subsequent growth appears unaffected in my garden. Originally planted as a 5ft (1.5m) specimen, in six years it has reached 16ft (5m), which gives an idea of its growth rate in a fairly fertile soil. Much of the crown is also now high enough to be unaffected by ground frosts in early spring.

While *C. japonicum* is a fine foliage plant throughout its leafing period, it is valued particularly for its autumn color, which varies considerably in seedlings, from pale yellow through orange to dark red and smoky purple, some slightly disappointingly only developing a purplish overlay to the green foliage before falling. This mix is extraordinarily attractive, enhanced by the evocative scent of caramelized sugar that emanates from the coloring leaves, but is lost soon after they fall.

Liquidambar styraciflua (Hamamelidaceae) (6A–7B)

The American Sweet Gum, *Liquidambar styraciflua*, occurs in the eastern United States and Guatemala in moist, sometimes swampy, areas, but in cultivation seems content with fairly ordinary garden soils, preferring those rich in leafmold, but it is unsuitable for dry, alkaline conditions. It is a very handsome deciduous tree, even in winter, with its gray, fissured, sometimes corky bark and rough-winged branchlets, and later its maplelike, alternately placed, glossy, dark green leaves, but it is in autumn that it comes into its own.

As the days shorten, the foliage of the American Sweet Gum erupts into a bonfire brilliance of claret red, crimson, and orange. *L. styraciflua* varies considerably in the quality of its coloring, and it is important not to rely on seed-raised plants to color uniformly well but to purchase clones like 'Lane Roberts,' 'Palo Alto,' 'Worplesden,' and 'Rotundiloba' – which does not produce the undesirable fruits – or to pick out plants from nursery rows in autumn. Remember, too, that it is preferable to plant young trees only 3 or 4ft (1–1.2m) high since they should establish quickly.

A tree of more or less pyramidal habit, *L. styraciflua* will in time reach 60 to 80ft (20–26m) or more, but it is relatively slow growing and may be enjoyed in the garden for many years before a decision needs to be taken on its future. Since it holds onto its autumn foliage for five or six weeks, and even when the leaves have fallen, spreads a colorful carpet of purple, red, orange, and yellow beneath the bare branches, *L. styraciflua* gives amazing value for very little care.

Liquidambar styraciflua

AUTUMN COLOR

The recipe for a fine display of bonfire colors begins with adequate summer rain and a sunny dry autumn with a long period of cool, but not frosty, nights. A sheltered site is important for those species with foliage likely to be damaged by severe winds or frost, and a position in full sun allows the red pigment to develop in plants that, in shade, usually turn only pale orange-yellow.

Most species appear to produce their best tints in moisture-retentive (not waterlogged) soils. A good supply of potassium favors good autumn color, while excess nitrogen, particularly applied in late summer, reduces pigment development.

Nyssa sylvatica (Nyssaceae) (4A–9B)

Like *Liquidambar*, *Nyssa sylvatica*, known as the Black Tupelo or Black Gum, thrives in eastern North America in wet and swampy areas and appreciates similar sites in cultivation. However, it will grow in any fertile, humus-rich soil as well as in sandy to mildly alkaline conditions provided moisture is not lacking. It is reasonably tolerant of pollution and is not averse to areas near the coast.

A deciduous, broadly conical tree seldom more than 50ft (15m) high in cultivation, but to 100ft (30m) in the wild, sometimes with swept-out "skirts" around its base, *N. sylvatica* is grown mainly for the beauty of its autumn tints, but is also handsome in spring and summer with usually shining, deep green, obovate leaves 5in (12cm) or so long. The leaves of some plants are dull-surfaced and lack the burnished sheen that is so attractive both in the young foliage and in the autumn, so it is well worth visiting a number of nurseries to make sure you purchase a plant that satisfies your requirements. Choose young specimens, if possible, as older *Nyssa* do not always settle quickly.

In midautumn, sometimes early autumn, the Black Tupelo will unleash its glorious display, starting quietly as the foliage becomes a mix of green, yellow, and orange before turning scarlet for two to three weeks, usually as *L. styraciflua* takes over its mantle.

TWO OR MORE SEASONS

Deciduous trees with long-lasting ornamental fruits and handsome bark begin to demonstrate their true value as late autumn and winter reveal the garden's skeleton.

If there is space enough, I would recommend *Malus* 'Golden Hornet,' whose white spring blossom ultimately yields a splendid crop of bright yellow crab apples that last throughout the winter months. For smaller gardens, *Betula* 'Silver Shadow' is a good choice – its white bark seeming to sing out in winter after the shimmering spring and summer foliage. *Cornus kousa* var. *chinensis*, a fine deciduous dogwood, is probably unequaled in its repertoire of long-lasting flowers (sometimes followed by fruits), brilliant-red autumn leaves, and fine winter bark.

SPRING OR SUMMER FLOWERS/AUTUMN FOLIAGE

Cornus kousa var. *chinensis* (Cornaceae) (6A–8A)

If I could have but one small tree in my garden, it would almost certainly be this marvelous deciduous dogwood. No more than 25 or 30ft (8–10m) high, *Cornus kousa* is a somewhat variable species found not only in China but also in Korea and Japan, var. *chinensis* being considered to be more open and treelike in its growth than the forms introduced from Japan.

For more than sixty years, there have been some fine specimens of the Chinese plant at Wisley that can be relied on annually to develop their astonishing display of flower heads in early summer. The show continues for well over six weeks because the four large bracts surrounding each tiny knob of greenish flowers expand from green to pure white, sometimes touched cream, and as they age change to pink and eventually brown.

The bracts of each inflorescence are broad and almost overlapping in the best forms, and frequently the great majority of the horizontally placed branches

Cornus kousa var. *chinensis*

Eucryphia glutinosa

of *C. kousa* var. *chinensis* are virtually hidden by the vast quantities of flower heads. In hot summers this extraordinary flowering is normally followed by ornamental, strawberrylike fruits, unfortunately unpalatable. In addition, there is the brilliant, deep red of the autumn foliage and later, when the leaves have fallen, the pleasant, slightly flaking bark on old plants.

Cornus kousa var. *chinensis* is not hard to grow, tolerating the sandy, well-drained soil at Wisley and flourishing in richer, loamy conditions and acidic, well-drained, high organic level soils; its hardiness is undoubted, and it is certainly a plant of extraordinary quality.

Eucryphia glutinosa (Eucryphiaceae) (8A–9B*)
This southern-hemisphere genus of great ornamental value provides a dozen or so species and hybrids cherished not only for their delightful blooms in mid- to late summer but also for their handsome foliage.

Eucryphia glutinosa is evergreen in its native Chile, yet its successful cultivation in North America is restricted to the West Coast and it must be grown in acidic soil to thrive. It is not always easy to establish or transplant. It has pinnate leaves with three to five shining, dark green leaflets that color burnished-orange and red in autumn. A small, spreading, bushy tree to 20ft (6m) or more, suckering at the base, it is often considered the

finest of its race, although there are now several hybrids which might lay claim to that title. The purity of its four-petaled, white, 2–3in (5–8cm) blooms, centered with prominent tufts of yellow-anthered stamens contrasting with the dark green foliage, is, however, difficult to better. Its beautiful autumnal foliage would perhaps be its winning card.

Propagation by layers and less readily by cuttings are the most satisfactory means of increase, although seed is produced in some seasons. Unfortunately quite a number of seed-raised plants have semidouble blooms; avoid them like the plague as they cannot compare with the purity and simplicity of *E. glutinosa*, single-flowered as one assumes nature intended.

Prunus 'Shirotae' (Rosaceae) (6A–7A)
Japanese flowering cherries contribute enormously to the beauty of our gardens in spring, and many also have fine autumn color. The majority form relatively small trees, which are not exacting in their cultivation requirements and grow well in any reasonably fertile, well-drained garden soil, preferably alkaline.

Among a plethora of cultivars, three have particular appeal for me. First among these is 'Shirotae,' also known as 'Mount Fuji,' which forms a spreading, almost flat-topped tree of some 15ft (4.5m) in height, often spreading to over 30ft (10m) across when mature with the branchlets arching at the tips. It produces fragrant, pendulous, dazzling white, semidouble (occasionally single) 2in (5cm) blooms in great profusion in midspring. As they fade, the fresh, pale green, long-tipped leaves appear, adding to the garden value of 'Shirotae' with their vivid yellow autumn coloration. It is best grown as a standard, if possible on a 5 or 6ft (1.5–2m) stem, to balance the spreading crown.

Equally fine is the cherry long known to me as 'Shogetsu' or 'Shimidsu,' but now called 'Okumiyako.' It is a most distinctive tree, eventually perhaps 15ft

Prunus 'Shirotae'

(4.5m) high and as much across, of rounded, bushy habit with the outer branches on mature trees gently weeping. Later flowering than 'Shirotae,' it produces its graceful, pendulous, pink-budded, then pure white, semidouble flowers in late spring. The effect is enhanced by the frilled edges of the petals and the 5–6in (12–15cm) flower stems as the bunches of up to six blooms sway gently in the wind. With its bronze-tinted young foliage unfolding as the flowers appear and turning red and gold in autumn, 'Okumiyako' ranks highly in my list of garden indispensables.

'Shirofugen' makes a fine companion for 'Okumiyako,' having a similar flowering period but with large, double blooms that open pink, turn white, and eventually change to purplish-pink before the petals fall. The foliage, bronze initially, expands fully with the flowers, producing a mellifluous combination of copper-bronze and pink over a period of several weeks, later producing autumnal tints of orange and copper-bronze to add to its attractions. More vigorous than 'Okumiyako,' reaching 25ft (8m) more in height, 'Shirofugen' develops into a wide-spreading but fairly upright tree, with the arching lower branches showing off to perfection the long-stalked, pendulous cluster of blooms.

OTHER PLANTS

Oxydendrum arboreum (Ericaceae) (5A–9A)

The Sorrel Tree, *Oxydendrum arboreum*, from eastern North America, is appreciated not only for its red and yellow autumn foliage but also for its white, urn-shaped flowers borne in late summer and autumn. *Oxydendrum* will not withstand alkalinity, requiring moist, humus-rich, acidic conditions in which it develops slowly, seldom reaching more than 30ft (10m) tall. Mature specimens are also attractive in winter, with their sinuous, gray-buff branches.

Prunus 'Kursar' (Rosaceae) (6B–9A)

Among the earliest flowering of the ornamental cherries are two superb hybrids, both ideal small-garden plants. 'Kursar' is a 15ft (4.5m) tree of vigorous, upright then later spreading growth, with beautiful single blooms, the rounded petals a dark cerise-pink with dark red calyces. It flowers in abundance in early spring, then toward midautumn the foliage turns orange-red for several weeks before falling. 'Okame' (6B–9A) is similar in habit and is useful to carry on the cherry season after 'Kursar,' usually blooming in midspring, with frilly-edged, shell-pink flowers and maroon-red calyces.

FLOWERS IN SPRING/FRUIT

Malus 'Golden Hornet' (Rosaceae) (4A–8A)

From the huge numbers of ornamental crab apples grown both for their flowers and fruit, *Malus* 'Golden Hornet' ranks very highly with me because its bright yellow fruits stand out on the dullest of winter days. The true plant (there are imposters about) almost certainly has as one parent *M. prunifolia* var. *rinkii*, because it has the curious, fleshy, "stemmed" calyx of this species, which is persistent in the fruit, a characteristic shared with 'Golden Hornet.'

'Golden Hornet' is one of the most decorative of all crab apples, with upright branches that tend to arch downward with age and bear a mass of pure white, typical apple flowers in midspring, followed by regular annual crops of deep yellow, 1in (2.5cm) long, ovoid fruits borne in clusters of two to four and lasting in good condition – unless it succumbs to fire blight, because it is somewhat disease-prone – from midautumn until mid- or even late winter. Its qualities have been recognized by the accolade from The Royal Horticultural Society of the Award of Garden Merit.

For those who may not be able to accommodate a tree of this size – *Malus* 'Golden Hornet' will achieve 30ft (10m) or more in height – the equally ornamental 'Yellow Siberian' and 'Red Siberian' clones of *M.* x *robusta*, with cherrylike, globose, yellow and bright red fruits respectively, provide a very similar effect on a smaller scale.

Sorbus cashmiriana (Rosaceae) (5A–6B)

Few genera provide so many good autumn-fruiting trees for gardens as *Sorbus*. While the brilliant red fruit clusters of *Sorbus aucuparia*, the European Rowan or Mountain Ash, and its allies gain great praise for their autumn splendor, less is heard about the white-fruited, Kashmiri *S. cashmiriana*, which, unfortunately, is still not widely distributed in the United States.

A small, open branched, deciduous tree usually no more than 12 to 15ft (3.5–4.5m) high and as much across, *S. cashmiriana* is hardy and easily grown in moisture-retentive, well-drained conditions, and may also be grown on sandy soils if mulched and irrigated in dry weather. The rich green, pinnate leaves consist of six to nine pairs of leaflets that are gray-green beneath and are well developed by the time the flowers appear in late spring. These are ½in (1–2cm) across, and pink in bud. They remain suffused with pink when they open, and each inflorescence, 6in (15cm) or more across, consists of forty or more upright, cup-shaped flowers held erect on long stalks. As the season advances the large white fruits develop and, once the russet leaves have fallen in midautumn, stand out against the bare, dark-hued branches, pendent clusters of globular, ½in (1–2cm), fleshy, dark-eyed "marbles" that last long into winter, because one of their assets is their lack of interest to birds.

Sorbus cashmiriana comes true from seed, and, with its ease of cultivation, very regular, long-lasting displays of both flower and fruit, and limited stature, rates highly as one of the best of all small-garden trees.

Malus 'Golden Hornet'

Sorbus cashmiriana

FLOWERS OR FRUIT/ FOLIAGE/HABIT

Davidia involucrata (**Davidiaceae**) (**6B–8B**)

A magnificent tree from western Sichuan and western Hubei in China, *Davidia involucrata* has huge, white, delicately veined inflorescence bracts that have given rise to the common names Dove Tree and Hand-kerchief Tree. A mature specimen in full dress is one of the most arresting and lovely sights in gardening.

The true flowers appear as a small green ball of sta-mens flecked with reddish anthers, at the base of the two, long-pointed, white bracts, the lower one 7 to 8in (18–20cm) in length with the upper bract about half its length. They appear in late spring from buds on the previous year's shoots, and remain in condition for sev-eral weeks before falling, leaving the green ball-like fruits, each containing four or five seeds, to develop to their full size of 1in (2.5cm) or more, when they become russet-brown with darker spots and hang like small cannonballs from the leafless growths in autumn.

Seed provides the simplest method of increase, pro-vided the defences of the hard "nuts" can be breached. One method is to bury the fruits shallowly in the soil in autumn. Several seedlings clustered together may then appear in two years' time and will need to be carefully separated and grown on. *Davidia* seeds need to undergo two periods of cold, the initial period allowing the radi-cle to appear, a further cold period, usually after a sec-ond winter, then encouraging shoot production.

A robust tree of over 50ft (15m) with spreading branches, *D. involucrata* and its marginally distinct var. *vilmoriniana* are also valuable as foliage plants, both having handsomely and deeply veined, deep green, ovate leaves, grayish-white beneath in the type, but

Davidia involucrata

almost without hairs beneath in var. *vilmoriniana*. Even out of flower they are statuesque and hardy specimens and woodland trees that may have their early growth clipped by frost but quickly recover and otherwise come to no harm. They tend to perform best in the less humid West Coast climates.

Drimys winteri (**Winteraceae**) (**7B–9B**)

A southern-hemisphere genus of evergreen trees and shrubs related to the magnolias, *Drimys* contains a number of fine garden plants that seldom receive much praise because of a reputation for being tender in cold gardens. This is true of some species, but the tough, dwarf *Drimys winteri* var. *andina* and the much taller but less reliably hardy *D. winteri* var. *chilensis* (also known as var. *latifolia*) are well worth garden space.

While some forms of *D. winteri* will succumb to severe cold, others remain unperturbed by the worst frosts and even if cut back in a really severe winter, re-sprout vigorously from the base the following spring. *D. winteri* var. *andina*, which occurs in the Chilean Andes at an altitude of about 4,000ft (1,200m), never seems to be touched by frost and as a miniature version of var. *chilensis* is ideal for small gardens, flowering freely even when only 1ft (30cm) or so high.

Var. *chilensis* itself is a rapid-growing evergreen with large, lustrous, dark green leaves, oblong-oblance-olate in shape, up to 6in (15cm) or more long and glau-cous beneath, extremely handsome when its strong upright stems 20ft (6m) or more high are densely clothed in foliage, rather like a soft-leaved evergreen magnolia. The flowers, produced from the upper leaf axils in late spring to early summer in cooler areas, are borne in umbellike heads with twenty or more of the yellow-centered, white, 1in (2.5cm), starlike blooms each with nine to eleven petals on reddish stems, with the additional benefit of a very pleasant fragrance. Cuttings root readily, so an annual insurance of a root-ed cutting or two will ensure that you do not lose your stock if a disastrously cold winter occurs.

Paulownia tomentosa (**Scrophulariaceae**) (**5A–9B**)

Paulownia tomentosa, the Empress Tree, or Royal Paulownia, is one of the most beautiful of all deciduous flowering trees that can be grown without protection in Britain. In addition to the large, terminal panicles of purple-blue, fragrant, 2in (5cm) blooms shaped like tubby foxgloves, *Paulownia* has magnificent foliage, opposite pairs of dark green and shallowly lobed leaves, with long petioles and softly hairy leaf blades 1ft (30cm) long, even on older trees. The growth rate is

Paulownia tomentosa

astonishing: a seedling planted at no more than 1ft (30cm) high in my garden reached 7ft (2m) in its first season and continued at a similar rate, so that five years on it is now some 30ft (10m) high and 20ft (6m) across, and providing the shade I required of it.

The rate of growth and capacity to regenerate from the base has led to its use purely as a foliage plant, particularly in colder areas, where flowering seldom occurs. One-year-old plants, cut to ground level or nearly so, will produce a number of vigorous shoots that develop huge leaves, over 2ft (60cm) across, and make an imposing mound of foliage. By rubbing out all but the strongest shoot when they are only 2 or 3in (5–8cm) long, the one stem will often achieve 10ft (3m) in a season, a striking feature with its enormous leaves.

The flower buds are produced at the tips of the branches in late summer or early autumn, but are often injured or killed between 0° and 5°F and do not always survive until late spring, when they would normally open. My own plant has three times produced flower buds, and these all succumbed to frost, but since the crown is now well above ground-frost level I hope within a season or two to see this very fine oriental tree in all its spring magnificence. If not, I am content with its stately habit and the shade of its imposing foliage.

Styrax obassia (Styracaceae) (6A–8B)

The genus *Styrax* provides us with a number of small trees of considerable garden value, most requiring acidic or neutral, lime-free soil. *Styrax officinalis* from eastern Mediterranean countries, source of the fragrant resin storax much used by the Ancients, occurs in alkaline soils and so is an exception, but although attractive, it does not match *S. obassia* from Japan, Korea and northern China and the equally lovely *S. hemsleyana* (6A–8B) from central and western China.

Both species are deciduous small trees 20ft (6m) or so in height and of conical habit with more or less rounded crowns, equally valuable for their fine foliage and their racemes of neat, white, bell-like flowers in early summer. I have a slight preference for *S. obassia* with its larger, more imposing, rounded, velvet-backed leaves and fragrant blooms, borne in 6–8in (15–20cm), spreading, semipendulous racemes, the purity of the white, 1in (2.5cm) flowers set off by the dark calyces and yellow anthers. *S. hemsleyana* has rather shorter, more upright flower sprays, and I have not been able to detect any fragrance, but both have found a place in my garden for their grace and poise, appearing quite happy in humus-rich conditions in partial shade.

Seed is the easiest way to increase these *Styrax*, if obtainable, although growth is fairly slow, and one must wait patiently for their first flowering.

Tilia 'Petiolaris' (Tiliaceae) (6A–7B)

The graceful pendulous habit of this, to me, most attractive of all the lindens makes it one of the most spectacular large deciduous trees. The weeping or pendent Silver Linden, *Tilia* 'Petiolaris,' will grow to over 100ft (30m) in height and, even on the very sandy, dry soil of Wisley on a minimal diet, has reached well over 60ft (18m). Once its 4in (10cm), heart-shaped leaves,

Tilia 'Petiolaris'

dark green above and white-felted beneath, appear in spring it remains attractive right through summer, the silver-backed foliage shimmering in the slightest breeze, to autumn when the foliage turns butter-yellow and falls to leave a golden carpet beneath the canopy. Even in winter, its pendent, elegant branch structure is most effective grown either as a specimen or parkland tree. There is a drawback, however, because the nectar of the sweetly scented flowers is known to be fatal to bumble bees (not hive bees), which fall to the ground in a stupor, yet still eagerly seek its nectar, as they do from the upright European White Linden, *T. tomentosa*, of which 'Petiolaris' is probably only a variant.

OTHER PLANTS

Eucryphia x *nymansensis* 'Nymansay' (Eucryphiaceae) (7A–9B)

Although the evergreen *Eucryphia cordifolia* from Chile is cultivated successfully only in the less humid climates of the West Coast, its hybrid with *E. glutinosa*, *E.* x *nymansensis*, is one of the finest flowering trees available, and is rarely damaged by cold. It arose at Nymans in Sussex, home of another outstanding hybrid, *Camellia* 'Leonard Messel.' *E.* x *nymansensis*, like *E. cordifolia*, grows well on alkaline soils provided they are moist and humus-rich; it also inherits its dark evergreen foliage, an ideal backcloth for the beautiful, pure white, four-petaled, 2 to 3in (5–8cm) wide, cupped flowers with their prominent boss of stamens. These are borne in late summer, and a mature plant of 'Nymansay,' the first clone named, which may reach 50ft (15m) in height after many years, is a breathtaking sight in flower. Easily raised from cuttings, 'Nymansay' is one of the most desirable of evergreens.

Morus nigra (Moraceae) (6B–10A*)

Black Mulberries thrive in warm, loamy, well-drained soil in West Coast areas, sometimes living to a great age (over 300 years in one recorded case) but are less happy in cool climates. The origin of the Black Mulberry is unknown, obscured by its tenure in cultivation in the Orient and Europe over thousands of years.

The gnarled branches and often leaning trunk of old specimens of the Black Mulberry give a pleasant feeling of age. The glossy, coarsely toothed, heart-shaped, rough-surfaced leaves turn a warm yellow in autumn after sheltering the blackberrylike fruits that during summer will have turned from green to dark blackish-red. It is not a plant to sit under in late summer, because the ripe fruits are liable to plop down with no warning, staining any clothing they touch.

EVERGREEN CONIFERS

Abies koreana (Pinaceae) (6A–7A)

Conifers have never featured largely in my gardens, perhaps because of the funereal aspect of so many and the plethora of named clones that are distinguished by minutiae of interest to collectors, but which have insufficient appeal to me to compete for garden space.

That does not, however, mean the banishing of all things coniferous, because there are many that have great ornamental merit as well as a considerable number that are very important structurally in any garden as hedges, screens, and windbreaks.

The genus *Abies*, the silver firs, almost in its entirety, provides ornamental foliage, cones, and distinctive shapes of great value to gardeners. For those who cannot accommodate the very large and extremely attractive species such as *A. grandis* (4A–7A), *A. concolor* (4A–7A) and *A. procera* (6A–7A), there is a suitable alternative in the slow-growing Korean Fir, *A. koreana*.

In the wild, *A. koreana* may reach 50 or 60ft (15–18m) in height, but it does not often exceed 30ft (10m) in cultivation and that only after many years. A less desirable, taller-growing plant is sometimes sold and may turn up from seed, but the neat, compact, pyramidal form is stocked by reliable specialist nurseries. It is densely clothed in dark, glossy green leaves, startlingly white beneath with the added merit of producing, when no more than 3ft (1m) tall, beautiful, upright, young cones, 2 to 3in (5–8cm) long, sitting like so many violet-purple candles on the branches and freely borne sometimes even on smaller plants. Like

Abies koreana

most silver firs, *A. koreana* should be grown in well-drained, moisture-retentive soil, but is more adaptable than some of its larger-growing brethren.

Over a dozen selected clones, vegetatively propagated by grafting, are now offered, one of the most distinctive and attractive being the very slow-growing 'Silberlocke,' in which the leaves twist almost vertically to reveal the gleaming undersurfaces, turning the plant into a patchwork of dark green and silver.

Pinus wallichiana (Pinaceae) (6A–7B)

Although eventually forming a large, broad-headed tree of 90 to 100ft (30m) in cultivation, the Himalayan or Bhutan Pine, *Pinus wallichiana*, is one of several species that are so beautiful they are well worth planting, even if they will one day outgrow the space available.

Easily raised from seed, *P. wallichiana* will grow rapidly, often putting on 2ft (60cm) or more in a season, to form a broadly pyramidal tree, which, if grown as an individual specimen, will retain its spreading lower branches for many years. Set densely with its five-needled groups of long, gray-green, slender, semi-pendulous leaves and bearing its solitary or bunched, pendulous, slightly curved cones up to 10in (25cm) in length at a reasonably early age, it is a most elegant and handsome tree, growing well even on light, sandy soils as well as succeeding in alkaline conditions, although not in limestone, dry gardens.

Equally as attractive is the related *P. ayacahuite* (7A–8B) from Mexico, differing in its hairy, not glabrous, shoots and in other minor characteristics of the cones from its Himalayan relation. Plant either of these species or the hybrid between them, *P.* x *holfordiana*, and you will gain year-round pleasure.

Related plants The Scots Pine, *Pinus sylvestris* (3A–7A), is, in its own right, a most beautiful tree for garden cultivation, particularly used as top cover for woodland plants. With the sun shining through its stems and highlighting the fine red-brown bark above undercover of rhododendrons, it performs a useful as well as ornamental role, well repaying its ground rent.

Among a considerable number of cultivars selected from *P. sylvestris*, one that I find particularly attractive is 'Aurea,' a very slow-growing clone which in summer maintains the normal gray-green, slightly glaucous coloration of the species. As winter approaches it gradually turns to bronzed-yellow and finally to gold, retaining its gilt throughout winter, before returning to its quieter summer garb. It is an ideal plant for small gardens, seldom exceeding 8 to 10ft (2.4–3m) after many years, although larger specimens are known.

Placed among heathers or to act as a focal point in winter, it is a delightful foliage plant that provides a warm glow in the garden on the dullest of winter days.

Tsuga mertensiana (Pinaceae) (6A–7A)

While all the hemlocks are extremely attractive trees of elegant habit, some species, such as *Tsuga canadensis*, the Eastern Hemlock, are particularly valuable as they produce numerous, often slow-growing variants of horticultural merit. It is, however, the beautiful spirelike growth and dense, gray-green foliage of *T. mertensiana*, the Mountain Hemlock, that appeals to me most, partly for its habit and relatively slow growth and partly for its unusual, radially arranged leaves, particularly in those forms in which they are strongly glaucous, giving the tree an overall blue-gray sheen. These seedling variants are grouped under the name forma *glauca* and, although lacking total uniformity, have great garden value.

Although *T. mertensiana*, which occurs wild in mountain areas from southern Alaska to northern California, may reach 80ft (25m) or more in height, it will take many years to do so. Several good specimens at Wisley, the largest now about 30ft (10m) tall, are well over fifty years old, the dry climate of Surrey and the eastern USA being less suited to *T. mertensiana* than parts of Scotland, where its growth is somewhat faster; in the moist conditions of Perthshire a specimen of nearly 100ft (30m) high has been recorded.

Another feature of this species is the size of the cones, which are often 2 to 3in (5–8cm) long, rich purple when young and red-brown once mature. Although a most decorative conifer, *T. mertensiana* is much less frequently seen or grown than it deserves.

Tsuga mertensiana

BARK OR STEMS/FOLIAGE

Betula 'Silver Shadow' (Betulaceae) (6A–7A)

The European White Birch, *Betula pendula*, has a particular appeal in the landscape, the rugged white and black-shadowed bark and the weeping habit of old trees are of great ornamental value both in the wild and in the garden. A number of other species, particularly from the Himalaya, with beautifully textured stems and peeling bark have also gained great popularity with gardeners for the remarkably intense winter effect of their bark and also for their handsomely veined foliage and overall elegance.

One of the loveliest of all the white-stemmed birches is a tree originally distributed as *Betula jacquemontii* (now *B. utilis* var. *jacquemontii*) that has been given the clonal name 'Silver Shadow.' The bark is almost startling in its intensity in winter and contrasts

beautifully with the large, dark green foliage in spring and summer. 'Silver Shadow' is one of several clones selected and now vegetatively propagated that provide pleasure throughout the year from their form, bark characters, and elegant foliage. All are small to medium-sized trees, ultimately likely to reach 50ft (15m) or more in height, but relatively slow growing and excellent for gardens where a single specimen tree is required to act as a focal point at the end of a vista or in a lawn. Among the rivals to 'Silver Shadow' are 'Inverleith,' 'Jermyns,' and 'Grayswood Ghost.'

Eucalyptus pauciflora subsp. niphophila (Myrtaceae) (7B–10B)

Various views exist about the suitability of *Eucalyptus* for gardens, some gardeners considering that they look alien anywhere in the garden landscape, but much depends on how they are placed. Few are totally hardy in most areas of the USA, but in mild areas, especially in California, many species grow well and most survive all but the severest winters. *Eucalyptus pauciflora* subsp. *niphophila*, the Snow Gum, has proved totally hardy and is ideal for small gardens because it seldom exceeds 30ft (10m) in height and has one of the most beautiful barks of any tree, the main stems peeling to reveal a mixture of silver, gray-green, cream, and pale green, sometimes tinted red, that varies through the year. In spring the young branches are initially a shining dark red covered in a glaucous bloom, which is often maintained until the bark begins to flake.

Add to these delights the orange-red growth buds, the shaving-brush tuffets of white flowers in summer,

Eucalyptus pauciflora subsp. *niphophila*

COLD-HARDINESS IN RELATION TO ORIGIN

In plants with a wide geographical range, there is sometimes a "character gradient," whereby botanical characteristics of the species may vary from one end of the range to the other without there necessarily being clear dividing lines between populations. This is known as clinal variation. Particularly important for horticulturists, is the character of hardiness when related to altitude, where populations of a species found at high altitudes are often hardier than those found at lower altitudes. *Eucalyptus niphophila* (meaning snow-loving), which grows in the aptly named Snowy Mountains of southeast Australia, and *E. pauciflora* (illustrated below), which is usually seen at lower altitudes, are generally considered to represent clinal variation of one species.

and the scimitar-shaped, glossy, gray-green, pendent foliage that unfolds green with bronze-red tints, and you have an ornamental of year-round beauty.

Propagated from seed which usually requires a cold period of stratification to germinate freely, the Snow Gum may initially be fairly slow-growing, but soon it begins to grow strongly and, instead of developing a tall, single trunk, may often branch naturally at a low level, forming a multistemmed tree on a short trunk. As with all eucalypts, it is important to plant out young, one- or two-year-old, specimens that have not become rootbound in pots; older pot-grown specimens may not prove root-firm and may be blown out of the ground by strong winds. Although tolerant of almost all well-drained soils, the Snow Gum is not happy in dry, limestone conditions.

Parrotia persica (Hamamelidaceae) (5A–8B)

Although often described as a large shrub, the northern Iranian and Caucasian *Parrotia persica*, in nature and often in gardens, is a deciduous, wide-spreading tree, perhaps best grown in moist, leaf-rich soils akin to those of the wet Caspian forests where it occurs wild, but equally at home on acidic sands and limestone soils, a tree of great character and beauty for any garden.

At Wisley there are two large specimens, one over 40ft (12m) high, which in winter show off their flaking bark, pale cinnamon over gray, to perfection. In late winter, the bare branchlets are covered with bright red stamens set in velvet brown bracts that reflect a warm crimson haze as the winter sun shines through the branches. As the flowers fade the young foliage unfolds a glossy bronze-green, with indented veining and slightly waved edges, that loses its coppery flush for the summer before donning its magnificent autumn tints that last for several weeks in beauty during midautumn. The attractive flaking bark is then revealed once again, quietly hidden while *P. persica* is in leaf. At different stages, the leaves may be green, gold-bronze, orange, or scarlet on the same branches, their burnished surfaces enhancing their resplendent exit into winter.

OTHER PLANTS
Acer griseum (Aceraceae) (5A–8A)
The Paperbark Maple, *Acer griseum*, is ornamental at any season. Just to touch its curling flakes of warm, orange-brown, older bark and stroke the rich reddish-cinnamon, firm young bark beneath is uplifting in winter. The attractive foliage, each leaf consisting of three toothed leaflets, fresh green above and bluish-green below, covers the rounded but gently irregular crown

all spring and summer before producing its marvelous, long-lasting, autumn tints of warm orange and red. The brownish-red, winged fruits are often freely produced, but only a very small percentage normally germinate and then only after stratification. However, my first *A. griseum* was a seed-raised plant.

Betula medwediewii (Betulaceae) (5A–7B)
Betula medwediewii from the Caucasus is a large, spreading, erect, branched shrub, which may reach 15ft (4.5m) in height (occasionally much more), and almost twice as much across after many years. Its distinctive habit admirably suits its use as a small specimen plant. In spring and summer, its spreading habit and large, handsome, rounded-ovate, corrugated, dark green leaves with deeply indented veins are most attractive, the foliage turning to a cool yellow in autumn. After leaf-fall, the large, bright, shining green buds, standing out among the silhouetted, upright, glossy, pale brown branches create a striking winter picture.

Parrotia persica

SHRUBS

Shrubs form the framework of many gardens, and one of the most important attributes we look for is their ability to provide interest throughout the year. Some shrubs – most *Deutzia* and *Philadelphus* species, for example – provide magnificent displays of flowers in mid-summer but little further garden value. Luckily, however, there are many shrubs with two or even three distinct characteristics valued by gardeners. They may combine attractive foliage with a profusion of colorful, sometimes fragrant flowers, perhaps followed by ornamental fruits. Yet others pay their way with autumnal tints, while *Rubus* and *Stephanandra* species are among those that provide beauty in winter with the color of their willowy stems or peeling bark, in addition to pleasant flowers in spring or summer.

Shrub plantings on their own may, unless carefully planned, have a few seasonal "dead spots". The inclusion of other types of plants can "lift" these areas and add to the beauty of the overall picture. Late-flowering perennials and bulbs with the elegance of cimicifugas and the autumnal purity of *Colchicum speciosum* var. *album* will provide white pools around the bases of deciduous azaleas and other shrubs that are past their own main season of beauty. Lilies are classic bulbs for combining with shrubs, as many like their bases in shade and their tops in sun.

Newcomers to gardening often fear that shrubs are demanding in their maintaintance, and it is true that some shrubs require a regular pruning routine; others, however, need little more than formative pruning.

SPRING

So many flowering shrubs of all shapes, sizes, and colors are at their peak in late spring that it is difficult not to yield to temptation and fill (in my case overfill) the garden with impulse buys. Unless you make sure in advance that any shrub you obtain will blend effectively with the plants you already possess, and that you have space for it, you will find yourself wandering the garden in search of a suitable site for your new acquisition.

It is easy to forget, too, the value of foliage plants to offset or complement the brilliance of azaleas, rhododendrons, camellias, and forsythias that dominate the spring scene. My choices here include *Spiraea japonica* 'Goldflame,' with bronze-red young foliage, and the evergreen *Photinia* 'Red Robin,' with its vibrant red spring growth.

Corylopsis sinensis

FLOWERS

Corylopsis sinensis (syn. *C. willmottiae*) (Hamamelidaceae) (6B–8B)

Deservedly valued for their attractive yellow tassels of fragrant flowers borne in early spring, the five or six species of *Corylopsis* in cultivation are all hardy shrubs from China and the Himalaya. They will grow well in acidic or neutral, leaf-rich woodland soils, and some may also be tried in alkaline conditions, if well supplied with humus.

Unfortunately, confusion has led to some species being currently grown under two or more names; the Chinese *Corylopsis sinensis* is now held to include plants grown as *C. willmottiae* in the past and is very often still cultivated as such in gardens. Nomenclatural problems aside, *C. sinensis* is an attractive, more or less upright, deciduous shrub that may reach 12ft (3.5m) or so in height, its neat, oblong-elliptic leaves, hairy beneath, arising from slightly red-tinted buds, which are often flushed purple as they unfold. A variant with striking, plum-purple, young growths has been selected and given the apt name 'Spring Purple.' Before the leaves emerge, however, a profusion of 4in (10cm) racemes of tightly packed, cup-shaped, soft yellow blooms appears

in early spring, sweetly scented and hanging gracefully among the pale brown branchlets.

Equally fine, and distinctive because of its conspicuous red anthers and glabrous foliage, is *C. veitchiana*, now saddled with the long-winded name *C. sinensis* var. *calvescens* forma *veitchiana* which, while it may indicate its botanical status, does nothing for its horticultural popularity. Like the erstwhile *C. willmottiae*, it is an extremely pleasant and useful scented early-flowering shrub, comparable in growth, but usually with slightly shorter racemes of a similar color.

Paeonia suffruticosa 'Rock's Variety' (Paeoniaceae) (5A–8B)

This superb tree peony has been described as a species, *Paeonia rockii*, and also as a subspecies and botanical variety of *P. suffruticosa*, all within the last ten years. This difference in botanical opinion leads me to retain the original name, 'Rock's Variety,' under which it was grown by Sir Frederick Stern who was sent a seedling, it is understood from Joseph Rock's original collection, from China in 1936. A very fine painting of the original plant in the RHS Journal for August 1959 shows it as a semidouble with white petals, heavily marked dark red-purple at the bases with the coloring suffusing slightly into the petal blades. Seedlings vary somewhat in both flower and leaf characters, sometimes having more pink in the petals than is permissible for 'Rock's Variety.'

Passing over the history of this much sought-after plant, there is never any dispute as to its horticultural merit, and it is one of the finest late spring-flowering shrubs, sometimes opening its sumptuous, 6in (15cm) blooms in midspring. It normally has between twelve and fourteen slightly frilled, firm-textured petals and a delicious scent, bearing its blooms just above the young, much-divided, slightly bronze-tinted foliage, which turns to a deeper green when mature. All the specimens I have seen are spreading shrubs of compact growth, seldom more than 6ft (1.8m) in height and 8 or 9ft (2.4–2.7m) across. A mature plant may well bear 100 blooms during the flowering period, a marvelous spectacle that, when its propagation requirements have been unraveled, will, one hopes, be more commonly seen.

Once obtained, 'Rock's Variety' is not difficult to grow. Good specimens may be found in very alkaline soils as well as in acidic conditions; sharp drainage, and an open, sunny position, where frost drains away rapidly, are this very desirable shrub's main requirements.

OTHER PLANTS

Daphne genkwa (Thymelaeaceae) (6A–8A)

The deciduous *Daphne genkwa* is much valued for the clusters of lilac-purple, slightly scented, small blooms that wreathe the bare branches in midspring. Native to various areas in northern and central China and Korea, *D. genkwa* has long been known in North America, but has proved less easy to grow than other species, although it does root fairly readily from semiripe cuttings. When at Wisley, I obtained several seedlings with larger, rather softer lilac flowers than those from which most stock in Britain had previously been derived. These proved more adaptable and easily propagated and will perhaps soon become more commonly seen. *D. genkwa* seldom grows more than 3 to 4ft (1–1.2m) tall, and given a well-drained but moisture-retentive soil in open conditions is certainly not the impossible plant that some would have us believe.

Exochorda x *macrantha* 'The Bride' (Rosaceae) (5A–8B)

A genus of four or five species from northern Asia, *Exochorda* contains several late spring-flowering, lax-growing, elegant shrubs. All prefer acid soils and open, sunny positions, but one or two succeed on alkaline soils if humus-rich.

'The Bride,' a hybrid of *E. racemosa* and *E. korolkowii*, produces long racemes of pure white, 1in (2.5cm) wide, five-petaled flowers from short, leafy twigs on the previous year's growth. If a few of the older branches and flowered shoots are pruned out after blooming, further long, arching shoots are produced to carry the following year's display.

Viburnum carlesii 'Aurora' (Caprifoliaceae) (5A–8A)

In this versatile genus, the selections made from *Viburnum carlesii* rate highly for their hummocklike inflorescences crowded with scented, white, usually pink-tinted blooms. A dense, rounded shrub 4 to 6ft (1.2–1.8m) high and as much across, *V. carlesii* is, out of flower, of no great import with its grayish, downy, ovate leaves, apart from an occasional sparkle of purple, red, and yellow before the leaves fall. However, it comes spectacularly to life in midspring when the embryonic inflorescences, developed in autumn, expand and for a few weeks scent the air around. Although the existing stock was of good quality, fresh seed from Korea to the Slieve Donard nursery led to the introduction of excellent clones with larger individual flowers. 'Aurora' (originally 'Donard Pink') has a very strong, sweet fragrance and deep red flower buds with the open blooms gradually changing to pink, while the equally lovely 'Charis' ('Donard Variety') has brighter red buds that open pure white.

Paeonia suffruticosa 'Rock's Variety' (see p.32)

FOLIAGE

Spiraea japonica 'Goldflame' (Rosaceae) (4A–8B)

A genus of very accommodating, easily-grown shrubs, spiraeas thrive in any reasonably fertile soil and, despite preferring fairly moist conditions, many will flourish on dry soils, although tending to become chlorotic in dry limestone areas.

While a number of species have only fleeting beauty when at their best in bloom, there are a few, such as *Spiraea japonica*, that are virtually trouble-free, provide very welcome late flowers, and, in some clones, are also beautiful foliage plants.

'Goldflame' is one of these, and is now very widely planted for the brilliance of its young foliage in spring. As the leaves unfold, they are reddish-bronze, suffused orange gradually changing to paler hues of orange and yellow before reverting to the light green of the mature foliage. If allowed to grow naturally, 'Goldflame' will develop into an irregularly rounded shrub some 4ft (1.2m) in height and as much across, but the young shoots on older plants are shorter and less colorful. To achieve the most effective leaf coloring, it is best to prune the whole plant to within 3 or 4in (8–10cm) of ground level in early spring before the buds break. This produces a burst of spectacular young growth, but does entail generous fertilizing, mulching, and watering to obtain the long, bright-hued shoots from which 'Goldflame' received its name. With more gross fertilizing it is also worth cutting back all the growth that develops after early spring, pruning to 5 or 6in (12–15cm) when the lighter colors of the foliage have faded. This will not only encourage a second crop of foliage color but almost certainly also avoid development of the rosy-pink flower heads that blend uncomfortably with the foliage.

With such treatment, replacement of a planting of 'Goldflame' may be necessary after a few years, but as it is very easily rooted from soft or semiripe cuttings this rejuvenation process is not usually a problem, and at its hard-pruned best 'Goldflame' is worth much time and trouble.

OTHER PLANTS

Photinia 'Red Robin' (Rosaceae) (8A–9B)

The unsung genus *Photinia* contains a number of both evergreen and deciduous species of considerable garden value, but most are surpassed by the hybrids between *P. glabra* and *P. serrulata*, grouped under the name *P. x fraseri*, all evergreens with handsome foliage and which grow well on alkaline soils.

Spiraea japonica 'Goldflame'

Outstanding among the selected clones is 'Red Robin,' raised in New Zealand and valued for its superb foliage, which matures a deep, glossy green, but has young growth of a startling, shining red, matching that of *Pieris* 'Wakehurst' (see below) in brilliance. It makes a particularly good hedge plant, and I vividly recall seeing both 'Red Robin' and the more coppery-red 'Robusta' being used prolifically for hedging in Australia, even if a little overdone in some cities. Trimmed annually, the hedges were spectacular in spring, gradually mellowing to the more sober but still very fine, deep green leaves of maturity. Left unpruned as an open-ground shrub, *P.* x *fraseri* and its various clones make large, rounded shrubs often 8 to 10ft (2.4–3m) or more high, but are readily maintained at lesser heights if required. They are all excellent shrubs that could replace many of the duller evergreens that lack the brilliance of 'Red Robin' and its allies.

FLOWERS AND FOLIAGE

Pieris formosa var. *forrestii* 'Wakehurst' (Ericaceae) (5A–8A*)

Although only suitable for growing in acidic conditions or in soil slightly on the acidic side of neutral, the genus *Pieris* as a whole provides us with plants of exceptional beauty, unifying evergreen foliage with elegant flower sprays and often brightly colored young shoots into shrubs of the first quality.

Pieris formosa is a variable, wide-ranging species from the eastern Himalaya to southwest China, usually a spreading shrub of 10 to 12ft (3–3.5m), occasionally twice as high in very favorable sites. A number of horticultural selections have been made, the most popular, and to many eyes the most beautiful, being 'Wakehurst.' A dense-habited, rounded or semiupright shrub often 6 to 8ft (1.8–2.4m) tall, 'Wakehurst' is well-clothed in shining, dark, evergreen, oblong-lance-shaped, finely-veined leaves, and in late spring, when the young shoots appear, it seems almost to burst into flame. The brilliant coloration of the new growth lasts for several weeks, gradually passing to salmon-pink, then yellowish-green, before adopting the fresh green of the mature leaves. Quite frequently 'Wakehurst' will produce a second flush of young growth in late summer, which, unlike the spring foliage, is safe from frost damage, this vulnerability being the only drawback of this fine shrub.

It is also greatly valued for the terminal flower pani-

Pieris formosa var. *forrestii* 'Wakehurst'

cles, large sprays of gleaming white, slightly scented lily of the valleylike flowers borne just after or sometimes with the developing shoots. These are formed in autumn, normally overwintering unharmed, although in very severe winters all forms of *P. formosa* may suffer foliage damage. Luckily, they rejuvenate very well if cut back hard in early spring, to 12in (30cm) or so above ground level, but must be fertilized and watered well to ensure strong new growth.

'Wakehurst' is best grown in slight shade and cool, moist, humus rich soil, where its brilliant red spring growths shine out, contrasting very effectively with the glossy, dark, older foliage.

Related plants Requiring very similar conditions to 'Wakehurst,' although better in more open sites, the white-flowered, sometimes pink-flushed *Pieris japonica* (5B–8A), 8 to 10ft (2.4–3m) or more in height, has a wide range of attractive clones of distinctive habit and shades of flower color. 'Flamingo,' which was raised in the United States about 30 years ago, is probably the deepest colored of all, with initially upright, then pendent, large sprays of its small, urn shaped flowers, dark red in bud and opening to a deep pink that pales as the flowers age, eventually becoming almost white before falling. These striking blooms, together with its bronze-red new growth, make it very distinctive among a range of white- and pink-flowered cultivars.

As with all *Pieris*, it is important to remove the developing seed pods so that energy is not wasted and the display from next year's flowers is not affected adversely. This is particularly relevant for the very profuse-flowering clones such as 'Flamingo' (deep rose-red non-fading flowers) that give sparingly of their magnificent flowers otherwise.

SUMMER

There is a great abundance of woody flowering plants that come into bloom in midsummer, among them such treasures as the delightfully scented and graceful *Buddleja alternifolia* and the many *Cistus* species, evocative of the Mediterranean. The glorious scent of *Philadelphus* and *Syringa* wafts over the garden, the pink froth of *Kolkwitzia amabilis* is at its peak, and *Spartium junceum* provides blooms of long-lasting yellow.

Hypericum species and hybrids are major contributors to the summer garden. Also valuable, and similarly continuing into autumn, are the hardy fuchsias that derive from the ubiquitous but indispensable *Fuchsia magellanica*. The silvers and gray-blues of *Artemisia* 'Powis Castle' and *Ruta graveolens* 'Jackman's Blue' are ideal for softening more strident colors in sunny sites.

DECIDUOUS SHRUBS FOR FLOWERS

Buddleja alternifolia (Buddlejaceae) (5B–8B)

In a genus that contains a considerable number of excellent flowering shrubs, the lovely *Buddleja alternifolia* from Kansu in central northern China stands apart from all other cultivated species, not only in its alternately placed leaves but also in having the trailing shoots of the previous year wreathed in bloom along their considerable length.

It has been described by Reginald Farrer as "like a gracious, small-leaved weeping willow when it is not in flower, and a sheer waterfall of soft purple when it is." It is difficult to better this description, except to refer to the sometimes silvered appearance of the lanceolate, dark green, willowlike foliage and the fragrance of the abundant clusters of early summer-borne, lilac-purple blooms with their tiny yellow eyes, which attract butterflies and bees, as with many others of its genus.

In the wild, *B. alternifolia* is found as a cliff dweller in very dry areas as well as in hedgerows, where its graceful, pendulous shoots spread widely. As a garden plant, this lax growth makes it difficult to place satisfactorily. Left to its own devices it will form a wide-spreading, mounding shrub, but it is probably at its most natural if allowed to tumble down a bank.

It makes a fine south-wall plant if carefully trained, but this may be regarded as a waste, for *B. alternifolia* is perfectly hardy. I have also seen it trained over an arch, which involves considerable work, because, unlike the well-known *B. davidii* and its relatives which flower on the current year's wood, *B. alternifolia* blooms on shoots that have grown the previous summer; hence, immediately after flowering the old flowered shoots must be cut out so that next year's blooms are assured. Best of all, grow *B. alternifolia* as a weeping standard. It may, with a little patience, be trained into this form on a stem 5 or 6ft (1.5–1.8m) high. *B. alternifolia* is very versatile in use and tolerant of the widest range of soil types, provided that drainage is sharp.

Related plants Commonest and best-loved of this diverse genus, the midsummer-flowering *Buddleja davidii* is an extremely variable plant found wild in central and western China, its lilac plumes of scented, butterfly flowers familiar from its ability to colonize virtually any piece of waste ground where seed lands.

Garden selections are legion, ranging from the huge panicles of the white-flowered, orange-eyed 'Peace' to the long, narrow racemes of the lilac 'Fortune' and the dark red-purple 'Royal Red.' My personal favorite is 'Black Knight,' deepest violet with contrasting orange-yellow eyes. All are beautifully fragrant, of the simplest cultivation, and requiring only hard spring pruning of the flowered wood back to 1ft (30cm) or so from the base to flower abundantly each season. Less vicious pruning will result in less vigorous growth, but will allow *B. davidii* to reach 12 or 15ft (3.5–4.5m). Removal of the spent flower-spikes before seed has developed will save much weeding out of seedlings the following spring, but the pale brown seed heads have a certain charm in winter.

Closely related to *B. davidii*, but differing, in particular, in the densely white-felted stems, *B. fallowiana* in its best forms is a very fine foliage plant as well as being valuable for its strongly scented, lavender flowers borne in narrow panicles on the current season's shoots and often up to 10 or 12in (25–30cm) long. A lovely, pure white, orange-eyed variant is also available.

Buddleja fallowiana (8A–9B*) is said to be rather tender, and a hard winter may establish whether or not this is true, but there is great enjoyment to be derived from its ghostly growth and the fragrance of its pale

Buddleja alternifolia

Kolkwitzia amabilis 'Pink Cloud'

lilac flowers in early autumn, which is its flowering season in its native China. In gardens the original introductions have crossed with *B. davidii* to produce two fine hybrids: 'Lochinch,' with deep orange-eyed, violet-blue flowers and gray, hairy foliage and stems, and 'West Hill,' paler flowered and with a grayish-white tomentum, both of relaxed growth that sets them apart from stiffer-growing *B. davidii* and its cohorts.

Kolkwitzia amabilis 'Pink Cloud' (Caprifoliaceae) (5A–9A)

Kolkwitzia amabilis, known particularly in the United States as the Beauty Bush, is in the top rank of China's hardy flowering shrubs. Easily cultivated and reveling in limestone as well as any other soil where drainage is not impeded, it forms a densely branched, deciduous shrub, eventually reaching 10 to 12ft (3–3.5m) in height and more across, with long, gracefully arching shoots, which bear myriads of its 1in (2.5cm) bell-shaped

blooms in small clusters along the twiggy laterals in early summer. The flowers vary from pale pink to a much deeper bright pink, always marked yellow in the throat and set off by the hairy, lobed calyx that remains persistent in fruit.

Curiously, this adaptable and most attractive shrub with its opposite pairs of neat, hairy, grayed-green, small leaves did not make much impact in British gardens until after World War II, although very popular in the United States since the early 1900's. The reason for its early lack of appreciation in Britain may have been the pale blooms of some seedlings, which do not compare in beauty with the very fine clone 'Pink Cloud' that was raised at Wisley from seed sent from the United States in 1946. This had developed into a plant well over 10ft (3m) high and across when Frank Knight, then Director of Wisley, and I were looking at it in full bloom in early summer 1963. He decided to exhibit it at the RHS halls in Vincent Square in London, because he felt it was clearly superior in color to any other variant he knew, and on 11 June 1963, named at my suggestion, it received a First Class Certificate, an unusual accolade on its first showing.

Propagating material was passed to the nursery industry, and it is now widely available, a charming and prolific plant that, in addition to rooting easily from semiripe cuttings, sends out basal suckering shoots that may be lifted in winter to pass on to any who admired its grace and beauty the previous summer.

Lavandula stoechas subsp. *pedunculata*

Lavandula stoechas **subsp.** *pedunculata* (**Labiatae**)
(**7B–9B**)

One of our oldest garden plants, the Spanish Lavender
(so-named although widespread in the Mediterranean
countries) was grown in Britain by the sixteenth century, and although regarded as somewhat tender, is still
greatly favored for its gray-downy, narrow, pine-scent-
ed foliage and for the angled, tightly packed inflorescence of tiny, deep purple flowers surmounted by a
conspicuous and attractive top-knot of broad, purple,
usually upright bracts standing up like rabbits' ears.

Even more striking is its subspecies *pedunculata*
(once accorded specific rank in its own right), which
differs in having a slightly shorter and broader flower-
spike produced on very long stalks held well above the
gray-green, strongly aromatic foliage and in its longer
but perhaps slightly narrower, violet-purple bracts.

Both are evergreen shrubs of 2 or 2½ft (60–75cm)
in height and, given sharp drainage and a bright sunny
position, are hardy enough in the south of England, and
if they succumb to winter damage are readily raised
from the abundantly produced seed.

Lavandula stoechas subsp. *pedunculata* (as now
defined) is restricted in the wild to certain areas of
north-eastern Portugal and central Spain, where I have
seen it growing in calcareous, rocky areas in quantity in
midspring, coloring great patches in the hillsides a
vibrant violet-purple. In cultivation in North America,
it is best restricted to the less humid West Coast. In
mild areas it makes a fine low hedge, the foliage when
crushed releasing a fragrance that, to me, smells like
a cross between that of Common Lavender and
eau-de-cologne, as refreshing as its longlasting flower-
spikes are beautiful.

Magnolia liliiflora 'Nigra' (**Magnoliaceae**) (**6A–9A**)

Nowadays, you may find this lovely deciduous flowering shrub under the name *Magnolia quinquepeta*
'Nigra,' but to most gardeners who know and grow it,
M. liliiflora 'Nigra' it will remain. It is one of the most
reliable and long-flowering of magnolias and is ideal for
small gardens, because it grows slowly, flowers at an
early age and its eventual height is seldom more than
10ft (3m). Some specimens are fairly upright but it is
not unusual to see more rounded specimens almost as
wide as high.

M. liliiflora 'Nigra' is certainly no more difficult to
grow than *M. stellata*, and has many advantages over it.
M.l. 'Nigra' usually begins to bloom in early summer,
its large, cylindrical, rich red-purple buds opening to
reveal their pale purple, almost white, velvet-textured

Magnolia liliiflora 'Nigra'

interiors. The buds continue to be produced for many
weeks, and, although the quantity of the exquisite 4–5in
(10–12cm), elongated, narrowly vase-shaped flowers in
summer and autumn is seldom great, there is rarely a
day or two until leaf-fall when one or more flowers in
varying stages of development are not to be seen. Add
to this long succession of bloom the dark glossy green
leaves that unfold with the first flush of flowers, and
you have a plant of great quality and garden merit. Its
only fault, if such it be, is that it will not tolerate limestone soils, requiring neutral to acidic, moisture-retentive, fairly fertile soils to give of its best.

Not surprisingly, 'Nigra' has proved to be a popular
parent and has passed on some of its qualities to a
group of magnolias with ladies' names ('Betty,' 'Ann,'
'Jane') raised in the United States, but none of these
has, to my mind, quite the same flower quality, particularly in the breadth and substance of the petals,
although their freedom of flowering and toughness as
garden plants are admirable characteristics.

Philadelphus 'Beauclerk' (**Philadelphaceae**)
(**5A–8B**)

What gardener is there who could do without at least
one *Philadelphus* in their garden, if only for the
exquisite fragrance of the blooms of many species and
hybrids? Known by the common name mock orange, all
the sixty or so species and a mass of hybrids are among
the most accommodating of deciduous shrubs, providing fine displays of their shallowly cup-shaped flowers
in early and midsummer whether on acidic or alkaline
soils or anything in between.

Among the species, the strongly perfumed European *P. coronarius* and its cultivars 'Aureus,' with golden young foliage, and 'Variegatus' with white edges to the leaves, the early-flowering *P. magdalenae* with deep, fragrant, cupped blooms, and the equally strongly perfumed *P. delavayi* forma *melanocalyx*, with its pure white petals set off by dark purple calyces, are favorites of long standing, all fine garden plants.

But it is 'Beauclerk' that I consider the most outstanding hybrid, raised from crossing the lovely, purple-stained 'Sybille' with 'Burfordensis,' enormous and almost gross with its rather flattened blooms on graceful, arching shoots. A shrub 6ft (1.8m) in height and as much across, 'Beauclerk' produces short sprays of three to seven very fragrant, large, white, saucer-shaped blooms, 2½ to 3in (6–8cm) across, with a delicate suffusion of purplish-pink at the base of each of the four evenly matched petals.

Like all *Philadelphus*, 'Beauclerk' is readily propagated from semi-ripe cuttings and will normally start to flower in its third year. Aftercare, apart from routine mulching and pruning out of a few of the oldest stems to ground level or nearly so, is minimal.

In addition to 'Beauclerk,' it would be churlish not to mention 'Belle Étoile,' as fragrant as 'Beauclerk' but smaller-flowered and a little less robust, distinguished by the conspicuous red-purple central patch in the blooms, and 'Virginal,' with double cup-shaped 1½–2in (3–5cm) blooms, equally well scented but more upright in habit.

Phygelius aequalis 'Yellow Trumpet' (Scrophulariaceae) (7A–9B*)

Two species of Cape Fuchsia, the common name given to this attractive genus of subshrubs from South Africa, both excellent garden plants, have also been deliberately crossed to obtain worthy hybrids.

Phygelius aequalis 'Yellow Trumpet' is very popular, a clone collected wild in the frost-prone Marwaga Mountain in southwest Natal. Found to be hardy in Britain, it was launched onto a willing market that clearly appreciated its long, yellow, tubular, trumpet-shaped flowers borne in profusion throughout the summer and autumn months.

Phygelius aequalis is an evergreen subshrub 2 or 3ft (60–90cm) high that is best cut to ground level each spring to renew basal growths. It sends out runners just below soil level, making propagation easy, although semiripe cuttings root readily. Occurring wild, often by streams, the various introductions all seem hardy, although the top growth is killed to ground level in

Phygelius aequalis 'Yellow Trumpet'

severe winters. The strongly four-angled shoots are clothed with opposite pairs of broadly ovate, toothed leaves, dark green above and light green beneath in the wild form, but light yellowish-green in *P. aequalis*.

The terminal, 9–12in (23–30cm) panicles bear slender, tubular, well-spaced flowers, 1½in (3.5cm) long, pendulous with even, slightly reflexed lobes. In flower color the populations of *P. aequalis* vary to some extent, but are usually in shades of delicate coral-salmon with the inner surface of the lobes bright yellow with a strong red edge, a color mix that further distinguishes it from the bright red *P. capensis*, although this often has a yellowish throat as well.

Both *P. aequalis* and 'Yellow Trumpet' are superb garden plants, but the charms of *P. capensis* should not be overlooked. Trained against a sunny wall, it will reach 6 or 8ft (2–2.5m) and will flower continuously through summer and autumn. The hybrids of those two fine plants, grouped as *P.* x *rectus* and with evocative clonal names like 'Elf,' 'Moonraker,' 'African Queen,' and 'Devil's Tears,' are proving their worth.

Spartium junceum (Leguminosae) (7A–9B*)

Astonishingly, the long-flowering Spanish broom is known to have been in cultivation in Britain since the sixteenth century, although its habitats in the southern Mediterranean might indicate suspect hardi-

Spartium junceum

ROSES AND OTHER SHRUBS WITH AN EXTENDED FLOWERING PERIOD

Rosa 'Graham Thomas' (Rosaceae) (5A–9B)

Among a yearly plethora of worthy rose introductions and multitudes of fine roses from the past, it is extremely difficult to pick out a few, let alone a single rose, to grow if you were allowed only one variety in your garden. 'Graham Thomas' would be my first choice, partly because he has been a friend and mentor for over thirty years and partly because the extremely fine rose named after him exemplifies not only his great love of the old roses but also his constant search for plants of quality that perform well in the garden.

Appropriately classed as an English Rose, for Graham is very much an English gentleman, 'Graham Thomas' is a gorgeous variety. It forms a tall shrub reaching 5 to 8ft (1.5–2.5m) in height and as much across, with dark, glossy green foliage. The sumptuous, fully double, many-petaled blooms are of the richest yellow, touched with honey shades in the center and shaped in the old-fashioned style. Flowering right through the summer, this is a plant that will thrive even on poor soils and in partially shaded locations It has a delightful, strong fragrance – one of Graham Thomas's particular enthusiasms being fragrant roses, which he often wears as a buttonhole.

ness, because it occurs on dry, stony hillsides from the Iberian Peninsula to Syria. It can frequently be seen in Spain and Greece, its elegant, rushlike, dark green wands of light yellow blooms appearing in late spring on rocky hillsides and roadsides.

A shrub often 8 to 10ft (2.4–3m) tall if left unpruned, *Spartium junceum* produces its elegant display of 12in (30cm) long, terminal racemes of scented, rich yellow, 1in (2.5cm) peaflowers continually from midsummer to frost in the north and from early spring to late summer farther south. Seed is abundantly produced and is the best method of raising new stock. As with most legumes, though, make sure seedlings are planted out in their permanent site as soon as possible; pot-bound plants do not form good root systems later and, when older, may well keel over in strong winds.

Untroubled by any drained soil, *S. junceum* is a marvelous coastal plant as well as growing well in hot, dry, limestone sites. But it is also an admirable plant for the ordinary garden, particularly in groups with lower evergreens in front of it to conceal the rather scraggy bases of old specimens. I prefer to leave *S. junceum* virtually unpruned apart from the removal of any dead or damaged shoots. If necessary, provided you do not cut into the old, brown parts of the stems, it may be pruned hard back and it will still repay you, in spite of such cruelty, with a splendid summer and autumn display.

Rosa 'Graham Thomas'

ROSES IN MIXED PLANTINGS

There is a tendency to forget that hybrid tea and floribunda roses *are* shrubs, because of the strict pruning regimes imposed on them as bedding plants, but allowed to grow unrestricted – apart from removal of dead and diseased wood – they will outdo many a flowering shrub by producing myriads of blooms over long periods. Old-fashioned and shrub roses are, of course, used in this way, but one seldom sees such cultivars as 'Madame Butterfly,' 'Hugh Dickson,' 'Shot Silk,' 'Grandmère Jenny,' 'Sutter's Gold,' and 'Peace' grown as shrubs. By initially pruning to provide a strong basal, branched framework of "permanent" stems, I have grown both 'Madame Butterfly' (illustrated below) and 'Shot Silk' as freely flowering, 6–8ft (1.8–2.4m) shrubs. True, the blooms are smaller than if pruned for bedding, but they add much color to borders.

Syringa microphylla 'Superba' (Oleaceae) (5A–8B)

A charming, deciduous shrub no more than 5 or 6ft (1.5–2m) high and as much across, *Syringa microphylla* has a neat, fairly dense habit, and rounded-ovate, dark green leaves no more than 2in (5cm) long. In late spring it produces terminal 4in (10cm) panicles of very sweetly scented, lilac-pink, slender-tubed flowers with spreading lobes on the previous year's shoots; later in the summer it will, unusually for a lilac, bloom again on the current year's growth. Like all lilacs, it is undemanding, and grows as well in limestone as in acidic soils, but it does appreciate fertile, well-drained conditions in full sun. It also tolerates heat and humidity. Its selection 'Superba' is much freer-flowering, with larger, slightly more lax flower trusses of brighter rose-pink that still provide a strong, sweet fragrance. It flowers profusely in late spring and, is seldom without some bloom until early autumn. Selective pruning of older branches to stimulate strong young shoots will carry the flowering season on until autumn.

OTHER PLANTS

Fuchsia 'Corallina' (Onagraceae) (7A–9B*)

One of the oldest and finest fuchsia hybrids in cultivation, 'Corallina' has a pedigree dating back over 150 years. Almost certainly a hybrid of *F. magellanica*, it has the same long, glossy red sepals and light purple petals or "skirt," but the flowers are much larger, over 2½in (6cm) in length. Its long, dark, arching, reddish shoots bear red-veined, deep green, channeled leaves at each node, from where the pendent, graceful blooms appear on leaf stalks more than 1in (2.5cm) long.

Pruned back to ground level each spring, it grows 3ft (1m) or more in the season, but 'Corallina' can also be grown as a wall plant, where it may develop a short trunk and reach 8 to 10ft (2.4–3m) high.

A direct selection of *F. magellanica* is 'Thompsonii,' with narrow, long-tapered, red sepals and the usual purple petals of this species on 1½–2in (3–5cm) stalks. The narrow leaves and overall slender, delicate appearance is belied by its hardiness.

Hydrangea arborescens 'Annabelle' (Hydrangeaceae) (4A–9A)

This *Hydrangea* species from the eastern United States has proved to be a very hardy, easily grown shrub, flowering from midsummer to early autumn. The clone 'Grandiflora' with a 6 or 7in (15–18cm), shallowly domed inflorescence of creamy white, sterile flowers has long been valued for its long-lasting display. Its one fault is the weakness of its flower stems, and it has now been largely superseded by 'Annabelle,' with even larger domes, well over 12in (30cm) across in some cases if the stems are pruned back annually. To some, it may appear top-heavy but, as it has much stronger flower stems than 'Grandiflora,' they are held upright, and a group of plants of this clone is a fine sight in summer and early autumn.

Hypericum bellum (Hypericaceae) (6A–8B)

Of the many shrubby St John's worts, *Hypericum bellum* has always appealed to me for its very neat, restrained growth and small flowers of bright gold, freely produced during early summer and beyond. A densely branched shrub growing to 2ft (60cm) or so in height, set with rounded ovate, fresh green leaves, slightly undulate and often red-lined at the edges, it proffers cup-shaped, 1½in (3.5cm) blooms that may vary in depth of color from a pale to deep yellow.

Often semievergreen, *H. bellum* also provides pleasant autumn color, the older leaves turning red and matching the bronze-red ripe seed capsules.

Syringa microphylla 'Superba' (see p.42)

Rosa 'Felicia' (Rosaceae) (5B–9B)

Among the hybrid musk roses, all of great garden merit, I find 'Felicia' one of the most pleasing, with its rich, dark green foliage and sweetly scented, fully double blooms a delightful mix of warm pink, salmon, and apricot, gradually fading to paler shades. No more than 6ft (1.8m) in height and of dense rounded habit, 'Felicia' produces bunches of blooms for much of the summer and, like many of its kin, makes an ideal flowering hedge.

Rosa 'Madame Butterfly' (5B–9B)

This sport from the equally well-known 'Ophelia' is, in my view, one of the best cultivars, with its exquisitely scented, shapely blooms of deep blush-pink, deeper in the center with a flush of yellow at the base of the petals. Although usually hard-pruned as a Hybrid Tea, I prefer it as a large shrub: it will grow to 6ft (2m) with ease, flowering all summer and into autumn, in mild areas sometimes producing a few blooms in December.

Rosa 'Peace'

A classic rose, 'Peace' is indispensable for the beauty of its large, high-centered, fully double blooms, opening widely to display the pink-flushed petals of pale gold, its deep green, glossy foliage providing a fine foil. Of great vigour, 'Peace' makes an admirable tall shrub if only lightly pruned and, although not of show standard, its flowers will still be of great substance and size, amply compensating for its lightness of scent.

FOLIAGE

Artemisia 'Powis Castle' (Compositae) (5A–8B)

There is a dispute over the correct clonal name for this plant, but little disagreement over the quality and popularity of *Artemisia* 'Powis Castle', with its dense mounds of silvery, filigree, ever-gray foliage some 2ft (60cm) high and often 3 to 4ft (1–1.2m) across.

Its growth may be somewhat lax, and it is best to pinch out the tips of young plants to encourage a more bushy habit, and subsequently nip out any wayward, long shoots that may spoil its slightly irregular, hummocky appearance. If you do so you will also benefit from the (to me) pleasant fragrance on your fingers, a rather less sharp scent than that of the related wormwood, *A. absinthium*. Although plants do occasionally produce flowering spikes, I am pleased they do not do so in profusion, because they are of little value.

I have found it to be hardy in sunny, dry, open sites, although some reports suggest it is not always so, perhaps supporting the theory that it is related to the generally tender *A. arborescens*. 'Powis Castle' withstands hard spring pruning and quickly refurbishes itself from its woody basal shoots, it comes through even severe winters with only minor damage, if any. It is clearly always eager to replace any lost growth, the embryonic shoots already forming on woody stems, as often occurs with the cotton-lavender, *Santolina*.

Used as a ground cover on dry soils in full sun, as a paving plant on a large terrace where its fragrant leaves may be enjoyed, or in hanging baskets, structured shrub plantings or borders, it is one of the most effective hardy foliage plants introduced in recent years.

Artemisia 'Powis Castle'

Ruta graveolens 'Jackman's Blue' (Rutaceae)
(4A–9B)

The only species commonly cultivated, the eastern European *Ruta graveolens*, known as rue or the herb of grace, has long been grown and valued for its medicinal uses. Gerard's account in *The Herball* of 1597, sets out its efficacy as a cure-all for virtually any complaint – an antidote to various poisons and a reputation for endowing clear-sightedness being among its listed virtues. If used or even handled, however, great care should be taken, because particularly in hot weather, it produces from glands in the foliage a volatile, acrid oil that may prove a very powerful irritant. It should be used, therefore, for ornament, not for medical experiment.

Ruta graveolens is, of course, also an attractive and compact dwarf ornamental shrub, seldom over 2 or 3ft (60–90cm) high, valued for its gray-blue, aromatic, divided leaves as well as for the contrasting citron-yellow, terminal corymbs of ½in (1cm), cup-shaped flowers with separated petals.

Best grown in an open, sunny, well-drained site, alkaline or acidic, it may be used as a fine foliage plant in shrub or mixed borders, in herb gardens and, not least, as a low hedge, where, kept gently pruned, its evergreen, glaucous foliage provides an attractive alternative to lavender or rosemary.

The Common Rue has now been replaced almost completely by the selection 'Jackman's Blue,' which is distinguished by its compact habit and vivid, gray-blue foliage that far surpasses that of any previously grown stocks of rue in beauty.

Ruta graveolens 'Jackman's Blue'

VARIEGATED FOLIAGE/ FLOWERS

Fuchsia magellanica 'Sharpitor' (Onagraceae)
(7A–9B*)

On vacation some twenty years ago in South Devon visiting the National Trust garden Overbecks (once known as Sharpitor), near Salcombe, I noted (but of course did not take!) a variegated shoot on a plant of the white-flowered form of *Fuchsia magellanica* now called var. *molinae*, but known in many gardens as var. *alba* or 'Alba,' which has white sepals and very pale pink petals. By chance a former member of the staff at Wisley became head gardener at Sharpitor the following year and, as the variegated shoot, somewhat surprisingly, was still there, he rooted cuttings and distributed material, so that now it has become an established clone in the trade. 'Sharpitor' was chosen as the name, after the garden, which was itself derived from Sharp Tor, a rocky headland close by.

Like other forms of *F. magellanica*, this plant has proved quite hardy, the foliage a mix of green, gray-green, and creamy white associating well with green or purple-foliaged companions. Some reversion occurs occasionally, as well as the production of a few albino basal shoots, but these are readily removed and, if so, do not mar the attractive effect of the muted, variegated foliage.

Weigela florida 'Variegata' (Caprifoliaceae)
(5A–8B)

Confusion reigns over the identity of three distinct, variegated-leaved *Weigela* clones that have variously been ascribed to *W. florida* and *W. praecox*. They are mentioned together here, because all are very attractive foliage plants, hardy and vigorous, and easy to grow in any well-drained fertile soil in a sunny situation.

All are also deciduous shrubs usually 5 or 6ft (1.5–1.8m) high (although somewhat lower in one clone), that flower on short laterals produced from the previous year's growth. Mainly grown for foliage they may be pruned fairly hard after flowering, removing flowered and weak shoots to stimulate strong growth with larger, and hence more effective, foliage.

Weigela florida is native to northern China and Korea and flowers in early to midsummer, producing its very decorative 1–1½in (2.5–3.5cm) tubular, bell-shaped, deep pink blooms. The variegated clone that derives from it, probably a hybrid, but known as *W. florida* 'Variegata,' has broad foliage with regular,

AUTUMN

As summer passes into autumn, our interest is compelled by the marvelous leaf coloring of shrubs such as *Euonymus alatus* and the Smoke Bush *Cotinus coggygria* (see p.57). These are matched by an abundance of fruiting shrubs, among them cotoneasters, berberis, skimmias and viburnums, and my particular favorites the red-berried *Daphne retusa* (see p.58) and pink-berried *Sorbus reducta*, the latter providing accents of color for two months or more before falling prey to the local bird population.

The strongly aromatic foliage of *Caryopteris* and *Perovskia* species and hybrids is complemented by a haze of blue flowers: in the selection below I highlight *Perovskia atriplicifolia*, which I hope never to be without for as long as I am still able to garden.

Of the many hydrangeas that offer autumn color, I find the larger types such as *Hydrangea villosa*, with its blue lacecap flowers, much more appealing than the mopheads.

FLOWERS

STABILITY OF VARIEGATION

Variegation in plants, the patterning of their usually green leaves with various colors, has long been appreciated, the variants being propagated and introduced as new cultivars. Most variegations are due to genetic mutations, "sports" or chimeras, which result in a change in the chemical composition of the green pigment in leaves, or its inhibition. Many are quite stable, although occasionally producing reverted shoots with all-green leaves. It is rare, for example, to see reverted shoots on *Weigela florida* 'Variegata' or *Philadelphus coronarius* 'Variegatus,' but the white-variegated *Fuchsia magellanica* 'Sharpitor' (illustrated below) will fairly frequently produce all-green shoots.

quite wide, creamy white edges and pink blooms similar to those of *W. florida*.

Another clone, also almost certainly a hybrid and known as *W. praecox* 'Variegata,' has narrower leaves slightly irregular in outline, but the foliage with its creamy white edging is often suffused pink, which blends with the very freely borne clusters of flowers, usually blush pink suffused a deeper pink.

Still without a valid name is a third variegated plant, which is of more spreading habit and very similar to *W. florida*. The leaves have a clean, bright, yellowish-white edging that gradually turns white, and the flower is a pleasant red-pink opening from much darker buds. It may be found under various names including the two mentioned above, as well as *W. florida* 'Albovariegata' and 'Aureovariegata.'

All the plants are of high garden value. To be sure of which one you are buying, go to your local nursery when they are in leaf. As things stand the names are irrelevant: the plant's the thing.

Caryopteris x *clandonensis* **(Verbenaceae) (5A–9A)**
Autumn-flowering shrubs are particularly welcome, bringing a fresh look to the garden as the long season of summer-blooming shrubs falters. Among the pleasantest is *Caryopteris* x *clandonensis*, a low-growing shrub that occurred in about 1930 in the garden of the then Secretary of The Royal Horticultural Society, Arthur Simmonds. The parent plants, *Caryopteris incana*, native to China and Japan, and the northern Chinese and Mongolian *C. mongolica*, grew together in his garden, and the resulting offspring of their liaison has provided gardeners with a fine shrub, more vigorous than either parent and approximately intermediate between them in flower and leaf characters.

Only some 2 to 3ft (60–90cm) tall, *C.* x *clandonensis* is a finely branched, rounded shrub clothed in soft, matt green leaves, grayish beneath and strongly scented, like those of *Lavandula stoechas*. During late sum-

Caryopteris x *clandonensis*

Hydrangea villosa

mer vigorous flowering shoots develop bearing, in the upper leaf axils, clusters of tiny bright blue flowers with exserted anthers that open in late summer or early autumn and remain in beauty for several weeks.

In early spring, it is advisable to cut the flowered shoots back to within one or two buds of the old wood, because this stimulates strong young shoots to flower later in the year. Hardy and growing in any well-drained soil in an open position, it is an excellent garden shrub and has given rise to a number of other good seedlings varying in habit and flower. The original clone described above was named 'Arthur Simmonds,' and since then the much deeper violet-blue 'Kew Blue,' 'Ferndown' with darker green foliage and deep blue flower clusters, 'Longwood Blue' from Longwood Gardens – selected for upright growth, sky-blue flowers and silver foliage, 'Heavenly Blue' with rich blue flowers and upright stance, and, most recently, 'Worcester Gold' with foliage of straw-yellow paling as the flower-spikes form, have been introduced. All are plants of equal merit that make *C.* x *clandonensis* one of the finest dwarf hybrid shrubs available to gardeners.

Hydrangea villosa (Hydrangeaceae) (7A–8B)

This, the finest of the shrubby species of *Hydrangea* for general garden use, has been sunk into the catch-all species *H. aspera* and sits uncomfortably within it both botanically and horticulturally. *H. aspera*, as currently defined, has a vast range from Nepal eastward to central China then south to Taiwan, and then appears again in Java and Sumatra. So many apparently different garden plants grown under distinct specific names are now, we

are told, merely *H. aspera* that it seems sensible, horticulturally at least, to retain the name *H. villosa* for this plant, which occurs wild in Sichuan province in western China and is the loveliest of this race of late summer-flowering hydrangeas.

It is a much less coarse plant than *H. aspera*, with soft, dark green, velvety, narrowly oval leaves up to 9in (23cm) long, and develops into a spreading shrub, eventually up to 8 or 9ft (2.4–2.7m) high and more across with short, flaking, papery branches. In late summer and on into early autumn the terminal, spreading lacecap inflorescences, often 9in (23cm) or more across, are produced on the current season's young shoots, the central mass of bright blue, fertile flowers bordered by lavender or rosy-lilac sterile florets.

Usually preferring fertile, cool, leafy soil and partial shade, *H. villosa* will nevertheless grow well under both acidic and alkaline conditions. Sir Frederick Stern, in *The Chalk Garden*, says that it was at home on his limestone cliff and seeded around among mats of *Arenaria balearica*. Unlike the Hortensia hydrangeas, it maintained its flower color even under these conditions. If you have neither a limestone cliff nor the space to allow it to spread, try it trained on a north or east wall.

Perovskia atriplicifolia (Scrophulariaceae) (5A–9A)

One of the plants that attracts most attention from visitors to Wisley in late summer and early autumn is *Perovskia atriplicifolia*, the Russian Sage. The plants were aged when I first went to Wisley for a vacation job in 1952 and, although their date of planting is now lost, they have to be at least sixty years old.

Found wild in hot, dry areas in Afghanistan and the western Himalaya, *P. atriplicifolia* has obviously found its niche at Wisley, where it forms very upright, rather stiff stems clothed in white, downy hairs and set with opposite pairs of strongly toothed, gray-green leaves, like those of *Caryopteris* very aromatic. The elegant shoots elongate to 3 or 4ft (1–1.2m) during late summer to display their small, but very beautiful, violet-blue flowers in long branched pairs, blending with the foliage to provide a haze of gray and lavender-blue lasting for many weeks and still attractive in midautumn.

In my own garden, I grow *P. atriplicifolia* close to the purple-lilac *Dahlia merckii* and *Indigofera heterantha* (*I. gerardiana*) with its rosy-purple pea-flowers, providing a soft color mix that I find blends well, both *Perovskia* and *Indigofera* being cut to near ground level each spring to maintain the balance. This treatment, regularly carried out, is always recommended for *Perovskia* and is essential, from the garden viewpoint, if the plants are not to deteriorate into a mass of untidy branches of uneven height.

Although often setting seed in North America, *Perovskia* can be easily propagated from cuttings of short shoots 2 or 3in (5–8cm) long that are produced after spring pruning. Named clones 'Blue Spire' and 'Blue Haze,' probably direct selections from seed-raised *P. atriplicifolia*, the names describing their attributes well, are available, and like the species itself are high in my league table of late-flowering shrubs.

Perovskia atriplicifolia

FOLIAGE AND/OR BERRIES

Euonymus alatus (Celastraceae) (4B–8B)

For sheer brilliance of color in autumn it is difficult to equal the display mounted by *Euonymus alatus* (see p.48) during midautumn and often into late autumn. Its small ovate leaves change from dark green, first to rosy-pink touched cerise, then to a vibrant crimson-pink, the foliage remaining long on the bush before dropping to form a brightly colored carpet, a gesture of defiant splendor before winter closes in. In winter, *E. alatus* also provides its distinctive skeleton of rather stiff branches with their conspicuous, flattened, corky wings sometimes up to ½in (1cm) wide, leaving you in no doubt as to the identity of the plant. There is also a form that lacks these corky extrusions, var. *apterus*, which usually appears less stiff in habit but has equally good autumn color. But I prefer the winged original, which provides more variation in form among other deciduous shrubs in winter.

After warm summers and reasonable pollination of the inconspicuous greenish flowers, there is often a good display of the purplish fruits opening to reveal the scarlet seeds, which flicker among the bare branches once the leaves have fallen.

Euonymus alatus, which occurs as a woodland and mountainside plant in Japan and China, is relatively slow-growing; although it may eventually reach 6 to 8ft (1.8–2.4m) in height and more in width, it will take many years to do so. Even slower-growing is the dwarf 'Compactus,' which was raised in the United States and is an ideal plant for small gardens as well as making a fine dwarf hedge.

Adaptable to soils of almost any pH, with reasonable drainage, an annual mulch and occasional fertilizer being provided, *E. alatus* can be relied on to provide its rich, striking autumn color year after year.

Related plants Although not particularly well-known in gardens, the European *Euonymus latifolius* (6A–9A), I find, is the most reliable of the spindle trees for a fine display of fruit each year. A somewhat upright, open shrub with gently arching branches, it will reach 7 or 8ft (2–2.4m) in height, and in autumn the ovate, 4–5in (10–12cm) long, fresh green leaves color a brilliant red, and when they fall they leave the very attractive, long-stalked, pendulous, rosy-crimson fruits swaying in the branches. These are five- or occasionally four-winged, and in early or midautumn split to reveal the bright orange-red seeds that remain in the open capsules for some time.

Euonymus alatus (see p.47)

OTHER PLANTS

Sorbus reducta (Rosaceae) (5B–7A)

Among the many mountain ashes or rowans that provide both autumn color and very attractive fruit to brighten the shortening days of the year are two fine dwarf species, *Sorbus reducta* and *S. poteriifolia*, both of which I have been fortunate enough to see in the wild in Yunnan province, China. They were growing in leaf-rich soil among other low-growing shrubs, conditions they appreciate in gardens.

S. reducta, well-known in cultivation, is a dwarf, usually suckering shrub growing to no more than 2ft (60cm) in height with typical mountain ash, pinnate leaves with four to seven pairs of shining, dark green leaflets covering the grayish-brown shoots. The hawthornlike, white, sometimes pink-flushed clusters of flowers are borne in late spring, and by early autumn the clusters of green, globose fruits are turning pink, remaining on the bare twigs long after the leaves have assumed their red-bronze autumn color and fallen. Readily raised from seed, preferably stratified, *S. reducta* is a charming small shrub suitable for even very small gardens.

The similar but even more diminutive *S. poteriifolia* (5B–7A) scarcely reaches 1ft (30cm) and differs in its pink flowers and initially red fruits that turn white as they mature. An uncommon plant in cultivation, it is well worth obtaining if the chance occurs.

WINTER

Great emphasis, and rightly so, is nowadays placed on winter performance, and particularly on plants that flower or are in fruit in the dog days of the year. Less often publicized are shrubs with attractive forms or bark features. Examples are the peeling, cinnamon-barked *Stephanandra*, the glaucous-stemmed willows such as *Salix daphnoides*, and the red-and green-stemmed forms of *Cornus alba* and *C. stolonifera*. However, my own special choice in this category is the white-stemmed bramble *Rubus cockburnius*, well worth growing for its winter display alone.

My other personal choice of shrub for winter has to be the superlative, fragrant winter-flowering *Daphne bholua* 'Jacqueline Postill', which deserves to be much more widely grown.

FLOWERS OR ORNAMENTAL STEMS

Daphne bholua 'Jacqueline Postill' (Thymelaeaceae) (7B–9A)

This superb winter-flowering plant is worth every award in the book. Any form of the eastern Himalayan *Daphne bholua* is worthy of cultivation, and some of the selected clones that have been propagated in recent years have proved extremely fine garden plants.

A plant of 'Jacqueline Postill' with long, undulating, dark green leaves has been growing outside our front door for the past seven years, and is now 7ft (2m) tall from a 9in (23cm) grafted plant. It begins to flower in early winter, and continues until early spring, neither flowers nor foliage touched by frost. The intense, sweet fragrance from the clusters of large purplish-pink flowers, almost white and crystalline in texture within, spreads for yards around, and on a mild day with the door open pervades the house.

Equally good, if slightly smaller-flowered, is 'Gurkha,' originating from a seedling brought back from Nepal in 1962. The flowering period matches that of 'Jacqueline Postill,' and apart from flower size the main difference is the deciduous nature of 'Gurkha,' which seems as tough and hardy as the Nepalese people after whom it was named. The evergreen 'Jacqueline Postill,' apart from the natural shedding of yellowing, older leaves, has remained untouched in many gardens even in very severe winters.

If you are lucky enough to obtain fresh fruit of *D. bholua*, it is essential to remove the fleshy exterior carefully, wash the remains off, and sow the seed immediately. Within two or three weeks, germination should occur, and the young seedlings should be potted on separately and protected for the first winter in a cold frame or greenhouse.

Various clones of *D. bholua*, however, are available either grafted onto seedlings of *D. longilobata* or on their own roots from cuttings that, from experience at Wisley, produce just as good plants with no likelihood of suckering occurring.

Rubus cockburnianus (Rosaceae) (6A–9B)

Gardeners regard any *Rubus* with suspicion because of their take-over tendencies, but among the more restrained brambles are several white-stemmed species that, while generally unspectacular in leaf, prove extremely effective winter ornamentals.

Rubus cockburnianus is a Chinese native originally discovered in western Sichuan, and is a very elegant plant producing graceful, long, upright then arching shoots that may extend to 7 or 8ft (2–2.4m) or more in one season. These stems, maroon-purple beneath, are coated with a pure white, waxy cover and, after leaf fall, show clearly why this and related species are known as the "white-washed brambles." The pinnate leaves are a pleasant fresh green above and white-felted beneath, producing an attractive effect in summer winds.

The stems of this group of species are biennial, like those of raspberries, and my preference is to cut them to the base once their ghostly winter whitewash is no longer attractive, when the young foliage develops. Others prefer to leave them to flower and fruit in their second year and cut them out after fruiting, leaving the new canes to take over their winter role. It is often more difficult and certainly a lot pricklier to delay the pruning of old stems, because they become tangled with the fresh canes and may damage their white covering.

Equally ornamental is *R. biflorus*, a Himalayan species that crosses deep into China and has been long cultivated. It has a more widely spreading habit and green, white-wax-covered stems that perhaps stand out more against dark backgrounds than those of *R. cockburnianus* (6A–9B), but appear to become more tangled. If allowed to fruit, the small yellow raspberries are pleasant tasting but of no real garden value.

WINTER FRAGRANCE

It is not difficult to plan a garden for year-round fragrance, not only from flowers, but also from foliage that you may touch or brush against as you pass.

Winter presents no problems, as so many shrubs provide not only color and brightness but also delicious scent from their blooms. There are all the witch hazels, *Hamamelis* (see p.62); *Viburnum x bodnantense* (p.61), and its parents *V. farreri* and *V. grandiflorum*; the well-named Wintersweet, *Chimonanthus praecox*; *Mahonia japonica* and its allies the sweet boxes, *Sarcococca* (p.61); and my particular favorite, *Daphne bholua* ('Jacqueline Postill' is shown below), whose blooms scent the air all around right up to late winter.

Rubus cockburnianus

TWO OR MORE SEASONS

Many shrubs are noted for their fine blooms or the high quality of their fruiting display. Relatively few, however, provide consistent displays of beautiful flowers in spring or summer followed by attractive, long-lasting fruits, as does the fragrant *Daphne retusa*.

Even more prized, especially for small gardens, are those exceptional "three-in-one" shrubs that add attractive foliage to their characteristics. One such plant of the highest merit is *Berberis darwinii*, with its glossy, evergreen leaves, orange-gold spring flowers and blue-black autumn fruits. Also outstanding is *Viburnum opulus* 'Xanthocarpum,' with flowers like hydrangea lacecaps, translucent yellow berries and rich autumn leaf color.

SPRING FLOWERS/ EVERGREEN FOLIAGE

Berberis darwinii (Berberidaceae) (7A–9B*)

The Chilean *Berberis darwinii* is one of the finest of all evergreen flowering shrubs, named after Charles Darwin, who, in 1835, collected specimens in Chile during the voyage of the *Beagle*. Its glossy, dark green, spiny leaves, characteristically with three terminal spines and a few spiny teeth either side, clothe an evergreen of dense habit, that will fairly slowly reach 10 to 12ft (3–3.5m) high, occasionally more, and as much wide. It has proved over many years to be perfectly hardy, and will thrive in any well-drained soil, preferring humus-richness, and some shelter from wind. In the US it is loyally restricted to West Coast areas.

It may selfseed, producing offspring slightly differing in leaf and flower characteristics. Chance cross-fertilization with related species has given us the well-known and very valuable *B.* x *stenophylla* (6A–9B) from an encounter with *B. empetrifolia*, and the natural hybrid *B.* x *lologensis* (6A–9B) has *B. linearifolia* as its other parent. Both are much appreciated for their wealth of orange or orange, and, yellow flowers in spring, and are offspring of which *B. darwinii* could justifiably be proud.

Berberis darwinii

In mid- to late spring, *B. darwinii* produces huge quantities of its 2in (5cm) long, pendent racemes of orange- gold, rounded flowers, often tinged flame-red in bud. The display lasts several weeks, followed frequently in early autumn by an equally profuse crop of the attractive fruits. These are rounded-ovoid and a shining blue-black in color, and are sometimes accompanied by a second but smaller crop of flowers.

I have yet to see a poor form of *B. darwinii*. Unusually nowadays, the plant has not been subject to the proliferation of cultivar names applied to minor variants of other species described as "improved." If you obtain plain *B. darwinii*, you will have one of the most glorious of garden shrubs with flowers, fruit and foliage all of top quality: an all-rounder *par excellence*.

Camellia x williamsii 'Donation' (Theaceae) (7A–9B)

Camellia 'Donation,' raised from a deliberate cross between *Camellia japonica* 'Donckelaeri' and *C. saluenensis*, stands out for its vigor and the freedom with which it unfailingly produces its 4–5in (10–12cm), semidouble blooms of soft pink with distinctive darker veining and a central boss of pale yellow stamens.

In midspring or earlier, 'Donation' provides an initial cascade of flowers, the season extending toward late spring. An added advantage of all *C.* x *williamsii* selections is that they drop their spent flowers, unlike many cultivars of *C. japonica* where the dead flowers need to be picked off as otherwise they hang on like bits of brown paper. 'Donation' has neat, glossy, dark green, narrowly ovate leaves; for informal hedging, it may be readily shaped and will still flower each spring. It requires a soil on the acidic side of neutral, preferably moisture-retentive and leaf-rich, where it will grow to 10 to 12ft (3–3.5m) high and as much across. This outstanding shrub, easily raised from late-summer cuttings, has received every available gardening award.

Another great favorite is 'Leonard Messel' (7A–9B), a hybrid between *C. reticulata*, a somewhat tender plant, and *C.* x *williamsii* 'Mary Christian.' It produces slightly larger, but looser-formed, slightly fluted, semi-double flowers of a rich, clear pink, pleasantly veined, from early spring often into late spring. More open in habit, it has matt, dark green, net-veined leaves and is most at home in the woodland garden, although, trained on a north or east wall, it will flower profusely given adequate moisture and humus.

Of very different habit is the old but still very fine clone *C. japonica* 'Lady Clare' (7A–9B). It is seldom more than a few feet high, but has a bushy, spreading, mounded habit that makes it ideal for many landscape situations where its glossy, deep green foliage is valued year round, with a spring bonus from its 5–6in (12–15cm), semidouble, deep peachy pink flowers.

Camellia x *williamsii* 'Donation'

Osmanthus delavayi (Oleaceae) (8A–10A*)

Osmanthus delavayi is certainly one of the finest evergreen shrubs for gardens, with its dense covering of opposite pairs of neat, leathery, dark glossy green, minutely scrately-toothed, ovate leaves no more than 1in (2.5cm) long, and its abundant clusters of both terminally borne and axillary flowers that turn the bushes to snow during late spring each year. Each flower is no more than ½in (1.5cm) long and the same across, with four spreading, then reflexed, lobes, looking like a pure, white miniature trumpet and with the most glorious sweet scent imaginable. Occasionally in cultivation a few of the ovoid, small indigo fruits may be found, but seldom if ever in quantity.

O. delavayi is agreeably tolerant of a range of soils and conditions. Unhindered by pruning, it will develop into a large spreading shrub 10 or 12ft (3–3.5m) high and more across. It is, however, fairly slow-growing, and because it flowers freely, even as a young plant, *O. delavayi* is well worth growing in small gardens, especially as it is also very amenable to pruning, flowered growths being gently cut back once the blooms have

Osmanthus delavayi

faded but before the fresh young growths appear. Try it also as a hedging plant, but always prune the hedge immediately after flowering, or next year's display, always a thing of great beauty, will be affected adversely. To see *O. delavayi* at its best, visit Bodnant Gardens in north Wales in late spring, where the huge hedge of this species is an unforgettable sight.

MEDITERRANEAN SHRUBS

The rich, colorful flora of the Mediterranean has for centuries been a source of garden plants, many proving cold-hardy in North America. Curiously, other species from the same habitats either sulk miserably or die when brought into cultivation.

Phlomis fruticosa, cultivated recently in parts of North America, is a fine example. Like most Mediterranean plants it requires sun, good drainage, and a spartan diet to give of its best. Most striking of all is the way in which *Euphorbia characias* and its subspecies *wulfenii* (illustrated below) have adapted to our conditions. Perhaps one day someone will raise a clone or seed-race of the lovely pink Cretan clover bush, *Ebenus creticus*, which occurs on the same hillsides as *P. fruticosa* and *E. characias* subsp. *wulfenii* yet resists outdoor cultivation.

OTHER PLANTS
Euphorbia characias subsp. *wulfenii* (Euphorbiaceae) (7A–10B)
In Greece and the Balkans this fine, shrubby spurge colors limestone hillsides yellow during spring, and it is equally well known as a garden plant, hardy in spite of its southern Mediterranean origins.

Self-sown seedlings are frequent, but vary in the size, quality, and depth of color of the bright yellow-green inflorescences.

An evergreen shrub, some might say a subshrub, up to 4 or 5ft (1.2–1.5m) high, it forms a compact mound of upright stems that grow throughout the season to develop their large, terminal, typical spurge inflorescences, often 12in (30cm) high and 6in (15cm) across. After the seed is ripe, or before if seed is not required, cut back the unsightly old stems to the base. The strong, new growths, with their densely set, narrow pairs of 5in (12cm) beautiful blue-green leaves, soon replace them. A sunny site and even some shade suits this plant provided the soil is well drained.

SUMMER FLOWERS/ EVERGREEN FOLIAGE

Callistemon subulatus (Myrtaceae) (9A–10B*)
The bottlebrushes from Australia and Tasmania have intrigued me since I saw *Callistemon subulatus* in flower at Wisley, forty years ago. In the USA its presence is virtually restricted to the low humidity areas of the West Coast. A bone-hardy shrub 4 to 5ft (1.2–1.5m) high with willowy branches covered densely with 2in (5cm), very narrow, glossy, deep green leaves, it produces its crimson, spikelike inflorescences about 3in (8cm) long and 1in (2.5cm) wide in midsummer at the ends of branches and on side shoots. The beauty of the flower heads lies almost totally in the colorful bunches of stamens, the sepals and petals being insignificant. After the blooms fade, hard, woody, small capsules are produced, but remain closed and firmly fixed to the branch, in nature only opening after bush fires, the plants regenerating from seeds in due course. Curiously, the terminal bud continues to grow beyond the faded inflorescence to produce young shoots to flower the following season.

Callistemon subulatus is probably best sited by a sunny wall or fence, where it receives maximum heat to ripen the young wood and initiate flower formation the following year. In nature, it occurs in open sites by damp creeks, but does not require very moist conditions in garden locations, growing well in acidic and neutral soils, less happy in strongly alkaline conditions. Like other bottlebrushes, it may be hard-pruned to keep it in bounds or to make it more shapely, either in spring or after flowering, although in the latter case the young shoots may not have time to ripen before winter.

The totally hardy *C. sieberi* (9A–10B) is a rounded bush some 3½ft (1m) high and across, covered in rather dumpy flower-spikes of cool yellow in early summer. While lacking the brilliant coloring of the red-flowered species, it is a very worthwhile, unusual garden shrub.

Cistus ladanifer (Cistaceae) (8A–10B*)
There are few lovelier sights in summer than the *Cistus* species and hybrids, with aromatic foliage and cheerful, open flowers like single roses. Many are not fully hardy but will survive winters if grown in very free-draining soil, alkaline or acidic, and given an open, sunny position with some winter protection around the stems, because bark-split is a common reason for their demise.

Since most are readily raised from semiripe cuttings (*Cistus ladanifer* and *C.* x *cyprius* are sometimes less obliging), it is worth propagating one or two plants each year to overwinter in a cool greenhouse in case of tragedy outside. All *Cistus* should be planted out from pots when young: older, larger pot plants are not always easily established. None transplants very well: bear this in mind when siting initially.

Of the numerous species and cultivars available, *C. ladanifer* (sometimes called *C. ladaniferus*) with its huge, solitary, white flowers, slightly crumpled in bud, and up to 4in (10cm) across with prominent maroon-red markings at the base of each petal is, to me, the

Cistus ladanifer

most spectacular. An evergreen shrub to 5ft (1.5m) high, it has attractive dark green foliage, with linear, almost stalkless leaves up to 4in (10cm) long, noticeably three-veined and very sticky from the gum that gives off a Mediterranean aromatic fragrance.

If *C. ladanifer* will not grow for long in your garden, then its offspring, *C. x cyprius*, should prove hardier. It is a hybrid with the white-flowered *C. laurifolius* (8B–10B) and, although very like *C. ladanifer*, it has somewhat broader leaves and clusters of three to six slightly smaller flowers, similar to those of *C. laurifolius* yet retaining the red markings of *C. ladanifer*.

Both are very free-flowering during early to mid-summer, and although they may have a short garden life, it is a merry one, for their blooms are beautiful and prolific.

Related plants Both in the wild and in gardens, the closely related genera *Cistus* and *Halimium* hybridize where some of their species meet, and have provided a number of excellent garden plants requiring similar treatment to *Cistus*. One of these, x *Halimiocistus winto-*

nensis (8B–10B), is a dwarf shrub about 2ft (60cm) high and more across with small, gray-woolly, young foliage, later green above. In late spring and early summer it produces a succession of cupped, 2in (5cm), clear white flowers with yellow basal marks separated from the rest of the petals by a narrow crimson-maroon zone. A sport from it, 'Merrist Wood Cream,' has pale creamy yellow petals with the same internal markings. I have grown both outside in sunny, well-drained sites for several years without protection, but in the severest winters they may be damaged or killed. Like *Cistus*, they are well worth the trouble of propagating annually as an insurance.

Hebe topiaria (Scrophulariaceae) (8B–10B*)
Having arrived in Britain only some twenty-five years after it was first described, *Hebe topiaria* has caught the imagination of nurserymen and is now propagated in considerable numbers and widely available.

I have grown it now for seven years in well-drained soil and full sun, and have found it to be totally unconcerned by severe frost or wet conditions. In that time it has grown into a tight dome 1½ft (45cm) high and 2ft (60cm) across, with semierect, intensely gray-green leaves, at the most ½in (1.5cm) long and usually less, and year-round it is a most attractive foliage shrub.

As with many of this group of *Hebe* species, the leaves are borne in opposite pairs at right angles to one another all the way up the stems, giving a four-ranked effect as you look down on the top of a shoot. This arrangement adds to the overall neatness of *H. topiaria*, which would be worth growing for its foliage alone.

In summer, however, it produces in the axils of the upper leaves of each shoot its 1in (2.5cm) spikes of small white flowers, and for a time the glaucous dome looks topped with snow. It is a tedious job to remove the developing seed pods that for a time spoil the symmetry of the bush, but, by the time I think about doing so, the plant has solved the problem by producing fresh young growth that covers them.

While one is often suspicious that lauded new introductions will turn out to be geese rather than swans, this is certainly not so with *H. topiaria*, which has more than proved its worth as far as I am concerned.

Related plants *Hebe ochracea* (8B–10B), one of the whipcord species, so called because of their shoots with tightly congested leaves, was previously known as *H. armstrongii* (8B–10B), and has arching, old-gold shoots, forming a vase-shaped shrub of 2ft (60cm) or so. More recently, an even finer dwarf clone, 'James Stirling,' has been introduced, with brighter, seasonally variable foliage color. It has a similar arching habit with rather stiff branchlets that are a mix of old-gold and yellowish-brown in spring and summer, and from autumn to early spring assume orange tints that gleam in the sunlight. The white flowers are unremarkable and seldom appear to interrupt the clean lines of its fine foliage.

The exact origins of *H.* 'Pewter Dome' (the name was my suggestion) are unknown, but this beautiful foliage plant was grown for some years simply as *H. albicans*, to which it is clearly related, differing in its rather narrower leaves and other minor characters. A dense, rounded shrub, usually 1 to 2ft (30–45cm) high (occasionally more), 'Pewter Dome' is totally hardy, easily cultivated, and valued not only for its glaucous leaves, which are neater and narrower than those other

Kalmia latifolia 'Ostbo Red'

derivations of *H. albicans*, but also for its freely given, white, 1–2in (2.5–5cm) long spikes of flowers that are produced in midsummer and complement the foliage well during their relatively brief appearance.

Kalmia latifolia 'Ostbo Red' (Ericaceae) (5A–9A)

The Mountain Laurel, *Kalmia latifolia*, native to the eastern United States, is certainly one of the most beautiful of all shrubs. Very old specimens, probably planted 100 years ago, still exist at Wisley, including a huge

plant of forma *myrtifolia* with much smaller leaves than is normal, 7 or 8ft (2–2.4m) high, although only supposed to reach half that height.

Kalmia latifolia occurs wild in relatively open positions, forming dense stands in acidic, sandy soil or rocky areas among, but not usually under, the dense shade of forest trees. In gardens it is grown in acidic to neutral soil but under a tree canopy, which probably explains why it sometimes has a reputation for sparse flowering, as to set flower bud it requires good light.

Similar in growth habit to many rhododendrons, it will form a shrub 10ft (3m) or more high and more across, but is often much smaller, with alternate, rather leathery, glossy dark evergreen leaves. In late spring and early summer, the domes of deep saucer- or cup-shaped flowers, 1in (2.5cm) across, open from angled buds, the angles formed by the ten stamen pouches.

Owing to breeding and selection programs, combined with tissue culture propogation, many named clones are available in the USA. 'Ostbo Red' is one of the finest, a magnificent plant in full bloom with iridescent, deep pure red buds that open to pale pink within and quickly become white apart from flashes of pink from the stamens. The color is intensified if grown in good light – full sunlight is fine if in leaf-rich, moist soil and well mulched. As with rhododendrons, it is also helpful to remove the spent flower heads before seed is set so that the young growth is not inhibited.

The selected clones of *K. latifolia* are garden plants of great beauty, and there exist some of the exciting color combinations, such as the beautifully banded 'Carousel' and 'Minuet.'

Phlomis fruticosa (Labiatae) (8A–9B*)

The eastern Mediterranean Jerusalem Sage is so often seen that it is perhaps somewhat undervalued. It is, in my view, still one of the best evergreen shrubs, particularly in those forms that have intensely silvered rather than gray-green leaves, although all forms provide mounds of attractive foliage all year long. The opposite leaves, up to 5in (12cm) long in some forms, are ovate-lanceolate, with prominent veins, woolly-surfaced, especially on the undersides, with a mild scent.

Variation is not uncommon in seed-raised plants. A clone cultivated as 'E. A. Bowles' or 'Edward Bowles' differs in its very large, handsome, rich green, hairy leaves and paler flowers, light yellow compared with the much richer yellow, deadnettlelike flowers of the "normal" plant, borne in tiered whorls above the foliage in early summer.

Related plants Not far removed from *Phlomis fruti-*

Phlomis fruticosa

cosa is the Lebanese *P. chrysophylla* (8B–9B), until recently scarcely known in gardens but now much valued for its fine foliage and clear yellow flowers, with white-woolly leaves and a yellowish stem. A shrub of some 3 to 4ft (1–1.2m) with more closely set foliage and a neater appearance than *P. fruticosa*, it has proved hardy at Wisley, and like *P. fruticosa* it is easily raised from cuttings or seed.

Prostanthera cuneata (Labiatae) (9A–10B)

One of the plants, like Lemon-scented Verbena, that one always touches when passing is this hardy Australian mintbush, *Prostanthera cuneata*, which has come through the severest frosts in parts of the West quite unruffled. It forms a mounded shrub to about 3ft (1m) in height and half as much again across, with shiny, dark, evergreen, opposite leaves, much paler on the lower surface, obovate in shape and only ¼in (6mm) long at most, densely borne on upright, much-branched shoots. As with the other species in the genus, its foliage is strongly aromatic, the scent being variously described as minty and smelling of wintergreen; my nostrils are, as yet, undecided between the two aromas!

In midsummer, or earlier under glass, *P. cuneata* produces a fine crop of its two-lipped, bell-shaped, white flowers, that are attractively suffused and patterned violet-purple in the throat, interspersed with a few yellow spots, and with two yellow marks at the base of the lower lip, which is prominently three-lobed. The flowers may be borne simply in the leaf axils or in short axillary spikes, and when in full bloom *P. cuneata* is a very pretty plant that is apparently much hardier than most reference books allow. Certainly its alpine habitats in Tasmania and in New South Wales undergo very cold periods, which may account for its adaptability to at least some West Coast climatic areas.

Rhododendron yakushimanum 'Koichiro Wada'

Rhododendron yakushimanum 'Koichiro Wada' (Ericaceae) (5B–8A)

Probably no rhododendron has been more fêted, at least in recent years, than the dwarf *Rhododendron yakushimanum* known only, it seems, from the small mountainous island of Yakushima, south of Kyushu, Japan. Two plants of this species were sent from Japan, prior to World War II, and one was evidently translated to Wisley at a later date. At the Chelsea Show in 1947, it was exhibited from Wisley in full flower and awarded a First Class Certificate. Since then, it has been shown to be somewhat variable in habit, leaf and flower quality, and the name of the sender, Koichiro Wada, was given to this clone. None of its many hybrids, in my view, has surpassed the parent.

It forms a dense mound of evergreen, 3–4in (8–10cm) long, convexly curved, dark green leaves that on the undersurface are coated with a thick white felt that gradually turns to a pale warm brown. In spring, if bud set in autumn has been good, it will be covered with swollen, brown-tinted flower buds that open to reveal up to twelve bell-shaped 2 or 2½in (5–6cm) blooms of apple-blossom pink, faintly flecked brown before turning white. Unless seed is required, the trusses of spent blooms should be carefully picked off, not too laborious a task on a shrub of 4 or 5ft (1.2–1.5m) high and 7 or 8ft (2–2.4m) across when mature. This will divert food that would otherwise have been used for seed production into preparing next year's flower buds, and also allows the young growths, white-felted on both surfaces, to emerge unhindered.

Rhododendron yakushimanum does, of course, require acidic soils to thrive, but will grow and flower well in full sun as well as dappled shade, given humus and moisture. It is certainly worth any trouble to please this aristocrat within a genus that has provided us with so many plants of the highest garden merit.

Related plants *Rhododendron* 'Polar Bear' (7A–9A*) blooms in late summer after the majority of its kin have long finished flowering. A hybrid of *R. auriculatum* and *R. diaprepes*, it is a very vigorous shrub or even a small tree to 20ft (6m) or more, but when in bloom it is a marvelous sight, with huge trusses of very fragrant, pure white trumpets with green-marked throats and speckling, and soft green foliage.

'Azor' (6A–9B), a shrub of some 8 or 9ft (2.4–2.7m), also late-flowering, is a hybrid of the deep-red *R. griersonianum* and the white *R. discolor*, producing in midsummer slightly lax trusses of up to eight, large, trumpet-shaped, deep pink blooms, red in the throat and slightly speckled red on the upper lobe.

SPRING OR SUMMER FLOWERS/ AUTUMN FOLIAGE

Cotinus 'Flame' (Anacardiaceae) (5B–8B)

Almost all forms of the Smoke Tree or Smoke Bush, *Cotinus coggygria* (*Rhus cotinus*), are attractive garden plants with fine foliage, filmy inflorescences in summer and brilliant autumn tints before leaf-fall.

C. coggygria is widespread through Europe with a distribution across the Himalaya to northern China, usually a plant of mountain slopes, where in autumn it provides great daubs of orange, yellow, and red on the landscape. A deciduous, open shrub or small tree of 15ft (4.5m) or so with rounded, alternate, slightly blue-green leaves when young, it produces its terminal, intricately branched, threadlike inflorescences in late summer, like brownish-pink smoke all over the crown, gradually turning grayish-pink as the autumn foliage display starts. In some of the selected clones which have foliage of varying shades of purple and copper through-

Cotinus 'Flame'

out the growing season, such as the deep purple-red 'Royal Purple,' the inflorescences have a similar coloring to that of the leaves, but usually of a paler hue, the whole plant taking on a more translucent appearance with the foliage reddening before it falls.

Cotinus coggygria is happy on fairly impoverished soils, and in overrich conditions will seldom color as satisfactorily. The stricter diet and the opportunity for shoots to ripen in sunny open sites seem to intensify the autumn color, particularly with 'Flame.'

The rather taller *C. obovatus* (4B–8A) (also called *Cotinus* or *Rhus americanus*) occurs in only a few sites in the southeastern United States and is an endangered species. Its foliage is much larger than that of *C. coggygria*, but the leaves are downy beneath when young, and much wider at the top than the base. Its chief merit lies in its brilliant autumn color, a mix of claret, scarlet, orange, and yellow, similar to that of 'Flame,' and it is likely that 'Flame' is a hybrid of the two species. Recently, the two species were crossed, using the dark-foliaged *C. coggygria* 'Velvet Cloak' with *C. obovatus*. One of the seedlings, now called *C.* 'Grace,' has received a First Class Certificate from The RHS. It is a very vigorous plant with the soft purple-red foliage of 'Velvet Cloak,' which turns scarlet in autumn, and large inflorescences of purplish pink in summer.

OTHER PLANTS

Hydrangea quercifolia 'Snowflake' Hydrangeaceae (5B–9A)

Native to the southeastern United States, the Oak-leaf Hydrangea needs a moist, quite rich, woodland soil and forms a fairly open, loosely branched, deciduous bush some 3 to 4ft (1–1.2m) high and somewhat wider spreading, distinctive in its large, scalloped, long-stalked, oaklike leaves often 8 or 9in (20–23cm) long and 6in (15cm) wide. In autumn the foliage turns brilliant shades of purple, red, and orange, but before that *Hydrangea quercifolia* produces its large, conical, upright flower panicles, often 6–9in (15–23cm) high and sometimes so heavy they arch over. This is evident with 'Snowflake,' a new clone in which the outer, sterile, "lacecap" flowers are not only double but also with up to six rosettes on a stalk. The uppermost ones are pure white with a tiny green center changing in the middle to a light green with the basal rosettes bronzed; by autumn they are all bronze-pink and last long after leaf-fall in good conditions. 'Snowflake' thrives in full sun and shade and performs superbly, its panicles measuring over 12in (30cm) in length and ornamental from late summer until late autumn.

SPRING OR SUMMER FLOWERS/ AUTUMN FRUIT

Daphne retusa (Thymelaeaceae) (7A–9B*)

This neat, easily grown, evergreen *Daphne* easily falls into my list of Five Best Shrubs. One of the most amenable species in a reputedly difficult genus, and best suited to the cool, low humidity areas of the West Coast, it produces richly fragrant, attractive flowers in abundance in spring followed by a profusion of shiny, succulent, red fruits in late summer and early autumn. *Daphne retusa* is one of the finest hardy dwarf shrubs that I know, forming a dense, compact mound seldom more than 2 to 3ft (60–90cm) high and as much across. It grows well in any humus-rich soil where drainage is not impeded, but it is less likely to thrive in extremely acidic or alkaline conditions. However, it is known to bloom and fruit freely for many years even on alkaline soils; and in Yunnan province in China I found it in fruit at the edge of a pine and rhododendron woodland, where the soil was undoubtedly acidic.

Daphne retusa was originally discovered in western Sichuan province in 1889. It has been collected more recently in Bhutan and Tibet at altitudes of 10,000 to

Daphne retusa

14,000ft (3,000–4,500m).

The dark glossy green leaves are usually no more than 1 to 2in (2.5–5cm) long and about ¾in (2cm) wide, with the apex rounded and notched. During early summer (and occasionally again in late summer), clusters of small, rosy purple and white, intensely fragrant flowers

are produced in abundance. These are succeeded by bright red, polished, globose fruits, which are rapidly taken by birds once ripe. If seed is required for propagation, you should gather the fruits just before they develop their full color. If the flesh is removed and the seeds sown as soon as possible and plunged in pots out of doors, germination usually occurs the following spring. The plants normally take three to five years to flower after germination.

D. retusa may also be raised from softwood or half-ripe cuttings, but if seed is available this is a more trouble-free method of propagation.

Viburnum opulus 'Xanthocarpum' (Caprifoliaceae) (4A–8B)

Viburnum opulus, is the European cranberry-bush widespread through much of Europe and into central Asia. A vigorous, deciduous shrub, it forms thickets of erect stems, clothed in maple-like three- to five-lobed leaves, and produces its terminal, cymose inflorescences, 3 or 4in (8–10cm) across, in early summer. The showy, outer, white, sterile flowers bordering the tiny, greenish, yellow-anthered, fertile blooms are like those of a lacecap hydrangea in miniature and give way in late summer and autumn to bunches of bright red, succulent, globose fruits, each about ⅓in (1cm) across. The brilliance of the fruits is matched by the beauty of the autumn foliage, which turns to bronze-purple and then reddish-pink before falling, leaving the fruit clusters standing out against the bare branches.

Viburnum opulus is particularly accommodating in its requirements, growing well on limestone and even tolerating poorly drained, although not waterlogged, ground. It will also grow well, but flower only sparsely, in very shaded conditions, and to obtain the best results it should be given an open, sunny site.

In its double form, well-known as 'Sterile' but as a result of nomenclatural quirks correctly called 'Roseum' (which it is not, except on fading), it is commonly and very sensibly called the Snowball Tree, with rounded masses of sterile white flowers and, following them, very rich autumn leaf color. Among other variants of garden value is the excellent 'Compactum' (not 'Nanum,' which is a poor creature), which is extremely free-berrying and about half the height of the normal plant, at 5 or 6ft (1.5–1.8m), occasionally higher. But best of all is 'Xanthocarpum,' with translucent, rich yellow or apricot-yellow berries, free-fruiting and, in my eyes, surpassing the red-fruited forms in beauty and longevity, the berries remaining on the branches, usually untouched by birds, long into the autumn.

Viburnum opulus 'Xanthocarpum'

Related plants The Chinese *Viburnum betulifolium* (5B–8B), a tall deciduous shrub with long arching branches to 10ft (3m) high or more, has, as its name suggests, birchlike leaves clothing its red-brown young shoots, strongly veined and dark green, setting off the 3–4in (8–10cm) flattened heads of small white blooms that appear in early summer. In autumn, the scene changes from summer quiescence to autumn abundance as the great pendent bunches of translucent, bright red berries drip from the upper branches like fat strings of red currants, a marvelous sight during midautumn and lasting well into late autumn on occasion. Although easily cultivated, *V. betulifolium* often does not fruit unless two or more plants, preferably different seedlings, are grown together. Then all should be well.

OTHER PLANTS

Rosa moyesii 'Geranium' (Rosaceae) (5B–8A)

The Chinese *Rosa moyesii*, with blood-red or pink flowers and flagon-shaped, freely produced, shiny bright red fruits, is one of the most beautiful rose species, providing interest from early summer to late winter. It is a tall, hardy, upright, branched shrub, often to 10ft (3m) high in the wild but rather less in gardens.

'Geranium' was raised at Wisley in the mid1930's, and although most forms of *R. moyesii* in cultivation had until then been pink-flowered, it produced bright geranium-red blooms, with waxy-textured petals and a ring of creamy yellow anthers. It has a more compact habit than many forms of *R. moyesii*, usually no more than 7 to 8ft (2–2.4m) in height, with slightly squatter, equally brilliant fruits.

AUTUMN TO SPRING FLOWERS

Coronilla glauca (Leguminosae) (8B–10A)

Now sometimes considered a subspecies of *Coronilla valentina*, it is under the name *Coronilla glauca* that most gardeners will recognize this superlative Mediterranean shrub. Although not widespread in North American gardens, it is a long-time denizen of British gardens, having been grown there for over 270 years in spite of the fact that in very severe winters it will often be killed, even if grown as a wall plant. It is easily raised from cuttings, however, and like *Cistus* is best propagated each year as an insurance against total loss.

A small, evergreen, bushy shrub that in the wild may reach 7 or 8ft (2–2.4cm) in height, *C. glauca* is usually no more than 3 or 4ft (1–1.2m) in cultivation, but may readily be trained up a wall, where its intensely glaucous, pinnate leaves provide a superb backdrop for the clusters of light yellow pea-flowers that will appear sometimes in late autumn, but more often in early winter and through into midspring, frequently blooming intermittently later in the year. It has puzzled me, ever since I first grew *C. glauca* some twenty-five years ago, that most references grandly state that it "flowers mid-

Coronilla glauca

spring to early summer," because I regard it as part winter-, part spring-flowering – the flowers are there for all to see and very sweetly scented into the bargain, at least in the daytime.

C. glauca should be placed at the base of a hot, sunny wall or under a south-facing windowsill where, when you open the window, you can not only see the joyous combination of blue-gray foliage and bright yellow flowers but also savor its perfume as well.

There is also a pale yellow clone, 'Citrina,' that I do find more tender, although equally lovely, and with the pretty creamy-variegated clone added – also marginally hardy – you have a charming trio of very worthwhile shrubs, valuable for foliage, flower scent, and an ability to flower over long periods of the year.

OTHER PLANTS

Skimmia japonica 'Rubella' (Rutaceae) (7B–10B)
Of many named clones of *Skimmia japonica*, the male 'Rubella' has always appealed to me more than the female, berrying clones. There is a neatness about 'Rubella,' which forms a bushy shrub up to 4ft (1.2m) high, densely set with dark green, glossy, elliptic leaves with deep red leaf stalks, that separates it in garden quality from its close relatives. Its conical flower heads, green at first, then becoming red-brown in bud, often cover the crown of the bush and remain in color right through autumn and winter before opening, in spring, to reveal their white interiors and yellow anthers, emitting a characteristic strong, sweet fragrance.

Although very easily grown, *S. japonica* 'Rubella' is better in slightly shaded, moist conditions, as its foliage is sometimes affected adversely by hot sunny weather.

Viburnum x *bodnantense* 'Dawn' (Caprifoliaceae) (5A–7B)
Among winter-flowering shrubs, *Viburnum* x *bodnantense* probably has the longest flowering season, occasionally coming into flower in late summer when still in leaf and producing a modicum of bloom right through until early spring to midspring. A large, upright, somewhat gaunt shrub, *V.* x *bodnantense* will quickly reach 6 or 8ft (1.8–2.4m) or more. The clusters of scented, tubular, pink-budded, white flowers are amazingly frost-resistant unless fully open, taking short breaks in very cold spells, when the closed buds wait patiently for more clement weather to continue their display.

The original clone, 'Dawn,' from Bodnant, and the rival clone from the Royal Botanic Garden Edinburgh, 'Charles Lamont,' are joined by 'Deben,' with pink buds opening to pure white flowers.

AUTUMN OR WINTER FLOWERS/ EVERGREEN FOLIAGE

Fatsia japonica (Araliaceae) (7A–9B)
Among the most ornamental of all hardy shrubs, *Fatsia japonica* is a magnificent evergreen that provides a sub-tropical effect in the garden and is also much valued as a pot plant for indoor decoration. The handsome, leathery, long-stalked, dark, glossy green, palmate leaves, cut for the house, last for several weeks in water, acting as a backdrop against which a succession of more ephemeral cut flowers may be displayed.

A large spreading shrub, *F. japonica* will reach as much as 12 to 15ft (3.5–4.5m) but is usually only 6 to 9ft (1.8–2.7m) high, and produces leaves in proportion, often over 15in (38cm) long and across, that form a dense canopy of polished foliage, ideal as a platform for the large panicles of milky white, globular flower heads that appear in midautumn. When open, the flower heads are a fine sight with the dark foliage as a foil, but in frosty weather do not, unfortunately, survive long, a good reason for growing one or two specimens as pot plants for a sunroom, if space allows, so that they may develop to the full undamaged.

Fatsia japonica

One of the toughest evergreens, this fine Japanese shrub will grow well in any well-drained soil and makes an admirable coastal plant as well as being useful as a lawn specimen and for blending into shrub borders. While I would never wish to grow the blotched, varie gated form, I would equally never wish to be without *F. japonica* in unadulterated dark green.

Mahonia x *media* 'Winter Sun' (Berberidaceae) (7B–9A)

The fortuitous selection by Sir Eric Savill, creator of the Savill Gardens in Windsor Great Park, Berkshire, of three seedlings from Russells nursery at Windlesham led to the development of one of the best races of win-ter-flowering plants imaginable. The original seedlings were being grown at the Slieve Donard nursery in Northern Ireland where the two parents, *Mahonia lomariifolia* and *M. japonica*, were planted close to one another and had clearly hybridized when the plants had reached flowering size and were examined.

The seedling picked out became *Mahonia* x *media* 'Charity,' certainly one of the finest of all evergreen shrubs, valued not only for the long glossy leaves borne on upright stems to 10ft (3m) or more, but also for the initially upright, then spreading 12in (30cm) racemes of

Mahonia x *media* 'Winter Sun'

lemon-yellow, slightly scented flowers borne in termi-nal sprays during late autumn and early winter, rarely touched by the frost, the display lasting for many weeks as new inflorescences succeed old.

Stimulated by the introduction of 'Charity,' other gardeners, notably Lionel Fortescue at The Garden House in Devon, made deliberate crosses of the same two parents and selected the best seedlings. Two of these, the bright yellow, upright-racemed 'Lionel Fortescue' and the more lax-flowered 'Buckland,' are now widely distributed and much valued for their deco-rative contribution in winter.

One of the original seedlings of *M.* x *media*, called 'Winter Sun,' is now considered to be a better garden plant than 'Charity,' having more erect racemes of larg-er individual flowers that eventually spread quite wide-ly but do not droop and are apparently impervious to light frost, at least in Britain. In most seasons its flow-ers open at the end of late autumn and continue on right through early winter.

It is difficult to choose between these admirable selections, because all the clones of *M.* x *media* have proved equable garden plants, thriving in leafy soils in sun or light shade, and if they exceed their allotted space they will withstand severe pruning. With stems cut back in spring to a few feet from ground level, they will quickly break from dormant stem buds to refurbish themselves and bloom again within two years.

OTHER PLANTS

Sarcococca hookeriana var. *digyna* (Buxaceae) (6A–8B)
The genus *Sarcococca* contains a number of species of fine, small, evergreen, shade-loving shrubs with sweetly scented winter flowers, giving rise to their common names, sweet box or Christmas box. All are Asian species that will grow as well in alkaline soils as in acidic and, with one or two exceptions, are totally hardy in the zones outlined.

Sarcococca hookeriana var. *digyna* is a willowy shrub no more than 3 to 4ft (1–1.2m) high with narrow, lanceolate leaves, producing axillary flowers in mid- to late winter, sometimes earlier – little tuffets of white that peer out between the leaves and waft their sweet fragrance through the garden. It occurs in two forms, one with green stems, the other with reddish stems and leaf midribs, known as 'Purple Stem,' both are equally good in the garden. Look also for the rather denser and sometimes taller *S. confusa*, with its glossy, ovate leaves, which in addition to its creamy anthered, strongly fra-grant white flowers, fruits freely, the whole bush often laden with showy black berries by summer.

WINTER FLOWERS/
AUTUMN FOLIAGE

Hamamelis x *intermedia* 'Diane'
(Hamamelidaceae) (5A–8B)

The witch hazels, species and hybrids of *Hamamelis*, are, with an odd exception, all winter-flowering and among the most beautiful shrubs available to gladden the dull days of winter in the garden and, as cut branches, in the house.

Hamamelis mollis, the Chinese Witch Hazel, with its spiderlike, bright yellow, citron-scented flowers is in any form a fine garden plant, but its hybrids with *H. japonica*, known collectively as *Hamamelis* x *intermedia*, are gradually replacing it as many fine selected clones are now available. 'Diane,' raised in Belgium by Robert and Jelena de Belder, is among my favorites, a spreading shrub with out-flung branches that, from mid- to late winter, sparkle with large, bright rich-red, spidery flowers, sharply but pleasantly scented and, with the winter sun shining through them, a sight to lift the heart. 'Jelena,' an earlier selection from the same stable, is in its color range still the best I know, an orange-red, suffused copper. A bonus from both 'Jelena' and 'Diane' is the superb autumn foliage.

'Pallida,' once assigned directly to *H. mollis*, was raised at Wisley before 1930 and is still one of the finest selections available – if you obtain the correct plant, which has pale sulphur-yellow flowers and a delicious, if slightly sharp, scent. Seedlings of like character currently being sold as 'Pallida' often inferior in the texture of the petals, which in the true plant are larger than those of most of the imposters. The autumn color is yellow, only occasionally flushed red.

Apart from the more usual winter-flowering *Hamamelis* there is one species grown in gardens that normally flowers in late winter or early spring: *H. vernalis*, which produces its tiny yellow, orange or red blooms in late winter, sometimes earlier. The species is not, in bloom, very spectacular, and the scent of the flowers is rather pungent, although not unpleasant. In leaf, however, the selection 'Sandra' is outstanding in autumn, almost breathtaking in the brilliance of its deep red, scarlet, and orange foliage in midautumn, and also attractive in spring as the coppery-purple leaves unfold before turning green with only hints of purple remaining in the summer.

All the witch hazels grow well in humus-rich, acidic to neutral soils, but are seldom happy in alkaline conditions, although if you garden on lime they may still be grown as tub plants if well fertilized and watered. They

Hamamelis x *intermedia* 'Diane'

Hamamelis x *intermedia* 'Diane' (detail)

will flower very well both in open sites and in light woodland, and although expensive to purchase, as they need to be grafted and are slow-growing, give tremendous value for very little outlay over many years. Their flowers are remarkably frost-resistant and never seem to suffer even if frozen solid for several days – what more could be asked of any plant?

VARIEGATED EVERGREEN FOLIAGE

Ilex x *altaclerensis* 'Lawsoniana' (Aquifoliaceae) (7B–9B)

If I had to choose just one variegated holly to grow in my garden it would almost certainly be 'Lawsoniana,' one of many clones of the Highclere Holly available, because it is one of the most cheerful plants imaginable to brighten winter days in the garden and indoors, if cut for the house.

It is a sport of the rather dull, dark green, broad-foliaged 'Hendersonii,' which is very vigorous and forms a more or less conical, well-clothed shrub, eventually becoming a tree of 30ft (10m) or more. 'Lawsoniana' retains the dark green edge of the leaf, very slightly spiny if at all, but the center is broadly marked with gold and bright green that lightens up the whole shrub. A female clone, it will, with a male close by, produce good crops of large red berries, but it is, of course, mainly grown as a foliage plant and for its compact bushy habit. It is prone to reverting to 'Hendersonii,' and an occasional sortie to remove any branches or shoots that have sported back to plain green is essential.

'Golden King,' somewhat perversely a female clone, with its broad gold edges and dark but bright green center to the leaf, I would also choose to provide variation in leaf pattern. However, as with so many genera where numerous clones have been named and marketed, the choice has to be personal to accord with your own likes and dislikes, particularly within a large and varied genus such as *Ilex*.

OTHER PLANTS
Rhamnus alaternus 'Argenteovariegata' (Rhamnaceae) (8A–9A)

The green-leaved form of this hardy Mediterranean shrub is now seldom seen, although with its glossy foliage it would be useful for maritime climates and for hedging. The best of its variegated forms, 'Argenteovariegata' is, however, frequently grown, although said to be slightly tender, and will reach 6 or 8ft (1.8–2.4m) high, a dense-foliaged shrub with the green leaves overlaid gray and irregularly but fairly deeply edged creamy white. It is an excellent foliage plant that should be grown sheltered from very cold winds, because these may brown the foliage to some extent. Used to brighten up other shrubs, or individually to provide a highlight in a mixed border, it will serve the gardener well for many years.

Ilex x *altaclerensis* 'Lawsoniana'

CLIMBERS AND WALL SHRUBS

Trained on a wall, trellis or arbor, climbers present their glories in a way that the gardener can control, directing their growth as necessary to clothe a surface or wind the plant sinuously in a pleasing asymmetry: it is their very need for support that allows them to be so persuaded. For foliage, flowers, scent or ornamental fruits or seed heads, or various permutation of these attributes, the climbers selected here are the ones I would least willingly do without, and the same personal yardstick has been applied to the choice of wall shrubs.

With genera as rich as *Rosa* and *Clematis* the process of picking out favorites has been particularly painful: omitting a plant altogether, or even giving it an undeservedly brief description as a "related plant" (as I have done with the indispensable *Clematis* 'Perle d'Azur'!) has often made me feel as if I had badly let down an old friend. However, giving rein to my enthusiasm in such cases would have led to a book more than twice as long.

Many of my choices here, such as *Wisteria floribunda* 'Mulitjuga' or *Lonicera perclymenum* 'Serotina,' are perfectly easy to grow, but I also list a number of plants that require a little more encouragement – such as *Tropaeolum polyphyllum*, with its lovely glaucous foliage and cool yellow flowers in summer – as well as some that amply repay the pampering they need to survive the winter.

SPRING

In cool temperate climates spring-flowering climbers and wall shrubs are often exiled under glass, where their tender attributes take refuge from frost. The excellent perennial *Tropaeolum tricolorum* is a small climber that produces a mass of red and yellow, maroon-mouthed blooms in a cool greenhouse. The very fine *Clianthus puniceus* puts a braver face on things: it can be grown outside successfully against a sunny wall in mild areas, so long as it receives some winter protection.

The early-flowering *Rosa* 'Helen Knight,' whose yellow blooms are delicately scented, may be grown as a shrub, but benefits from being trained to grow on a sunny wall. It was introduced to nurseries soon after its first flowering, but curiously thirteen years elapsed before it became widely available – despite the fact that at Wisley over 500 requests for a supplier were once monitored in a three-week period during its flowering season!

FLOWERING CLIMBERS AND WALL SHRUBS

Clianthus puniceus (Leguminosae) (8A–11)

Clianthus puniceus, a native of the North Island of New Zealand, is known commonly as Parrot's Beak. Although more at home in the cool greenhouse or sunroom in frost-prone climates, it is worth planting against a wall in mild areas, where its evergreen foliage covered in bright scarlet blooms in spring and early summer presents a magnificent sight.

Naturally growing in sandy, well-drained, and sometimes rocky sites, *C. puniceus* has a somewhat spreading habit, the base and lower branches becoming woody and the younger, lax, often semipendent shoots bearing elegant, glossy, or gray-green, pinnate, fernlike leaves. Training against wires on a support from an early stage ensures that the pendulous clusters of up to fifteen, 2–3in (5–8cm), pea-shaped blooms with upright, swept-back standards and long, clawlike keels are seen to best effect against the handsome foliage.

Red-flowered forms, from deep scarlet to vermilion, are most frequently grown, but variants with flowers from white to deep pink are also available. The ivory-white, green-tinted forma *albus* appears to come true from seed, and makes an attractive foil for the red of the common Parrot's Beak if they are grown together.

Given a sheltered, sunny position and some winter protection, *C. puniceus* is easy to grow and in gardens in our warmer regions I have seen specimens 10 to 12ft (3–3.5m) across and as much high. In less clement gardens, it is sensible to raise seedlings regularly as a precaution against winter loss. Spring-sown seed raised in a propagator at 60 to 65°F (15–18°C) normally germinates freely, but the seed coat is fairly tough and gentle scarification may be needed. Snails seem inordinately fond of the foliage, so appropriate controls are needed.

This is one of the most spectacular of all spring-flowering plants, irresistible when seen in its full glory. **Related plants** *Clianthus formosus (C. dampieri)* (9A–11), known as the Desert Pea from its habitat in western and northern Australia, is as beautiful as its New Zealand relative but in the USA, at least, much more demanding. A spreading subshrub or woody-based herb, it has gray, silkyhairy, pinnate foliage and 3in (7.5cm), lobster-claw flowers of brilliant scarlet, each with a contrasting, glossy, purplish-black mark.

Clianthus formosus is easily raised from seed but requires very sharp drainage. At Wisley it has been grown successfully in hanging baskets watered via an empty 3in (7.5cm) clay pot centered in the basket. A gorgeous winter- and spring-flowering plant for the cool greenhouse, *C. formosus* is worth every effort to grow even though it is doubtful if, even in Southern California where it is hardy, it will ever emulate the amazing display of bloom I was once fortunate enough to see in Western Australia.

Rosa 'Helen Knight' (Rosaceae) (7B–9B)

I have a particular liking for *Rosa* 'Helen Knight' because not only is it an outstanding, early-flowering rose but it also provides happy memories of two people for whom I had great affection and respect, Frank Knight, Director of Wisley from 1955 to 1969, and his wife Helen, after whom this fine rose was named. The seed parent was *Rosa ecae* from Afghanistan and northwest Pakistan, a yellow-flowered species best grown as a wall plant in most areas, because it requires warmth to ripen the shoots and to flower freely each spring. In cultivation, it is rarely known to produce fruits, but in 1964 Frank Knight noticed a few hips on the plant growing against his house at Wisley, from which these

Clianthus puniceus

seedlings were raised early in 1966. In due course, one of these flowered, producing a profuse display of slightly cupped, 2in (5cm), bright yellow blooms during late spring for a period of about four weeks. On investigation it proved to be a hybrid with *R. pimpinellifolia* 'Grandiflora' (*R. spinosissima* var. *altaica*) and combines the best attributes of each parent.

An upright, somewhat arching shrub reaching 6ft (1.8m) or more in the open, 'Helen Knight,' although perfectly hardy, is perhaps more suitable for growing against a sunny wall, where it may be trained to cover an area 12ft (3.5m) high and across, but is also very easily restricted. The original plant at Wisley was a remarkable sight in late spring, the lacy, fresh green foliage awash with clear yellow, gently fragrant blooms. This superb rose is now stocked by a number of nurseries and, although some may regard its single, relatively short flowering period as a drawback, the abandon with which it blooms as a wall plant very early in the rose season makes up for any lack of remontant flowering.

OTHER PLANTS

Tropaeolum tricolorum (Tropaeolaceae) (8B–9B)
One of a group of seldom-grown, very fine, perennial nasturtiums with fleshy rhizomes or tubers, *Tropaeolum tricolorum* amply repays its rent in a cool greenhouse. Its slender, twining growths, with five- to seven-lobed, fresh green leaves, appear in late winter and will rapidly cover a support of twigs or canes to a height of 3 to 4ft (1–1.2m). From early winter for two months or more, bright red and yellow, maroon-mouthed blooms, about 1in (2.5cm) long with puffed-out flower tubes and long, upcurving spurs, appear from the leaf axils in profusion.

Regrettably, the tubers are not hardy and probably derive from coastal areas of Chile, although a stock from mountain populations that survives winter snows has recently been introduced and may prove hardy. There is, though, a record of *T. tricolorum* being grown unprotected for six or more years by the foot of a south wall in dry conditions in southwest England, so those with surplus tubers might experiment in a similar site.

SUMMER

Flowering climbers come into their own in summer, draping curtains of color and scent on walls and fences. Roses and later-flowering, older varieties of clematis can be planted in combination to great effect, trained over frames or allowed to climb freely through trees. To my mind, the canary-yellow flowers of *Rosa* 'Mermaid' associate particularly well with the light-blue *Clematis* 'Perle d'Azur,' but permutations are virtually endless.

A number of fine selections from *Wisteria floribunda* and other wisteria species have been introduced, mainly from Japan, but none surpasses 'Multijuga' at its peak (p.72).

Among my choices of summer-flowering wall shrubs is the superb evergreen *Alyogyne huegelii* (p.74). Undoubtedly one of the finest introductions of recent years, it has yet to be fully tested to see whether it will face winters in favored sites with equanimity: if not, I am more than happy to enjoy its beauty in a pot or as a summer visitor only.

FLOWERING CLIMBERS

Clematis 'Étoile Rose' (Ranunculaceae) (5A–9A)

Although very popular in the early part of this century, 'Étoile Rose' and a number of other hybrids of *Clematis texensis* with considerable garden merit had virtually disappeared from cultivation by the end of World War II, and it is only in relatively recent years that they have become available again through specialist nurseries.

My first sight of 'Étoile Rose' was in southern England, scrambling through shrubs and intermingled with climbing roses to a height of some 7 or 8ft (2–2.4m). In late summer, it was providing a fine display of its nodding, deep cherry-red blooms edged with silver-pink, a sight that remains vivid in my memory more than thirty years later.

As with so many of the excellent *texensis* and *viticella* hybrids, it requires only moderate attention in order to thrive. Apart from the provision of a cool, well-drained root run and adequate support to enable

its long-spreading shoots to wander sinuously toward the light, the only treatment necessary is an annual spring pruning to ensure it does not deteriorate into a tangled bird's nest of unruly growth. In early spring, all the old stems should be cut back to within 12 to 16in (30–40cm) of ground level, preferably to developing, near-basal shoots, which will then grow vigorously through spring and early summer before presenting the colorful elegance of their fluted, open blooms until the first frosts bring the year's display to an end.

Related plants Few genera of climbers apart from *Rosa* can hope to compete as garden plants with *Clematis*, known to many gardeners as 'The Queen of Climbers.' Countless hybrids have been bred since the advent of the ubiquitous but very beautiful, deep purple *C.* x *jackmanii* (4A–9A) in 1860, and have in their ancestry the genes that endow them with longevity of flowering. 'Perle d'Azur' (4A–9A) is one of these I could not do without. The profusion of china-blue blooms from midsummer until midautumn render it invaluable late in the year. It looks particularly fine against a yew hedge, where its purity of color warmed by hints of purple and green makes it one of the most effective plants in my garden at this time of year.

Clematis 'Ville de Lyon' (4A–9A), with its long flushes of dark crimson, cream-anthered blooms both early and late in the summer, I also find very appealing. Like the delicate and lovely 'Étoile Rose,' hybrids of *C. viticella* such as 'Ville de Lyon' have a delicate charm and indefinable quality that contrasts markedly with the very colorful, but to me sometimes gross, platelike blooms of many modern cultivars.

Codonopsis vinciflora (Campanulaceae) (6A–8A)

Codonopsis species provide attractive small climbers or twiners for a variety of garden situations and are by no means difficult to please. Many species occur wild in alpine areas of the Himalaya and those cultivated are tuberous, herbaceous perennials with usually solitary, often nodding blooms borne terminally. *Codonopsis vinciflora* differs in having upright, saucer-shaped blooms that, in forms introduced in the 1950's, were a bright, clear blue with flowers 1½in (4cm) across. A fine-foliaged plant with both opposite and alternate, toothed, thin-textured leaves on sinuous stems, *C. vinciflora* seldom achieves more than 2 to 3ft (up to 1m) in height and is best grown in humus-rich soil among dwarf rhododendrons, daphnes, or other low-growing shrubs, where it provides mid- and late summer color.

Seed germinates readily in spring if autumn or winter sown with the pots plunged outdoors to undergo a cold period. The tiny seedlings are difficult to prick out as they are rather fragile, so the whole pot is best transferred into a larger container of humus-rich potting mix or the seedlings pricked out as small clumps into a similar mixture. Once the plants go dormant, the small tubers that form during the summer may be potted up individually or the process left until early spring. Seedlings usually take three years to reach flowering size and, although tolerant of alkaline conditions, thrive better in humus-rich, peaty soils. They will not accept heavy, poorly drained soils.

Codonopsis vinciflora occurs naturally from Bhutan across to Tibet and into southwest China and is often confused with the more robust *C. convolvulacea* (6A–8A) which is twice as tall with larger flowers and entire, leathery leaves, but is equally as good a garden plant both in its blue and white forms.

Several other species are very desirable, particularly *C. ovata* (6A–8A) with its elegantly flared, pendent bells of dark-veined midblue, and the tufted, nonscandent *C. meleagris*, its bluish-green, nodding flowers veined deep reddish-brown and marked internally with purple or yellow-green. Almost all are very gardenworthy, although the foxy-smelling foliage of *C. clematidea* (6A–8A) and one or two other species may deter some gardeners from growing members of this most attractive genus of bellflower relations.

Lonicera periclymenum 'Serotina' (Caprifoliaceae) (5A–9A)

The woodbine or common honeysuckle of hedgerows and woodland, lauded by poets in romantic mood, is distributed naturally through much of Europe and across to western Asia. Not surprisingly it is very variable, and several selections have been made, notably the clone known as 'Serotina,' 'Late Dutch,' or 'Late Red.'

Confusion reigns, as two clones at least are marketed as 'Serotina,' both flowering from early or midsummer until midautumn with blooms a rich purple-crimson without, cream ageing to yellow within, and intense evening fragrance. The young stems are red-brown and somewhat glaucous, and the leaves are glaucous beneath. The main differences appear to be in habit, the clone now called 'Florida' (or 'Serotina Florida') being dwarfer, almost shrubby, with slightly less bronzed flowers, while the other, simply sold as 'Serotina,' is a vigorous twiner that will reach 12 to 15ft (3.5–4.5m) or more with ease.

Both grow in slight shade in humus-rich soil with plenty of water during the growing season to maintain strong, fresh-looking foliage and an abundance of flower. If pruning is required, it should consist merely of cutting back flowered shoots to encourage further flowering wood to be produced, the removal of tired, old, straggling branches, and the tying-in of strong new growths. Shearing over the growth completely, as sometimes recommended, may result in great "birds' nests" of twiggy growth. If more formal training is required, it may, however, be useful to trim back all shoots in spring to encourage flowering shoots to be produced over the whole "surface," a treatment I have seen very effectively applied to the clone 'Graham Thomas,' which has large, pure cream flowers turning yellow with age and entirely lacking any purple coloration, but still intensely fragrant in the evening.

While there are many fine honeysuckles available, none has quite the same appeal to me as *L. periclymenum* and the superb clones grouped under 'Serotina,' which, together with 'Graham Thomas,' form a trio of flowering climbers of the highest quality.

Related plants If the magnificent Chinese *Lonicera*

Lonicera periclymenum 'Serotina'

tragophylla (6A–9A) had the scent of *L. periclymenum*, it would be among the most sought-after of climbing plants. In spite of its lack of fragrance, *L. tragophylla* is valuable for the huge, terminal heads of up to twenty bright yellow, typical honeysuckle blooms up to 3½in (9cm) long and 1in (2.5cm) or so wide at the mouth. Add to this the handsome, slightly glaucous, mature foliage and the bronze coloration of the young leaves, and you have one of the finest deciduous garden climbers available. Grow it with its roots shaded and its main growth in full sun to obtain the best effect. *L. tragophylla* will also flower well in semishaded positions, but better for this purpose is its somewhat smaller-flowered hybrid, *L. x tellmanniana* (6A–8B), with bright yellow, orange-budded blooms.

Mutisia oligodon (Compositae) (8B–9B)

During my early years at Wisley I was lucky enough to visit two great gardeners, Norman Hadden and Bertram Anderson, who had adjacent gardens near Porlock in southwest England. *Mutisia oligodon* was one of many memorable plants I first saw there, grown as a low hedge some 30ft (10m) or more long and 3ft (1m) high, theoretically separating their two gardens. It was an astonishing sight in full bloom, the dark green, toothed, narrow foliage, gray-woolly beneath, a superb foil for the salmon-pink, yellow-centered, 3in (7.5cm), daisylike flower heads borne in profusion in summer and early autumn.

Like most species of this fascinating South American genus, it is a tendril climber and in the wild in Chile and Argentina occurs in rocky areas and dry pastures at altitudes between 3,000 and 5,000ft (1,000–1,500m). Mutisias are best suited to the drier, less humid climates of the West Coast.

Like many of the species, *M. oligodon* spreads by basal suckers from which it may sometimes be propagated, although it is better to leave these shoots untouched, since they often resent disturbance. Increase by semiripe cuttings or from seed is preferable, and normally presents no problems. Although few of us will have the opportunity to grow *M. oligodon* as an informal hedge, it is ideal for growing against a low wall, because it seldom exceeds 3 or 4ft (1–1.2m) in height; it may sometimes be persuaded to scramble a little higher given an open trellis support. It is altogether a most satisfactory and very beautiful climber that should be more widely grown.

Related plants Few who see the 4–5in (10–12cm), brilliant orange daisies of *Mutisia decurrens* (8B–9B) can resist attempting to grow it, but it is less easy to please

than *M. oligodon*. Having killed three specimens, I still hope to succeed by growing it against a west wall, its base in cool shade and its top growth in full sun.

It resents any disturbance of the suckering shoots, which in healthy plants are freely produced. They act as replacements for worn-out flowering shoots and, if removed, debilitate the plant, which may well eventually be lost. Propagation from cuttings of flowered shoots as well as semiripe cuttings may be successful, but if seed is available this is by far the easiest method of obtaining young plants, which should be placed in their permanent position as soon as they are growing well, with as little root disturbance as possible. Although a tricky plant to grow, *M. decurrens* provides such a long and glorious summer display that successful establishment is worth every effort to achieve.

Rosa 'Mermaid' (Rosaceae) (7B–9B)

High on my list of climbing roses to grow with limited wall, fence, or pergola space comes the hybrid of *Rosa bracteata*, christened 'Mermaid' when introduced in 1918 and now a worldwide favorite.

My first plant was a purchase never regretted, even though it made a very large hole in my schoolboy pocket money allowance. Although reputed to be slightly tender, as is its *R. bracteata* parent, once established with a strong woody framework only very minor damage is likely in the severest of winter conditions. Certainly the specimen on the Wisley laboratory building has been there for sixty years or more, since it was an old plant when I first saw it there in 1949.

In most years, 'Mermaid' remains evergreen, or virtually so, and, although its foliage may in some years be prone to black spot, it is normally covered with deep green, somewhat leathery, lustrous leaves which are beset from early summer until midautumn with enormous single blooms of fragrant, soft, clear, canary-yellow, often 4 or 5in (10–12cm) across, with the central boss of orange-yellow stamens remaining in beauty for some time after the petals fall.

Against a wall, it will reach 25 to 30ft (8–10m) in height, but is equally as good trained semihorizontally along a high fence or over a shed or carport. If no support is available, it may be used to form a large, spreading shrub on a bank or sunny, open site, where it will need some control, but beware the vicious, hooked thorns when training or pruning its strong, wilful shoots. Only limited pruning is necessary or desirable on trained plants. Apart from removing damaged, diseased, or dead wood when seen, a limited spurring back of unwanted shoots is all that may be required.

Magnificent in its own right, 'Mermaid' also combines beautifully with the light-blue *Clematis* 'Perle d'Azur,' an association I have found very effective.

Related plants At one time *Rosa* 'Albertine' (5A–9A) was an almost obligatory inhabitant of new gardens, but now this very floriferous hybrid derived from *R. wichuraiana* is less frequently seen. It is still an outstanding garden plant, putting all its energies into one sumptuous, midsummer display of its distinctive, coppery-pink, red-budded blooms that emit a delicious, fruity fragrance and scent the air for many yards around. Like 'Mermaid,' it may be treated as a somewhat sprawling shrub and will reach 5 or 6ft (1.5–1.8m) in height, but is better grown with support where its glossy, bronze-tinted leaves set off the loosely double blooms to perfection. Minor pruning to maintain it within its allotted space is all that is required.

A semievergreen *Rosa sempervirens* hybrid of great charm, *Rosa* 'Félicité Perpétue' (5A–9A) provides a single but long-lasting display, its huge swags of rosetted, double, creamy white blooms, red-tinted in bud, appearing for several weeks in midsummer. It will readily climb to 20ft (6m) or more through a tree, but is not difficult to keep within bounds on a house wall or arbor, forming masses of strong basal shoots that should be loosely tied into place. Without support, 'Félicité Perpétue' will form a rounded, spreading bush

of great beauty in bloom. Plant with it one of the hybrids of *Clematis viticella* or *C. texensis* that, cut to the ground each spring, will flower in late summer and autumn through the foliage of the rose. It is credited with having a delicate, primroselike perfume, but it is more akin to an antiseptic cream, according to my wife. This obviously detracts in no way from its charm as it is her favorite rose.

Schizophragma integrifolium (Hydrangeaceae) (6A–9A)

The well-known *Hydrangea petiolaris* (4A–8B) is a valuable selfclinging climber, particularly as it will thrive on shaded north or east walls. Its period of bloom, however, is limited and far surpassed by the superb *Schizophragma integrifolium* from central China, which is equally accommodating, but flowers for several months rather than a few weeks.

A vigorous deciduous climber attaching itself to its support by aerial roots, it may take a little time to establish. Once suited, in a moist, humus-rich, well-drained soil, it quickly sends out long shoots, well clothed with attractive, long-pointed, ovate, alternate, bright green, 5in (12cm) leaves, the edges minutely toothed. A plant four years old against our house is now 10ft (3m) up an east wall and half as wide, although it has yet to flower. A mature plant grown for fifty years at Wisley was

Rosa 'Mermaid'

Schizophragma integrifolium

Wisteria floribunda 'Multijuga' (Leguminosae) (5A–9B)

Often listed as *Wisteria floribunda* 'Macrobotrys,' this is remarkable for its flower racemes that may reach 3ft (1m) in length, although in Britain it does not always achieve such magnificence.

A Japanese plant cultivated for over a century, it should be grown either on a very stoutly constructed arbor or allowed to clamber by means of its twining stems through established deciduous trees, where its racemes of blue-violet and mauve pea-flowers, marked yellow at the base of the standard petal, may be displayed to perfection during early summer. It may also be trained to clothe a house wall, but needs to be very carefully placed and controlled to avoid damage to gutters and other structures from the intertwining, woody stems – they can be several inches thick, with the crushing capacity of a python. Rather than take such risks, it is better to train the main stems up, along and across an arbor so that the long racemes of bloom hang down like curtains of purple mist.

Pruning wisterias seems to baffle many people. The aim is to produce as many flowering spurs as possible, and this is achieved by two straightforward operations. In mid- to late summer, all the young shoots, including the very long extension growths, should be pruned back with hand pruners (or finger and thumb) to five or six leaves. After leaf-fall, these same shoots and any others that have developed in the interim are cut back to two or three buds. This will encourage the formation of spur systems and flower buds from which the following year's racemes should develop.

Apart from a well-drained, reasonably fertile soil and ample water during the growing season, nothing more is required to provide a fine display. If no structure is available, it is also possible to grow this and other wisterias as a large bush, training young plants to develop a strong, woody framework by regularly pruning back redundant shoots to the main branches, then instituting a regime of spur pruning, as described above, which is easier to carry out on a large shrub than on a wall or arbor. I have seen a number of wisterias grown successfully this way at Wisley and Kew.

OTHER PLANTS

Tropaeolum polyphyllum (Tropaeolaceae) (7B–8B)

It is, perhaps, misleading to call this delightful, if somewhat touchy, plant a climber as it grows naturally in the high Andes of Chile and Argentina as a spreading mat-former in scree conditions, spraying its elegant trails of five- to seven-lobed, very glaucous foliage far and wide.

restricted at 30ft (10m), having reached the eaves of the main building, and it is likely that it would have exceeded 40ft (12m) if left to its own devices.

In full bloom, *S. integrifolium* is a magnificent sight, with huge, flat inflorescences up to 12in (30cm) across produced abundantly from sideshoots along the main branches. Each is like a large head of a lacecap hydrangea, the fertile, inconspicuous flowers in the center surrounded by a galaxy of larger, sterile, creamy white, ovate bracts each over 3in (7.5cm) long, gently moving like small handkerchiefs in the slightest breeze. As they age, the bracts turn pink before fading to a warm, light brown, eight or more weeks after they first unfold.

Viable seed is seldom produced in cultivation, but cuttings of young, semiripe sideshoots root reasonably well, and layers from basal shoots may also provide a supply of young plants. It is also now readily obtainable from nurseries. Awards from The Royal Horticultural Society of a First Class Certificate in 1963 and an Award of Garden Merit in 1993 indicate its tremendous garden value, judgments I fully endorse.

Wisteria floribunda 'Multijuga'

In gardens, it will do the same, but will also scramble through low vegetation and with gentle encouragement may reach 5 to 6ft (2m) in height.

I have found it difficult to establish from the slender, fleshy tubers, but, when it approves of the position and diet provided, *Tropaeolum polyphyllum* is likely to take over a considerable area although never becoming a nuisance because, soon after flowering in midsummer, the foliage dies back for an autumn and winter rest period. It is worth growing for its beautiful glaucous foliage alone, but add to this the terminal 6–12in (15–30cm) sprays of cool yellow blooms, neater, refined versions of the common nasturtium, and you have a garden plant of great ornamental quality.

Propagation from the tubers requires a little patience, because they may need to be established in pots before being planted out, and disturbance, apart from very careful removal of dormant tubers for propagation, upsets their equilibrium in my experience. But even if it does take time to persuade *T. polyphyllum* to grow well, it is more than worthy of star treatment.

FLOWERING WALL SHRUBS

Abutilon vitifolium 'Veronica Tennant' (Malvaceae) (7B–9B)

Cultivated since 1836, when it was raised from seed obtained in Chile, *Abutilon vitifolium* is one of the most spectacular late spring and early summer-flowering shrubs, producing showers of mallowlike blooms varying in color from lavender-purple to white. I find 'Veronica Tennant' particularly attractive, its shallowly bowl-shaped, 4in (10cm) blooms a soft, almost luminous lavender with a hint of pale pink contrasting well with the orange anthers and purple-tipped stigma.

Although normally described as a shrub some 6 to 10ft (2–3m) in height, *A. vitifolium* will, in favorable conditions, reach 25 to 30ft (8–10m). The six-year-old plant of 'Veronica Tennant' growing on our house wall has passed the eaves at 20ft (6m), and is attempting to cover a similar breadth. The beautiful, clean white var. *album* planted in an open site is, however, much more restrained at only 10ft (3m). It is often relatively short-lived, but even in more severe winters healthy plants usually come through unscathed. The older leaves often become yellow and fall in winter, but the softly hairy, long pointed, vinelike, gray-green leaves at the ends of the branches remain evergreen and in early to midsummer produce, from their leaf axils, clusters of five or more long-stalked blooms, creating billowing curtains of lavender or white.

Abutilon vitifolium forms an irregularly pyramidal, upright-stemmed shrub with open, spreading, gray-woolly branchlets, and even when grown against a wall is best pruned only very lightly to curtail wayward branches. If severely cut back, it usually loses its graceful habit, although still regenerating and flowering reasonably well. Seed is abundantly produced, and seedlings are frequent around my own plants. Cuttings of young semiripe shoots taken in mid- to late summer root readily and should be used to propagate named clones like 'Veronica Tennant' and 'Tennant's White.'

There are two minor drawbacks. Firstly, the soft-wooded stems are very attractive to our cats, who like to sharpen their claws on them daily, luckily with no visible harm to the plants. Secondly, the fallen flowers quickly go mushy and need to be cleared daily to avoid anyone slipping on them; but do not let these caveats put you off growing one of the most beautiful and prolific of all flowering shrubs (see p.74).

Related plants *Abutilon* x *suntense* is a relatively new hybrid between *A. vitifolium* and another small-flow-

Abutilon vitifolium 'Veronica Tennant'

ered Chilean species, *A. ochsenii* (7B–9B), with dark blue-mauve flowers, which has proved to be an outstanding garden plant in the twenty or so years since it was introduced. While I was working at Wisley specimens of what were thought to be an unusual form of *A. vitifolium* were sent to me for identification. Examination proved it to be of hybrid origin, and it was subsequently named after the garden in which it was grown, Sunte House. The same hybrid has now been raised elsewhere, and a number of clones, including the rich mauve 'Jermyns,' 'Violetta' in violet-blue, and 'White Charm,' are now offered. All have proved to be tough shrubs that will reach 8 to 10ft (2.5–3m) in height, and, in my garden, have proved hardy in the open, very free-flowering with cupped blooms 2in (5cm) or so across, the foliage somewhat less gray in aspect than *A. vitifolium* with smaller, less lobed, brighter green leaves.

Semiripe cuttings may be rooted very readily in summer to perpetuate the clones and, if raised from seed, minor differences in flower color, size, and shape will occur. One such variation, which I have named 'Ralph Gould' after the raiser, appears to be a backcross with *A. vitifolium* and has much flatter, more open flowers than other forms of *A.* x *suntense*, the flowers being up to 3in (7.5cm) across.

For those who feel unable to cope with the exuberant *A. vitifolium*, any of the named clones of *A.* x *sun-*

tense will provide excellent substitutes, equally as free-flowering but of somewhat more demure behavior.

Alyogyne huegelii (Malvaceae) (9A–10B)

Also known as *Hibiscus huegelii* and called in its native South and Western Australia the lilac hibiscus, this superb evergreen shrub has been grown in California for many years but is normally grown as a cool greenhouse plant or used for summer display, planted out or in a container.

I first came across this species in Western Australia some twenty years ago, a shrub some 6 to 8ft (1.8–2.4m) tall covered in exotic, satin-textured, deep purplish-lilac, open trumpet-shaped blooms that expanded to over 4½in (11cm) across. One of the most popular clones grown in California is named 'Santa Cruz.' The furled buds are reddish-purple and the base of each petal marked darker red-purple, with pale yellow anthers and style branches. The neat, attractive, three- to five-lobed foliage is somewhat oaklike in shape, and matt dark green above and paler beneath.

Alyogyne huegelii will grow in any well-drained, open potting mix and will readily survive short periods of mild frost. Trained against a sunny south wall and given winter protection, it should sit out all but the severest winters. I maintain a plant in a large pot in a cold greenhouse each winter, and after being housed in late autumn it continues in bloom almost until Christmas, has a short rest and starts to flower again in late winter and early spring. It is then returned outdoors to continue its display until rehoused again in late autumn. In Australia, it appears to flower only in spring and early summer, and its nine-month display in Britain may perhaps be due to the cooler climate.

Alyogyne huegelii

My own plants have yet to set seed, but there is no problem in increasing *Alyogyne* from semiripe cuttings of short sideshoots.

Ceanothus 'Skylark' (Ramnaceae) (8A–10B)

Among a number of fine evergreen *Ceanothus* I obtained in California some nine or ten years ago for Wisley were three clones that to date seem hardy, as well as being very floriferous and ornamental.

A specimen of 'Skylark' grown against a wall on my house is now some 10ft (3m) high, with glossy, dark green, semiupright foliage, strongly three-veined and clearly akin to *C. thyrsiflorus*. It has dense, bright, deep blue clusters of flowers borne two or three weeks after various forms of *C. thyrsiflorus* and the excellent hybrid 'Concha,' which normally flowers with me in late May and is similar in flower color. In open ground, 'Skylark' forms a spreading mound over 6ft (2m) tall and more across, an amazing sight in early summer and sometimes again in late summer, its honey-scented blooms massed with bees. After flowering it may be pruned hard, though not into the oldest wood, to keep it within bounds against a wall.

'Millerton Point,' another derivative of *C. thyrsiflorus*, is even more vigorous than 'Skylark.' Planted against a wall in my garden but allowed to roam free, in six years it was over 10ft (3m) tall by 18ft (5.4m) along the wall and 12ft (3.5m) out from it. The foliage is rather paler green and borne more or less horizontally. In late spring, it produces strongly fragrant, long, white flower sprays, touched cream in bud and a haven for bees. It needs considerable restriction, but regular pruning of the flowered shoots immediately the blooms fade and perhaps a further trim in midsummer will contain it without difficulty against a wall.

This trio is completed by 'Dark Star,' the flowers of which usually have a red tint in bud but open to an intense dark blue, relieved by the tiny white anthers. The small leaves are very dark, glossy green, and rugose, indicating that *C. impressus* is one of its parents, and its rather rigid, slower growth lends itself to tight wall training, the clusters of dense, globular flower heads covering the foliage in early summer.

All three of these superb *Ceanothus* are readily increased from semiripe cuttings in summer.

Dendromecon rigidum (Papaveraceae) (8A–10B)

Not as well known as *Romneya coulteri*, the Californian tree poppy, *Dendromecon rigidum*, the Bush Poppy, is restricted to West Coast regions. A specimen outside a south-facing window on my house at Wisley formed a spreading, open shrub 4 to 5ft (1.2–1.5m) tall, and flowered for many years given a protective basal bracken mulch in winter. Occasionally, some of the shoots were frost-killed, but suckers from the base appeared the following spring, freely sending up their willowy shoots set with alternate, very glaucous, ovate, evergreen leaves. The shoots begin to branch naturally low down, and in the same year produce the brilliant yellow, poppylike flowers singly on long stalks during midsummer. Each bloom reaches 2½ to 3in (6–8cm) across when mature, slightly fragrant, with four petals, irregularly toothed at the apex, and with a fat central boss of darker yellow stamens.

Firm regulation of the older shoots by pruning them back immediately after blooming, and training the young shoots into any gaps, meant that the Wisley plant often flowered very freely for a month or so in midsummer, but rarely produced more than an occasional bloom later. When treated with less rigidity, it flowers over many months, and a plant less than a year old in

---

PLANT HUNTING IN CALIFORNIA

The richness of the Californian flora is matched by the enthusiasm, dedication, and hospitality of some of its plant-loving inhabitants. Pre-eminent in my experience is Wayne Roderick: without his guidance it would not have been possible to see many rarities as well as fine stands of more common plants. The thrill of seeing trilliums, erythroniums, and many of the beautiful *Calochortus* and *Fritillaria* species in the wild, some in very considerable quantities, is difficult to equal. While bulbs were the focus of our trips, other plants were not neglected, among them swathes of *Ceanothus thyrsiflorus* by stands of redwoods not far from San Francisco.

Many Californian plants of high garden potential have been been brought into cultivation, such as *Ceanothus* 'Skylark' (illustrated below); many more plants remain to be introduced and tested for hardiness.

Dendromecon rigidum

my garden has produced a modicum of flowers in ten of the past twelve months. I now have a second specimen, which will be wall-trained to see if I can achieve a similar display of gold and gray in midsummer.

Availability of this attractive, if tender, plant is limited, but root cuttings or suckers may be established reasonably well, although semiripe heel cuttings of young side growths are more often used to obtain stock.

Erythrina crista-galli

Erythrina crista-galli (Leguminosae) (7B–10B)

One of the most exciting and arresting plants that gardeners can attempt to grow outdoors in North America is the Cockspur Coral Tree, *Erythrina crista-galli*, which may attain well over 20ft (6m) in height in the subtropics but is normally reduced to herbaceous status in frost-prone climates.

Spectacular though this South American species may be as a tree, with its large, dark red, pealike blooms, borne both in long, leafy, terminal racemes as well as in axillary clusters, it is comforting to know that it flowers on the current season's growth. Even if cut back to the rootstock, in a sheltered and, if possible, protected site, it will almost always send up basal shoots often 3ft (1m) or more long. In late summer or early autumn these terminate in the huge inflorescences that are characteristic of all species of this most ornamental genus. The foliage is also very handsome, the dark green, pinnately three-parted leaves admirably complementing the 2ft (60cm) sprays of bright coral-red.

A well-drained site under a south wall and a protective winter covering at the base should allow *E. cristagalli* to grow happily, if at a low level, for many years outside while, for the less adventurous, it also makes an excellent sunroom plant, either planted out or in a pot. Seed is not often available, but heel cuttings of the young shoots in spring are not too difficult to root – and worth every effort to do so.

Solanum crispum 'Glasnevin' (Solanaceae) (7A–9B)

One of the most attractive and prolific of wall plants, *Solanum crispum* 'Glasnevin' spreads its arching, scandent growths high and wide, often reaching 15ft (4.5m) or more in height and spread. The large sprays of mid-violet, orange-centered, potatolike flowers of this fine Chilean native first appear in late spring and are still to be found on plants in sheltered positions in mid- to late autumn, occasionally venturing forth for Christmas if the weather has not been too inclement.

Solanum crispum was first introduced to England around 1830, but the forms then grown have now largely been superseded by the more prolific, longer-flowering clone 'Glasnevin,' which arrived in Britain from the Irish garden of that name just prior to World War I. It has an undeserved reputation for being slightly tender and will thrive and prosper even in poor alkaline soils, often with an exuberance that demands restriction by relatively drastic pruning. While usually grown as a wall plant, where firm training to provide a basic woody framework and spur-pruning are essential if it is not to fling its long, sinuous shoots in all

Solanum crispum 'Glasnevin'

directions, *S. crispum* 'Glasnevin' may also be successfully, but more unusually, grown as an open-ground shrub with little or no support, provided ample space is available. Left to its own devices, it will form a great mound some 20ft (6m) across and covered in bloom for much of the summer and autumn.

Related plants Somewhat more tender than its Chilean relative, the evergreen *Solanum jasminoides* (7A–9B), which attaches itself to supports by means of its leaf stalks to climb to 15ft (4.5m) or more, is a very attractive species from Brazil, Paraguay, and neighboring regions of Uruguay and Argentina, where it inhabits forest edges.

In its albino form, 'Album,' it is one of the most beautiful climbers for a sunny, sheltered site, with bright, fresh green, simple or slightly lobed leaves, producing from midsummer to autumn truss after truss of the glistening white, yellow-anthered, shallowly cup-shaped, 1in (2.5cm) wide flowers. In severe winters, it may be cut to ground level, but with the protection of a deep basal mulch will quickly regenerate the following spring, although it is wise to root a cutting or two in late summer to overwinter in a frost-free greenhouse. The pale bluish forms I have seen are scarcely worth growing, with slaty, miserably small flowers; the white clone now offered is, however, superb.

AUTUMN

In autumn the repeat-flowering roses produce their second flush; *Clematis texensis* and *C. viticella* hybrids are still in fine form; *Campsis* x *tagliabuana* 'Madame Galen' remains resplendent where she has sufficient warmth; and *Solanum crispum* 'Glasnevin' delights until the first frosts. But there are two shrubs I would choose for their special merits in this season: *Vitex agnus-castus* (at Wisley the forma *latifolia*) and *Leonotis leonurus*.

FLOWERING CLIMBERS AND WALL SHRUBS

Leonotis leonurus (Labiatae) (9A–10B*)

My first acquaintance with this brilliantly colored South African subshrub was in a range of frames attached to one of the old Wisley greenhouses, where it was grown for protection. For several weeks in midautumn, until the frosts, it flaunted its brilliant orange-red whorls of 2in (5cm), long-tubed flowers carried terminally on woody-based stems 5 to 6ft (1.5–1.8m) high. The stems were then cut to near ground level, the plants tucked into a coat of dry bracken and the frames closed for winter, although air was admitted on mild, frost-free days to avoid stagnation and possible rotting. In the USA, its successful cultivation is restricted to the West Coast.

Basal cuttings from spring growths rooted easily, giving me an opportunity to try it in my own garden, where it flowered and then succumbed, because my winter protection for it was inadequate. I have since successfully used the technique of planting it against a warm, south wall behind an evergreen shrub such as *Euphorbia characias*, which takes the worst of the cold leaving the dormant rootstock of *Leonotis* reasonably safe under a further precautionary wire-mesh, bracken-filled mat. This probably seems a great deal of trouble to protect what some might consider to be merely a glorified orange deadnettle – but to me it is worth it to obtain the brilliance of its orange-scarlet foliage as the year moves to a close.

Leonotis leonurus may also be grown as a pot plant to flower from late spring until midautumn either outdoors or in a cool greenhouse. But beware red spider, to which it is a martyr in a protected environment.

Vitex agnus-castus

Vitex agnus-castus (Verbenaceae) (6B–9A)

The deciduous *Vitex agnus-castus*, commonly known as the Chaste-tree, is a delightful plant grown not only for its elegant flower panicles but also for its fragrant foliage. Common in southern Europe across to central Asia, the Chaste-tree flowers over a long period from early to late autumn in the wild and is extremely variable in flower color, from violet to pinkish-lavender and sometimes a rather dirty white, so it is important to select and propagate the more attractive color forms rather than rely on seed-raised plants.

Easily grown in any well-drained soil, *V. agnus-castus* is a shrub of open, spreading habit and about 6 to 9ft (2–2.7m) high in cultivation. It comes into leaf rather late in spring, producing from the gray-downy, fairly slender shoots opposite pairs of digitate leaves, each with up to seven radiating, lance-shaped, dark green leaflets that are gray-felted beneath and, when gently rubbed, strongly aromatic.

It is best grown as a single specimen, when it forms a fine small tree 15 to 20in (6–8cm) high. In hot summers it will flower freely, producing numerous branched panicles of fragrant, small, tubular, open-mouthed flowers terminally on the current season's shoots in mid- to late summer. In wet, cold summers, the display is likely to be delayed and less abundant. The botanical variant, forma *latifolia*, with broad leaflets, said to be hardy, has at Wisley produced great sprays of its midviolet flowers set in woolly calyces in a most effective display.

Pruning is rare; if required the frost-damaged stems may be cut back in midspring before the leaf buds expand. As seed-raised plants may vary in color, make sure that purchased plants have been propagated from a selected clone, such as 'Blue Spire.'

WINTER

Winter-flowering wall shrubs planted against or very close to a door or window can bring the delights of scent and bloom to even the most housebound in the darkest months of the year. The scented flowering shrubs I have chosen – *Chimonanthus praecox*, *Abeliophyllum distichum*, *Prunus mume* cultivars and the winter-flowering viburnums – are all hardy and can be grown freestanding in open ground, but they will often flower more profusely against a sunny wall. (Remember, though, to avoid walls with an east-facing aspect, on which frosted buds and flowers can easily be damaged by early morning sun.)

Jasminum nudiflorum is so forgiving of cold and shade that it will grow almost anywhere. Its untidy habit is best indulged by allowing it to tumble over a low wall or bank.

FLOWERING WALL SHRUBS

Chimonanthus praecox var. *luteus* (Calycanthaceae) (6B–9A)

China has provided some winter-flowering shrubs of great beauty, of which the Winter Sweet, *Chimonanthus praecox* (also known as *C. fragrans*), can be classed as indispensable with its superbly scented, midwinter blooms. A native of Hubei and Sichuan, it is hardy in the open, forming a compact, densely branched, deciduous shrub, 6 to 8ft (1.8–2.4m) or more tall, bearing opposite pairs of deep green, narrowly ovate, lustrous leaves, 4 to 5in (10–12cm) long with elongated tips.

It is best grown in a sheltered location allowing the wood to ripen thoroughly in summer, which often enhances flowering. It can also be trained as a fan and, once a basic framework has been established, pruning consists of shortening back the flowered shoots in late winter or early spring to encourage fresh growth on which the following season's flowers should be borne. Train new shoots into the spaces in the framework and allow some short shoots to develop as breastwood to avoid too formal a pattern developing.

Considerable variation in the form and coloring of the flowers occurs; the most usually seen variety has bell-shaped blooms 1in (2.5cm) across consisting of about ten almost translucent, long, outer, pale yellow segments, the inner five or six petals being shorter and purplish-red. In var. *luteus*, which I prefer, all the segments are yellow, and somewhat darker than in other varieties. The flowers are borne singly on short stalks arising in the bud axils of fallen leaves on last season's shoots and appear any time between late autumn and late winter but are usually at their peak in early winter.

Chimonanthus praecox is easy to grow in reasonably fertile, well-drained soils and is raised from seed without difficulty. Layering is a slow but effective way of increasing good forms but requires patience. Cuttings of semiripe shoots with a heel, hormone treated, or softwood cuttings may be rooted, but the failure rate is often considerable. The effort is worthwhile, however, if only because of the exquisite scent of this fine, flowering shrub on a midwinter's day.

OTHER PLANTS

Abeliophyllum distichum (Oleaceae) (5B–8A)
One of the finest early-flowering deciduous shrubs, *Abeliophyllum distichum* produces elegant, arching sprays of fragrant, white, or occasionally pale pink flowers that brave the winds and frosts of late winter. It is perfectly hardy but in colder areas is best grown as a wall plant where its spreading, *Forsythia*-like shoots may be trained to 6ft (1.8m) or more, so that the short axillary racemes of four-petaled blooms with recurving petals are shown to best advantage. Flowers are produced on shoots of the previous season but also on older wood from nodal swellings botanically called "wens" (as with *Forsythia* and *Cercis*). Care must be taken, therefore, not to prune out all flowered shoots, since wood three years or more old may still bloom freely. Weak or old, worn-out shoots can be removed immediately after flowering. A fine wall plant, thriving even in poor soils and readily propagated from semiripe cuttings in summer, *A. distichum* will grow well on walls of any aspect but prefers a south- or west-facing site, to some extent reminiscent of the hot summers of its native Korea.

Jasminum nudiflorum (Oleaceae) (6B–9B)
Although I look forward to its long display, from late autumn until late winter in good years, I find *Jasminum nudiflorum* difficult to place in the garden. It is untidy and angular in winter when its long, dark green shoots are bare of the deep green, three-parted leaves, yet all is redeemed when its solitary, 1in (2.5cm), warm yellow, tubular blooms, with five spreading lobes, appear in profusion along the branchlets in early winter. *J. nudi-*

florum is almost always recommended as a wall plant and may be trained to 12ft (3.5m) or more in height and as much across, yet it always reminds me of someone with a very tight collar who wishes he could burst free. It is best planted to tumble over a low wall or down a bank as it does in its native western China.

After several unsuccessful attempts to find a pleasing site for *J. nudiflorum*, the problem was solved by the plant itself. Unnoticed by me, it had layered itself in several gaps near the top of a brick wall, where it was happily growing and flowering with no other source of nutrients and has continued to do so for six years.

Jasminum nudiflorum is bone-hardy and shows a remarkable tolerance as to soil and aspect, thriving even in shaded, cold positions. Pruning, particularly of elderly specimens, is sometimes puzzling. Any dead, damaged, or weak shoots should be cut out, then immediately after flowering any flowered shoots should be cut back to a strong pair of growth buds beyond the spent blooms. These will produce strong lateral shoots that will bear next winter's flowers. In time, the long main growths will become scraggy and should be pruned out to the base or back to a vigorous near-basal replacement shoot. If you allow *J. nudiflorum* to grow over a sunny bank, simply cut out any dead or unsightly shoots after flowering.

Prunus mume 'Beni-chidori' (Rosaceae) (5B–10A)
Selections of the Japanese Apricot have been cultivated in China and Japan for many centuries and are valued for the beauty of the delicately scented, single, semi-double, or double, white, pink, or crimson, almondlike flowers and for their fruits that are dried and used for preserves. In colder areas, fruit is rarely formed, but the four or five cultivars of *Prunus mume* available are worth cultivating, either as open-ground shrubs or as wall-trained specimens, just for their attractive late winter or early spring-borne flowers.

Although *P. mume* eventually reaches 20 to 30ft (6–10m) in height, it is mostly grown as a tall shrub, pruned after flowering to maintain a steady supply of bright green shoots that will bear the following year's flower display. It is best given a sheltered, well-drained, preferably sunny site, because the flowers are, like those of peaches and nectarines, damaged by frost.

It takes well to wall-training as an informal fan, preferably on a south or west wall, and with the young branches awash with bloom it is a marvelous sight for several weeks in late winter, severe frosts allowing, particularly the beautiful 'Beni-chidori' (also listed as 'Beni-shidon' or 'Beni-shidare'), with massed, single, rich crimson, ½in (1cm) blooms with a delicious fragrance, likened by some to that of hyacinths. Some confusion over the identity of 'Beni-chidori' has occurred. The plant that received an Award of Merit from The RHS in 1961 was single-flowered and crimson in color, but a double pink clone is doing duty for it in some nurseries. My suspicion is that this is a sport from the white, semidouble or double 'Omoi-no-mama' ('Omoi-no-wac'), which produces shoots with pink blooms among the white in my garden. If these attractive, early-flowering wall plants are a little dull in summer foliage, they will not mind if the annual *Thunbergia alata* or another short-term climber shares their wall space.

Viburnum foetens (Caprifoliaceae) (6A–8B)

Apart from the winter-flowering *Viburnum grandiflorum* and *V. farreri* (*V. fragrans* of old), there is a further unsung species that, to me, is in many ways a better garden plant. While it has a long flowering period, it does not spread its favors spasmodically from early autumn to midspring as do these species, their hybrid *V.* x *bodnantense* and its named clones. Instead, it produces its large trusses of well-scented, clean white flowers, very occasionally flushed pink at the base, in a steady supply from early until late winter. Like all the winter viburnums, even after severe frosts, it continues to produce flower from undamaged trusses of bloom in tight bud.

Although *V. foetens* is now available from a number of nurseries it was seldom offered ten years ago, possibly because of the off-putting specific epithet *foetens*, meaning evil-smelling, which, in flower at least, it is not. A Himalayan species, it is distinguished from the closely related *V. grandiflorum* (7A–8B) by its much more compact, rounded habit and in having generally stouter branches, and leaves lacking hairs beneath. Most variants of *V. grandiflorum* have thinner shoots and a gawky, taller habit with less symmetrical flowers and smaller flower trusses.

Horticulturally, these are distinct species, and it is better, I believe, to maintain their separateness to avoid confusion. Taxonomy apart, *Viburnum foetens* is a fine garden plant, perfectly hardy in the open but often grown by a wall (although not trained against it, as its habit is too rigid), growing steadily to 6 or 7ft (2m), although often less. Cuttings of semiripe shoots may be rooted in summer, but usually take some time to reach planting size. It is well worth the wait – *V. foetens*, now well over forty years old, still grows outside my old room at Wisley, where it wafts its sweet scent through the open window on sunny winter days.

TWO OR MORE SEASONS

My selection of long-flowering climbers and wall plants includes *Tropaeolum tuberosum* 'Ken Aslet,' which is somewhat tender but a marvelous selection for summer and autumn display.

The attractions of colorful foliage can easily be overlooked. Throughout spring and summer both *Actinidia kolomikta* and *Stachyurus chinensis* 'Magpie' have pretty crimson-pink tints in their variegation, which fades only in autumn. The bright-golden-leaved *Humulus lupulus* 'Aureus' gradually pales to lime-yellow as summer progresses, while the leaves of *Parthenocissus henryana* change from a spring and summer coloring of dark green veined with silver to a striking red in autumn. For fragrance the lemon-scented leaves of *Aloysia triphylla* and honey-scented *Itea ilicifolia* are difficult to surpass.

SUMMER TO AUTUMN FLOWERS

Campsis x *tagliabuana* 'Madame Galen' (Bignoniaceae) (6A–9B)

The mainly subtropical and tropical family Bignoniaceae includes some of the most resplendent of climbing plants. Of these, *Campsis grandiflora* (6B–9A) from China, *C. radicans* (5A–9A) from the southeast United States, and the hybrid between them, *C.* x *tagliabuana*, originally raised in Italy, can be grown and flowered outdoors in cooler areas given a warm south- or west-facing wall and ample space to develop. In the United States, *C.* x *tagliabuana* forms a vigorous and compact climber.

Campsis x *tagliabuana* 'Madame Galen' is the most reliable clone, providing a long succession of striking, trumpet-shaped blooms, borne in large, open, many-flowered clusters during early to late summer. A deciduous climber with thick woody stems, 'Madame Galen' attaches itself to supports by short aerial roots and will rapidly cover a wall or fence, reaching 30ft (10m) or more if permitted, and is amply supplied with large, opposite pairs of pinnate leaves over 1ft (30cm) long consisting of seven to eleven toothed, dark green leaflets. The sumptuous, open tubular-campanulate blooms are often more than 3in (8cm) long, externally orange-red with the five expanded lobes, deep red with a hint of brown, spreading to nearly 3in (8cm) across.

Grown in well-drained loam, and allowed to extend its shoots toward the sun, 'Madame Galen' has flowered freely on a wall at Wisley for many years. It is spring-pruned, the previous season's growth cut to within two to four buds of the main framework, ensuring a good supply of strong, flowering shoots, the blooms being produced terminally on the current season's growths. A magnificent plant in bloom, *C.* x *tagliabuana* has few, if any, competitors among hardy climbing plants in summer and early autumn.

Campsis x *tagliabuana* 'Madame Galen'

Tropaeolum tuberosum 'Ken Aslet' (Tropaeolaceae) (7B–9A)

Although halfhardy this is one of the most satisfactory climbing plants as not only does it produce its orange-yellow flowers in quantity from early summer until early autumn or later, but the rate of tuber increase is rapid, numerous offsets being formed each season. They need to be lifted annually once the top growth yellows and either planted 4 to 6in (10–15cm) deep in a sheltered site with a mulch, or stored in frost-free conditions until midspring, when they may be planted out.

Tropaeolum tuberosum is a variable species from Peru, Ecuador, Colombia, and Bolivia, and the initial introductions proved to be very late-flowering, and were really only of value as a greenhouse plant. *T. tuberosum* 'Ken Aslet' was named after a superintendent of the rock garden department at Wisley, who, just prior to World War II, acquired a stock that regularly flowered in summer, and distributed it widely to friends.

Climbing by means of its leaf stalks, *Tropaeolum tuberosum* may reach 6 to 8ft (1.8–2.4m) or more in a season, preferring to scramble through trellis or early-flowering deciduous shrubs than undergo formal training on a wall. It is also possible to pinch the shoots back when young and use it as ground cover in sunny or lightly shaded positions, although I have never tried this.

The gray-green, five-lobed leaves are less distinctive than those of *T. polyphyllum*, but nonetheless very handsome against the elegant, orange-yellow, scarlet-spurred, 1½–2in (3–5cm) blooms that stand well above the foliage on red, slightly arching pedicels.

OTHER PLANTS

Abutilon 'Kentish Belle' (Malvaceae) (7B–9B)
The very attractive *Abutilon megapotamicum* has given rise to several hybrids and has passed on both its graceful arching habit and its somewhat exotic red and yellow coloring to 'Kentish Belle,' which has been recently honored by The Royal Horticultural Society with the Award of Garden Merit. It is an ideal plant to grow on a wall under a window where, allowed 3 to 4ft (1–1.2m) to grow upward and a little more to spread outward, it will be in bloom from late spring until late autumn. A very neat shrub with long-pointed, slightly lobed leaves and a constant succession of pendent, ocher-yellow, tubular bells, 1½in (4cm) long with the large, muted red calyx extending over halfway down the petals, it has proved hardy in relatively protected sites in colder areas but, like *A. megapotamicum*, if cut to the ground it obligingly produces fresh shoots from the base the following spring. In less favored areas, 'Kentish Belle' is well worth growing as a sunroom or patio plant.

Buddleja crispa (Buddlejaceae) (7B–9B)
One of the finest of all wall plants, *Buddleja crispa* is valuable for a number of reasons, not least its very long flowering period that stretches from early summer until frosts intervene. A deciduous, white-woolly shrub with young stems, inflorescences, and neat heart-shaped, ovate, toothed leaves covered in a floccose down, it will grow to 10ft (3m) or more in height, and in the USA it is most suited to West Coast climates with lower

humidity and lighter soils. It is, however, best grown against a wall where the gently spreading young growths, terminating in 4–5in (10–12cm), slightly nodding flower-spikes, provide waterfalls of tiny, lilac, white-eyed, very fragrant blooms, in bunched whorls, each of forty or fifty individual flowers. Originally recorded from Afghanistan and the adjacent Himalaya, *B. crispa* flowers on the current year's shoots, providing a superb display if the previous year's flowered shoots are pruned back in early spring.

Rosa 'Golden Showers' (Rosaceae) (5A–9A)

Now almost forty years old, this fine pillar or wall rose has outlasted many of its competitors, providing a more or less constant succession of large, semidouble, fragrant, bright yellow blooms, set off by glossy, usually disease-free foliage, from early summer until midautumn, with a few stray flowers appearing even later. Against a fence or wall, it will reach 8 to 10ft (2.4–3m) in height, but it may also be grown as a free-standing shrub, although it becomes somewhat bare at the base.

Rosa 'New Dawn' (Rosaceae) (5A–9A)

Reaching over 20ft (6m), this plant looks superb trained over an arch or on an arbor where its long shoots, densely clothed in glossy, distinctive foliage, are not too constricted. 'New Dawn' is also suitable for growing through small, open-centered trees such as some crab apples that often have rather dull summer foliage; equally, given space, it will develop into a mounding, wide-spreading "shrub" that will flower from early summer to midautumn, with some blooms appearing up until the New Year in mild areas. It is a sport of 'Dr Van Fleet', differing only in its remontant habit, producing cluster after cluster of the sweetly fragrant, well-formed, semidouble blooms of deep silvery pink. An outstanding rose on all counts, it is seldom affected by black spot, although late in the season young growths may suffer from mildew.

Rosa 'Madame Grégoire Staechelin' (Rosaceae) (5A–9A)

Although this vigorous and very attractive rose produces only one crop of its large, semidouble, glowing pink blooms, paler within than without and markedly veined on the reverse, it provides them in such abundance and with such a fresh scent akin to that of sweet peas that its nonremontant habit is of no real consequence. Happy in any aspect, even north-facing, it also contributes to the autumn scene with its huge, deep orange-red, long-lasting hips.

ORNAMENTAL FOLIAGE

Actinidia kolomikta (Actinidiaceae) (4A–8A)

One of the most striking of foliage plants, this Far Eastern relative of the Chinese gooseberry or kiwifruit, *Actinidia deliciosa*, occurs wild in Manchuria, China, and northern Japan and is there tremendously vigorous, climbing to considerable heights through trees by means of its strong, twining, sinuous stems.

In shade, its 5–6in (12–15cm), ovate leaves, purplish when young, are pleasant enough, but in strong light they are very colorful during spring and summer, much of the leaf-blade becoming white and pink before fading, then falling, later in the year. It is sometimes suggested that male plants may produce more colorful foliage than females, but to my knowledge there is no real evidence of this. Certainly, young plants propagated vegetatively can take some time to demonstrate their parents' attributes so plant age may play a part, but as yet there is no definitive answer for cases where the foliage does not color well, although ample light as well as the provision of good drainage and not too rich a diet may trigger the appropriate response.

Actinidia kolomikta

Actinidia kolomikta is easily grown and propagated from semiripe cuttings, and if it does produce its small, white, fragrant, cupped blooms hidden behind the foliage these provide an added bonus, and also allow you to check the sex of your plant. It does not normally grow too vigorously further north, reaching perhaps 15 to 20ft (4.5–6m), but if restriction is needed prune back wayward shoots early in the dormant season and shorten back side growths and breastwood to within two to three buds of the main framework branches to maintain a dense cover of the attractive foliage.

If you are a cat lover, it is also useful to protect young plants until they have grown some distance up the support. Only when I saw our two cats rolling on the remains of what had been a strong, young specimen of *A. kolomikta*, recently planted, did I recall an evocative passage in the *Botanical Magazine* describing cats slavering over charcoal made from its woody lianas in its native woodlands.

Aloysia triphylla

Aloysia triphylla (Verbenaceae) (8B–10A)

For over 200 years, lemon-scented verbena (also grown as *Lippia citriodora*), an introduction from Chile, has been popular in the United States, where it is cultivated particularly for the delightful fragrance of its leaves. It will not usually withstand very severe winters, although in sheltered spots it is known to have survived temperatures as low as 23°F (–5°C), despite being cut to the ground.

Grown against a sunny south wall in well-drained, not too rich soil, it is worth trying in any garden that is not subject to regular very cold spells. Small, soft-grown specimens raised from cuttings are offered commercially and these should be grown on in a loam-based potting mix in a cold or cool greenhouse to develop a woody base before planting out in midspring. It is useful to use the basin planting technique suggested for *Cosmos atrosanguineus* (see p.187) so that the base is eventually 2 to 3in (5–8cm) below normal soil level. If the disaster of a very cold winter occurs and the top growth is killed, it will then have a good chance of breaking again from the base.

Aloysia triphylla will sometimes develop into a rather spreading, straggly shrub and from a fairly early age it is important to pinch out the growing shoots to encourage it to bush out. The pale green, lanceolate leaves are usually borne in whorls of three, and if left unpruned will produce late in the summer or autumn slim panicles of tiny, very pale, purplish-lavender blooms. My own preference is to take out the growing tips regularly and forget the flowers, so that all the

plant's energies are put into developing fresh shoots and a bushy habit. This also provides useful cutting material to root and overwinter in case of loss. Pot-grown lemon-scented verbena from midsummer cuttings is very welcome on the kitchen window sill or in a sunroom where it will retain its leaves and provide its marvelous fragrance for the household to enjoy all winter and beyond.

Humulus lupulus 'Aureus' (Cannabaceae) (5B–9B)

Some people will be familiar with the sight of hopfields in parts of Oregon where the crop is grown on poles, a twining herbaceous perennial with rough, three- to five-lobed leaves followed by the well-known hops of commerce. Easily grown in any fertile, well-drained soil, *Humulus lupulus* itself is not very often grown in gardens, but the golden-leaved form known as 'Aureus' is a most attractive foliage plant. It will rapidly climb in spring to 10 or 12ft (3–3.5m) or more and is suitable for a variety of garden sites to cover fences, walls, or clamber up trees. It may also be used on tripods or similar structures, where, having reached their allotted height, the long stems will cascade down to provide pillars of bright yellow, deeply lobed leaves that gradually pale to lime-yellow as the season advances. The best planting of *H. lupulus* 'Aureus' I have seen was where it was used to cover an arched arbor and was a most effective feature, planted sufficiently densely to ensure virtually complete coverage of the structure. Easily raised from cuttings, the essential

Parthenocissus henryana

method to increase this male clone, the golden hop may also be used to relieve the gloom of large, dark-foliaged conifers that have little decorative value in summer. Planted a few feet from the base and encouraged to make the initial move onto the conifers, *H. lupulus* 'Aureus' may reach 20ft (6m) or more, clinging to the skirts of the tree and covering it with a sheet of pale gold for several months. The herbaceous nature of the golden hop allows the conifer to continue its not very merry way without too much damage being done to its foliage. Care should be taken, however, to use it only on large Leyland cypresses or similar conifers that will shrug off any minor effects of the hop with equanimity.

Parthenocissus henryana (Vitaceae) (7B–8B)

The common Virginia Creeper, *Parthenocissus quinque-folia*, and the allied but distinct Ivy Boston *P. tricuspi-data* are very familiar and often rampant wall climbers that are spectacular autumn-coloring plants of great merit if sensibly planted so that they do not take over huge areas of garden or house walls to the detriment of other plants. Having removed from my present garden many barrow-loads of both species that had smothered much of the ground and walls in their vicinity, the decision to plant the deciduous, very decorative *P. hen-ryana* instead was not difficult to make.

It is still a vigorous species, attaching itself to the surface it is covering by tendrils with adhesive pads at their tips, but more readily controlled and certainly of equal if not greater beauty as a foliage plant. Introduced from central China early this century, it will reach 15ft (4.5m) or so, and requires a northerly or easterly aspect to develop to perfection its palmate, three- to five-part-ed, velvety dark green leaves, beautifully veined silvery gray, sometimes touched pink. Not only is the foliage exceedingly decorative all spring and summer, but in autumn its leaves turn to a bright vinous-red, the sil-vering being retained to some extent and enhancing the overall effect. The small clusters of greenish flowers are scarcely noticed, but in autumn after warm summers a further bonus of dark blue berries may result.

Although not difficult to grow in fairly moist and

fertile, well-drained soil, *P. henryana* takes a little time to learn that it is intended to climb, sometimes preferring to remain near ground level. The use of a few peasticks should soon persuade it to move in the correct direction, and in a relatively short time the quality of this glorious foliage climber becomes apparent.

OTHER PLANTS

Stachyurus chinensis 'Magpie' (Stachyuraceae) (7A–8B)
Surprisingly, this attractive sport of *Stachyurus chinensis*, which first occurred in the mid-1940's, was seldom seen in gardens until the last ten years or so. Its elegant shoots are set with ovate, long-tapered, gray-green leaves edged with an irregular, creamy white edge, suffused pale green and rose, a beautiful effect from spring until late autumn when the variegation fades before the foliage falls. In addition, the bare, purplish branchlets are enhanced by 4–5in (10–12cm) racemes of soft yellow bells hanging down like those of *Corylopsis* in early spring before the young foliage expands.

Although hardy enough to be grown outside as a freestanding shrub, where it will reach 7 or 8ft (2–2.4m) in height, I prefer to grow 'Magpie' against a wall, where its arching growth may be fanned out informally to provide a delightful mélange of pastel coloring for more than half the year. On a hot, sunny wall or fence, the foliage may be scorched; an east wall with some shade for part of the day is ideal.

FLOWERING EVERGREEN WALL SHRUBS

Garrya elliptica 'James Roof' (Garryaceae) (8A–9B)

Almost always recommended as a wall shrub, this evergreen shrub or small tree from California and Oregon reaches 15ft (4.5m) or more with ease, but is unsuitable for growing in the humid Eastern and Midwestern regions. As a wall plant, it thrives even on north- or east-facing aspects, and if pruned in spring after flowering, is readily kept in check; this also removes any unsightly, winter-damaged foliage. Although indifferent to soil types, it needs relatively sharp drainage. It is very long-lived in cultivation: plants well over fifty years old are often recorded.

A fast-growing evergreen with shining, undulate-edged, handsome foliage, dark green above and gray-

Garrya elliptica 'James Roof'

woolly beneath, it is particularly valued for its beautiful silvered catkins that begin their development in late summer as pale green clusters of "caterpillars" that gradually increase in length until by early winter they are almost 1ft (30cm) in length in the best clones. By then, they have changed to a silky, silvery gray-green with yellow anthers peeping out between the scales and have lost the stiffness of their youth, and sway elegantly in the winter breezes to provide from late autumn into late winter a fine contrast with the glossy foliage.

Garrya elliptica is unisexual and, in this instance, the male is more beautiful than the female because the catkins are much longer and conspicuous, particularly in the selected clone 'James Roof.' Another fine clone with catkins over 1ft (30cm) in length and with very undulate-edged leaves is named 'Evie.'

The female of the species is by no means to be despised, however, because while its catkins are unremarkable in comparison with the male, they produce later in the year elongated bunches of hard, blackish, red-juiced fruits, covered initially in silky-gray hairs.

Itea ilicifolia

Garrya elliptica is one of the finest evergreens available for our gardens, readily propagated from late summer cuttings, accommodating in its cultural requirements and ornamental at all times of year.

Itea ilicifolia (Escalloniaceae/Iteaceae) (7B–9B)

Although not fully hardy without some form of shelter from severe frosts and icy winds, the western Chinese *Itea ilicifolia* will withstand the majority of winters in colder areas and is a charming evergreen fit to grace any wall, the dark glossy green, hollylike foliage, paler beneath, edged with tiny, sharp teeth carried on initially upright, then elegantly arching, long shoots. More normally seen as a shrub some 7 or 8ft (2–2.4m) tall and sometimes as much wide, *I. ilicifolia* is best left untrained apart from minor pruning to maintain it within bounds, and in a well-drained, reasonably fertile, and moisture-retentive soil will reach 12 to 15ft (3.5–4.5m) or more against a wall.

A fine plant of this beautiful evergreen, now well over forty years old, grows by the staff entrance of the Wisley laboratory, and although severely damaged in a harsh winter some fifteen years ago, it recovered well and now flowers abundantly during mid- to late summer, producing near the ends of the shoots its long, slender racemes of tiny, greenish-cream flowers. These are attractively honey-scented, and the catkinlike inflorescences may reach 10 to 12in (25–30cm) in length, lasting in beauty well into the autumn.

Readily increased by late summer cuttings, *I. ilicifolia* is much less planted than its qualities deserve. It is one of the finest and most attractive of evergreens, valuable for its very handsome foliage and sweetly-perfumed streamers of flowers that, if there is a floral arranger in the household, will certainly be greeted very favorably once it has reached flowering size.

FLOWERS AND ORNAMENTAL FRUIT OR SEED HEADS

Clematis tibetana subsp. *vernayi* 'Orange Peel' (Ranunculaceae) (6A–9A)

This long-flowering, vigorous clematis is remarkable not only for the astonishing profusion of the deep orange-yellow, pendent, bell-like flowers, each 2 to 3in (5–8cm) long, produced from early summer until late autumn, but also for the mass of silvered, fluffy seed heads that continue in beauty through the winter.

Once known as the "orange-peel form" of *Clematis orientalis*, it has now been placed under the Nepalese and Tibetan *C. tibetana*. This species is noted for its finely divided, glaucous foliage as well as the fleshy, thick-textured sepals, which resemble pieces of orange peel, giving rise to the cultivar name. 'Orange Peel' appears to be quite indifferent to soil type, although poorly drained soils are not suitable. Its vigor is so great that it should be given ample room to send its sinuous shoots into a small tree, onto a strong arbor or cascading down a steep bank, where its tangled growths will provide virtually year-round interest with a mélange of bright yellow flowers, silver seeds, and grayed foliage.

As with other members of this group of *Clematis* species such as the long-sepalled *C. tangutica* and the open-flowered *C. serratifolia* (6A–9A), it flowers on the previous year's shoots. Pruning, unless essential to maintain it within bounds, should be confined to cosmetic removal of wayward shoots. Normally *C. tibetana* and its allies will continue to flower and fruit for many years with little attention – although an annual mulch of well-rotted potting mix or manure is helpful on poor soils. Propagation by halfripe cuttings of young shoots provides a ready means of increase, and the abundance of seed produced annually may also be germinated without difficulty if sown in autumn and plunged in pots outside in the garden. Seedlings may not match the high quality of the parent plant, and if plants identical to the parent are required, vegetative propagation by cuttings or by layering is essential.

Related plants *Clematis cirrhosa* (7A–9B), a climber to 12 or 15ft (3.5–4.5m) in height, is widespread in the Mediterranean region and has proved to be very variable both in leaf and flower characters. Its main value to gardeners lies in its flowering period, from midautumn until midspring depending on the individual plant, when the pendent, bell-shaped, slightly scented, greenish-white or creamy blooms, which may be virtually unspotted to heavily endowed with reddish flecks, appear above the often finely cut, lobed foliage.

'Freckles' is a relatively new clone with very large flowers for this species, up to 4in (10cm) across, with the outside of the blooms pinkish-cream, while internally they are heavily flecked purplish-red with a hint of brown in the coloring. It has a long flowering season, often from early summer until late autumn and attractive, glossy green, usually trifoliate leaves that are evergreen or virtually so. All forms of *C. cirrhosa* and its variety *balearica*, with finely divided leaves that turn bronze in autumn, are very welcome in the winter months when very few climbing plants are in flower.

HERBACEOUS PERENNIALS

A year's intense exposure at the start of my horticultural career firmly imprinted a love of perennials on my gardening psyche. In the nursery I remember rows of double white and double lilac primroses in the shade beds, while the field beds were planted with the bellflowers *Campanula lactiflora* 'Loddon Anna' in pink and 'Prichard's Variety' in deep violet-blue. These, together with the intense gentian-blue flowers of *Anchusa azurea* 'Loddon Royalist,' remain firm personal favorites.

In the last twenty years perennials have often received, undeservedly, a bad press. The swings of fashion, and a mistaken idea that growing perennial plants is very time-consuming and unrewarding, made planting shrub beds and borders a more popular activity. In fact, perennials are among the most versatile of garden plants. There are species and cultivars for all situations – sun or shade, limestone or acidic soils, wet or dry ground. In foliage and flower, perennials provide a vast range of form and color.

There is no shortage of published advice on planning combinations of hues and textures. Often this encourages overdesigning, with too much emphasis on contrast of foliage or consciously juxtaposed flower colors. I prefer to follow a more flexible approach, keeping in mind the example of Gertrude Jekyll: justly famed for her use of perennials, she would delicately adjust her designs over a number of seasons to achieve the effect she required.

SPRING

Many of the spring-flowering herbaceous perennials are woodlanders in origin, and so need moist, humus-rich soils and cool shade to thrive in the garden. Solomon's seals, *Uvularia grandiflora*, *Glaucidium palmatum* and the trilliums are all very satisfying.

Polygonatum curvistylum always intrigues garden visitors who find it difficult to believe that it is a "proper" Solomon's seal.

My selection for spring also includes the early-flowering primrose *Primula vulgaris* 'Alba Plena' and the lilac-pink *Cardamine pratensis* 'Flore Pleno.'

FLOWERS

Cardamine pratensis 'Flore Pleno' (Cruciferae) (3A–8A)

Lady's Smock, *Cardamine pratensis*, known to some by other colloquial names, including Cuckoo Flower, Meadow Cress, and Spinks, is widespread through much of Europe as a plant of damp meadows and ditches. It is often found coloring large areas of meadowland and other grassy areas lilac-pink or blush-white during mid- to late spring, with its 12in (30cm) high racemes of four-petaled, typically cruciferous flowers. When naturalized in the garden, *C. pratensis* not infrequently gets out of hand if conditions are too much to its liking. However, it dislikes excessive heat and humidity. The various double-flowered forms are much more restrained, although quickly forming vigorous clumps in moist, cool, leaf-rich soils or in wet grassland.

Double-flowered variants are quite frequent in the wild, and one at least was known to the Tradescants, great plantsmen of the seventeenth century, who referred to it as "Cardamine flore pleno, double Ladyes-smock." The clone usually grown as 'Flore Pleno' today (almost certainly not that grown by the Tradescants) is a most attractive and floriferous plant with upright, sparsely branched stems arising from rosettes of the pinnate, cresslike leaves, terminating in bunches of lilac-pink, many-petaled, double blooms, which lack any normal styles or stamens. It only really thrives in moisture-retentive soils, and in drought years, as I know to my cost, will die out completely.

Although *C. pratensis* 'Flore Pleno' produces no seed, it may readily be propagated by division of the densely fibrous rootstocks and, most unusually, from leafy, congested shoots that arise at the bases of the leaflets or occasionally in the axils of the narrow-segmented stem leaves. Young plantlets will form in a couple of weeks if a small stone is used to weigh down basal rosettes so that they are in contact with damp soil.

Two good, recently introduced double clones are 'William,' deep lilac in flower with dark green, bronze-tinted foliage, and 'Edith,' white but pink-tinted in bud, with broad petals and a green eye formed from the bud of a tiny flower within the primary flower.

Glaucidium palmatum (Paeoniaceae/Glaucidiaceae) (6A–9A)

Glaucidium palmatum is often described as "choice" in catalogs, a description which usually indicates that the plant is going to be expensive and difficult to grow. For *G. palmatum*, the former, sadly, is often true; the latter not so, if this gorgeous Japanese relation of the peony is offered conditions similar to those of the high mountain woodlands of Hokkaido and Honshu, to which it is endemic. It prefers cool, moisture-retentive, neutral to acidic soil, amply supplied with leaf mold and shelter from scorching sun or cold drying winds (as do so many woodland plants). Otherwise it is no more demanding than herbaceous peonies. It is perfectly hardy, down to 5°F (−15°C); the best groups I have seen were in a garden near New York, the huge clumps, growing in shade, having withstood the climatic extremes of the eastern United States.

A clump-forming deciduous perennial, 8 to 10in (20–25cm) high, slowly increasing from stout, short rhizomes, *G. palmatum* pushes up fleshy, arching stems in mid- to late spring. The flower buds are then still furled within the leaves, which rapidly unfold to reveal the solitary, cup-shaped, four-petaled flowers, which are often 3 to 4in (8–10cm) across, their beautiful satin sheen and violet-blue set off by the central boss of golden stamens. The flowers may vary somewhat in color from pale lilac to violet; the exquisite white-flowered var. *leucanthum*, which apparently comes true from seed, is also (occasionally) available.

Although the beauty of the flowers is relatively short-lived, the maplelike foliage is very handsome from the time it unfolds until midautumn when the plant goes into winter rest; the leaf blades, with seven to eleven lobes, are sharply toothed and crinkled when young, expanding eventually to 8 or 9in (20–23cm) across with a rugose, strongly veined surface.

Propagation by careful division of the rhizomes is a slow method of increasing stock. Seed sown as soon as possible after it is ripe in autumn will normally germinate the following spring. Seedlings may not appear for two years and young plants, like peonies, are often slow to establish and may take a few years to reach flowering size, but it is well worth the wait to see the sumptuous flowers in a woodland setting or on a peat bank.

Polygonatum x *hybridum* (Liliaceae) (3B–9A)

Solomon's seals have been favorites of mine since my childhood. Although not particularly showy plants, all exhibit an elegance of habit and have an accommodating nature, growing well in humus-rich soils in sun or shade and even in more barren sites, intermingled with the roots of trees or shrubs.

Polygonatum x *hybridum*, best called "Garden Solomon's Seal," is the commonest of this race in cultivation. It is a vigorous hybrid of *P. multiflorum* (3B–9A), and *P. odoratum* (4A–9A), with slightly ridged, arching stems, 4 to 5ft (1.2–1.5m) in length, and glossy, ovate, strongly veined, horizontally and alternately placed leaves, 3 to 4in (8–10cm) long. In late spring the pendent clusters of two to four slightly waisted, tubular flowers, white with green tips and faintly fragrant, are produced in the upper leaf axils. This hybrid rarely develops the globose, blue-black berries characteristic of the two parent species, which remain on the seed stems after the foliage has turned to butter-yellow in autumn and dropped.

Propagation by division of the fat, far-seeking rhizomes in early spring presents no difficulty, the only problem in some areas being attack by the gray larvae of

Polygonatum x *hybridum*

a sawfly, which will strip the foliage within a few days if not located and destroyed when the first chewed leaves are seen, usually in early summer.

Apart from its garden value as an ornamental of graceful habit and elegantly poised flowers, *P.* x *hybridum* is a useful plant for forcing. Clumps of rhizomes lifted in autumn, boxed up in leafy soil, and brought into gentle heat in a greenhouse may be induced slowly into growth to provide material for cut floral arrangements a month or two prior to normal flowering. The spent rhizomes should be replanted in the garden to recover, although it will usually be two years before they flower again.

Related plants A newcomer to cultivation, the distinctive *Polygonatum curvistylum* (4A–9A), from Nepal and western China, has very slender, sinuous, dark purple stems, 12 to 18in (30–45cm) high, clothed with whorls of linear leaves about 1–1½in (2.5–4cm) long, which in summer produce in the leaf axils clusters of two or three mauve, long-tubed flowers ⅓in or so (8–10mm) long. It increases rapidly from the thin rhizomes and happily pushes its flexible stems through low shrubs in my garden to bloom freely each year in early or midsummer.

Very closely related to *Polygonatum*, the small genus *Disporopsis* is virtually unknown in gardens apart from the evergreen *D. pernyi* (5B–9A). It is perfectly hardy and forms dense mats of rhizomes that produce dark mottled stems, 12 to 15in (30–38cm) high, bearing shining, dark green leaves and, in late spring or early summer, large, white, scented flowers that are flared at the tips. Normally, the current year's stems and foliage remain evergreen for a further season but may die back in severe winters, the rhizomes remaining unaffected.

Primula vulgaris 'Alba Plena' (Primulaceae) (5B–8A)

Double forms of the Common Primrose were much sought after as long ago as the Elizabethan era, when the English Primrose, *Primula vulgaris*, was highly regarded as an ornamental, as a salad vegetable, and for its medicinal properties. The Elizabethans also appreciated all the curiosities like Jack-in-the-Green and Hose-in-Hose, variations of which are still occasionally grown today.

'Alba Plena' was well known before Gerard published his famous herbal in 1597, and plants under this name are still grown today, although it is doubtful if it is the same clone that was available during the sixteenth century. I grow a number of variations of the English Primrose, but 'Alba Plena' will always remain my favorite, partly for its links with great gardeners of the distant past, but also for its continued good behavior and precocity in flowering. In early spring, sometimes earlier in mild winters, the clean white, double flowers, with, usually, two or three rows of the deeply notched petals and a slightly muddled center, are produced in profusion, just above the light green foliage, the whole clump standing about 6in (15cm) high. 'Alba Plena' continues to flower for several weeks and will often produce a few blooms later in the year.

Although 'Alba Plena' will thrive in any moisture-retentive, preferably humus–rich soil, it should be rejuvenated by division every three years because it quickly forms congested clumps and, particularly in drier soils, tends to become "woody" and die out unless divided regularly and planted in a fresh position. Some gardeners prefer to divide primroses after plants have flowered, but my own experience has been that splitting the clumps in late autumn or waiting until the flower buds are just showing deep in the leaf clusters in early spring is more successful if the divisions are to be planted straight out in the garden. However, if the divisions are potted up and cared for in a shaded cold frame, time of division is much less important.

Related plants Although in the past most double-flowered primroses were mules, unable to produce seed, a few produce fertile pollen, and there has been a fairly recent influx of named double clones, selections from Barnhaven Double seed races and others. *Primula* 'Miss Indigo' (5B–8A), is one of a large range obtained from New Zealand in the early 1980's, and it has proved very vigorous in my garden, forming dense clumps of dark green, slightly purple-flushed foliage. The flowers, which are almost inky blue with white-edged petals, appear in early spring, with secondary crops late in the season.

The well-known Drumstick Primula, *Primula denticulata* (5A–8A), from the Himalaya and western China, is one of the most reliable and earliest flowering of the *Primula* species and one of the easiest to grow. It prefers moist soils, where it will often naturalize from self-sown seedlings, but is at home in ordinary garden soils that do not dry out. The dense globes of small lavender, purple, pink, red, or white primrose blooms appear in early spring at ground level among the developing leaves, the flower stems gradually elongating to thrust the rounded flower heads 4 to 6in (10–15cm) above soil level. Increase by seed, which is copiously produced, will quickly provide masses of plants, but the flower colors and form of the flower heads will vary enormously. Many seedlings provide wishy-washy dull

MICROPROPAGATION AND TISSUE CULTURE

This specialized method of propagating plants by culturing tiny pieces of plant tissue, under sterile conditions and using an artificial growth medium, is widely used in commercial horticulture.

Tissue culture allows the production of large quantities of an individual plant in a much shorter period by more conventional propagation methods, and may be used as a conservation aid to increase rare plants. It has also improved the availability of plants that are difficult to propagate by other means, or are slow to increase vegetatively – for example, double primroses such as *Primula vulgaris* 'Miss Indigo.' Additionally, it is possible to free plants from virus infection by tissue culture using meristems (growing points). A number of virus-free clones, such as double forms of *Hesperis matronalis*, are now freely available.

lilacs, and careful selection should be made to retain only those with well-formed flower heads of good color. Always buy seedlings in flower. Increase these by division of the clumps, which is slow, or by root cuttings taken during the dormant season.

The almost legendary *Primula forrestii* (6A–8A) has now become readily available as a result of recent expeditions to northwest Yunnan, China, having been first introduced from the area by George Forrest in 1906. I have seen it in abundance in the Lichiang area in dry limestone habitats, often in rock crevices. The subshrubby clusters of golden-green foliage bearing umbels of up to twenty-five deliciously scented, orange-eyed flowers on 6in (15cm) stems in late spring and early summer. In the garden, an ideal position for this enchanting, hardy species is a crevice in a south-facing limestone wall with an overhang giving protection from excess moisture. *P. forrestii* certainly achieves the gold standard in its genus.

Trillium grandiflorum

Trillium grandiflorum (Liliaceae/Trilliaceae) (4B–9A)

One of the joys of early spring is to see the emergence of the shoots of *Trillium grandiflorum*, the North American Wake Robin, the three ovate leaves initially down pointed before rising to the horizontal on stems that are 12in (30cm) or more high. The pointed flower buds are poised in the center of the trinity of leaves that gives it another of its common names, Trinity Flower. By late spring the large flowers, 2 to 3in (5–8cm) long, have opened to reveal their pristine white and neatly veined petals, which, initially, are encased in the three narrower green sepals, upright at first and then gently nodding, with the petal tips recurved.

A native of the woodlands of eastern North America, it is the easiest trillium to cultivate and is extremely long-lived and undemanding, steadily forming large clumps by increase of the stout rhizomes.

Trillium grandiflorum is usually propagated by dividing the clumps of rhizomes when dormant, preferably in early spring, ensuring that each split has at least one strong dormant bud. Increase may be hastened by scoring partially around the rim of a dormant bud in late summer with a sharp knife and applying a little fungicide. A number of tiny offset rhizomes will form along the wound, and these may be carefully detached and grown on separately or left to swell the clump so that more divisions are eventually available. Seed, ripening usually in late summer as the leaves die down,

should be sown as soon as possible and given a period of cold either artificially or by exposure of the seed pots to frost during winter. *Trillium* seed often exhibits "double dormancy," requiring two periods of cold separated by a milder period for germination to take place. Seedlings of *T. grandiflorum* and the larger species may take five or six years to reach flowering size; some of the more delicate species like *T. rivale* (5A–8B) will bloom within two or three years from seed.

Related plants The whole *Trillium* tribe is one of the most satisfying plant genera that I know. Similar in stature to *T. grandiflorum* is a beautiful plant usually grown as *T. sessile* 'Rubrum' (5A–8B), almost certainly a form of the variable *T. chloropetalum* (4B–8B), from California. 'Rubrum' is distinguished by the claret petals and the beautifully mottled leaves. It is possible that a number of clones are grown under this name; but all are magnificent spring-flowering woodland plants.

The charming *T. rivale* is usually less than 4in (10cm) in height with dark glossy leaves, about 1in (2–3cm) long, and white or pale pink flowers, also 1in (2–3cm) long, freckled a deeper pink. In hilly country on the California-Oregon border I have found it growing in moist seepage areas seeding into the leafmold of *Rhododendron (Azalea) occidentale* (6B–9A). It is easily pleased in humus-rich acidic or near-acidic soil, but is best grown in a peat bank or woodland position where it will not be overwhelmed by bullying neighbors.

Trollius europaeus (Ranunculaceae) (3B–7B)

Although to some extent replaced in cultivation by its hybrids with various Asiatic species, the European Globe Flower makes a very fine garden plant in northeastern North America, suitable for any moist, fairly rich soil and flowering well in sun or shade. The large, three- to five-lobed, basal leaves arise from a fleshy rootstock and soon build up into mounds of handsome, deeply cut foliage as the flowering stems elongate to 2ft (60cm) or more. The cool lemon-yellow, globelike flowers (see p.94), up to 2in (5cm) across, are made up of ten to twenty incurved, overlapping petallike sepals surrounding the smaller, pale orange-yellow nectaries and stamens, and are borne terminally and singly 2 to 3in (5–8cm) above the foliage in late spring. In many regions of Europe *Trollius europaeus* may be seen growing in subalpine meadows, coloring extensive areas during late spring and early summer, or even into late summer at higher altitudes. Easily grown, readily propagated by division or seed, *T. europaeus* ranks among the most beautiful of herbaceous plants, giving no ground in quality or reliability to its hybrid offspring.

Trollius europaeus (see p.93)

Uvularia grandiflora (Liliaceae) (4B–9A)

The North American Merry Bells, a suitable common name for this elegant lily relation, a plant of quiet beauty, occurs naturally in deciduous woodland, spreading gently through the leaf-humus. As the arching shoots thrust upward and the stem-clasping, fresh green leaves unfold in mid- to late spring, the bright yellow, pendent bells, 1in (2.5cm) long, with propellerlike, markedly curved tepals, light up the woodland floor for a week or two, fading and falling as the stems reach their allotted height of 18in–2ft (45–60cm).

In gardens it has proved amenable, growing and increasing well in any reasonably fertile soil in sun or shade, although giving of its best in cooler, moister sites. Division of the tangled rhizomes in autumn or early spring provides a ready means of increase for both the more commonly seen bright yellow-flowered plants and the sulphur-yellow var. *pallida*.

OTHER PLANTS

Lathyrus vernus 'Albo-roseus' (Leguminosae) (5A–9A)
The Spring Vetch, *Lathyrus vernus*, widely distributed in Europe and into eastern Siberia, is one of the toughest and most accommodating herbaceous plants available for spring display. It produces sprays of small pea-flowers, purple, blue, pink, or white, in midspring as the pinnate feathery leaves unfurl to form dense clumps about 12in (30cm) high. My preference is for 'Albo-roseus,' with bi-colored bright pink and white blooms. It thrives in any reasonably well-drained soil, even flowering regularly in semishade. It comes true from seed. Division of the very tough rootstock is difficult but can be undertaken in early spring.

Uvularia grandiflora

SUMMER

There is an abundance of excellent summer-flowering perennials, and when confronted with the challenge of selection it is inevitable that I rely partly on personal associations. Some of my choices are old favorites first encountered in my early gardening days.

Anchusa azurea 'Loddon Royalist,' with its deep gentian-blue blooms, was a new form when I first saw it over forty years ago at Carlile's Nursery. As it lacked the sprawling habit of the species, it needed no support, and was eagerly welcomed for this characteristic.

It was at Carlile's, too, that I encountered the four clones of *Leucanthemum* x *superbum*, recommended here (p.96) for their long flowering season. *Phlox paniculata* 'Bright Eyes,' with lovely flowers in midsummer, and *Hemerocallis* 'Golden Chimes,' with rich yellow, mahogany-backed flowers and ornamental foliage, are fine cultivars with which I have had an equally long acquaintance.

Among more recent introductions that have particularly impressed me for their garden-worthiness is *Scabiosa* 'Butterfly Blue.'

FLOWERS OVER A LONG SEASON

Astrantia maxima (Umbelliferae) (5A–7B)

The masterworts, species of *Astrantia*, are among the easiest of herbaceous plants to grow, accommodatingly settling down in any well-drained soil in sunny or partially shaded sites, and contributing very effectively to the summer display over a long period.

Even the *Astrantia minor* (5B–7B), which I know well from acidic woodland south of Lake Como, Italy, with its miniature white and green flower heads and finely cut leaves, blooms more or less continuously through the summer.

Pride of place, however, goes to *Astrantia maxima* from the Caucasus, Iran, and Anatolia. It forms spreading mats of basal leaves with three divisions (five in one subspecies), from which the sparingly branched, flow-

ering stems, 1 to 2ft (30–60cm) high, arise for several months during the summer. These carry the broad-bracted, strawberry-pink umbels with their central clusters of tiny, pink, fertile flowers that make *A. maxima* such an attractive plant for use as a cut flower and for floral arranging. In nature *A. maxima* occurs in damp meadows and woods and, although happy in most sites, underachieves when grown in sandy, poor soils unless mulched regularly.

Astrantia maxima seems a cleaner and more fastidious plant than some of the mongrel seedlings of *A. major* (5A–7B). There are, however, two clones of this widespread central and southern European species that deserve star rating. 'Sunningdale Variegated' first occurred as a sport of *A. major* in a London garden, a pressed leaf being sent to me at Wisley for identification in 1965. Its beautiful, yellow and cream splashed foliage at its best in spring in an open, sunny site. This is a marvelous plant to meld into the border and to use for floral arranging.

The startling black-stemmed, dark ruby-red *A. major* 'Ruby Wedding' has appeared more recently. It should be vegetatively propagated rather than seed-raised to retain its remarkable coloring and its repeat-flowering characteristic. The latter distinguishes it from 'Rubra,' which is often raised from seed and does not always live up to its name as it is seldom rogued to retain its coloration.

Astrantia maxima

Leucanthemum x *superbum* 'Esther Read' (Compositae) (5A–8A)

The Shasta daisies, formerly known as *Chrysanthemum maximum*, have not only changed their generic name but also are now purported to be of hybrid origin between the large-flowered *Leucanthemum (Chrysanthemum) maximum* from the Pyrenees and the closely related, smaller-flowered *L. lacustre* from Portugal. Both species have long been cultivated, and their unwitting union has given rise to a very valuable race of garden plants, justifying fully the epithet *superbum*. Some cultivars, notably 'Esther Read,' may also carry genes of *L. vulgare*, the common Ox-eye Daisy.

Shasta daisies are, I believe, much undervalued by gardeners, partly, perhaps, because of the ease with which they grow and partly because all are white or near-white in flower. All the selected clones (and seed-raised stocks) behave with an equanimity matched only by some of the related genera in the same family. Their hardiness is unquestioned, and they will grow and increase well in virtually any soil conditions, provided drainage is not impeded. Most clones tolerate dry, poor soils and, even when neglected, bloom for long periods in summer. They amply repay normal herbaceous-border treatment, blending well with pastel and richer colors, and providing long-lasting cut flowers.

Division of the robust rootstocks is advisable every two or three years, discarding the woody centers and replanting the vigorous outer portions, to maintain the quality and quantity of the blooms. Well over fifty clones and a number of seed selections have been named, from "singles," with yellow central disc florets and long, white, marginal ray flowers, often 5in (12cm) or more across and sometimes markedly fringed, to semidoubles, anemone-centered and full doubles, all with increased numbers of ray florets.

The forerunner of this garden-worthy race was 'Esther Read,' at one time grown extensively for the cut-flower trade. The true stock is available today but in many commercial outlets has been ousted by an impostor that is about 3ft (90cm) tall. The original, 20in to 2ft (50–60cm) in height, with double blooms that are 4in (10cm) across and glistening white, touched with lemon in the center as the flowers open, is one of the stalwarts of the border. Given good soil, sharp drainage and regular division, it will flower from late spring until the first frosts, provided the old flower stems are cut as the blooms fade.

Equally valuable is 'Wirral Supreme,' a full double, with slightly shorter ray petals in the center, on strong stems 2½ft (75cm) tall, with variations from the fringe-

Linum narbonense

petaled, double 'Aglaia' to 'Cobham Gold,' also a double but with a raised yellow center and white marginal petals, both 18-24in (45–60cm) tall. All four are old favorites, familiar to me from Carlile's Nursery where I worked over forty years ago.

Linum narbonense (Linaceae) (5A–8A)

One of the memorable features of farming in recent years in Britain has been the increase in growing flax for linseed oil, spreading a heart-lifting summer haze of pale blue over the countryside. It is very difficult to recreate this beautiful effect in the garden but, on a small scale, the use of the perennial blue-flowered flaxes in group plantings comes close to it. Supreme among these is the ethereal *Linum narbonense* forming mounds of azure-blue all summer, if given an open, sunny, well-drained site.

Native to southern Europe, from Portugal to the former Yugoslavia, and also occurring in North Africa, *L. narbonense* varies from 15in to 2ft (38–60cm) in height and may need staking. It forms a cloud of delicate but wiry, gracefully arching stems with very narrow, glaucous leaves and sprays of bright blue, white-eyed flowers of open funnel shape that are often 1½–2in (4–5cm) across. As with a number of *Linum* species, the blooms usually close in midafternoon, but the following morning provide a further display of brilliance, a cycle that is repeated more or less continuously from early summer right through to early autumn. Cut back hard after flowering.

Selected, named clones, like the compact, vivid sky-blue 'Six Hills,' appear to have been seed-raised rather than vegetatively propagated in recent years and have probably been lost because they do not come true from seed. Stocks raised from seed vary to some extent in stature, flower size, and depth of color but are all delightful plants for the front of the border.

Primula florindae (Primulaceae) (6A–8A)

The vast family of primroses contains numerous plants of great garden merit, some difficult to please, others thriving without difficulty and sometimes becoming naturalized in cultivation. Among the latter the firmly perennial *Primula florindae* stands out as one of the finest and certainly the largest, having been recorded as reaching 4½ft (1.4m) in height, although 12in (30cm) or so less under normal garden conditions. Ideally it should be grown in partial shade as a waterside or bog plant to achieve its full potential but is perfectly at home in moderately rich, moist soils and, given ample water in the growing season, will succeed in sandy, humus-rich soil.

Young seedlings quickly build up into large rosettes of the distinctive foliage, with ovate-cordate leaf blades and very long leaf stalks, the whole often measuring 15in (38cm) or more in length. The robust flowering stems begin to appear in midsummer, each terminating in a huge, spreading umbel of up to eighty pendent, open-funnel shaped, fragrant, clear citron-yellow flowers, each up to 1in (2.5cm) long, dusted inside with creamy farina. The display extends into late summer, when the farina-covered seed heads are in themselves most attractive.

Color variations with orange-brown or pinkish flowers are sometimes available, almost certainly hybrids, with *P. alpicola* (6A–8A) and *P. waltonii* (6A–8A) as the suspected infiltrators. I have no time for these mongrels because they lack the purity of *P. florindae*. Seed is abundantly produced, but *P. florindae* is virtually self-sterile, so it is important to grow several seedlings together to obtain a good supply. Division of clumps in early spring is also a practical method of propagation, but the availability of self-sown seedlings usually makes this unnecessary.

Primula florindae, which is sometimes called the Himalayan Cowslip, was discovered in southeast Tibet

FLOWERS FOR CUTTING

The range of cut flowers nowadays stocked by florists embraces many easily grown border plants. The florist's display may include *Aconitum henryi* 'Spark's Variety,' in dark purple, the delicate, white-sprayed *Aster* 'Monte Cassino,' achilleas such as 'Coronation Gold,' the papery, blue *Catananche caerulea*, *Crocosmia masonorum* in orange-red, and the fiery red *Crocosmia* 'Lucifer.' All provide excellent, long-lasting cut flowers.

It is worthwhile planting in groups of five, seven or nine so that the removal of a few blooms will not affect the overall display. "Cut-and-come-again" plants such as *Scabiosa caucasica* ('Miss Willmott' is illustrated below) provide a continuum of blooms from summer into autumn, particularly if the spent flower heads are removed regularly. *Schizostylis coccinea* in red, pink, or white, will often bloom into late autumn.

by the plant collector Frank Kingdon Ward. Introduced in 1924, it was one of his greatest contributions to our gardens.

Scabiosa caucasica 'Miss Willmott' (Dipsacaceae) (4A–9A)

The Caucasian Scabious, like *Leucanthemum* 'Esther Read' and her allies, has been highly prized for many years, combining extended flowering (early summer to early autumn) with long-lasting qualities as a cut flower. At one time vast acres were grown for floral arrangements and many cultivars selected from a color range varying from deep blue to lavender and white. The main survivors now are the stalwart, ever-popular 'Clive Greaves,' a prolific, reliable lavender-blue now over sixty years old, the darker 'Moerheim Blue,' and, to my mind the best of the whites, 'Miss Willmott.'

One lesson that I learned in my nursery days, when helping to cut blooms for staging at flower shows, was to cut only those blooms in which the marginal florets were just developing, while removing to the base any spent flowers, to stimulate a continuing supply of fresh growth and further flowers to lengthen the season. The main clones grown were 'Clive Greaves,' 'Penhill Blue' (now seldom seen) and my favorite, 'Miss Willmott.'

'Miss Willmott' is often described as having creamy white blooms, but although in bud there is a hint of cream and green, the flower heads open pure white and when grown well may be as much as 3in (7.5cm) across. She has a strong constitution (as does 'Clive Greaves') lacking in many cultivars, and, given a well-drained reasonably rich soil, preferably alkaline, will flower very freely through the summer. She is not the best of performers in hot climates, so in such areas grow in partial shade. Propagation by division is vital to maintain true stocks and is best carried out in midspring (splitting plants in autumn often brings winter losses) using vigorous shoots with strong fibrous roots for replanting, while discarding weak and woody material.

Related plants One might suspect that strong marketing rather than quality explains the ready availability of *Scabiosa* 'Butterfly Blue' (5A–8B) since its introduction in 1985. Having grown and enjoyed its continuous summer supply of 2in (5cm), lavender-blue flowers on cobby, 18in (45cm) high clumps of the deeply cut foliage for some nine years, and found it reliably perennial and hardy in an open, sunny, well-drained site, my fears have been allayed. In South Carolina it produces blooms year-round, but do not cut back too hard. An excellent plant for the front of the border or alpine garden, this purported child of the British native *S. columbaria* (5A–8B) has certainly come to stay in my garden.

OTHER PLANTS
Linaria triornithophora (Scrophulariaceae) (7A–9A)
This beautiful toadflax from Spain and Portugal is grown less than it deserves. An elegant perennial 3 to 4ft (90–120cm) in height with strong, upright, simple or branched stems clothed with whorls of three, occasionally five, lance-shaped, bluish-green leaves, it produces terminal inflorescences of up to fifteen enchanting birdlike blooms. The individual flowers are often 2in (5cm) long including the curved spur, varying from violet-purple to lavender-purple or pink, with darker stripes lightened by the yellow palate.

Best grown in full sun in well-drained soil, it may be propagated by division in early spring, or raised easily from seed, plants sown under glass in early spring often blooming by midsummer. Mulch well for valuable winter protection.

EARLY SUMMER FLOWERS

Aconitum x *cammarum* 'Bicolor' (Ranunculaceae) (5A–8A)
Opinions differ as to the correct name for this superb border plant (and cut flower), which regularly goes on the nomenclatural merry-go-round and may also be grown as *Aconitum napellus* 'Bicolor,' *A.* x *bicolor* or, less commonly, as *A.* x *stoerkianum*. The parentage for the various clones grouped under *A.* x *cammarum* is considered to be *A. napellus* x *A. variegatum*. Regardless of its botanical persuasion, 'Bicolor' is one of the most vigorous and reliable of the monkshoods, the usual common name for this very varied and useful genus, derived from the shape of the flowers.

'Bicolor' initially grows stiffly upright, the sturdy stems well clothed with deeply divided, glossy, dark green leaves, gradually becoming more wide-spreading as it reaches full height of 4ft (120cm) and the inflorescences develop. The 1in (2.5cm) high, helmet-shaped flowers are white, margined and suffused violet-blue, a most attractive contrast, and are carried in dense racemes 4 or 5in (10–12cm) high with a number of subsidiary racemes developing below the main spike, continuing the flowering season from early to midsummer.

Monkshoods require a well-drained and moisture-retentive soil of reasonable fertility. Apparently indifferent to soil pH (except extremes), they will also grow well in full sun or light shade, *A. napellus* and its relatives occurring both in open meadowland and at woodland margins in Europe, a tolerance passed on to their garden offspring. Somewhat shorter, to 3ft (90cm), are two other excellent clones bred by Alan Bloom, 'Blue Sceptre,' in violet-blue and white, and 'Bressingham Spire,' a dark violet-blue, that have a much more upright habit, spirelike flower-spikes derived from *A. napellus*, and require no staking.

'Bicolor' has a tuberous rootstock (which is poisonous, as in all monkshoods) that quickly develops offset tubers. These may be divided in the dormant season to increase stock, preferably as the foliage fades or during mild spells in winter, as monkshoods start into growth early in the year. All the named clones should be vegetatively propagated to maintain true stock.

Anchusa azurea 'Loddon Royalist' (Boraginaceae) (3B–8A)
One of the first plants I handled during my early gardening training was *Anchusa azurea* 'Loddon Royalist,' a recent introduction at Carlile's Nursery in 1949–50,

when I worked there. Several clones of this very valuable race were grown, including 'Dropmore,' 'Opal' and 'Pride of Dover,' all fine standard selections of the widespread southern European and North African *A. azurea* (*A. italica*), worthy of cultivation in any of its forms for the summer glory of its terminal spikes of blue, white-eyed blooms. Most, however, are 4 to 5ft (1.2–1.5m) high and tend to sprawl over other plants in the border if not staked. The advent of 'Loddon Royalist,' an erect three-footer (90cm) with large flowers of deep gentian-blue that does not require support, was a milestone in the garden development of this species, particularly as it also begins to flower in late spring and continues in bloom all through early summer and onwards, if the old spikes are cut out as the flowers fade.

Any coarseness in 'Loddon Royalist' and its relations, all of which have hispid, rasping, lanceolate leaves and thick stems, counts for naught when their azure display of flowers is at its height. Its qualities were recognized by an RHS Award of Merit in 1957.

Anchusa azurea 'Loddon Royalist'

In nature *A. azurea* occurs in dry, open sites by roadsides and in grassland, as many visitors to the Mediterranean countries will have seen in spring and early summer. Good drainage and soil that is not over-rich in open, sunny sites suit all forms of the species best. Overfertilized plants tend to be short-lived and, although this is a reliable perennial, in wet conditions the thick, fleshy rootstock may succumb to fungal rots, particularly if the crowns are covered during winter with the decaying foliage remains of neighboring plants. Root cuttings, preferably taken in midwinter when fully dormant, provide an easy means of propagation. Young roots about 2in (5cm) long placed in pots in a propagator will take four to six weeks to produce shoots; those planted in the open ground need to be twice as long to provide adequate food reserves for the three to four months they take to regenerate.

Dactylorhiza elata (Orchidaceae) (8A–5A)

Among the terrestrial orchids grown in gardens, the various species of spotted and marsh orchids are the most satisfactory as they are hardy, free of increase and not difficult to grow. The common European Spotted Orchid, *Dactylorhiza fuchsii*, and some of its close relatives will even seed around as they do in the rock garden and alpine meadow at Wisley, but none provides such a magnificent display as *D. elata* from south-west Europe (and, it is sometimes stated, North Africa) when its fat, rich purple or lilac-purple spikes up to 2ft (60cm) high or more appear in the summer months.

It has floated around in gardens under a number of names in the genera *Orchis* and *Dactylorhiza*, and has been confused with the closely related Madeiran *D. foliosa* (also known as *D. maderensis*). As the various *Dactylorhiza* species hybridize freely in the wild where species overlap, it is not surprising that gardeners have become confused over the identity of the plants they grow. The most reliable characters for distinguishing unadulterated *D. elata* from *D. foliosa* are that the inflorescence of the former is 6–10in (15–25cm) long with long green bracts protruding beyond the flowers; whereas in *D. foliosa* the inflorescence seldom reaches 6in (15cm) long and the bracts are hidden or just peeping out.

Whatever the botanical niceties, *D. elata* is a most beautiful plant for a humus-rich site in open woodland, on the rock garden, on a peat bank or at the front of a border. Once suited, it forms large clumps with narrow, spotted or unspotted leaves, from which the sumptuous flower spikes appear between early and midsummer.

TERRESTRIAL OR GROUND ORCHIDS

Ground orchids fascinate many gardeners, partly because of their innate beauty and partly for the curious formation of their flowers. But indiscriminate collecting by botanists and gardeners has led to the virtual extinction of some ground orchids in Britain. Not only is it illegal to collect these plants, but very few survive more than a year or two's cultivation without special care. And as seedlings of most ground orchids, in nature, do not reach flowering size for many years, depredation of populations of any orchids will almost inevitably lead to their decline as numbers decrease.

A number of species are, however, in cultivation already, and some, like *Dactylorhiza elata* and its allies, are not difficult to grow in woodland soils and will increase steadily from tuber division.

Propagation by division of the palmately lobed tubers in late autumn or early spring is easy. Seed is freely produced, but conventional methods of dealing with it are seldom successful. The simplest method is to scatter fresh seed in leafmold or peat mulch around the parent plants. Given time, germination may occur.

Dactylorhiza foliosa, which from the gardener's viewpoint is a more slender version of *D. elata*, with the lip of the flower often broader and with shorter flower-spikes, requires similar treatment to *D. elata* and is just as satisfactory as a garden plant.

Incarvillea mairei (Bignoniaceae) (5A–8B)

Few herbaceous perennials possess the flamboyance of *Incarvillea* species, members of the mainly woody *Bignonia* family and cousins of the tropical *Jacaranda* and the Indian Bean Tree, *Catalpa*, strange though this relationship may seem.

Incarvillea mairei, in its various forms, is widespread in nature from the mountains of western Nepal across to Bhutan, Xizang (Tibet), and southwestern China. In the Lijiang Mountains and the Zhongdian Plateau in northwest Yunnan I have seen it growing in profusion on sharply drained, stony hillsides, forming rosettes of handsome, deep green, pinnate leaves, to 12in (30cm) long, with up to nine, ovate, toothed leaflets, the terminal one being more rounded and larger than the lateral leaflets.

In early summer, the leafless inflorescences, with up to five large, showy flowers, are produced on stems up to 12in (30cm) tall, trumpet-shaped crimson-purple flowers, yellow- and white-throated, and up to 1in (2.5 cm) long with spread-back lobes, A natural variant, subsp. *grandiflora*, which is widespread almost across the whole range of the species, differs only in its slightly larger flowers and leaves with only five leaflets (sometimes fewer). Two very popular, low-growing selections, 'Nyoto Sama' from Xizang, with smooth leaves and bright pink blooms in late spring, and 'Frank Ludlow' from Bhutan, a rich, deep pink flowering on very short stems in early summer, are available, both coming virtually true to type from seed.

Propagation by division of the fleshy, tuberous rootstocks when dormant is possible, but, since seed is produced in large quantities and young plants will bloom in their third or fourth year, it is seldom practiced, particularly as divided plants are slow to recover.

All are marvelous garden plants, as is the commonly grown *I. delavayi* (5A–8B) from China, a taller species with narrow leaflets, and are often long-lived, withstanding at least 5°F (–15°C) if grown in well-drained soils in open sunny sites. Although sometimes said to prefer neutral to alkaline soils, they will also grow well in acidic conditions and are often recommended as peat-bank plants.

Lychnis flos-jovis (Caryophyllaceae) (4A–8B)

Hailing from the central and western European Alps, *Lychnis flos-jovis* has been maintained as a garden plant in Britain for over two and a half centuries, an unassuming, easily satisfied, and free-flowering campion that combines woolly, gray-white mats of ovate-lanceolate leaves, attractive in themselves, with neat heads of up to ten flowers, 1in (2.5cm) wide, ranging from bright purplish-red to scarlet, pink or white, on stems from less than 6in (15cm) tall to over 2ft (60cm).

Although variable, all forms are excellent border plants, provided they are not overfed, when they are liable to pass away as a result of too rich a diet. In nature *L. flos-jovis* inhabits dry, subalpine, rocky slopes and screes, usually granitic or siliceous, although in

Lychnis flos-jovis

gardens it seems perfectly at home in alkaline conditions as well. Semistarvation conditions in full sun suit it best and intensify the silver-gray effect of the leaves, as well as encouraging more compact growth. All forms are much-appreciated plants in my garden, but the clear pink 'Hort's Variety,' dense-growing and usually under 12in (30cm) high, and 'Nana,' with deep pinkish red flowers and usually only half this height, find particular favor with me.

Seed is freely produced and germinates readily. Although a proportion of seedlings come close in character to the parents, propagation in spring by basal cuttings or division of the rosettes is the only certain way to maintain selected color forms.

Meconopsis x *sheldonii* (Papaveraceae) (6A–8B*)

In a genus with so many beautiful and garden-worthy plants, it is not easy to pick one that stands out from such a range of outstanding candidates. Both *Meconopsis grandis* (6A–8B*), particularly in the form

known as 'GS 600,' and the fabled Himalayan blue poppy, *M. betonicifolia* (6A–8B*), have strong claims, but the prize as far as I am concerned goes to *M.* x *sheldonii*, a hybrid between these two Himalayan species. A sound perennial, unlike *M. betonicifolia* which tends to be monocarpic, it maintains the vivid intensity of its blue blooms, whereas some forms of *M. grandis* (6A*–8B*) (and also of *M. betonicifolia*) may produce less pleasing, purple-suffused flowers.

Meconopsis x *sheldonii* is a strong-growing perennial, reaching 4 to 5ft (1.2–1.5m) in height, and forms dense clumps of rosetted, ovate, basal leaves that are 12in (30cm) long and rough and bristly to the touch. In late spring and on into midsummer the nodding, cupped flowers of clearest, cleanest blue appear as the crumpled buds unfold and provide one of the loveliest sights that may be seen in any garden in summer (see p.102), particularly when sited in dappled shade among rhododendrons or placed close to water, for the mirrored reflection of the blooms. Sadly, for those with alkaline soils, it does not appreciate lime in any form, and a cool, humus-rich position in light shade is needed for *M.* x *sheldonii* to thrive. It is primarily suited to cool moist areas with low humidity, such as the Pacific northwest and limited areas of the northeast.

Propagation by division at fairly regular intervals of two to three years in early autumn or early spring is necessary to increase stocks. It is worth the effort to please, particularly if the clones 'Branklyn,' with huge flowers often 6in (15cm) across, or 'Slieve Donard,' slightly lighter blue and with more pointed petals, can be obtained.

Related plants The delightful *Meconopsis chelidonifolia* (6A*–8B*), from western Sichuan, is somewhat neglected in gardens as it has been overshadowed by its more sumptuous relatives.

A perennial with overwintering crowns, like swollen buds, in spring it produces sinuous stems, 3 to 4ft (90–120cm) high, set with pale green, prettily lobed, hairy leaves. For several weeks in summer it bears its freely branched inflorescences with many flowers of shallow cup shape, described in the early 1900's by Reginald Farrer as "crumpled pale yellow silk on stems fine as wire."

Meconopsis chelidonifolia detests cold winds and dryness and is happiest in moist, lime-tree, humus-rich soils where the delicate stems can find support from neighboring dwarf shrubs. Unusually, it produces vegetative buds in the upper leaf axils, which may be used (like lily bulbils) to increase stocks, in addition to spring division of the rootstock.

Meconopsis x *sheldonii* (see p.101)

Ranunculus aconitifolius 'Flore Pleno' (Ranunculaceae) (5A–9A)

Fifteen or so years ago both the single and double forms of *Ranunculus aconitifolius*, a plant of the mountain meadows in central and southern Europe, had become uncommon garden plants in Britain, although they were once treasured for their elegant growth and long-flowering display during the summer months.

The handsome clumps of neatly cut, shining foliage give rise to upright flowering shoots reaching 3ft (90cm) or more in height, which display the open sprays of single, clean white buttercups from midspring on into summer, often with further flushes of bloom later in the season. It varies somewhat in flower size and from seed-raised plants only those with larger flowers should be selected.

'Flore Pleno' has made a comeback in recent years. Reputed to have been brought to Britain by Huguenot settlers at the end of the sixteenth century, it is commonly known as Fair Maids of France or Fair Maids of Kent. It is a delightful plant, similar to the wild species apart from possessing formal, double, pure white blooms, sometimes with a green-tinted center.

All forms of *R. aconitifolius* will grow well as border plants but prefer a meadow soil – deep, cool, and moist – in which they will steadily form large clumps. These may be divided in autumn or early spring to increase stock. Ideal also for the woodland garden, both single and double forms impart airiness to any planting.

Related plants As a buttercup enthusiast, even for that dreadful weed *Ranunculus repens* (4A–9B) and its double form (when it is not in my garden!) I find it difficult to choose one from the range available. *Ranunculus bulbosus* (5A–8A) 'F. M. Burton' differs from the species in having creamy yellow flowers profusely borne in early summer over the neat, lobed, marbled foliage. In my garden it seldom exceeds 9in (23cm) in height and often flowers again in early autumn.

OTHER PLANTS

Hesperis matronalis 'Lilacina Plena' (Cruciferae) (4A–9B) Plants charged with history appeal to me, and ranking high among them are the double forms of Dame's Violet or Sweet Rocket, supposedly introduced by Huguenot refugees. Most of the old variants are now lost or rare, and all the doubles must be propagated vegetatively, the majority of them having succumbed to virus diseases. Recently, however, both the double white 'Alba Plena' and the double lilac 'Lilacina Plena' have been cleaned up and the viruses removed. In well-drained, alkaline but moisture-retentive soil they grow well in sunny, open positions, producing their abundant flowers, like small double stocks, on stems 2 to 3ft (60–90cm) high from early to late summer.

MIDSUMMER FLOWERS

Achillea 'Coronation Gold' (Compositae) (3B–8B)
Indispensable in the summer border are several species of yarrow, not least some of the color variants and hybrids derived from *Achillea millefolium* (3B–8B), pilloried as a turf weed in its more rampant mood.

The stately *A. filipendulina*, a plant of wet meadows from the Caucasus and parts of central Asia, is frequently grown, its large platelike heads of bright yellow produced on tall stems, 4 to 5ft (1.2–1.5m) high, from midsummer until early autumn, striking in flower and excellent when cut for drying. A chance cross with the gray-leaved plant grown in gardens as *A. clypeolata* (3B–8B), (although not, it appears, the species entitled to the name) produced the very attractive 'Coronation Gold,' a more freely branched plant of lesser stature, reaching no more than 3ft (90cm), with filigree, gray-green leaves. In flower character it resembles *A. filipendulina* but with smaller, less densely set flower heads of bright gold that are freely and continuously produced from early until late summer, or later. An ideal plant for the small garden, 'Coronation Gold' is untroubled except by very wet or very dry soils.

In 'Moonshine' (3B–8B) it has a companion of equal merit, although it does not perform as well in hot, humid, summer conditions. The flower heads are of cooler coloring, a soft but bright yellow, with lovely silvered, feathery foliage on well-branched stems to 2ft

Achillea 'Coronation Gold'

(60cm) in height. Neither cultivar requires staking except in very windy locations; both increase freely and propagate readily by division in spring; and they provide long summer beauty as well as winter cheer from the dried inflorescences.

Agapanthus inapertus subsp. *pendulus* (Liliaceae) (6B–10B)
Summer would be much poorer without the ethereal colors of the African blue lilies, many of which have proved totally hardy in North America, in spite of a reputation to the contrary. This is true of the deciduous *A. campanulatus* (6B–10B), *A. praecox* (6B–10B) and the many fine cultivars derived from them. Many years have been spent breeding and selecting the best plants for garden use, and these have been distributed as named clones and as a seedling group called Headbourne Hybrids. Sadly, many of the seedlings now labelled as Headbourne Hybrids have not been rogued and now bear little resemblance to the original plants.

Among the species, the deciduous, late summer-blooming *A. inapertus* subsp. *pendulus*, from the eastern Transvaal, has particular appeal for me and is hardy to at least 14°F (–10°C), although in very cold areas it will benefit from some winter protection. Its upstanding stems, 3 to 4ft (90–120cm) tall, terminate in dense clusters of tubular, dark blue or violet-blue blooms up to 2in (5cm) long that are upright in bud but quickly become strictly pendulous. It is a most beautiful and distinctive plant, forming clumps of broad, rich green, basal foliage above the fleshy rootstock typical of all *Agapanthus*. Several other subspecies and color forms of *A. inapertus* are available but are of lesser merit. With all *Agapanthus* it is a wise precaution to see plants in flower before obtaining them: seed-raised plants may well be of hybrid origin. Division of the fleshy rootstock in spring is a slow but effective method of propagation.

Among *Agapanthus* clones and species I would pick out are the dark blue 'Lilliput,' 12in (30cm) or so high; 'Loch Hope,' almost four times as tall and of similar coloring; and *A. campanulatus*, with gray-green leaves and flowers ranging in shade from pale to dark blue. All these are reliable, in the sunny positions and fertile, moisture-retentive soils *Agapanthus* appreciate.

Anthemis 'Grallagh Gold' (Compositae) (4B–8B)
Widespread in Europe and the Near East on sandy, sharply drained soils, *Anthemis tinctoria* (4B–8B) is the progenitor of many fine garden plants. From late spring until midsummer all bear large daisy flowers with heads up to 2in (5cm) across in various shades of yellow and

cream carried on filigree-leaved, woody-based stems about 2ft (60cm) tall. These plants are valuable in the border but tend to be so profuse in flowering and so busy developing seed that they become exhausted and do not produce the basal growths needed for the following year's display. Thus, it is important to cut back free stems soon after the blooms fade so that basal shoot production is stimulated. Given good drainage, a relatively spartan diet and an open, sunny position, all are otherwise easy border plants. Taller varieties may require staking.

'Grallagh Gold,' one of several outstanding clones, raised nearly fifty years ago and still available from many nurseries, is valued for its flower heads of bright gold, touched orange, which may owe something to the influence of *A. sancti-johannis* (4B–9A), a bright orange species known only from Bulgaria in the wild, that hybridizes readily with *A. tinctoria*. It is likely that other richly colored clones, like the deep golden-yellow 'Beauty of Grallagh,' are derived from these two species, but other fine cultivars, like the lemon-yellow 'E. C. Buxton,' the paler yellow 'Wargrave Variety,' and 'Sauce Hollandaise,' a pale yellow changing to creamy white, are direct derivatives of *A. tinctoria*.

True *A. sancti-johannis* is a delightful plant, the rich orange of its blooms almost startling in intensity, but purchases that I have made latterly have always been of a yellow impostor of imperfect lineage.

In view of the variability of plants from garden-collected seed, it is better to propagate named clones from basal cuttings in late summer or early spring.

Campanula lactiflora 'Prichard's Variety' (4A–8A)

Among the most reliable and striking of herbaceous perennials is the variable *Campanula lactiflora*, from the Caucasus and adjacent areas of Turkey and Iran. A plant of subalpine meadows and forest margins it thrives in a range of garden conditions, from the formal border to grassland and light woodland.

In summer and early autumn it is a magnificent sight, its stately 5–6ft (1.5–1.8m) stems topped by huge domes of inch-long (2–3cm) bells, that vary from the deepest violet-blue to pale milky blue, soft pink, or white. In informal plantings, the various forms provide a marvelous melange of late color for weeks, just as the equally prolific *C. latifolia* (4A–8A), with larger tubular bells in a similar range of colors, will do earlier in summer. For borders, it is best to use named clones.

Although *C. lactiflora* is most frequently thought of as a tall plant for the back of the border, it has proved variable in height as well as in flower color. The mound-forming 'Pouffe,' described by its raiser, as "an attractive little freak," scarcely reaches 12in (30cm) in height, its dense, light green foliage beset with lavender-blue bells for weeks in summer. 'Loddon Anna' is a beautiful soft pink and 5ft (1.5m) or more in height.

Finest of all these clones is the deep violet-blue 'Prichard's Variety,' which only occasionally exceeds 3ft (90cm) in height and, although somewhat willowy in growth, with dense, heavy-branched flower heads, seldom requires staking. An alternative plant for further back in the border is the taller, but otherwise very similar, 'Superba.'

Anthemis 'Grallagh Gold'

Campanula lactiflora 'Prichard's Variety'

Propagation by division of the tough, almost woody, rootstocks or from basal cuttings in early spring should be used for named clones. Seed raised plants are perfectly acceptable for naturalizing; any unwanted color forms can be discarded once they have been given a chance to show their paces.

Related plants The unusual, almost smoky, coloring of the elegant hybrid *Campanula* 'Burghaltii' (4A–8A) does not appeal to everyone, but I would not want to be without this bellflower. Hardy, easily divisible, and free-flowering, 'Burghaltii' is no more than 2ft (60cm) tall, producing in early summer its large, tubular, pendent, grayish-mauve blooms, deep purple-mauve in bud, and up to 4in (10cm) in length when developed. 'Burghaltii' and the similar but slightly darker-flowered 'Van Houttei' (4A–8A) have considerable garden value, particularly as, if cut to ground level after the first flush, they will give a further burst of flower in autumn.

Digitalis laevigata subsp. *graeca* (Scrophulariaceae) (5A–8A)

Foxgloves in any guise are admirable garden plants, in many cases seeding freely, perhaps too much so in the case of the European native biennial *Digitalis purpurea* (4A–8A), but always welcome for the long racemes of tubular or bell-shaped blooms throughout summer.

I particularly like some of the species with puffed-up flowers (inflated-globose, botanically) with their net veined, tonguelike lips. The Balkan *Digitalis laevigata*, best known to me in its Greek form subsp. *graeca*, occurs at the edges of woodlands and at road sides. It is to be found in profusion on the lower slopes of Mount Parnassus in Greece, where I have seen large colonies still blooming in late summer and early autumn. A perennial, with basal rosettes of dark green, broadly lanceolate leaves, *D. laevigata* subsp. *graeca* grows to a height of 3 to 4ft (90–120cm), the strong stems, with linear leaves, terminating in long racemes of clear yellow-brown flowers, net-veined purple-brown, with pouting white lips.

Similar in many ways is the more widespread *D. ferruginea* (4A–8A), which, as the name suggests, has flowers of bright rusty-brown (sometimes yellowish-brown), with a network of darker veins and a larger lip, bearded but not white. They are borne in dense, long racemes during the summer months but, unlike those of *D. laevigata* subsp. *graeca*, seem only rarely to produce subsidiary inflorescences later in the year.

Both species are best raised from seed and, although they are often associated with woodlands in the wild, are best grown hard in fairly open positions in sharply drained soils to avoid the development of foliage that is too lush. Given these conditions, they are quite hardy and bloom regularly and freely each summer, providing an intriguing change from the European foxglove and its brighter flowers of more varied coloring.

Phlox paniculata 'Bright Eyes' (Polemoniaceae) (4A–8A)

Although the wild forms of the North American *Phlox paniculata* are seldom seen in cultivation, in spite of their vigor and hardiness, the cultivated offspring has gained great popularity in Britain and Europe. There has, however, been some decline in their cultivation, because of their susceptibility to nematode damage.

One of my earliest horticultural memories is of weeding among rows of phlox savoring the rich, distinctive fragrance which complements so well the profuse and colorful trusses of bloom, produced between midsummer and early autumn. The range of colors available is astonishing, particularly when one remembers that the wild species is recorded as varying only from purple to pink and white. Nevertheless, very few of the cultivars show characteristics of any species other than *P. paniculata*, although the related but distinct *P. maculata* (4A–8A) and *P. carolina* (4A–8A) have sometimes been cited as parents.

Requiring good drainage and growing well on sandy soils, border phlox suffer in drought conditions and, if possible, should be given a humus-rich, moisture-retentive soil. They are also at home on alkaline soils.

Even in good soils it is worth dividing clumps every third or fourth year, since most cultivars deteriorate after that period; the few wild forms available (in shades of lilac, mauve, and white) may remain undisturbed much longer. Always use fibrous-rooted young shoots to replant.

If nematodes are a problem (contorted shoots and leaves indicate their possible presence) propagation should only be from root cuttings (the nematode remains in the stems). Take sections 2 to 3in (5–8cm) long, preferably as complete individual roots. Burn the old plants, and plant the youngsters from root cuttings on fresh sites free from nematode.

'Bright Eyes,' with pyramids of pale pink, ruby-eyed, rounded "pips" (individual flowers) on 2ft (60cm) stems, is an admirable cultivar I have known for over forty years. Others that must have their place are 'Brigadier,' in bright orange-red with huge trusses on stems 4ft (120cm) high; 'Mother of Pearl,' about 3ft (90cm), with cool, white blooms suffused palest pink; and the chalk-white, red-eyed 'Graf Zeppelin.'

Platycodon grandiflorus (Campanulaceae) (3A–9A)

The Far Eastern Balloon Flower or Chinese Bell-flower, *Platycodon grandiflorus* (often wrongly spelt *grandiflorum*), the only species in the genus, has become a well-established denizen of our gardens in the last hundred years. It was first introduced from Shanghai, where plants were cultivated as a substitute for ginseng. The species occurs in mountain meadows in northern China, Manchuria, Korea, and Japan. In cultivation it has proved very variable in habit and flower color, some forms reaching 2ft (60cm) in height, while the sturdy, early-blooming dwarf var. *mariesii* from Japan is very free-flowering and seldom exceeds 10 to 12in (25–30cm), although many plants so offered are not true to type.

Platycodon grandiflorus accepts both alkaline and acidic conditions, preferring sharply drained, fairly

Platycodon grandiflorus

fertile soil. The young growth emerges late in spring to produce fleshy, purple-flushed stems. The blooms, described by Reginald Farrer as "fat-faced flowers of rich powder-blue," appear in terminal clusters, expanding from the balloon-shaped buds to display their bell-shaped interiors during mid- to late summer. In the best forms the flowers are 2in (5cm) across, deep blue or violet-blue and beautifully veined. White and pink selections, and some with double or semidouble flowers, are grown but lack the clean lines and simplicity of form that spell garden quality for me.

The usual means of propagation is from seed. Particularly fine plants may be maintained as clones by division of the fleshy, thick rootstock.

Veronica 'Crater Lake Blue' (Scrophulariaceae) (5A–8A)

Numerous speedwells have proved their worth in the perennial border and in the rock garden, some of the forms of *Veronica austriaca* and its subspecies *teucrium* (once accorded specific rank as *V. teucrium*) being at home in both situations. They produce enchanting spikes of small, open, white-eyed, blue flowers in profusion in midsummer on stems varying in height from 10in–2ft (25–60cm) or more. Native through much of Europe as a meadow plant or on stony slopes, *V. austriaca* subsp. *teucrium* has provided a number of cultivars that have been selected particularly for their compact habit, freedom of bloom, and the quality of flower

Veronica 'Crater Lake Blue'

color. Of these 'Crater Lake Blue,' massed with close-set spikes of intense gentian-blue to a height of 12 or 15in (30–38cm), is much in demand. It is an ideal front-of-the-border plant, straightforward to grow in any well-drained soil. Like most of its allies, it may readily be propagated by division in autumn after flowering or by cuttings of young shoots in spring.

Close relatives include 'Royal Blue' and 'Blue Fountain,' both taller and in slightly differing shades of azure. All will give pleasure year after year even on the poorest soils with minimal attention.

FLOWERS AND
ORNAMENTAL FOLIAGE

Acanthus mollis (Acanthaceae) (7A–9B)

Few herbaceous plants possess the presence required to stand alone in specimen groups, but there is no doubt that *Acanthus mollis*, known colloquially as Bear's Breeches or Branke Ursine, is one of the élite in this respect. The quality of its lush, handsome, lobed foliage is sufficient reason alone for it to be given a prominent place in gardens. Massive leaves, often 2ft (60cm) long by 6 to 8in (15–20cm) wide, arch elegantly from the fleshy rootstock to form glossy, dark green mounds from which the imposing flower-spikes, 4 to 5ft (1.2–1.5m) tall, arise in late summer. These are densely set with the white, purple-veined flowers, hooded within the 2in (5cm) purple bracts that are the dominant feature of the inflorescence.

Acanthus mollis is native to western Europe and northwest Africa but has become naturalized elsewhere, particularly in Greece, where the leaf shape in Corinthian capitals may have been derived from the plant. Considerable variation in the depth of leaf lobing may occur, the most commonly grown form, var. *latifolius*, having ovate lobes and shallow incisions, the leaf blades reaching 8in (20cm) or so across. This is probably the most satisfactory for general garden use, looking particularly fine if planted in large isolated groups as a focal point with brick or paving surrounds. It is also at home in the border or among shrubs, preferably in well-drained fertile soil in full sun. *A. mollis* and its variants are, however, very tolerant of shade.

Propagation is extremely easy, far too easy some would say, from root cuttings. Move *A. mollis* and the fleshy roots left behind will quickly produce young plants. Division of large clumps in early spring and autumn-sown seed can also be used to increase stock.

Other plants that can act as "anchor species," permanent features that link the ever-changing pattern of flowering plants within the overall scheme, include the eastern Mediterranean *A. spinosus* (6B–9B), with deeply divided, sharply spiny leaves, and the Balkan *A. hungaricus* (*A. longifolius*) (7A–9B), also with deeply cut foliage but with a broad, winged midrib and no spines.

Galax urceolata (Diapensiaceae) (3A–8B)

The sole member of its genus, *Galax urceolata* (also known as *G. aphylla*) is native to moist woodlands in the southeastern United States, where it forms dense mats of its attractive, glossy, evergreen foliage, which

develops red-bronze tints in autumn and winter. The leaves are up to 5in (12cm) long, rounded, slightly toothed, cordate at the base. The small white flowers are produced well above the foliage in slim spires, 1 to 2ft (30–60cm) high, lightening the woodland floor for several weeks between early and midsummer.

Galax urceolata needs acidic, moisture-retentive soil where its creeping rhizomes wander happily among leaf mold, in both dappled shade and full light, the autumn and winter coloration of the leaves being more pronounced in open positions. Careful division of the rhizomatous rootstock in spring, or autumn sowing of the very fine seed, uncovered on an acidic potting mix, provide effective means of increasing stock, although seedlings are slow-growing and can take a number of years to reach flowering size. A plant of quiet beauty, *Galax* is valuable in the garden for its burnished foliage; it is also sought after for floral arrangements.

Galax urceolata

Hemerocallis 'Golden Chimes' (Liliaceae) (3A–9B)

Vast numbers of day lilies are now available, with intense breeding programs, particularly in the United States and Australia, hourly adding, it almost seems, new developments in color, size, and shape, bewildering the newcomer to gardening. Many of them are excellent garden plants, but some are almost gross in flower size and somewhat unbalanced in the relationship of inflorescence to foliage. These are fine for the enthusiast and the show bench, but do not always sit comfortably with other plants in the garden.

'Golden Chimes,' however, now more than forty years old, is elegant, floriferous, and most attractive when displaying its branching sprays of red-brown flower buds opening to rich yellow, mahogany-backed, delicate, trumpetlike blooms, 2in (5cm) across. These appear in profusion from midsummer on stems 2 to 3ft (60–90cm) tall that thrust through the plentiful, arching, narrow, bright green foliage. The length of flowering possibly owes something to the genes of the late-flowering *H. multiflora* (5A–9B) in its parentage.

Like all day lilies, 'Golden Chimes' thrives in any reasonably drained soil, preferably somewhat moisture-retentive, but it is undeterred, even in drier soils, flowering freely whether in sun or light shade. Propagation by separating pieces of the interwoven, fleshy rootstock in autumn or spring (or indeed almost at any time of year) is quite straightforward, and the divisions quickly reestablish and develop into new large clumps.

Many other cultivars are excellent for the garden. It is largely personal choice of flower color, form and height (as well as future neighbors in the border) that will determine which of the vast range is chosen.

Related plants Scent is not normally associated with day lilies but *Hemerocallis lilio-asphodelus* (3A–9B),

graceful in growth and with beautiful, clear yellow, freely produced flowers with delicately recurved petals in early summer, has the bonus of delightful fragrance.

Another species that combines attractive flowers and plentiful ground-covering foliage with a delicious perfume is *H. citrina* (3A–9B), which flowers in late summer, opening its blooms in the early evening.

Lysimachia clethroides (Primulaceae) (3A–9B)

Quietly beautiful and much less frequently grown than many other herbaceous perennials of lesser quality, the Japanese and Chinese *Lysimachia clethroides* occurs on open, hilly grassland in nature. In gardens it prefers a reasonably moist soil but should also be tried in meadow conditions, perhaps in an old orchard, since it is tough enough to compete with other rumbustious perennials and quickly forms large groups from the gently creeping rhizomes. Under ideal conditions it can become weedy and invasive. The erect stems, clothed in alternate, narrowly elliptic, light green leaves, grow steadily during early summer to 3ft (90cm) and in late summer terminate in arching, swan-necked spikes, 4 to 6in (10–15cm) long, of small, white flowers. As the season progresses the inflorescences gradually straighten,

Lysimachia clethroides

providing a most attractive and unusual effect, unmatched elsewhere in the herbaceous border.

Lysimachia clethroides is untroubled by all but extreme soil conditions, although withstanding boggy ground better than drought. It is an easy, trouble free plant increased readily from division of its rhizomatous growths or from seed, which is abundantly produced.

In the same category, although of quite different aspect, is the glaucous, narrow-leaved, sentinellike *L. ephemerum,* from the Iberian Peninsula and the Pyrenees. The inflorescences of white flowers are as long as those of *L. clethroides,* but unbending and erect from the beginning. It is clump-forming rather than spreading and may reach 4ft (120cm) or more in the distinctly moist situations it prefers. As well as being decorative throughout the summer, it retains its narrow spires of small, rounded, light brown seed pods during autumn and early winter, unless these are carried off as a valuable prize by the resident flower arranger.

Morina longifolia (Dipsacaceae) (6B–9A)

The unusual scabious relative *Morina longifolia,* from the Himalaya, is a border plant that stands out from its neighbors. In nature it occurs on open hillsides and meadowland at altitudes of 10,000ft (3,000m) and more in many areas of Kashmir, Nepal, and Bhutan. In Britain it has proved hardy but is not always long-lived unless given well-drained and fertile soil, where it will form dense clumps of its very prickly, dark green, thistlelike leaves, 8 to 10in (20–25cm) long, that emit a spicy aroma when touched. By midsummer the strong, erect stems have developed to a height of 2 to 3ft (60–90cm), bearing prickly leaves low down and producing in the upper half dense whorls of the delightful, long-tubed, fragrant white flowers from midsummer until early autumn. As they age, the blooms turn rose-pink, then crimson, and gently bow downward to give place to further young flowers from the congested whorls, the whole in full fig resembling a series of small pink and white fireworks. Even then *M. longifolia* has more to give, because the stems dry well and provide very effective material for winter decoration. In northern states it is advisable to protect the plants with a mulch in winter.

This species is easily raised from seed but the young seedlings should be transplanted at an early age and planted out from pots as soon as possible, as too much root disturbance is likely to be resented.

Morina longifolia is not easy to place in the conventional border, because of its distinctive growth habit, and it should not be given aggressive, large-leaved

neighbors, as the dark atmosphere of smothering foliage may encourage rotting of the basal leaf rosettes. The best groups that I have seen have been in among rocks in scree, where *Morina* was benevolently lording it over its companions of lesser stature and flowering profusely in the sunny, open conditions.

Rodgersia pinnata 'Superba' (Saxifragaceae) (5A–7A)

The six or so species of *Rodgersia,* robust, rhizomatous perennials allied to the saxifrages, would be well worth growing if only for the decorative effect of their leaves, from spring to autumn. Add to that a summer display of elegant, frothy inflorescences made up of hundreds of tiny white or pink flowers, followed by attractive seed heads, and value for money is guaranteed.

Rodgersia pinnata is found wild in Yunnan and Sichuan, in China, growing by streams and in moist grassland. From the stout, creeping rhizomes it produces arching leaves 12in (30cm) or so long, each with five to nine 6 to 8in (15–20cm) leaflets, with dark green, rugose, deeply veined surfaces. Sometimes the leaves are not strictly pinnate, with clearly separated pairs of leaflets, but instead are partially joined; in cultivated

Rodgersia pinnata 'Superba'

plants this may result from hybridization with the palmate-leaved *R. aesculifolia* (5A–6B), which has foliage like that of a buckeye.

In midsummer the elegant, plumelike flower heads are produced on stems 3 to 4ft (90–120cm) high, often white or yellowish-white but not infrequently pale to deep pink in color. Undoubtedly the most desirable clone is 'Superba,' which not only has broad pyramids of bright pink flowers followed by copper-red seed heads but also bronze-tinted young foliage and often good autumn color. But, be warned, many plants masquerading as 'Superba' have been seed-raised, not vegetatively propagated by division, as they should be. Although these are often good plants in their own right, they seldom match 'Superba' in beauty.

All the species prefer moist, humus-rich soils in open or slightly shaded sites. Although ideal plants for waterside plantings, where their bold, spreading foliage looks most at home, they will grow well as border plants or in open woodland provided they are mulched in spring and kept well watered in dry periods, making thoroughly satisfactory plants for gardens where drought is not a problem.

Selinum tenuifolium (Umbelliferae) (5B–7B)

If cow parsley and Queen Anne's lace were not common roadside plants in Britain but rarities from the Himalaya, they would almost certainly be extolled as plants of great merit, valued for their lacy flower heads and "architectural" habit. *Selinum tenuifolium*, however, does hail from the Himalaya and, deservedly, was recognized by our Victorian forebears as a fine garden plant, ideal for grouping in turf beds, where its elegant poise could be fully appreciated.

A plant of mountain meadows, *S. tenuifolium* (possibly correctly known as *S. wallichianum*) is a hardy, clump-forming perennial, reaching 5 to 6ft (1.5–1.8m) or more in height, with strong, upright, sometimes bronzed, branched stems and very finely cut leaves, up to 12in (30cm) long. During mid- to late summer, sometimes later, the large, white terminal inflorescences are borne in irregularly tiered umbels both on the main stems and on the many side shoots, floating like lace above the surrounding vegetation.

Although division of the rootstocks in early spring is sometimes practiced, it is preferable to raise *S. tenuifolium* from seed sown as soon as possible after it is ripe. As with many Umbelliferae, the seed does not remain viable for long unless stored under cool, dry conditions, so autumn sowing is to be recommended to ensure reasonable germination.

An excellent plant for the back of a border, *S. tenuifolium* will grow readily in any well-drained soil, preferably in full sun, but it also makes a fine display in grassland or in light woodland, where its imposing stature, delicate foliage, and airy flower heads may be appreciated to the full.

Senecio smithii (Compositae) (7A–9A)

Many of the herbaceous groundsels that have been brought into gardens have proved to be rough, tough and on the way to being ugly, their ease of cultivation in no way making up for lack of aesthetic qualities. *Senecio smithii* from southern Chile and Argentina, however, is a garden plant of merit both for its ornamental foliage and bold, attractive flower heads.

My first sight of *S. smithii* was a somewhat wilted specimen sent to me for identification some thirty-five years ago with a letter of assurance that it was growing wild. Having eventually tracked down that, while naturalized in the west of Scotland, its true home was on the other side of the world, I asked for material to grow. This was sent willingly, planted in the Wild Garden and duly labeled. The appearance behind the label of one of the largest docks ever seen turned out to be an error on the part of the sender (duly rectified) rather than a misidentification on my part.

Ever since that episode *S. smithii* has been a perennial I have enjoyed growing (if snails and slugs allow),

Senecio smithii

partly for the memory but mainly for its attributes in the garden particularly by waterside plants or in boggy wet soils, where it is happiest. Dry soils suit it not at all, but it may be grown successfully, if well mulched and watered, in good garden soil, although not to maximum size. The short rhizomes produce dense clusters of oblong-ovate, dark gray-green leaves up to 12in (30cm) long that initially have a covering of white wool, particularly on the undersurface. Robust, leafy, unbranched stems reaching 5ft (1.5m) in height terminate during mid- to late midsummer in large, rounded, umbellike clusters, 8–12in (20–30cm) across, of white, yellow-centered daisy flowers, each up to 2in (5cm) wide.

Handsome in foliage and attractive in flower, *S. smithii* is easily propagated by spring division of the rhizomatous rootstock or raised from seed.

Thalictrum delavayi 'Hewitt's Double' (Ranunculaceae) (4B–8A)

All the meadow rues, characterized by their willowy growth, delicately divided leaves and light, colorful inflorescences, are worth growing if only for their maidenhairlike foliage. Excellent border plants in the genus include the 5ft (1.5m) European species *Thalictrum aquilegiifolium* (5A–8A), which has large fluffy flower heads with conspicuous stamens in purple or white, as well as *T. flavum* (5A–9A) in various shades of yellow and its subspecies *glaucum* (*T. speciosissimum*). All grow readily in any well drained soil.

The cream of the genus, however, come from Asia, and among a number of purple-flowered species *Thalictrum delavayi* (often confused with *T. dipterocarpum*) stands supreme. In Yunnan I have seen it still flowering profusely in midautumn, its wandlike, dainty-foliaged shoots surmounted by a haze of huge, airy panicles of bloom, swaying among shrubs in shaded, moist sites in the company of *Anemone hupehensis*. The pyramidal inflorescences may be as much as 12in (30cm) across and almost twice as high when well grown, and consist of delightful flowers, ½in (1cm) long, with pendent, creamy stamens surrounded by four lilac-purple sepals. Some variation in flower color occurs and there is an attractive white form available, as well as the beautiful 'Hewitt's Double,' with a cascade of double lilac-purple, pom-pom blooms, which lack stamens but are both prolific and long-lasting.

Thalictrum delavayi and its relatives flower from midsummer to early autumn. They like fairly rich, moist but well-drained soil and are best given support by neighboring plants. Staking may be needed in windy situations, but planting in a hollow about 6in (15cm)

Thalictrum delavayi 'Hewitt's Double'

deep and gradually filling this during the growing season with humus-rich soil encourages strong root development and helps provide an anchor for the stems.

With the advent of micropropagation 'Hewitt's Double' has now become readily available. In the past, spring division was the main means of increase, although, with patience, the tiny, swollen leaf buds ("bulbils") that form between stem and leaf may be grown on to flowering size. The single-flowered forms are readily raised from seed, which should be sown soon after it is ripe, since it is often short-lived. Seedlings will take three or four years to flower.

Veratrum nigrum (Liliaceae) (3B–7B)

The statuesque *Veratrum nigrum*, a member of the lily family (or, if you follow modern botanical thought, the split-off family Melianthaceae), captured my imagination in my early gardening days with its incredible plumes of dark chocolate-maroon flowers, both sinister and attractive at the same time. Like the other species in cultivation, it is best grown in deep, moist soil, happily accepting heavy alkaline soils, if reasonably drained, and thriving in sun or as a woodland plant in partial shade, as I have found it near Lake Como in Italy. Widespread in nature from much of Europe across to Siberia and China, *V. nigrum* is a robust, long-lived perennial. In early spring it develops a fan of striking, broadly elliptic, pleated, and deeply veined leaves a foot (30cm) or more long; it is well worth growing for the quality of its foliage alone. It is, however, susceptible to slug damage.

On established plants the shortly branched inflorescences, 4 to 6ft (1.2–1.8m) tall, appear in early summer and midsummer, closely set with numerous ½in (1cm) starlike flowers, variously described as black, blackish-purple, maroon, or red-brown, but in reality probably a subtle mix of them all. A slightly unpleasant scent does not detract from their overall quality, which is shown to best effect when they are backlit by evening sun.

Propagation by division in autumn or early spring is slow, but the most satisfactory means of increasing stock, because seed-raised plants take at least five to seven years to reach flowering size.

The only other species that is fairly readily available is *V. album* (4A–7B), known as the False or White Hellebore or Helleborine but with no direct relationship to either plant. It, too, is a very widespread species and is similar in habit and size to *V. nigrum* but, as the name indicates, with white flowers, although throughout its range these may vary from greenish- to yellowish-white. It is as handsome as its black-hued cousin. Both look good in a woodland setting or grouped in isolated plantings, though perfectly at home in the border.

OTHER PLANTS
Geranium macrorrhizum (Geraniaceae) (5A–9A)
One of my indispensable all-rounders, this easily grown and attractive species is among the densest and most effective of all ground-covering plants, spreading by thick, creeping rhizomes, with masses of intensely aromatic, light green leaves, deeply cut into five to seven jagged lobes and providing bright orange-red autumn color. It flowers in late spring and summer, color varying from dark magenta to the rose-pink 'Ingwersen's Variety' and the almost white 'Album.' *G. macrorrhizum* naturally occurs on limestone formations but is happy on acidic soils and thrives in sun or dry shade.

Geranium psilostemon (Geraniaceae) (4A–8A)
In early to midsummer this sterling performer for the border, also known as *G. armenum*, bears many-branched sprays of cup-shaped flowers that are about 1½in (3–5cm) across. These show-stopping blooms, bright magenta-crimson and black-centered, are carried on stems 3 to 4ft (90–120cm) high above the mounds of attractive, deeply cut, usually seven-lobed leaves, which assume orange and yellow tints in autumn. Even the swelling red growth buds, in early spring, are attractive. *G. psilostemon* has few foibles as to soil or situation.

WINTER

While several perennials – the bergenias and pulmonarias among them – retain their foliage throughout the season, hellebores are the only herbaceous plants that flower reliably in the depths of winter. Their clusters of cup- or bell-shaped flowers, usually pale green, white or shades of pinky purple, extend well into the spring, offset by handsome leaves.

FLOWERS AND FOLIAGE

Helleborus argutifolius **(Ranunculaceae) (6B–7B)**
The early flowering Christmas and Lenten roses are much sought after for modern gardens. Some are totally herbaceous, losing all their foliage by winter; some have overwintering leaves that are replaced in spring by vigorous young foliage; yet others are evergreen and almost shrubby in habit. Among the latter is one of the easiest and most attractive species, *H. argutifolius*, also known as *H. corsicus*, after its land of origin.

It produces subshrubby stems lacking any basal leaves and bearing only cauline (stem) leaves, each consisting of three spiny-toothed, leathery, markedly veined leaflets. These are mid- to dark green and on vigorous plants often measure 8in (20cm) long and nearly 3in (7.5cm) wide. The strong stems arise from a tough, rhizomatous rootstock and, if plants are well pleased with their environment, may reach 3 to 4ft (90–120cm) in height. The terminal inflorescences are produced between midwinter and early spring, each bearing up to thirty of the pale green, nodding, cup-shaped blooms, up to 2in (5cm) across, and are furnished internally with darker green nectaries surrounding the bunches of stamens and the pale yellow anthers.

As the abundantly produced seed is ripening, young growths spring from the rhizome replacing the spent, flowered shoots, which should be cut out once seed has been gathered. Seed sown in autumn will normally germinate the following spring, the seedlings taking two years to reach flowering size. Plants self-seed freely.

Helleborus argutifolius appears hardy, reaching near-perfection in fairly rich soil in sun or partial shade. It still grows well in less favored conditions, although in deep shade loses the stately compactness that marks it as a foliage and flowering plant of year-round quality. This plant does best on the West Coast, because it dislikes areas with hot, humid summers.

TWO OR MORE SEASONS

Some perennials have such wonderful flowers that the insignificance of their leaves is easily forgiven, but the border also cries out for ornamental foliage. Large perennials with well-defined, attractive leaves can provide a structure to underpin the more ephemeral attractions of flowers. My choice here includes *Kirengeshoma palmata*, with great maple-like leaves and waxy blooms which last from late summer into autumn, and *Cynara cardunculus*, a majestic plant with silver-gray foliage and towering late-summer flowers.

For small mounds of color and texture I would single out *Paeonia mlokosewitschii*, whose brief but beautiful flowers are borne on ground-covering foliage that changes color continuously well into autumn.

Rudbeckia fulgida var. *sullivantii* 'Goldsturm' deserves its great popularity for its late-summer to autumn flowers: at its glowing best, it beautifully complements *Artemisia* 'Powys Castle' or the more upright *Artemisia ludoviciana* 'Silver Queen.'

Helleborus argutifolius

Related plants *Helleborus foetidus* (3B–8B), the Bear's Foot or Stinking Hellebore, is widespread in central and western Europe, including Britain, occurring in limestone areas, usually in woodland. It differs from *H. argutifolius* in having petiolate leaves with seven to ten divisions, the leaflets being narrower and less coarsely toothed, and smaller, sometimes fragrant, bell-shaped, pale green flowers, almost always rimmed purple-red, which often remain attractive until late spring. 'Wester Flisk' is a particularly fine selection, with red brown stems and petioles that contrast well with the dark foliage and unusual flowers. In shaded, moist, humus-rich conditions it will grow to 2½ft (75cm).

In the twenty years I have grown it, *Helleborus purpurascens* (5B–8B) has never failed to push up at least the first of its flowers before Christmas. These are 2in (5cm) across, cup-shaped and dark purple-violet, although *H. purpurascens* is a variable species. The flowers nestle at ground level before their stalks elongate to 8 or 9in (20–23cm) in fruit. This, sadly, is not freely produced and increase by division is slow.

SPRING FLOWERS AND ORNAMENTAL FOLIAGE

Bergenia 'Silberlicht' (Saxifragaceae) (4B–8A)
The resurgence of interest in the old-fashioned Megascas or Elephants' Ears, as they were once known, a fanciful reference to their large leaves, has led to a spate of hybridization and seedling selection, with over fifty named clones as well as species being available commercially. Their value for evergreen ground cover (with the exception of *Bergenia ciliata* (5B–8A) and its var. *ligulata*, which are frost-deciduous in Britain and North America), fine foliage effect, and early season flowering is now fully accepted, although in the past they were often relegated to dark corners of the garden or dry areas under trees, where, in spite of neglect, they would flower cheerfully in late winter and early spring.

Bergenia 'Silberlicht'

I rate 'Silberlicht' (or 'Silver Light,' as it is also known) as one of the best hybrid bergenias in a very competitive field. It has large, handsome, leathery, dark green leaves, 6 to 8in (15–20cm) long, that are produced from the thick, slowly spreading rhizomes. In mid- to late spring, sometimes earlier, the large heads of pure white, narrowly bell-shaped flowers with dark calyces are produced on stems that are 12 to 15in (30–38cm) tall, the petals becoming suffused with pink as they age.

Like all bergenias, 'Silberlicht' thrives in any soil, acidic or alkaline, dry or damp, in sun or shade, making a trouble-free permanent resident, ideal for the border or as ground cover among deciduous shrubs. The rhizomes are readily divided to increase stocks, preferably in spring; splitting at other times (except in drought conditions) is tolerated, with few failures occurring.

If only I had sufficient space to accommodate more in my garden, there are very few of this easy-going race that I would reject. Among the others that particularly appeal to me are the Himalayan and Chinese *B. purpurascens* (5B–8A), with deep red-purple winter foliage and nodding, purple-pink, narrow bells; the pink- and white-flowered forms of the small-leaved *B. stracheyi* (4B–8A), from Afghanistan and north India; and 'Ballawley' (4B–8A), with large, shiny, fresh green leaves and crimson blooms.

Corydalis flexuosa (**Papaveraceae**) (5B–8A)

Few plants have gained such rapid popularity as this superb blue-flowered *Corydalis* from western China, which only arrived in Britain in 1989. Three clones were introduced by members of the expedition, who found it growing profusely in moist, leafy, woodland soil in the Baoxing (Moupine) and Wolong valleys in Sichuan. *C. flexuosa* has proved so easy to grow in humus-rich, well-drained soil and is so easy to propagate that it is certainly here to stay.

The rootstock consists of small, fleshy, tight-knit, cuplike leaf bases from which slender rhizomes extend, developing at their apices further plants, providing a ready means of increasing stock. The leaf rosettes often overwinter, expanding in spring to produce finely divided, glaucous purplish-green foliage and sparingly branched flowering stems. The showers of narrow, sky-blue or purplish-blue, elegantly tip-tilted flowers begin in early spring. The display continues until late spring or early summer, even, in cool conditions, intermittently through the summer. In very dry conditions *C. flexuosa* will retreat into dormancy, often re-emerging in autumn to flower again before frosts intervene.

Seed is freely produced, and many of the plants now sold are seed-raised, with variation in leaf and flower characters as well as habit unless a named clone is obtained. The tallest of these, 12in (30cm), is 'China Blue.' The name aptly describes the flower color, although there is variation from sky-blue to a more greeny blue, depending on the maturity of the 1in (2.5cm) flowers and the conditions (in all the named selections flower color tends to be intensified by cool weather). The foliage is purplish-green, particularly in winter, marked red at the base of the leaf lobes. The foliage of the slightly shorter 'Père David' is more glaucous, and the flowers about 1½in (3–5cm) long. The compact 'Purple Leaf,' 6 to 8in (15–20cm) high, has dark red marks on purple at the leaflet bases, and the flowers, 1in (2.5cm) long, are blue with a purple tinge.

Dicentra spectabilis (**Fumariaceae**) (3B–8A)

Bleeding Heart or Dutchman's Breeches has been a treasured denizen of our gardens since 1846, when it was sent back to the Royal Horticultural Society from China by its collector, Robert Fortune. It had been introduced some thirty years previously but was not established successfully, although it rapidly became a very popular garden plant from Fortune's collection. The Latin and common names have been etched in my memory since my first acquaintance with the plant, which was when I was at Carlile's Nursery. Tommy

Dicentra spectabilis

Carlile, the proprietor, had pulled apart the petals of a flower and shown me the "lady in the bath," the outline which has given rise to another of its colloquial names.

A woodland plant in nature, *Dicentra spectabilis* has taken readily to life in the perennial border, and increases steadily from the fleshy rootstocks to form strong clumps of delicately divided, graceful leaves, in flower reaching a height of 2–2½ft (60–75cm). The elegant, arching, 9in (23cm) pendent sprays, of heart shaped flowers are produced in late spring and early summer. Each flower has two outer, deep pink or rosy red, pouched petals, surrounding two exserted, narrow, white inner petals. The plant is a sight of great beauty when in full flower, and the foliage remains attractive afterwards. Left undisturbed and given well-drained, fairly rich soil and a cool position, *D. spectabilis* will continue to thrive for many years.

Propagation is usually by careful division of the brittle, fleshy rootstock, preferably leaving the main crown intact and only removing side pieces. Young shoots may also be used to increase stock if detached with a small piece of root and grown on in a cold frame. Seed is not usually produced in any quantity in Britain but, when available, should be autumn-sown.

The advent of micropropagation has increased the supply of the typical *D. spectabilis* and of its very lovely white form, usually sold as 'Alba' (the correct but undignified name is possibly 'Pantaloons'), which has pale green foliage and also apparently comes true, or almost so, from seed.

Among a race of very beautiful plants *D. spectabilis* stands supreme, but the genus as a whole has much to offer, from the undoubted challenge of the exquisite and tiny Japanese *D. peregrina* (4B–8A) to the easily grown, fern-leaved long-flowering *D. eximia* (3B–8A) and *D. formosa* (3B–8A), with the many named clones that derive from them.

Epimedium x *warleyense* (Berberidaceae) (4B–9A)

There is not one of the barrenworts ("happy mediums" was the name coined for them by the remarkable gardener E. A. Bowles) that I would not grow for their foliage and their delicate and unusually formed but fleeting flowers. Many are most effective as ground cover, spreading to form dense mats of interlocking, thin rhizomes, often smelling like mild ginger, from which, in early spring, the airy sprays of spreading, spiderlike, often long-spurred flowers arise. A few, like *Epimedium diphyllum* (6A–9A) and *E.* x *youngianum* (4B–9A), are fully deciduous and one or two, notably *E. perralderianum* (6A–9A), are evergreen but the majority retain their foliage, in various states of repair, over winter, the delightful hybrid *E.* x *warleyense* among them. By early spring the leaves should be cut away whenever practicable. If left, they will obscure the flowers and later detract from the beauty of the young leaves. *E. grandiflorum* and the hybrid *E.* x *versicolor* (of which there are several named clones) are exceptional for the bronze tints of the developing foliage.

The parents of *E.* x *warleyense* are *E. alpinum*, with red and yellow flowers, and a form of the yellow-flowered *E. pinnatum* (4B–9A). The hybrid produces gently arching racemes, 15in (38cm) long and occasionally branched, of coppery orange and pale yellow blooms above the fresh green, elegant leaves, which are divided into five to nine well-spaced, ovate leaflets. Although not absolutely impenetrable to weeds as is the case with some of its cousins, the foliage makes good ground cover. Seed, rarely produced, would not come true, but division of the slender rhizomes in autumn or winter presents no problem.

Some barrenworts thrive in the open provided they have humus-rich soil. In the poor soil of my Wisley garden, *E.* x *warleyense* grew well in full sun with no more than an annual sprinkling of leaf mold.

Related plants Two recent introductions from Sichuan in China that have taken well to cultivation are *E. davidii* (5A–8B) and *E. acuminatum* (6A–8B). The first is a gorgeous and vigorous evergreen, which has clear yellow spiders, with curving, downward-pointing spurs, and bronze young foliage produced over longer periods than is the case with most species. The equally delightful *E. acuminatum*, introduced from Mount Omei (Emei Shan), is deciduous (or virtually so in my garden) and has much longer leaflets than *E. davidii*, with spurs of red or brownish-purple that are 1in (2.5cm) long and capped by white sepals. Both species prefer a humus-rich soil, some shade and shelter from wind.

Lysichiton camtschatcensis (Araceae) (6B–9B)
The bold foliage of the two species of *Lysichiton* (sometimes spelt *Lysichitum*), members of the arum family, has become a familiar sight by waterside or in boggy ground in many large gardens, the huge, rich green, glossy, oblong-ovate leaves, often over 4ft (120cm) long, providing a striking contrast to the reedlike leaves of irises and other moisture-loving plants. The more frequently seen is *L. americanus* (7A–9B), widespread in western North America and much larger and more vigorous than the relatively delicate *L. camtschatcensis*, from Japan and eastern Siberia, with leaves that are seldom more than 2½ft (75cm) in length. In early spring the large arumlike, boat-shaped spathes, rich yellow and up to 16in (40cm) tall in *L. americanus*, pure white,

shadowed green and 8 to 9in (20–23cm) tall in *L. camtschatcensis*, appear before the foliage, which develops quickly, outstripping and soon hiding the last of the inflorescences as spring advances.

Lysichiton camtschatcensis is more suitable for small gardens and, in my eyes, is the better plant, the unpleasant scent and overegged yellow of *L. americanus* losing out to the sweet scent and purity of its relative.

Given permanently damp soil, neither species (nor the cream-spathed hybrid between them) is difficult to grow, although from seed, kept saturated to germinate, it will be five or six years before the seedlings flower. Increase by division is possible, but it requires an elephant or a machine of equivalent power to heave them out of the squelchy bogs in which they grow.

Meehania urticifolia (Labiatae) (5A–8A)
Many might consider this Japanese woodlander no more than a subprostrate deadnettle with long-tubed purple flowers. However, it is an ideal ground cover, spreading freely by long leafy stems that root at the nodes, and forming large patches of heart-shaped, dark green leaves that are strongly veined, rugose, and 2in (5cm) in length. During late spring and early summer it produces terminal and axillary clusters of flowers that are 2in (5cm) long and vary from blue-purple to purple, often with darker spots on the lobes. Its pleasant fragrance emanates from the calyx, not the corolla.

Provided it has leaf-rich soil, this easy-going plant will provide mounds of dense cover 12in (30cm) high, even in sunless sites. It is ideal in woodland as a companion for shrubs, but is to be avoided where more delicate species are being grown. Propagation scarcely needs comment: rooted runners that are dug up and replanted reestablish quickly. Tip cuttings taken from young growths in spring also root readily.

Paeonia mlokosewitschii (Paeoniaceae) (5A–7B)
In a race full of floral opulence, *P. mlokosewitschii*, often called "Mollie-the-witch," is outstandingly beautiful, particularly appealing for the simplicity of its lemon-yellow flowers. Known in the wild from only one small area in the southeast Caucasus, where it occurs in open hornbeam woodland, *P. mlokosewitschii* is perfectly hardy and easily grown in any well-drained soil, preferring sun, although slight shade often enhances the ethereal luminosity of the flowers.

Early in spring the vigorous shoots push through the soil and open to reveal the divided, biternate leaves with oval to obovate leaflets, attractively bronze-tinted at first, then forming a mound about 2ft (60cm) high of cool, glaucous green. The flower buds open in late spring, revealing the rounded perfection of the cup-shaped, 4–5in (10–12cm) lemon-yellow blooms, containing the central clusters of golden-yellow stamens and densely hairy, pink-tipped carpels. Sadly, as with so many single-flowered peonies, the petals are quick to fall but the foliage remains attractive throughout summer and in autumn turns to muted yellows and browns as the distinctive seed pods curl open to reveal their shining black seeds.

Seed is produced fairly freely and provides the readiest means of increase, although it will be five years from germination before the first blooms appear. Always sow in autumn because the seed of this species – and of almost all peonies – needs to be subjected to a period of cold to germinate. As *P. mlokosewitschii* will hybridize with a number of red-flowered peonies, it is important to see plants in bloom before purchasing them. *P. mlokosewitschii* is slow to develop into reasonably sized clumps but division of the rootstock in autumn or early spring is feasible. If dividing (most peonies take a fair time to reestablish and flower regularly after division), split into three or four portions of reasonable size rather than many small pieces.

Related plants The sturdy vigor of the brilliantly colored *Paeonia peregrina* (6A–8A) , native of southeast Europe and western Turkey, sometimes listed as *P. lobata* and known as 'Fire King' in my nursery days, is in marked contrast to the delicate *P. mlokosewitschii*. *P. peregrina* achieves 3ft (90cm) in my garden, rather than the 2ft (60cm) usually credited to it, producing during

Paeonia mlokosewitschii

late spring a regular and prolific display of magnificent scarlet, glossy-petaled blooms, globe-shaped and 4 to 5in (10–12cm) across, over mounds of shining dark green, strongly veined foliage.

Of the many lovely peony cultivars the one that I would never be without is the free-flowering 'Bowl of Beauty' (4B–8A), at its best in early summer, the rich pink, broad outer petals and the central ruff of creamy white petaloid stamens making a marvelous confection. In addition, the flowers, 5in (12cm) across, are beautifully scented and long-lasting, both in the garden and when cut, and the plant itself is easy to grow.

Pulmonaria longifolia 'Bertram Anderson' (Boraginaceae) (3B–8A)

Almost all the lungworts provide excellent ground cover, happiest in shade and moisture-retentive soil. With the exception of *Pulmonaria angustifolia* and some of its offspring, which tend to die back to the crowns in winter, they retain their foliage for much of the year.

They are prolific seeders, crossing with the utmost abandon to provide a range of plants with attractive foliage and often delightful early flowers in shades of blue, pink, and red as well as white. Most of the seventy or more clones now offered have been selected from seedlings that have arisen in gardens or nurseries rather than through deliberate hybridization. Many are distinct and worthwhile garden plants, although some differ only marginally from others already extant.

One of the finest and neatest, a selected clone of the western European *P. longifolia*, is 'Bertram Anderson.' This is distinguished by its narrowly lanceolate, silver-spotted leaves, producing early in spring 12ft (30cm) high stems with dense terminal heads of rich blue flowers that turn with age to violet-blue. Of the same persuasion, but with more silvered leaves and violet-blue flowers, is 'Dordogne.' I prefer the species and clones that do not become too leafy and coarse after flowering, which some of the more robust variants of the spotted-leaved *P. saccharata* (3B–8A) and the plain-leaved *P. rubra* (4B–8A) tend to do.

Increase by division of the rootstocks in autumn or early spring, or by root cuttings in winter. Pulmonarias from seed almost certainly will not come true.

Smilacina racemosa (Liliaceae/Convallariaceae) (4A–9A)

Related to *Polygonatum*, the genus *Smilacina* contains some twenty-five or so species from north and central America and central and eastern Asia, almost all of which are plants of horticultural merit. *Smilacina race-*

Smilacina racemosa

mosa is undoubtedly the best of the breed because this fine woodlander, unusually among herbaceous plants, is valued for its flowers, foliage, and fruits.

I have seen it in western North America at the margins of both deciduous and coniferous woodlands, seemingly preferring acidic soils, although there are records of it growing comfortably in heavy alkaline soils rich in humus. The handsome, strongly veined, dark green leaves, broad, elliptic to ovate and 5in (12cm) long, resemble closely those of *Polygonatum* x *hybridum* (3B–9A). They are borne alternately on arching stems up to 3ft (90cm) high, which develop from a tangle of shortly creeping rhizomes. In midspring and on into late spring branched inflorescences, borne terminally and 4 to 6in (10–15cm) long, burst into creamy white, starry blooms that are sweetly fragrant. As they age the flowers become pinkish-brown. The berrylike fruits are green at first, often becoming speckled purplish-brown, and in late summer are bright red and mottled red-purple. For this effect more than one clone is needed, because *S. racemosa* appears to be self-sterile.

Plants raised from seed will be clonally distinct, but young seedlings, like those of Solomon's seals, are slow-growing. The seed should be sown in autumn to provide a cold period for germination. In late autumn or early spring the dense clumps of rhizomes may be carefully teased apart to increase stock.

Symphytum 'Goldsmith' (Boraginaceae) (3B–8A)

The comfreys include a number of coarse and sometimes rampant perennials, but there are several noninvasive species and hybrids that provide excellent ground cover, pleasant if unspectacular flowers, and also thrive in unpromising sites. Those with variegated foliage in shades of cream, yellow, and green are useful for dark corners, particularly in reasonably fertile soil.

Some twenty or more years ago I was given a beautifully variegated *Symphytum*, with ovate, dark green leaves edged and heavily suffused cream and gold, and with occasional touches of pink late in the season. This spread well in fairly deep shade and more open conditions in the plentifully mulched sand of my Wisley garden and was passed on to many visitors who admired its very ornamental foliage.

This is now marketed as 'Goldsmith,' sometimes referred botanically to the somewhat invasive *S. caucasicum* (3B–8A) but probably a hybrid of *S. grandiflorum* (3B–8A), despite the fact that this has creamy yellow flowers while those of 'Goldsmith' are usually blue and pink. It is a delightful, trouble-free plant that may readily be increased by division and gives pleasure from early spring to late autumn with its low mounds of highly decorative leaves. To me, the pendent flowers detract from the foliage and it is worth cutting out the developing inflorescences.

Tiarella wherryi

Tiarella wherryi (Saxifragaceae) (4B–8A)

The foamflowers, species of *Tiarella*, are to me one of the great joys of late spring and early summer. *T. cordifolia* (4B–8A), native to eastern North American woodland and the most commonly grown species, quickly forms dense mats of its fresh green foliage as the creeping rhizomes spread through the leafy soils, which it prefers. Its leaves, 2 to 4in (5–10cm) long, are ovate-cordate with three to five gentle lobes. In early summer the delicate, upright, 4–6in (10–15cm) sprays of pink-budded, fluffy, white stars appear and remain in beauty for several weeks. It is an easy-going plant that will thrive in a variety of situations, provided it has light shade and a moist, humus-rich soil. In some gardens it spreads so rapidly that it is considered a weed.

Some judge the cream of the genus to be *T. wherryi*, also from eastern North America. It is distinguished from *T. cordifolia* by its maple-shaped leaves, with five distinct lobes, and in being clump-forming, with short rhizomes. Its propagation by division of the clumps is inevitably slower than that of *T. cordifolia*.

Excellent clones, all happiest in light shade, include 'Bronze Beauty,' which I obtained, simply as *T. wherryi* from a friend in North America who had found it in the wild. Its sharply cut leaves are a mélange of deep red-bronze and pale green, surmounted by spires of bronze-pink buds, opening to a delicate pale pink.

LATE SUMMER TO AUTUMN FLOWERS

Aster novi-belgii 'Fellowship' (Compositae) (4B–8A)

Indispensable as late-flowering border plants, Michaelmas daisies, derived from the eastern North American *Aster novi-belgii*, are now so numerous that it is impossible to do more than pick out one or two high-quality representatives. They vary in stature from the dwarf offspring of *A. dumosus* (3B–8A) and *A. novi-belgii* – 'Lady in Blue' is only 6 to 9in (15–23cm) high – to tall-growing kinds, of which the vigorous and aptly named 'Climax' achieves 5 to 6ft (1.5–1.8m). Flower color ranges from the deepest violets and blues through every shade of red and pink to pure white.

Satisfied by any well-drained soil and an open aspect, Michaelmas daisies rapidly form dense clumps of basal growths. These soon become woody and bare in the center and should be divided in spring at least every three or four years to maintain flowering potential and quality, all but vigorous, young outer shoots being discarded. Although very tolerant plants, the cultivars of *A. novi-belgii* benefit from regular fertilizing.

The major problem from which they suffer is powdery mildew, a disease that is particularly troublesome if plants are allowed to dry out at the roots: during the growing season keep the plants well watered and mulched. If necessary, use a benomyl fungicide or equivalent spray as soon as the slightest sign of mildew is seen; once established the mildew is very difficult to control. At the end of the season remove all the old growth and debris, preferably cutting the stems down as soon as the flowers fade and burning them. A preventive spray of a recommended fungicide should then be applied to the young growths.

In areas where powdery mildew is very prevalent it is best to grow cultivars that are wholly or partially resistant. I have found that the long-flowering, deep pink 'Fellowship,' 3 to 4ft (90–120cm) high and with flower heads each over 2in (5cm) across, is much less prone to this trouble than many of the red-flowered clones. 'Winston Churchill,' for example, is so susceptible that, sadly, it is not really worth growing. 'Climax,' an elegant, willowy six-footer (1.8m), with large panicles of powder-blue flower heads, is surprisingly resistant, in my experience. Although rather tall, it is a clone of considerable beauty and flower quality.
Related plants Probably a cultivar of *Aster pringlei* (5A–8A), although often listed under *A. ericoides*

(5A–8A), another North American species, *Aster* 'Monte Cassino' is representative of a range of small but very profuse-flowering Michaelmas daisies of considerable garden value and excellent for cutting. They normally bloom from mid to late autumn, lengthening the season with myriad sprays of pink, blue, creamy yellow or white flower heads no more than ¼–½in (6–12mm) across. Hardy, trouble-free, requiring no support and easily increased by division, 'Monte Cassino' is an midautumn snowstorm of white stars.

Aster novae-angliae(5A–8A), the New England Aster, like *A. novi-belgii* originating from eastern North America, has been less popular than that plant for borders but is as easy to grow and remains unaffected by powdery mildew. Division every three years is important to maintain flower quality and vigor. Dryness and lack of nutriment lead to discoloration of the leaves and browning on the stems before plants come into flower. Most cultivars are 5 to 6ft (1.5–1.8m) tall, with mauve-pink or purple flower heads. However, 'Harrington's Pink,' introduced in the 1950's, is a pure, clear pink of considerable quality and one of the few clones that will last well as a cut flower. Deservedly popular newcomers include the white-flowered 'Herbstschnee' ('Autumn Snow') and 'Andenken an Alma Potsche,' although its bilious cherryade color is not for me.

Cimicifuga simplex 'Elstead Variety' (Ranunculaceae) (4A–8A)

Bugbane is an unprepossessing common name for a genus of very attractive herbaceous plants that flower over several weeks in late summer and autumn, providing a marvelous display of their slender, arching inflorescences with white, occasionally pink-tinged, flowers. Dried powder from *Cimicifuga foetida*, least ornamental of the genus, was formerly used against bedbugs.

Cimicifuga simplex, widely spread in Japan and northeastern China, varies in height from barely 2–8ft (60–240cm). The various clones in cultivation are between 4 and 6ft (1.2–1.8m) tall and have biternate or triternate, much-divided leaves with up to eighty of the ovate, often trilobed and toothed leaflets forming a mass of ferny foliage, from which the elegantly sinuous flowering stems appear in midautumn. The racemose inflorescences, often with a number of side branches, may be 12ft (30cm) or more long, beset like slender bottlebrushes with small, white or creamy white, scented, stamen-filled flowers that lack petals.

Several named cultivars (sometimes offered under the invalid name *C. ramosa*) have been introduced, including the glistening 'White Pearl,' green-budded and snowy white in flower, and 'Brunette,' a selected clone with foliage, stems, and flowers of a rich, deep purple, only the inner parts of flowers retaining a degree of whiteness. The superb, free-flowering 'Elstead Variety' occasionally continues flowering into late autumn. It has purple-brown flower stems and flowers filled with creamy white stamens.

Cimicifuga species are are quite hardy, preferring cool, fairly deep, and continually moist soils. They are readily propagated by division in spring, the only way to maintain selected clones, but two forks used back to back may be needed to make the tough rootstock see reason. Seed should be sown fresh in autumn, but the selected clones will need to be divided, as seed-raised plants will vary.

Hedychium coccineum 'Tara' (Zingiberaceae) (7B–9B)

Although often regarded as tender plants suited only for the greenhouse, the beautiful genus *Hedychium* contains several species that will tolerate 14°F (–10°C), some surviving even very severe winters without any protection. In the wild, *Hedychium* species often inhabit forest edges or streamsides, flourishing in humus-rich soil. In gardens they prefer more open, well-drained, acidic soils, but will grow satisfactorily at pH 8.0–8.5. A plant suitable for these conditions is 'Tara,' a clone of the superb, late-flowering *H. coccineum*, from the central and eastern Himalaya. This was raised from seed collected in 1972 on the Nagarot Ridge of the Kathmandu Valley in Nepal at 7,250ft (2,280m).

'Tara' has proved quite hardy planted out in a sand-based, moisture-retentive soil in my own garden for the last eight years. The stout, fleshy rhizomes, planted 2 to 3in (5–8cm) deep, have steadily increased, in early summer producing attractive clumps of glaucous green, two-ranked foliage that obscures the reed-like stems, as much as 6ft (1.8m) high, from which the terminal inflorescences appear in late summer and early autumn. These are dense spikes, over 6in (15cm) long, of scented, bright orange-red, orchidlike blooms, with long exserted styles and stamens in the same color. The individual blooms are relatively short-lived, but established groups produce a considerable number of flower-spikes over several weeks, providing a fine display of unusual coloring late in the season.

Propagation by division of the rhizomes is best carried out in late spring, just before the young shoots break dormancy; division at other times of the year is unwise, since the cut surfaces of dormant rhizomes are prone to fungal attack and rotting.

Kniphofia 'Little Maid' (Liliaceae) (6B–8A)
Few plants give me as much pleasure as well-established groups of this marvelous, low-growing *Kniphofia*. It exemplifies the best qualities of a genus that contains numerous selected and named clones. It forms dense clumps of neat, narrow foliage, above which the slender, elegant flower stems, often 12ft (30cm) or so long, arise in profusion during late summer and autumn. Initially green, the downward-pointing, close-set buds open to tubular, ivory-white flowers, as the long flower-spikes mature, quickly to be replaced by fresh inflorescences thrusting up through the leaf rosettes. In 'Little Maid' the vast majority of the blooms on each inflorescence are at their peak at the same time; in some species and cultivars the spikes are somewhat unsightly, the older brown flowers of the lower half being retained while the upper blooms have still to open. The way the flowers age should be taken into account when new seedlings are being selected.

Many kniphofias are hardy to 14°F (–10°C) and will grow without difficulty in most well-drained soils, preferring those that are moisture-retentive. Some of the species and their close hybrids, however, are more tender and may need winter protection in more northern regions.

Although kniphofias fit well into borders, some are also happy among shrubs or as isolated groups, and they are useful close to the sea, withstanding salt spray and strong winds. Winter wet is their main enemy, particularly in cold gardens. In combination with frost, it may lead to rotting of the crowns. Propagation by division in spring is advisable; plants divided in autumn or winter are less able to withstand cold and wet. Seed sets freely, but even the species in cultivation hybridize readily and a motley bunch of offspring usually results.

Related plants Long known as *Kniphofia galpinii* (7A–8B), a related but distinct species, *K. triangularis* might well be taken for an elegant grass during summer, having leaves seldom more than 1/10in (2–3mm) wide. In early and midautumn stems rise to 3ft (60–90cm) above the foliage, and a profusion of dainty, bright coral-orange flower heads appear like miniature firecrackers, providing a pleasing warmth as the season closes. One of the hardiest species, *K. triangularis*, is also one of those with the greatest garden value.

Much more robust is *K. rooperi* (5B–8B). The common name red hot poker that is generally applied to the genus is particularly appropriate in this case: the strong stems it sends up from rather lax clusters of broad, green, channeled leaves are 4ft (120cm) tall and end in fat, jolly, 4in (10cm) red and yellow inflorescences. A parent of many of the taller hybrids, it has proved hardy at Wisley for over twenty years and in midautumn is a fine sight glowing in the sunshine.

Other worthwhile variations on the red-hot-poker theme include the scarlet 'Samuel's Sensation,' the deep tangerine-red 'Lord Roberts,' both 5 to 6ft (1.5–1.8m) high, and the rather shorter 'Bees Lemon' with 3–4 ft (90–120cm) spikes of bright lemon-yellow.

Romneya 'White Cloud' (Papaveraceae) (7B–10B*)
Although subshrubby in habit, the Californian tree poppies are frequently grown as border plants. From a garden viewpoint, they should be treated as herbaceous and the stems, which usually die back close to ground level in winter, removed during the annual cleanup. They may, however, prove too invasive for neat borders, their wandering rhizomes sometimes creating

Kniphofia 'Little Maid'

Romneya 'White Cloud'

havoc by sending up shoots in the middle of neighboring plants. Careful siting is, therefore, essential. Provided the position is open, sunny, and well-drained, romneyas make few demands, needing only an annual cutback and mulch. They are best in areas of low humidity such as the West Coast. Getting them established, however, sometimes presents a problem. Pot-grown plants do better than open-ground divisions, which, if taken, are also likely to make the parent plant sulk, root disturbance not being appreciated. Propagation is usually from root cuttings from the rhizomes carefully removed in winter or seed.

It is worth every effort to grow the Californian tree poppies wherever their escapist habit can be accommodated (the best stands I have ever seen were naturalized in short grassland). Mature plants, with willowy stems 5 to 6ft (1.5–1.8m) tall and clothed in very attractive, divided, gray foliage, provide a continuous display of huge white poppies, making one of the most beautiful sights in the garden during summer and autumn.

Romneyas are usually offered under the names *R. coulteri* or *R. trichocalyx* (*R. coulteri* var. *trichocalyx*) (7B–10B*), but most plants in cultivation are probably hybrids between these two taxa, which differ only in minor botanical characteristics. 'White Cloud' is an American-raised clone that has intensely glaucous foliage and sumptuous, fragrant, crinkled blooms that can be up to 8in (20cm) across; as the white flowers open they reveal the deep yellow pompon of stamens.

Rudbeckia fulgida var. *sullivantii* 'Goldsturm'

Rudbeckia fulgida var. *sullivantii* 'Goldsturm' (Compositae) (3A–9A)

Despite the burden of its botanical name, *Rudbeckia* 'Goldsturm' is undoubtedly one of the most effective and long-flowering border plants available for summer and autumn display. The botanical differences between the different forms of *Rudbeckia fulgida* – var. *sullivantii*, var. *deamii*, and var. *speciosa* – need not concern the gardener; but all are worthwhile garden plants, their differences only slight variations on the same theme.

The selection 'Goldsturm' is, so far at least, unequaled, forming neat mounds 2 to 3ft (60–90cm) high of ovate, dark green, strongly veined leaves and branched stems bearing very large heads, 5in (12cm) across, of deep yellow ray petals with slightly pendent tips, contrasting with the prominent central black cones that give rise to the common name Black-eyed Susan. Suited to any fertile garden soil with reasonable drainage, 'Goldsturm' is virtually trouble-free, although it will show some signs of distress in very dry conditions and in sandy soils it should be mulched to prevent the foliage wilting. 'Goldsturm' is also a very useful cut flower.

Schizostylis coccinea 'Sunrise' (Iridaceae) (6B–8B)

Thirty or so years ago the only generally available variants *Schizostylis coccinea* were the ubiquitous 'Mrs Hegarty' and 'Viscountess Byng,' both with relatively small pink flowers in midautumn and late autumn, and a crimson-flowered plant considered then to be "typical" of the species. Nowadays a range of some twenty selected clones has been introduced, mostly larger-flowered and blooming in late summer over a long period. 'Sunrise,' in particular, I have found tremendously prolific, constantly throwing up its gladioluslike 18in (45cm) spikes of cupped 2in (5cm), glowing pink blooms from midsummer until late autumn and even into early winter. This is a clone of great garden value and its flowers are excellent for cutting.

Commonly found wild in the Drakensberg Mountains of Natal and Lesotho growing as a streamside plant, *S. coccinea* has proved totally hardy in spite of its South African origin, preferring fairly rich, moisture-retentive soil, in which it quickly forms large patches, perennating by means of long, slightly swollen rhizomes. The obvious means of increasing cultivars is by separating the plentiful rhizomes in spring. Fair amounts of seed are produced, particularly from the early blooms. The named clones will not, of course, come true from seed (although white-flowered 'Alba' is an exception), but the chance of variation in flower color and size may be worth the trouble of waiting a few years for seed-raised plants to reach maturity.

The large-flowered, burnished rich crimson 'Major' ('Grandiflora') and the similar 'Professor Barnard,' both growing to about 2ft (60cm), are also excellent garden plants, long- and free-flowering.

Sedum 'Vera Jameson' (Crassulaceae) (5A–8B)

Among a plethora of fine garden sedums, all excellent ornamental flowering and foliage plants, one that has always stood out, though only by a short head in a high-quality field, is 'Vera Jameson.' It is ideal for a sunny position in the front of a border or island bed and is also suitable as an alpine garden plant, because it seldom exceeds 9in (23cm) in height. The graceful arching stems are closely set with opposite pairs of glaucous, fleshy purple leaves, rounded and about 1in (2–3cm) long, and, in late summer bear in abundance terminal, slightly curved 2in (5cm) heads of starry, dusky purplish-pink flowers.

The probable parents of this chance seedling are two other excellent garden sedums, the upright *S. maximum* 'Atropurpureum,' 2ft (60cm) high and with dark maroon-purple foliage, and the shorter 'Ruby Glow,' gray-foliaged and wine-red in bloom.

All are amenable plants thriving in any well-drained soil, but to obtain the most intense foliage coloring should be grown in sunny, open sites in poor soils. An excess of food encourages rather lusher growth and the purple coloration of the foliage is masked, the leaves becoming olive-green. A semistarvation diet will also ensure a compact habit. In late autumn the shoots die down to the somewhat fleshy rootstock, readily divided in autumn or spring if required.

Verbena patagonica (Verbenaceae) (7A–10B)

To most gardeners verbenas are spreading half-hardy perennials with tightly packed flower heads that are often raised from seed for use as border fillers, bedding plants, and in hanging baskets, applications where their wide color range is valued. *V. patagonica* (frequently but incorrectly labeled as *V. bonariensis*), widespread in temperate and tropical America, is in contrast a tall, slender species, 4 to 5ft (1.2–1.5m) high, which proves valuable as a border plant.

This plant flowers for much of the summer and autumn, the large, terminal, inflorescences a haze of purple-mauve from the numerous tiny, scented flowers, which are much loved by butterflies. A light airy plant, *V. patagonica* has narrow, but rigid, four-sided stems with well-spaced, opposite pairs of lanceolate, toothed, dark green leaves.

Young plants will often appear far from the parent plant from self-sown seed, particularly in the light soils and sunny positions where it seems most at home. Although a perennial, remaining so in many mild gardens, in cold areas it is best grown from seed annually.

Sedum 'Vera Jameson'

Verbena patagonica

OTHER PLANTS

Aconitum carmichaelii (Ranunculaceae) (4A–8A)
This beautiful tuberous-rooted monkshood is prized for its terminal racemes of violet-blue, helmeted flowers, 1in (2–3cm) long, that appear in midautumn and for its rich, glossy, cut foliage attractive all spring and summer. Height varies from 3–6ft (90cm– 1.8m), and flower color ranges from rich violet-blue to a paler purple-blue. The species, which occurs wild in central and western China, includes a number of variants; all are easily grown in well-drained, fairly rich soils.

Anemone hupehensis (Ranunculaceae) (5A–8A)
I have been fortunate enough to see this species (and collect its seed) by roadsides and among shrubs in Yunnan, China. Its shallowly cupped flowers were pure white internally, with prominent bosses of bright yellow stamens, but the reverse of three of the (usually) six segments was bright crimson-pink, providing a contrast between buds and open flowers. In the wild, blooms vary in color from white to deep crimson-pink, on plants 2 to 3ft (60–90cm) high. Spreading by short rhizomes from a central rootstock and readily raised from seed,this is among the best of the "Japanese" anemones for late summer and autumn color.

Gentiana asclepiadea (Gentianaceae) (5A–8A)
The graceful, arching 2 to 3ft (60–90cm) stems of the elegant Willow Gentian, bearing numerous pairs of azure blue tubular, 1½in (3–4cm) blooms in the leaf axils almost the length of the stems, is a familiar sight in the alpine woodlands and mountain meadows of Europe in late summer and early autumn. In cultivation it rapidly colonizes humus-rich, deep soils in dappled shade, seeding freely in both acidic and alkaline conditions. Reliable, long-lived, and varying in flower color from darkest blue, often marked white within, to pure white, sometimes tinted green – a plant of great beauty in cool areas with low humidity.

Salvia uliginosa (Labiatae) (6A–10B)
One of my all-time favorites, this graceful *Salvia*, 5 to 6ft (1.5–1.8m) tall, occurs wild in damp areas in Uruguay, Argentina, and Brazil. Although slightly tender, in my experience it seems unaffected by the worst winters in southern England if grown in a fairly rich, moist soil, where its forked, fleshy rhizomes spread freely and may be used for rapid propagation. The first of the clear sky-blue sage flowers, borne in small spikes on freely branching stems, appear in late summer and continue until late autumn.

SUMMER AND AUTUMN FLOWERS/ORNAMENTAL FOLIAGE

Euphorbia schillingii (**Euphorbiaceae**) (7A–9B)
Euphorbia schillingii is one of the most long-flowering and beautiful members of a genus that includes many fine garden plants. My own plant came some eight years ago from Tony Schilling, who in 1975 had collected material as *E. sikkimensis* (Schilling 2,060) in stony ground between 8,200 and 9,500ft (2,500–2,900m) in the Dudh Khosi Valley of eastern Nepal. In 1987 his plant was described as a new species, a clump-forming (not stoloniferous) plant, with warty fruits, and various other distinctive leaf and inflorescence characters.

Euphorbia schillingii produces robust 3 ft (90cm) stems that are clothed in oblong-elliptic, alternately placed leaves that are dark green with a conspicuous white midrib, up to 6in (12–15cm) long and more than 1in (2.5cm) wide. From early summer the stems are topped by bold, typical spurge inflorescences that are bright lime-yellow; astonishingly, these remain in beauty until at least midautumn in my garden. They produce an abundance of seed, which self-sows to my great pleasure, although not always in the places I would prefer. Seedlings transplanted at an early stage settle down quickly, but need to be moved before the fleshy, anchoring roots descend into the depths. *E. schillingii* may also be propagated easily from basal heel cuttings in spring or from nonflowering short side shoots with heels at almost any time during the growing season. Avoid getting sap on the skin (the milky exudation of all spurges can cause rashes) and allow the sap to dry before inserting the cuttings, preferably in a plant incubator with bottom heat. In addition to its incredibly long flowering period and overall aesthetic quality, Schilling's spurge thrives, given good drainage, in soils of a wide pH range. One marginal regret is that in Britain the leaves do not turn brilliant autumnal scarlet as they do on plants in the wild in dry sunny weather after monsoon.

Geranium '**Ann Folkard**' (**Geraniaceae**) (5A–8A)
In about 1973 the chance combination of the procumbent, trailing *Geranium procurrens*, from Nepal and Sikkim, and the Caucasian and northern Turkish *G. psilostemon*, which grows 3 to 4ft (90cm–120cm) high, resulted in an outstanding garden plant.

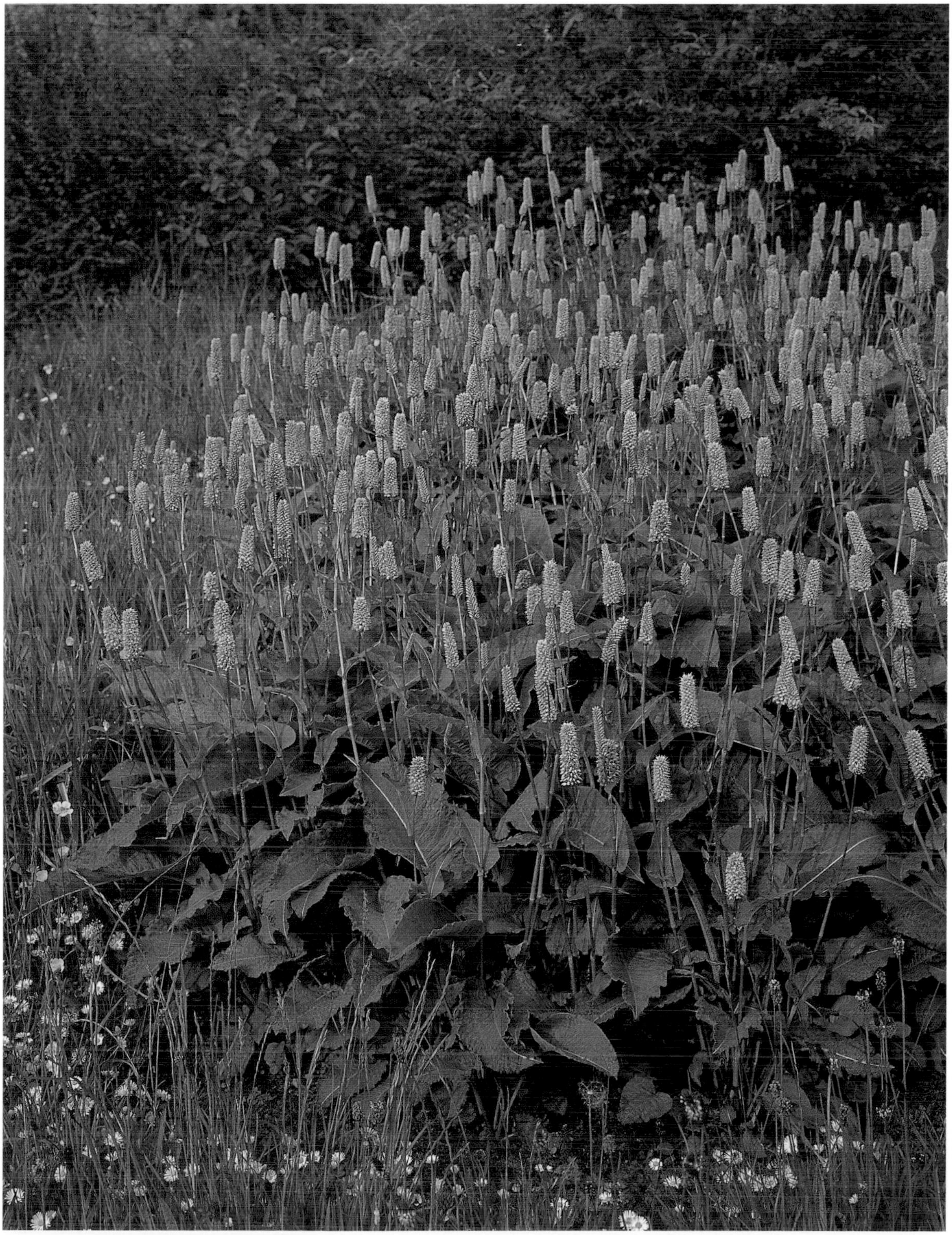

Polygonum bistorta 'Superbum' (see p.126)

Like its *G. procurrens* parent, it can spread both out-ward and upward, if support is available, extending about 4ft (120cm) from the central rootstock, to which in late autumn the growths die back. The green-gold of the deeply cut leaves starts to show in early spring.

The tips of all the shoots that fan out from the root-stock retain this coloring through the growing season, while the older foliage darkens and mounds densely to about 18in (45cm). From early summer there is a four-month performance of nonstop flowering, with saucer-shaped, five-petaled blooms, up to 1½in (4cm) across, velvety, rich magenta-purple, with black centers and veining. Seed does not develop, which may account for the marathon flowering period. Propagate by division of the tough, forked rootstock or by basal cuttings root-ed in a plant incubator, preferably with bottom heat.

Taking advantage of ground-covering potential, I placed my plants underneath shrubs, but they have also aimed at higher things, scrambling through a *Viburnum carlesii* 'Diana' to over 4ft (120cm) without harming it.

Polygonum bistorta 'Superbum' (Polygonaceae) (3A–8B)

Polygonum bistorta (sometimes listed as *Persicaria bistorta*) is a most accommodating ground-cover plant that grows happily in an open position in any well-drained soil, but particularly appreciates a moist, humus-rich medium, in which it will form dense, weed-proof clumps of wavy-edged, ovate to oblong, 6 to 8in (15–20cm) dark green leaves. The erect flowering stems may vary from 2 to 2½ft (60–75cm) in length and ter-minate in dense, bottle-brush spikes of deep, glowing pink flowers that remain in beauty from early summer to midautumn (see p.125).

Equally useful and attractive is the mat-forming and somewhat variable *P. affine* that occurs wild in the Himalaya from Afghanistan to Sikkim at 10,000–15,000ft (3,000–4,500m), where it tumbles down rocky slopes, a froth of pink and red flower-spikes. The clone 'Superbum' (not to be confused with the *P. bistorta* variant of the name) is a vigorous plant that produces a profusion of blush-white flower-spikes more or less continuously during summer and autumn, the flowers deepening to rich crimson with age.

The compact 'David Lowndes', with shorter 6in (15cm) inflorescences that open coral-pink and age to a dusky pink, and the slightly taller, rose-pink, 'Darjeeling Red', are also very useful for the front of the border or larger rock garden. Propagation by divi-sion of the rhizomatous growths of all these poygonums in spring is unproblematical.

AUTUMN FLOWERS AND ORNAMENTAL FOLIAGE

Kirengeshoma palmata (Saxifragaceae/Hydrangeaceae) (5A–8A)

It is not often that gardeners are introduced to garden plants by seeing them depicted on china, but I clearly remember my first sight of this delightful plant, during my National Service days in Germany in the early 1950's: it was on a Rosenthal tea service, duly admired and purchased some time before I discovered the plant's identity.

Native to Japan, where it inhabits mountain wood-land, *Kirengeshoma palmata* is a stately herbaceous plant some 3 to 4 ft (90–120cm) in height, valued both for its handsome foliage and for its cool butter-yellow, waxy blooms, which are produced in arching terminal and axillary sprays during late summer and autumn. The maplelike leaves, irregularly and sharply cut, with seven to ten lobes, are arranged in opposite pairs and can measure up to 12in (30cm) across. The elegant individual flowers are semipendent, 1 to 2in (3–5cm) long and narrowly bell-shaped, each consisting of five, fleshy, overlapping petals slightly recurved at the tips.

Seed is seldom available from cultivated plants, and spring division of the fairly tough rootstock is the nor-mal means of increasing stock. If seed is available, how-ever, it is best sown as soon as it is ripe in late autumn unless stored in cool, dry conditions, when spring-sow-ing may also be successful.

The late-flowering habit of *K. palmata* is a very valuable asset, particularly in woodland, where, in dap-pled shade, and given acidic to neutral, leafy, moist soil, it thrives, complementing the turning foliage of the woody understorey, particularly when accompanied by the equally rewarding late-blooming *Cimicifuga* and *Aconitum* species, as may be seen on Battleston Hill at Wisley.

If woodland planting is not possible, *K. palmata* may also be grown in more open sites but it should then be given some shelter, particularly in spring, when the unfolding young foliage is vulnerable to cold winds unless grown in the protection of a more robust shrub companion.

Saxifraga fortunei (Saxifragaceae) (6A–8A)

One of the most beautiful of woodland plants, often grown also in the alpine garden, *Saxifraga fortunei* (also known as *S. cortusifolia* var. *fortunei*) is noted not only for its late-flowering habit, frequently coming into

Kirengeshoma palmata

bloom in midautumn and continuing into late autumn, but also for its fine foliage.

Native to northeastern Asia, particularly Japan and north China, *S. fortunei* occurs by streamsides on wet rocks or in similar sites in partial shade from sea level to the mountains, varying considerably in plant size as well as in foliage characters.

The shortly creeping rhizomes give rise to clumps of attractive, more or less rounded, dark green, glossy leaves, up to 5in (12cm) across. The margins are cut into ten or more bluntly rounded lobes, the overall effect reminiscent of an open fan. The leaves are often purplish-red beneath, and in some selected forms the whole leaf surface is suffused reddish-bronze.

In midautumn the airy sprays of white flowers, with unequally sized petals that give them the appearance of tiny butterflies, are borne on delicate, red-tinted stems occasionally 18in (45cm) or more tall, but usually no more than 9 to 12in (23–30cm).

Two selected variants, 'Wada' and 'Rubrifolia,' have foliage of purple-red that contrasts beautifully with the clean white flowers. 'Windsor' is 2ft (60cm) tall, green-leaved and white-flowered. All three are well worth obtaining both as foliage and flowering plants.

Some shade is preferable, either in light, deciduous woodland or in cool, moist conditions among rocks by water, where they provide welcome color and beauty at a time of year when most herbaceous plants have already shut up shop for their winter break.

OTHER PLANTS
Sedum spectabile (Crassulaceae) (4A–9A)
Sedum spectabile, a bone-hardy plant from northeast China and Korea, is easy to grow in any well-drained soil in sun, and is often undervalued, despite its very long season of beauty. Fat, succulent buds give rise to stems 12 to 18in (30–45cm) tall, densely clothed in fleshy, glaucous green leaves and, by late summer, carrying platelike flower heads, often 4 to 6in (10–15cm) across. The massed, long-lasting, starry flowers, which open in late summer and continue on into early autumn, attracting nectar-seeking butterflies and bees, vary from deep to pale pink and pure white. My favorite, 'Brilliant,' is bright rose-pink, enhanced by darker stamens and ovaries.

Propagation by division is easy. Cut portions of mature stems laid, on trays of potting mix in a plant incubator, will root readily.

ORNAMENTAL FOLIAGE, FLOWERS SECONDARY

Cynara cardunculus (Compositae) (6A–8B)

Few plants contribute as much to the summer border as the majestic cardoon, *Cynara cardunculus*, supremely beautiful both for its magnificent foliage and brilliantly colorful flower heads. Native to dry, stony slopes and grassy areas in south-west Europe, *C. cardunculus* will often reach 7 to 8ft (2–2.5m) in height if well suited in gardens, preferring fertile, well-drained soils in open, sunny positions. It forms huge mounds of arching, deeply and elegantly cut, silver-gray leaves, often over 3ft (90cm) long, to which flower arrangers are drawn like bees to a honeypot. In early summer the strong, gray-woolly flower stems thrust through the basal foliage, bearing similar but smaller leaves, and terminate in late summer in branched sprays of huge, nectar-rich, thistlelike flower heads, 4in (10cm) or more across. These great tuffets of deep purple-blue surrounded by spiny, sometimes purple-tinted bracts, tower above the surrounding vegetation. Plants that have been grown in very rich soils may become too lush to withstand strong winds and some staking may be

Cynara cardunculus

required. Use short stakes, putting them in early in the season, so that they will quickly be covered by the foliage, and tie in the flowering stems as they develop.

Readily propagated by division of the fleshy rootstocks, in spring rather than autumn, particularly in cold gardens, *C. cardunculus* and its less spiny but very similar relative the globe artichoke, *C. scolymus*, may also be propagated successfully from root cuttings.

A superb plant for the border, *C. cardunculus* is also ideal planted in a group of five or seven to make a striking focal point. If the developing flower stems are removed early, the great mounds of silvered foliage are on their own most impressive for many months.

A bonus from a plant that already provides so much garden value is that the flower heads, if cut just before the flowers expand, open and last well in water and may be air-dried for winter decoration.

Heuchera 'Pewter Moon' (Saxifragaceae) (4A–9B)

The species and hybrids of coral bells or alum root, members of the North American genus *Heuchera*, are seldom lauded in garden literature in spite of their value as border, woodland and rock garden plants. Some, it must be admitted, are rather dull, but there are a number that are decorative in flower and foliage.

The most exciting of the recent introductions that I have grown is 'Pewter Moon,' raised in the Netherlands from a cross between 'Greenfinch' and 'Palace Purple.' It forms gently mounded mats 2 to 3in (5–8cm) high of rounded scalloped leaves up to 2in (5cm) across, dark ruby-purple beneath and with a pewter-sheened upper surface offset by markedly darker green veining. To date it has not flowered for me, but I am happy to grow it for the attractive foliage.

An equally fine foliage plant, *H. micrantha* 'Palace Purple,' was raised from seed at Kew by Brian Halliwell. Much larger-leaved than 'Pewter Moon,' it is valued for the dark red-bronze, puckered foliage, slightly lighter on the reverse, which retains its distinctive coloration from early spring until late autumn, quickly forming clumps 12in (30cm) or more across. 'Palace Purple' flowers very freely, producing a continuum of the delicate, airy, dark flowering stems, 15in (38cm) high and spangled with tiny white flowers all summer. Seed is freely formed and many of the seedlings resemble their parent; any that develop pale-hued or green leaves should be discarded.

All heucheras develop rather woody rootstocks, and after two or three years should be split to maintain vigor. Replant the young crowns with fibrous roots in humus-rich soil and discard the old material.

Related plants In contrast to most of the other cultivated heucheras, with their feathery sprays of tiny, bell-shaped flowers, *H. cylindrica* has, stiffly upright spikes, 1 to 2ft (30–60cm) tall, of cream, brown, rose or green, more or less tubular flowers borne well above the neat clumps of dark green leaves. The leaves are rounded, heart-shaped and shallowly scalloped. The veteran plantsman Alan Bloom has selected from seedlings of *H. cylindrica* the very handsome 'Greenfinch.' Its flower color is more green than cream, and the tall, 2 to 3ft (60–90cm) stems, with evenly spaced blooms, are usefully distinctive to flower arrangers while the upright lines contrast attractively with more rounded or less formal neighbors in the border or woodland.

Hosta sieboldiana 'Elegans' (Liliaceae) (3A–9B)

The plantain lilies, long-time Cinderellas of the plant world, are now among the élite of herbaceous plants, valued for their tolerance of soil conditions and position as well as for their handsome, often striking foliage and stately stems of trumpet- or bell-shaped blooms.

Hosta sieboldiana, particularly in the form known as 'Elegans,' has ranked as a classic foliage plant of the highest ornamental value for almost a century and stands up to competition from new cultivars, of which there are several hundreds, offering a wide range of foliage shape, size, texture and color. 'Elegans' slowly forms large clumps of spreading, rounded, blue-gray leaves (see p.130), cordate at the base and often over 1ft (30cm) long, with the leaf surfaces deeply veined and puckered, making a superb sight from late spring until the autumn, when the mounded foliage turns to honey-gold. The spires of trumpetlike flowers, white with a lilac flush, appearing in late to midsummer on stems 2 to 2½ft (60–75cm) tall, almost seem to intrude on the perfection of the elegant leaves.

Like most of its kind, 'Elegans' will thrive in sun or partial shade, preferring, but not insisting upon, humus-rich, moist soil, particularly in more open positions in the garden.

Division in early spring or autumn by splitting clumps into crowns with one to three buds, using back-to-back forks, will provide maximum increase without difficulty. Using a spade to cut out cakelike slices from established plants to give to friends is practicable at almost any time of year, but care should be taken to avoid damaging the main crown buds. Filling the resultant hole with fertile soil will encourage the development of new shoots.

Plants raised from seed will not be identical to the parent, although seedlings are sometimes offered as var. *elegans*, a name used to cover a number of clones that differ from each other in minor ways.

'Halcyon,' with more pointed foliage and leaf blades only 6in (15cm) or so long, also has deep glaucous blue foliage, although the leaves are not strongly puckered. It increases rapidly, and in addition to its very fine foliage has attractive, broad flower-spikes of deep lavender in midsummer.

Related plants Among a plethora of gold variegated clones, *Hosta* 'Gold Standard,' a sport of *H. fortunei* (possibly the var. *hyacinthina*), stands high in my personal *Hosta* chart for the clean quality of the bright gold foliage, narrowly margined dark green. In shade the color is somewhat dulled, and in intense heat the plant may lose color and become almost white. In my sandy Wisley garden, given moisture and annual mulches, it grew rapidly and withstood full sun without bleaching, but normally it is more comfortable in slight shade. Well worth a little trouble to maintain at its brilliant best, 'Gold Standard' is a plant I would not willingly do without, although voracious snails believe I should.

One of the giants of the *Hosta* world, the American selection 'Sum & Substance' has huge, broadly ovate, sharp-pointed, chartreuse-gold leaves that are deeply and elegantly veined and of satiny texture. Initially the foliage, which is glaucous beneath, has a somewhat crumpled look and is greenish-yellow before developing to full size. The magnificent foliage, which develops its best color in full sun, is supplemented in midsummer and sometimes also in early autumn by tall, arching flower-spikes of pale lavender-mauve. This most attractive plant is less prone to slug and snail damage than most of its cousins.

OTHER PLANTS

Polygonum virginianum 'Painter's Palette' (Polygonaceae) (4A–8B)

This plant may also be listed under *Tovara* or *Persicaria filiformis*, but it is well worth obtaining, both for its ground-covering capacity and the decorative effect of its foliage. Some of its close relatives may become pernicious garden weeds, but *Polygonum virginianum* spreads gently to form low mounds of ovate 6 in (15cm) leaves in 'Painter's Palette,' a delightful mélange of shades of green, ivory, cream, and pink. The centers of the leaves have a strong, red-brown, V-shaped mark that becomes darker as the foliage matures. Wispy, thin, brownish flower-spikes appear in late summer on stems 2–2½ft (60–75cm) high, but are best removed to avoid distraction from the foliage, which delights the eye from spring until autumn.

Hosta sieboldiana 'Elegans' (see p.129) and *Polystichum setiferum* (see p.132)

FLOWERS AND ORNAMENTAL FRUIT

Actaea alba (Ranunculaceae) (3A–9A)

The various species of baneberry provide quiet beauty from their fluffy, powder-puff inflorescences in late spring and, in autumn, from the shining, colored berries that are poisonous if eaten and have given rise to the common name for the genus.

All are hardy perennial, woodland herbs with short, woody, rhizomatous rootstocks from which the strong, upright stems, 2 to 3ft (60–90cm) high, appear in late spring. The foliage is dissected and fresh green, and the shoots terminate in rounded or cylindrical tight clusters of flowers, with conspicuous white or creamy white stamens. As the season advances, these gradually develop attractive fruits that vary from black to red or white, depending on the species.

Actaea alba

The most spectacular is *Actaea alba* (also known as *A. pachypoda*), the White Baneberry or Doll's Eye from eastern North America, a fascinating plant in fruit with spikes of glossy white, pea-sized berries, each black-dotted at the apex and borne on thick, fleshy, scarlet stalks. The berries appear in autumn and remain attractive until the frosts. A less commonly seen red-fruited variant, forma *rubrocarpa*, has glossy red rather than white fruits, but still has the thick scarlet stalks so characteristic of this species. Another good garden plant, the North American *A. rubra*, is also red-fruited but has slender green stalks.

Cultivation presents no problems in any moisture-retentive, cool, shaded position, all the species preferring humus-rich conditions. Propagate by division of

the rootstock in autumn or early spring or from seed sown in autumn to provide a winter chilling period that encourages germination the following spring.

Although the fruits of *Actaea* species are poisonous, the root of the European *A. spicata*, Herb Christopher, a fine, black-fruited woodlander, was at one time used to treat complaints ranging from arthritis to asthma.

Dictamnus albus var. *purpureus* (Rutaceae) (2A–8B)

Sometimes listed as *Dictamnus fraxinella*, this attractive herbaceous member of the rue family is also commonly known as Gas Plant, a reference to the way in which the volatile oils in the warty glands of the inflorescence and fruits may be ignited on still, hot, sunny days. A very desirable garden plant, thought to have been cultivated since Roman times, *Dictamnus albus* var. *purpureus* occurs wild in dry rocky places and open woodland from Spain through most parts of Europe across to Turkey and the western Himalaya. Closely related species extend the range of the genus through much of central Asia to northwest China.

I was surprised by the starkness of its habitat in the wild when I saw it in northern Greece on open, sun baked, limestone mountainsides growing in company with the Madonna lily, *Lilium candidum*. However, in a sunny, open position in well-drained acidic or alkaline soil, *D. albus* var. *purpureus* steadily increases and will eventually form large clumps of erect stems 3ft (90cm) high and set with alternately placed, pinnately divided, ashlike leaves, 6–9in (15–23cm) long, that emit a strong lemony aroma. The young shoots emerge later than those of many other herbaceous plants: protect clumps by covering with a wire-netting dome from autumn until the shoots are well up in late spring. The 5–6in (12–15cm) racemes of five-petaled, flattish blooms, purple-pink with dark veins and tufts of prominent stamens, appear from early to midsummer, unfolding from the base of the spike first, a superb sight when seen *en masse* in well-established groups. The pure white *D. albus* var. *albus*, sometimes green-touched with lighter green foliage, is just as lovely and is especially good in mixed plantings of the two color forms. As the flowers fade, the unusual star-shaped, five-lobed, glandular seed capsules develop, snapping open when ripe to release the hard black seeds.

Propagation by careful division of the woody rootstock is possible, but plants tend to sulk if disturbed. Young, pot-grown plants raised from autumn-sown seed, however, establish readily and once planted are best left to their own devices, except for the application of an annual mulch.

GRASSES AND FERNS

Hakenochloa macra 'Aureola' (Gramineae) (7A–9B)

The transition from wet mountain cliffs in Japan on the main island of Honshu to the conventional herbaceous border is a long step for one of the most attractive of ornamental grasses now settled in American gardens. In spite of its somewhat specialized natural habitat, *Hakenochloa macra* takes well to cultivation, preferring a neutral to acidic, moisture-retentive soil in moderate shade or full sun, but also tolerant of less than ideal sites. In my early days at Wisley the green-leaved *H. macra* and its most frequently seen cultivar 'Aureola' grew well in the dry soil under the bamboos in the Bamboo Walk.

Slowly spreading from slender, tough rhizomes, *H. macra* forms dense masses of narrow, fresh green, arching leaves that are 12 to 15in (30–38cm) long. In autumn they often turn to orange-bronze, continuing in beauty long into winter. In late summer and autumn, too, the delicate, feathery, tiny sprays of pale green-brown flowers on stems 18in (45cm) high supplement the attractiveness of the turning foliage.

Division of the rootstocks in spring, rather than autumn, is advisable, as with all grasses. But do not be too greedy and split the clumps into very small pieces, unless potting separately and maintaining in a cold frame until established. I learned this the hard way, losing an entire stock in my eagerness to extend a planting.

The typical green-leaved *H. macra* is, in its own right, an extremely ornamental grass, but it is the variegated forms that claim most gardeners' attention, particularly 'Aureola,' its yellow foliage enhanced by narrow, longitudinal, dark green stripes. Its autumn color is equal to that of the species. Two other variegated forms are occasionally to be seen, 'Alboaurea,' with less distinctive paler yellow and off-white striping, and 'Albovariegata,' with white stripes.

Pennisetum alopecuroides (Gramineae) (5A–9B)

Most of the species of this large genus of annual and perennial, often very beautiful grasses occur in the tropics and warm temperate regions, and only a few are suitable to grow outdoors in frost-prone climates and then should be given the benefit of warm, open sites where the soil is well-drained and not too fertile. Soft growth often means sudden winter death.

Some forms of the variable *Pennisetum alopecuroides*, from China and Japan, but with a distribution spreading to Australia, have, however, proved reasonably tough, and several selected clones are now available, varying from 1½–4ft or more (45–120cm) in height. All are densely tufted perennials with short rhizomes, producing in spring fountains of slender foliage that arches over as the season advances. In midsummer the erect flowering stems extend above the foliage, producing cylindrical, fluffy, brushlike, terminal inflorescences, in color varying from greenish-yellow to dark purple and in length from 2–8in (5–20cm). These are usually at their peak in early autumn but will often last well into winter.

Propagation by spring division is the usual method of increase, but seed-raised plants provide the opportunity to benefit from the plant's variable nature. Regular division of clumps every three to four years may encourage plants to flower freely, but a key factor is thought to be the geographical origin of the stocks.

The free-flowering clone 'Hameln' – probably derived from the Australian plant originally described as *P. compressum* (now subsumed under *P. alopecuroides*) – produces flowering spikes 2ft (60cm) high from late summer, opening green with dark bristles and then slowly changing to pale brown by winter. The very attractive forms with dark purple-bronze inflorescences probably derive from the Japanese forma *purpurascens*, possibly by hybridization with variants adapted to cooler climes. The early-flowering 'Woodside' has dark-hued spikes, and in the 4ft (120cm) high 'Burgundy Giant' the whole plant is suffused dark red-bronze.

In climates where *P. alopecuroides* and its clones may be doubtfully hardy, and even where they do thrive unprotected outdoors, it is well worth growing them as container plants for terraces or patios.

Polystichum setiferum (Dryopteridaceae) (5A–8B)

Of the many ferns that add to the quality of a garden, the Soft Shield Fern, native to Britain and widespread through much of Europe, is remarkable for its tremendous variation, one British fern fancier in the late nineteenth century having described well over 300 forms with pseudo-Latin names! Few of these are available today, but those listed by nurserymen are among the most ornamental and beautiful of their breed.

Polystichum setiferum is normally a woodland plant of limestone soils, but is remarkably adaptable in cultivation, thriving even in moderately acidic, dry sites, remaining unperturbed in full sun, although best in dappled shade. The evergreen, graceful, soft-textured fronds, often 3ft (90cm) or more long, are lanceolate in shape, bipinnately divided and borne in spreading shuttlecocklike fashion (see p.130), arising from the short, erect rhizomes. The plant is sometimes confused with the Hard Shield Fern, *P. aculeatum*, but has much softer foliage and its pinnules ("leaf" divisions) are distinctly stalked, not decurrent. The grass-green fronds are enhanced by the conspicuous orange-brown scales on the rachis (leaf stalk) and are beautiful as they unfold, combining dense silver-brown scaling and pale green before they arch outwards to show their lacy elegance.

Propagation from fresh spores is relatively difficult, but some forms may be increased from "bulbils" (in reality embryonic plantlets) that are produced along the central rachis. Peg down cut fronds with bulbils on seed trays of a humus-rich potting mix and place in a cool propagator. Detach plantlets when well rooted.

Polystichum 'Acutilobum' (or Acutilobum Group, as several variations on this theme, also known as 'Proliferum,' occur), with long, spirally set, pointed, dark green fronds, is perhaps the most widely available. The Divisilobum Group, with rosettes of finely cut fronds, also contains cultivars that may be increased from bulbils. The tracery of the elegant fronds, set at 45 degrees or less and forming swirling mats of dark green, is a delight throughout the year, particularly in 'Densum,' where the frond divisions are multiplied and frilled.

Related plants Many species of *Dryopteris* are worthy of garden space, including the British native *D. filixmas*, the Male Fern, but none is more effective than the stately *D. wallichiana* from northeast Asia, a common plant in the Himalaya, where it inhabits woodlands and moist open areas up to 12,000ft (4,000m). This deciduous, hardy fern produces bold shuttlecocks of twice-divided, lanceolate, leathery fronds that extend to 5 or 6ft (1.5–1.8m) in height. They are green-gold as they unfold, later a deeper green, and contrast superbly with the black or dark brown, scaly rachis (stalk). Several similar species from Africa and South America are sometimes assigned to *D. wallichiana* and may prove more tender than those originating from the Himalaya.

Stipa gigantea (Gramineae) (6B–9B)
Few plants give me more joy than this gigantic and most elegant perennial grass from the Iberian Peninsula and North Africa. In Spain, where I saw it, alas not in flower, *Stipa gigantea* was the dominant species on some of the dry, rocky hillsides in Andalucia, where it formed great tussocks of its virtually evergreen, narrow, arching, 2ft (60cm) leaves. Later in the year it must have been a magnificent sight, with the relatively thin, but very sturdy, almost bamboolike stems topped by great airy sprays of long-awned, oatlike burnished flowers, well-spaced out on stems 6–7ft (1.8–2cm) high.

Stipa gigantea

The flowers start purplish-green but soon turn to purest harvest gold.

Stipa gigantea has proved quite hardy in British gardens, and seems to be more tolerant of a wide range of soil conditions than might be expected from a plant normally subjected to the rigorous heat of Spanish summers and inhabiting dry, sharply drained soils. Nevertheless it will grow perfectly well in a range of well-drained soils, although perhaps at its best on chalky or sandy soil in full sun. In the wild it comes into flower in mid- to late spring, but in cool temperate regions the first flower-spikes do not normally appear until early summer but then continue until early autumn, with the strong stems, still retaining many of the, by now bleached, spikelets through until late autumn or sometimes even later.

Seed is not often available but division of the tough rootstocks in spring (not autumn) provides a perfectly satisfactory means of increase. Offspring of a plant generously given to me over thirty years ago by the great plantsman Graham Thomas is with me to this day.

In spite of its stature, *S. gigantea* may be grown in relatively small gardens as its overall leaf spread, even on large clumps, is usually no more than 3 to 4ft (90–120cm). Grown as a specimen plant or in isolated groups it is superb, particularly with a dark evergreen background. Positioning it in a well-drained position by a pool provides doubled beauty from the reflection of its elegantly swaying flowering stems.

BULBS

Bulbs have given me some of my most memorable botanical encounters. (Like everyone else, I use the term "bulb" in the portmaneau sense, to cover other types of food storage organ: the corms, tubers, tuberous roots and rhizomes, as well as true bulbs). A particular interest in *Crocus* and *Colchicum* species has encouraged me to visit Greece and Turkey in spring and autumn with Brian Mathew, whose expertise on crocuses is unrivalled. I particularly remember one November twenty years ago in the Máni peninsula, where our excitements included, in an old olive orchard, the discovery of *Crocus niveus*, in cultivation since the early part of this century but poorly known in the wild.

Tulips from central Asia, daffodils from the Iberian peninsula and North Africa, lilies from China and the Caucasus, and numerous bulbs from South Africa and the Americas feature among my many enthusiasms, for the pleasures they will bring, with careful seasonal planning, all through the year in a variety of settings including formal beds, mixed borders, grass, and clumps of woodland.

The most commonly grown bulbs are the highly bred cultivars of tulips, narcissi, and lilies, but I incline towards the many species of bulbs with a simpler charm. The lovely spring-flowering *Cyclamen repandum* is one example, while for winter all gardeners should have at least one form of *Iris unguicularis*: even if the weather is miserable a few blooms picked out and brought indoors will lighten the gloom and scent the air around with its delicate perfume.

SPRING

Many outstanding dwarf spring bulbs have yet to achieve the popularity they deserve. Among my favorites are *Brimeura amethystina* and x *Chionoscilla allenii*, both easy to grow and free to increase. The exquisite *Tecophilaea cyanocrocus* is also a superb plant, but unfortunately not easy to obtain. From the popular genera, I have chosen *Narcissus bulbocodium*, *Scilla sibirica* and *Tulipa saxatilis*.

Dwarf-flowering bulbs may be allowed to naturalize in grass or woodland settings, or massed in groups in the alpine garden, according to cultivation requirements and the gardener's individual taste.

Gardeners who do not know or grow any species of the superb genus *Erythronium* can do no better than start with *E. revolutum*, not only for its attractions of flower and leaf but also for the ease with which it can be grown.

The larger-flowering bulb *Fritillaria imperialis*, with its terminal cluster of large red, orange or yellow flowers beneath a crown of leaves, is so striking that it is usually grown as a specimen plant in the border.

DWARF FLOWERING BULBS

Arum creticum (Araceae) (7A–10B)

Aroids have always held a curious fascination for me, partly because of the evocative common names of *Arum maculatum* (6A–9B), Lords-and-ladies, Devil-in-the-pulpit and Cuckoo-pint among them, and partly for the school-imparted knowledge of their curious pollination mechanisms. Apart from aroid enthusiasts, few would call most members of the genus *Arum* beautiful; some dislike the liver-pâté coloration of the spathes, particularly species like the Dragon's Arum, *Dracunculus vulgaris* (*Arum dracunculus*) (7A–10B), with inflorescences that give off an offensive smell.

The award of a First Class Certificate by The Royal Horticultural Society to *A. creticum* is an indication of the high quality of this very desirable and ornamental plant, which is blessed with a very pleasant fragrance that complements the bright to midyellow spathes. These appear from mid- to late spring and in general aspect are akin to *A. maculatum* but the inflorescences, 12in (30cm) and occasionally up to 18in (45cm) high, are held well above the broadly arrow-shaped, bright green leaves, and the spathe is reflexed at the tip when fully developed. The elongated, cylindrical spadix is usually slightly longer and a deeper yellow than the spathe and is particularly noticeable once the spathe tips are reflexed. Records of *A. creticum* with purple, or purple flecked with yellow, spadices and white or green spathes almost certainly refer to the similar *A. idaeum* (7A–10B) from Crete, which is unscented and does not have the noticeably reflexed spathe apex.

Arum creticum is not difficult to grow, forming dense clumps of tubers that come into growth in early autumn. Introductions from high altitudes, such as the Mount Ida region of Crete, have proved totally hardy for many years in less extreme climates of the USA.

Plants that seldom produce flowers although increasing rapidly from tuber offsets may be too well fertilized and probably need to be transferred to an open, sunny, well-drained site similar to the stony mountain slopes with garrigue vegetation in which *A. creticum* is found in nature.

Brimeura amethystina (Liliaceae) (5B–9A)

Banishment from the hyacinths botanically has done nothing to diminish the charm of this attractive and very floriferous small bulb, which is also extremely easy to grow. Native to subalpine meadows on limestone mountains in northeast Spain and recorded from the north-west of the former Yugoslavia (a curiously separated natural distribution), *Brimeura amethystina* (*Hyacinthus amethystinus*) is best described as a small, refined bluebell, with more slender, channeled leaves and more or less horizontally held, narrow, bright blue bells, ½in (1cm) long, borne in simple, one-sided racemes 6 to 8in (15–20cm) high. Like the English bluebell it flowers in mid- to late spring, but is readily distinguished from it by its tubular flowers that are joined and not split into separate segments. Variation in color from dark blue to pure white is known, but the cultivated stocks with Cambridge-blue flowers I find more appealing than the darker hues. The superb white form, of the utmost purity, is of equal merit and prolific both in bulb increase and in seed production.

Trouble-free and unperturbed by any but ill-drained soils, *B. amethystina* is one of spring's finest small bulbs and it well deserves a place being found for it in every garden.

Crocus sieberi subsp. *sublimis* forma *tricolor*

x *Chionoscilla allenii* 'Fra Angelico' (Liliaceae) (3A–8B)

Although seldom grown as a garden plant, this natural hybrid between *Scilla bifolia* and a *Chionodoxa*, probably *C. luciliae*, is one of the most attractive of early spring bulbs, much neglected although extraordinarily free to increase from offsets. My first acquaintance with it was at Wisley in 1958 when, soon after I had joined the Botany Department, it came into flower in early spring in the alpine house, creating pools of cool, deep blue, unmatched in beauty by its near relatives.

x *Chionoscilla allenii* was first recognized as a distinct entity at the Royal Botanic Gardens, Kew, London, England, where it had been received in a consignment of bulbs from Smyrna toward the end of the nineteenth century. The Wisley plant was grown initially as *Scilla sibirica* 'Fra Angelico,' presumably a reference to the blue coloring in this fine artist's paintings.

A robust plant with fairly wide-channeled, dark green leaves, it produces arching sprays, 6in (15cm) long, of eight to twelve broadly star-shaped flowers. These are 1 to 2in (2–5cm) in length, deep blue, and have greeny blue anthers. 'Fra Angelico' appears to have no foibles and must be rated as one of the top few dwarf, spring-flowering bulbs. It will thrive in virtually

any soil, alkaline or acidic, and is at home in the alpine garden, in woodland sites, or grown in containers – an outstanding all-rounder for any garden.

Other hybrids of these two genera have been recorded varying from purple-blue to pink, this latter color being found in *C. allenii* 'The Queen.' None, however, has the magic quality of 'Fra Angelico,' and my enthusiasm for this easily grown bulb remains undiminished after more than thirty years.

Crocus sieberi subsp. *sublimis* forma *tricolor* (Iridaceae) (3A–8B)

The wealth of spring-flowering *Crocus* species that gardeners are now able to obtain is astonishing, but from a gardener's viewpoint I feel that the Greek mainland forms of *Crocus sieberi* are very difficult to better. The species is widespread in Greece and extends into the southern Balkans, usually being found in mountain pastures and woodlands, in early to midspring, often carpeting the ground with its lilac flowers soon after the snows melt. The variation in depth of flower color is considerable, from dark violet-mauve to palest lilac, occasionally white, but the flowers always have a distinctive orange-yellow throat.

There are currently four subspecies recognized, but for horticultural purposes a number of selected clones have been named and multiplied commercially. 'Violet Queen,' with dark violet flowers and rich orange stigmata, and the paler 'Firefly' are two vigorous clones, but pride of place goes to the remarkably colored forma *tricolor*. Botanically it is a variant of *C. sieberi* subsp. *sublimis* and occurs in the northern Peloponnese in rocky areas or light deciduous woodland. The deep yellow throat and the lilac-mauve of the perianth segments are sharply separated by a band of white, providing an attractive three-colored effect, in some forms further enhanced by a darker tip to each segment. Each corm produces several of these lovely globular flowers.

Particularly vivid colored plants should be maintained from the steady proliferation of the corms from offsets. This method of increase is necessary also for the very fine *C. sieberi* 'Bowles' White,' which is orange and yellow in the throat and with broad clean white perianth segments of good substance.

These forms of *C. sieberi* thrive in any well-drained soil of reasonable fertility in an open position, but the corms (as with virtually all crocuses) do need some protection from mice, voles, and chipmunks. They may be grown in small-mesh wire cages about 6in (15cm) deep; another method is to "plant" mothballs (they need replacing after about three years) in between the corms.

Related plants One of the finest sights I have ever seen as a plant collector was *Crocus gargaricus* (6A–8B), coloring great areas of Ulu Dag, the Bithynian Mount Olympus, in western Turkey above the town of Bursa in midspring. Sheets of brilliant orange globes were emerging from the snow-melt on the alpine meadows and even spreading into pine woodland, co-habiting in some areas with the ethereal blue *Crocus biflorus* subsp. *pulchricolor* and the more somber green and olive *Fritillaria pontica*. Known only from three mountains in Turkey, where it is still plentiful in spite of the concrete carpets laid down for the ski hotels, this small-cormed species must not be dried out in the resting season or it will disappear. I have grown it successfully in a peat bank area and in leaf-rich soil, where it gently increased from the slim stolons that are produced from the corms of the Ulu Dag populations but not, it appears, from plants in the other sites it frequents.

Cyclamen repandum (Primulaceae) (7A–9B)

Sometimes saddled with a reputation for being slightly tender, *Cyclamen repandum* is normally hardy in milder regions of the USA, and may seed freely and become naturalized in woodland soils in some gardens. The cream of the spring-flowering species, it has elegant, crimson-magenta, scented blooms set amid silver or

Cyclamen repandum

gray-green patterned (occasionally all-green) lobed foliage, which is frequently red-purple below. Since it is found naturally in central southern Europe from France to Greece, it is perhaps wise to plant the corms several inches (5–8cm) deep in cold gardens so that some protection from very severe weather is provided, advice worth following for all forms. Otherwise leaf-rich soil in conditions akin to its native woodland home are all that it asks. Seed is usually freely produced from established corms and should be sown as soon as it has been gathered, if possible. Seed should either be scattered around the parent plants or pot-sown and plunged outdoors over winter.

There is some controversy over the botanical status of populations of *C. repandum*, sometimes quite distinct, in its various wild localities. A variant from Rhodes, recognized botanically as subsp. *rhodense*, is white (very occasionally pale pink) and pink-nosed, and the foliage is often only slightly white or silver-flecked. For general garden purposes it is a lesser plant than the "normal" *C. repandum* (and is probably not as hardy). Another subspecies, *peloponnesiacum*, found with the autumn-flowering snowdrop *Galanthus reginae-olgae* (5B–8A) in the gorge behind the archeological site of Mistra near Sparta and in the ravines by the Langada Pass in the Peloponnese, is a very fine variation to complement plantings of the crimson-magenta forms. The deep pink, magenta-nosed flowers stand above the marbled, strongly white-speckled, dark green foliage.

Erythronium revolutum (Liliaceae) (5A–8B)

The Trout Lilies, one of several descriptive common names given to the North American species of this attractive genus, never fail to delight me each spring with their beautiful foliage and elegant flowers. Many are woodland or mountain snow-melt plants; some of the latter, like the very fine white-flowered *Erythronium montanum* (5A–8B), the Avalanche Lily, and the yellow *E. grandiflorum* (5A–8B), prove recalcitrant garden plants, but the majority of woodlanders take to cultivation readily.

Among these *E. revolutum*, widely distributed in moist woods and by streams from California northward to British Columbia, is one of the easiest to cultivate, growing well in leafy soil in slight shade and increasing readily from seed. In some gardens it quickly naturalizes, as may be seen in early spring at Wisley, where it proliferates and spreads a pink haze through the woodland areas in which it is grown. The fleshy, elongated bulbs each produce a pair of basal, spreading, narrowly ovate, glossy green leaves, often beautifully marbled brown or darker green. The large flowers, 2 to 3in (5–8cm) across, pink with yellow centers, are pendent and reflexed slightly at the tips like mandarins' hats. One to four at a time are borne on slender stems, 5 to 6in (12–15cm) high, during early to midspring.

There is considerable variation in flower color, from deep to pale pink and occasionally to white; some forms with strong pink coloration (var. *johnsonii* and var. *smithii*) have been recognized as distinct entities. However, they cannot be distinguished adequately on the basis of flower color alone, and the names are best discarded, because plants with these names are unlikely to differ from stock simply sold as *E. revolutum*.

The freely produced seed should be sown as soon as ripe, the pots plunged outside, and the potting mix kept moist. Germination may be slow, and seedlings will take three to four years to reach maturity and flower.

Related plants Known from a small area in California, *Erythronium tuolumnense* (4B–8B) is one of the earliest species to flower, producing, in early spring, clusters of two to four bright yellow, pendent blooms, 1in (2.5cm) across, above pairs of glossy, plain green leaves, long-stalked and ovate. I have seen hundreds of these lovely plants in pinewoods above the Tuolumne River.

It takes a year or so to settle, but in a humus-rich, well-drained site in partial shade blooms regularly and freely each year, despite a reputation for being shy-flowering, and increases steadily from offset bulbs although it does not, in my garden at least, set seed.

Erythronium tuolumnense has been used as a parent of several delightful clones that are vigorous and free-flowering. 'Pagoda,' with soft sulphur yellow, internally red-ringed, slightly scented flowers and large, bronze-marbled leaves is one of these; its sister seedling 'Kondo,' with lemon-yellow, green-tinted blooms, is very similar but with slightly less mottled leaves that almost lose their marbled look after flowering. Both grow about 12in (30cm) tall and increase rapidly in ordinary garden conditions. A third hybrid, 'Jeanette Brickell,' named after my wife in 1978, is a strong-growing plant 9in (23cm) tall. In midspring it produces sprays of five to seven blooms 2 to 3in (5–8cm) across that are pure white but with greenish centers and brownish-red markings.

Erythronium 'White Beauty' (4B–8B), now considered a floriferous clone of *E. californicum*, is an outstanding garden plant, rapid of increase, with light green, white-marbled leaves and stems 6 to 8in (15–20cm) high, bearing two or three ivory-white flowers, 2 to 3in (5–8cm) across, flecked brownish-red in the center. It is sometimes sold as a clone of *E. revolutum* or *E. oregonum*.

Erythronium revolutum

Ipheion uniflorum 'Wisley Blue'

Ipheion uniflorum 'Wisley Blue' (Liliaceae) (6A–9A)

The constant shifting of *Ipheion* from one genus to another is a source of bewilderment to gardeners. I propose to ignore the latest pronouncement that it should now be *Tristagma*, as this delightful and prolific bulb deserves a little stability in its life.

Ipheion uniflorum, like most members of the genus, is native to Argentina and Uruguay. It displays its attractive, star-shaped, 1 to 2in (2–5cm) flowers singly on slender stems 6 to 8in (15–20cm) high amid clusters of linear, pale green, slightly glaucous foliage during early to midspring; and may be increased by division of the small, freely produced, onion-scented, white offset bulbs. What was once the most common form, with silver-blue blooms, has been replaced by a clone of equal vigor but with flowers of violet-blue, with slightly darker tips to the segments. The original plant of this clone was sent for naming to Wisley in the late 1950s, eventually "escaping" to the trade as 'Wisley Blue.'

Although often grown as a pot plant in the alpine house, *I. uniflorum* (in all variations) seems to be quite hardy in the open garden, given a sunny, or slightly shaded, well-drained site. At one time it was used at Wisley as an underplanting for hornbeam hedges, forming a haze of lilac in early spring, and often earlier, before the hornbeam burst into leaf. It proliferated well, even in the very dry soil below the hedges, with no care at all. Such sites are also suitable for several early-flowering bulbs, including *Scilla sibirica*, *S. bifolia*, and *Chionodoxa*, which will frequently naturalize under deciduous (but not too greedy-rooted) hedges.

Since the advent of 'Wisley Blue,' other fine clones have been introduced, all seemingly as even-tempered in the garden and now becoming commercially available. The best include 'Froyle Mill,' in dark violet-blue, and 'Rolf Fiedler,' a large-flowered, white-throated, clear blue. Add the superb, long-stemmed 'Alberto Castillo,' with large white flowers, to provide an excellent trio of early-flowering bulbs to grace any garden.

Iris 'Katharine Hodgkin' (Iridaceae) (4A–8A)

The *Reticulata* group of irises (so called because of the netted or reticulated bulb tunics) provides some of the best of all dwarf spring-flowering bulbs, both for gardens and as pot plants. Many are very easy to grow, free-flowering and hardy, quickly forming clumps from offset bulbs produced at the sides of the parent bulb. Some also produce numerous tiny bulblets, which may take two or three years to mature.

Almost all the species undergo a dry, summer ripening period in the wild, and in cultivation they should be given open, sunny sites with sharp drainage. In such conditions species like *Iris reticulata*, *I. histrioides* and various hybrids will usually form good clumps, flowering regularly in late winter and early spring each season. They are excellent for raised beds, the narrow, normally four-sided leaves seldom becoming untidy: they die away early and neatly, so that neighboring plants are not overwhelmed by their foliage. Each year I also grow a range of different named clones ('J.S. Dijt,' 'Cantab,' 'Joyce' and the like) in pots to bring into the house, where their delightful flowers, some pleasantly scented, may be more readily appreciated.

'Katharine Hodgkin,' a hybrid between the deep blue *I. histrioides* and the yellow *I. winogradowii*, raised in the mid-1960s by E. B. Anderson, is among the finest of the race. Whilst the flowers are 2½in (6cm) across with a white ground color, the broad falls and standards are suffused and veined lavender-blue, with dark purple-blue spots and orange-yellow markings on the ridges of the falls – an unusual and attractive color-mix repeated in 'Frank Elder,' a beautiful hybrid of the same parentage. Both clones proved vigorous and free-flowering in my Wisley garden, where they were grown with no special treatment, thriving in spite of being subjected to summer irrigation. Both freely produce "rice-grain" bulblets, which afford an easy means of increase.

Related plants Most of the many beautiful species of the Juno group of irises, distinguished by the fleshy, thick, persistent roots and the papery bulb tunics, only thrive if given bulb-frame or alpine-house treatment. Despite occuring in sun-baked, stony, mountainous sites in Tadjikistan and Afghanistan, *Iris bucharica* (4A–8A) is a perfectly easy and most attractive mid- to late spring-flowering garden plant, given sun and good drainage. The form most generally available is about 8 to 10in (20–25cm) high and has up to six creamy white or very pale yellow flowers with contrasting darker yellow falls that have longitudinal purplish-brown marks and flecks. A form with blooms a richer, deep yellow all over (sometimes grown as *I. orchioides*) is also very desirable. Both variants may be propagated by seed or by careful separation of the bulbs.

Leucojum vernum (Amaryllidaceae) (4A–8B)

Few bulbous plants are easier to grow than the Spring Snowflake, *Leucojum vernum*, which blooms as early as late winter in most years, and its larger relative *L. aestivum*, the Summer Snowflake, which, despite its name, flowers in mid- to late spring, and sometimes earlier.

Widespread in Europe and now naturalized in Britain, *L. vernum* inhabits rich deciduous woodlands and meadows. but in gardens seems indifferent to all but very dry conditions, although at its most luxuriant in heavy, damp soils, particularly by pools and streams.

The dark green, strap-shaped leaves push their tips above the soil as the 5in (12cm) scapes, each with one, occasionally two, of the 1in-wide (2.5cm), pendent, white, green-tipped blooms develop in late winter and continue into early spring. The flowers, unlike the closely related snowdrops, have six equal segments, are like slightly pleated, six-toothed, rounded lampshades.

Two variants are recognized that are also good garden plants; in var. *carpathicum* the tips of the perianth segments and style are yellow-tipped, and not infrequently there are two flowers per scape; var. *vagneri* is still green tipped but has two flowers to a stem. There is in fact no clear dividing line between the variations. All are well worth growing and are easily spread by division or from seed, often self-sown in suitable sites.

No less accommodating is *L. aestivum*, known as the Loddon Lily in Britain as it is found wild on river banks and water meadows, notably by the River Loddon in Berkshire. It is, however, widespread in Europe and eastward to the Caucasus, being distinguished from *L. vernum* by having smaller but more numerous flowers on each stem and a much taller habit. 'Gravetye' (or 'Gravetye Giant') is a particularly fine clone, its elegant stems, 2ft (60cm) and occasionally taller, bearing up to seven of the green-tipped flowers, only two-thirds the size of those of *L. vernum*.

Leucojum vernum

Muscari macrocarpum (5B–8B) (Liliaceae)

Known to gardeners and botanists since the seventeenth century, *Muscari macrocarpum* has never become widespread in cultivation in spite of its most attractive, sweetly scented blooms and the relative ease with which it may be grown.

Native to a number of islands in the eastern Aegean and recorded also from eastern Crete and southwest Anatolia, the present stock in British gardens results from a reintroduction by Dr Peter Davis from the island of Amorgos, where it was growing in limestone cliffs and where it is also cultivated in gardens.

The 8 to 9in (20–23cm) flower-spikes of bright yellow, purple-tipped blooms spread their strong but pleasant scent in midspring. By some the scent has been described as redolent of ripe bananas, but to me it is more like honey with a hint of musk. The slightly untidy, broad, strap-shaped, channeled leaves are deep green with a light glaucous tinge and appear before the flower buds develop, gradually extending to 12in (30cm) or so in length before dying down in early summer. *M. macrocarpum* also makes an excellent pot plant but needs a deep container to accommodate the large bulbs, which develop very fleshy thick roots similar to those of a Juno iris.

Although apparently tolerant of below freezing temperatures, *M. macrocarpum* is best given a sunny position in well-drained soil where the bulbs can be protected from summer rain. The "rain shadow" at the foot of a warm wall is ideal. However, the most impressive colonies I have seen were in Scotland, growing in a shaded bed with no shelter from rain when the bulbs were dormant.

Seed rarely seems to ripen satisfactorily in Britain, but bulb increase is reasonably rapid and stocks are regularly available in Britain, though rarely in the USA.

The similar but rather duller-flowered Turkish *M. muscarimi* (*M. moschatum*) (5B–8B), with greenish-white, faintly blue-flushed blooms, is valued for its strong musk scent.

Related plants *Muscari comosum*, the Tassel Grape-hyacinth, a very widespread plant in much of southern Europe and eastward into Turkey, is more interesting than beautiful, with 12in (30cm) high spikes of small, dull brown bells topped by tuffets of purple sterile flowers. Few would grow *M. comosum* today except in the delightful form known in our family as the "feather duster plant," *M. comosum* 'Plumosum' (5A–8B). In this form the dun-colored, fertile flowers have been entirely replaced by sterile flowers, so that the whole inflorescence is transformed into a mass of purple threads, an unusual and most attractive variant which remains in beauty for several weeks in midspring.

Narcissus bulbocodium (Amaryllidaceae) (6B–8B)

Few who have seen the magnificent displays of the Hoop Petticoat Daffodil, *Narcissus bulbocodium*, at Wisley would deny it a place as one of the finest of all dwarf spring bulbs. In the wild it usually occurs in mountain meadows, and is widespread in Spain, Portugal, western France, Morocco, and Algeria. Its extreme variability in flower and leaf characters has led to the development of a cumbersome system of nomenclature as botanists and gardeners have struggled to classify this variation satisfactorily.

The flowers, each 1 to 2in (3–5cm) across, are borne singly on scapes usually no more than 4 or 5in (10–12cm) high with several very narrow, dark green basal leaves. The bright to pale yellow, puffed-out corona is of broad funnel shape and often frilled, while the perianth segments are narrow. The Wisley meadow contains both the deeper yellow form known as var. *conspicuus* and the paler var. *citrinus* which now intergrade as both produce seed freely and naturalize in the short, acidic grassland through which moisture flows plentifully, particularly during the spring growing season. Although most forms of *N. bulbocodium* may be increased from bulb separation without difficulty, they are also readily raised from seed, flowering-sized bulbs being achieved in three or four years.

As well as being suitable for naturalizing in grass, *N. bulbocodium* may be grown very successfully in the alpine garden or in any open site where sufficient spring moisture is available. It also makes a very fine pot plant for alpine-house decoration.

Where I have seen it in the wild in Spain (possibly the smaller-flowered var. *nivalis*) it grows in acidic turf, flowering as the snows melt in the Sierra de Gredos and Sierra de Guadarrama. In cultivation *N. bulbocodium* tolerates more alkaline conditions, although then does not seem to be so prolific of increase.

Related plants *Narcissus cyclamineus* (5A–8A), with its sharply reflexed perianth segments and narrow frilled trumpets, is a beautiful dwarf bulb and an important parent, imparting the character of its swept-back "wings" to numerous excellent garden hybrids. In northern Spain and northern Portugal it occurs in damp, acidic, mountain pastureland, but it is now uncommon in the wild. It prefers acidic soils and damper conditions than *N. bulbocodium*. Its bright, rich yellow "shooting stars" are held on stems 4 to 6in (10–15cm) high. For those who lack suitable conditions, many good dwarf hybrids (such as 'Quince,' 'Jet Fire,' 'Snipe,' 'Jumblie') impart much of its character. Under the name *Narcissus* 'Bowles' 'EarlySulphur' (5A–8A), I have for many years grown a most attractive form of *N. minor* whose exact origin is unknown. The blooms, sulphur-yellow rather than the rich yellow of most forms of *N. minor*, are beautifully frilled and have a green-suffused base to the tube. Little more than 6in (15cm) high, it flowers in my Sussex garden in midwinter and offers its blooms for several weeks, increasing steadily from offset bulbs.

Narcissus 'Cedric Morris' (5A–8B) is also an outstanding garden plant, notable not only for its precocity but also for remaining in flower for more than six weeks in the open garden. The first trumpet daffodil to appear, it always produces its midgold flowers in early winter and in some seasons in late autumn. Although sometimes referred to as *N. minor*, it is almost certainly a variant of *N. asturiensis*, somewhat taller at 5 to 6in (12–15cm) than the usual plant available from the bulb trade, but similar in other ways, apart from its less "waisted" trumpet. Originally collected in northern Spain, it increases steadily from bulb division, but has yet to become widely available commercially.

Narcissus bulbocodium

Tecophilaea cyanocrocus (Tecophilaceaceae) (7A–9B)

The almost legendary Chilean Crocus, extinct or virtually so in the Cordillera of Santiago and Valparaiso in Chile, where it occurred at an altitude of 10,000ft (3,000m) in stony pastures, is undoubtedly one of the most beautiful and desirable of all spring-flowering plants. Its presumed demise is partly due to overgrazing by cattle and other stock that are turned out to feed on upland grasslands in the Chilean spring. Its main method of increase being from seed, grazing at flowering time over a number of seasons would inevitably lead to a drastic reduction in populations. Collecting for horticulture has undoubtedly contributed to the probable extinction of *Tecophilaea cyanocrocus* as a wild plant, but inadvertently its horticultural qualities have also ensured its conservation, albeit several thousand miles from its natural home.

The small, flattish corms give rise to two or three narrow, channeled, basal leaves; and in early to midspring, sometimes earlier, each of the 4in (10cm) stems bears one to three intense royal blue, open-campanulate, almost flat, 1½in wide (3–5cm), six-parted flowers. Of similar quality is a form known as var. *leichtlinii*, with slightly paler blue, white-throated flowers.

Although hardy and grown successfully outdoors in various areas of Britain in sandy, well-drained soil, the very rarity of *T. cyanocrocus* demands that it should be grown in a bulb frame or alpine house, where the summer dormancy essential to its well-being can be provided easily. Sunbaking is not required, the aim being to achieve conditions akin to those of the high, dry upland of the Chilean Cordillera following the snow-melt.

In bulb frames or pots a fairly rich, very sharply drained potting mix is required to plump up the corms; once seed has been gathered the plants should be rested until encouraged into growth again by watering in late winter or early spring. Hand-pollination to provide a reasonable seed-set should be carried out to bulk up stocks of this marvelous plant. In recent years some British nurseries have been able to offer limited quantities of the bulb as a result of horticultural conservation, particularly at the University Botanic Garden, Cambridge, and the Royal Botanic Gardens, Kew. It is still extremely rare in the USA.

Tulipa saxatilis (Liliaceae) (6A–9B)

Relatively few tulip species can be relied upon to remain undisturbed in the garden for many years and continue to flower reliably. The Cretan *Tulipa saxatilis*, which I have found growing around the edges of cultivated fields on the Omalos Plain, appears not only to be hardy but also very persistent, spreading freely by underground stolons although seldom, if ever, by seed, because mature seed capsules do not normally form.

The shining, deep green basal leaves appear in late winter or very early spring, and the unusual lilac-pink flowers, with a prominent yellow base internally, almost globular and 2 to 2½in (5–6cm) wide, are produced in midspring. The colors are often divided by a narrow white band, and with the contrasting purple-black anthers provide an unusual and attractive color mix. The flowers are borne on stems up to 12in (30cm) high that may have branched heads of three or four blooms (I have recorded a specimen in the wild with six), although one or two per head is more usual.

Tulipa saxatilis sometimes has the reputation of being difficult to flower, apparently being more intent in spreading by its strong stolons, frequently over 12in (30cm) long. I have not found it to be difficult in an open sunny position, and it has also performed well on acidic sands at Wisley. Once obtained and planted in a well-drained, warm site the bulbs should be left to settle; although they may take a couple of years to adjust, they should then begin to bloom regularly. If bulbs are slow to flower, restrict the area through which the stolons can wander, using slates or roof tiles sunk into the ground. Once the allotted area is thick with bulbs, regular flowering should occur.

Related plants The superb *Tulipa greigii* (3B–9A) from central Asia is the parent of numerous hybrids of great garden value. The large blooms, 3in (7.5cm) long, borne on stems that are 6in (15cm) tall, are brilliant vermilion-scarlet, with black and sometimes yellow basal markings. The purple-banded foliage is also extremely ornamental, and this characteristic has been passed on to many of the hybrids, such as 'Red Riding Hood,' 'Plaisir,' and 'Cape Cod' – all prolific garden plants valuable for their fine foliage as well as for their sumptuous flowers produced in early to midspring.

Originally found in one small area in northern Turkey, the delightful *Tulipa sprengeri* (3B–9A) has not been rediscovered in the wild but is well established in gardens: it is tolerant of both acidic and alkaline soils and of a range of sites, from alpine gardens to grassy meadows and lightly shaded woodlands. It also naturalizes readily from seed. The slender stems are 1½ to 2ft (45–60cm) high and in late spring bear elegant, rather narrow flowers, 2½in (6cm) long, that are crimson-scarlet within and a light straw-crimson without. Plants from seed will often flower in 3-4 years, a short period for tulips.

Tulipa saxatilis

OTHER PLANTS

Corydalis solida 'George Baker' (Papaveraceae) (6B–8A)
Although most forms of *Corydalis solida* produce flowers of a muted purple, it is a very variable species. 'George Baker' (also known as 'G. P. Baker') is an outstanding clone, in early spring displaying its racemes of deep brick-red, narrow, pouting, two-lipped blooms on stems 3 to 4in (7.5–10cm) high above neatly divided, fern-like foliage. As the lower flowers fade and the seed pods develop, the inflorescence elongates to reach 6in (15cm) or so in height. Any well-drained soil seems acceptable to this desirable plant. Germination is rapid if the seed is sown fresh, but 'George Baker' should be increased by division of the small tubers as the seedlings do not come true to color.

Fritillaria camschatcensis (Liliaceae) (3A–7B)
In late spring the Black Lily produces yellow-anthered bells that are usually blackish-purple (sometimes brown, green, or greenish-yellow) and about 1in (2–3cm) long. They are borne in clusters of two to eight at the apex of stems that may be as short as 5 or 6in (12–15cm) or well over 2ft (60cm) long. These are sup-

plemented by whorls of five or six glossy, lance-shaped leaves, the whole arising from a scaly bulb that produces masses of "rice-grain" bulblets and often sends out short stolons that make it simple to propagate. A plant of sub-alpine meadows and open damp woodlands from Kamchatka and Japan across to Alaska and western North America, it will sulk and eventually disappear if not grown in a cool, moist position in light shade.

Fritillaria michailovskyi (Liliaceae) (5A–8A)
Unknown in cultivation until 1965, when the Mathew-Tomlinson expedition brought it back from northeast Turkey, where it was growing in alpine grassland near the snowline, this is now one of the most readily available as well as one of the most beautiful of all the species. It seldom reaches more than 4 to 6in (10–15cm) in height, producing, in early to midspring, up to four (occasionally more) pendent bells, each about 1in (2–3cm) long with the basal half in brownish-purple contrasting with a broad, bright yellow band around the mouth. It thrives in any well-drained soil. Although often grown as a pot plant, it will grow perfectly well in an open site on the alpine garden. It is increased by small bulblets, from scaling the bulbs, or by seed.

Scilla liliohyacinthus (Liliaceae) (4A–8B)
I find this squill one of the most attractive of wood-landers, tolerant and very easy to grow and increase from the somewhat curious, yellowish, scaly bulbs. These steadily form large clumps of rosetted, shiny, bright green, strap-shaped leaves, 6in (15cm) or more long, which emerge in early to midspring to be followed shortly by the racemes of cup-shaped, midblue flowers on stems 6in (15cm) high. In addition to the normal blue form, there is an equally good white. Give it a position in moist grassland or leafy shade similar to its wild conditions in the French and Spanish Pyrenees, and it will give much pleasure in spring with no further care.

Scilla siberica (Liliaceae) (2A–8B)
There are few lovelier bulbs than the Siberian Squill from Crimea and the Caucasus, which is readily available and very easy to grow in virtually any position in the garden. The vivid, deep blue, bell-shaped, more or less pendent flowers are carried on 2–4in (5–10cm) stems, which develop just as the dark green, glossy leaves emerge, from early to midspring. Apart from the deep blue form (known as 'Spring Beauty' or 'Atrocoerulea'), paler blue and white variants are known. Bulb increase is rapid, and seed is freely produced. It is effective when naturalized in beds of deciduous shrubs.

LARGER FLOWERING BULBS

Fritillaria imperialis (Liliaceae) (5A–8B)
The stately Crown Imperial, introduced as long ago as 1576 by Clusius, was much appreciated by gardeners such as Parkinson in the seventeenth century, in spite of the strong, foxlike odor given off by the bulbs. *Fritillaria imperialis* has been recorded wild from the western Himalaya in Kashmir and Pakistan westward to southeastern Turkey, usually on dry rocky hillsides up to 8,000ft (2,400m) or more. Because of its long-time cultivation for ornament and in some areas for food (the bulbs, though poisonous raw, are said to be very nutritious when cooked), it is likely that some records refer to cultivated or naturalized stands.

In early spring the shoots burst through the soil, the sturdy stems clothed in whorled, sometimes alternate, glossy, bright green, lanceolate leaves rapidly reaching 2½ to 3ft (75–90cm) or more before producing terminal clusters of large, nodding flowers crowned by a tuffet of leaves (see p.146). Each inflorescence contains six or more 2 to 3in (5–7.5cm) long, bell-shaped blooms, brick-red, orange or yellow, with six glistening white drops of nectar in the throat.

Although tolerating a wide range of soils, *F. imperialis* does not always settle down immediately, and once planted it is best left undisturbed for a number of years. I plant the bulbs, which have a hollow central core through which the main shoot develops, on their sides so that water does not sit in the hollow when they are dormant. Increase by bulb offsets is steady, and it is also propagated from seed, which usually is produced in abundance only in warm, early seasons. Expect a wait of six years or more for seedlings to flower.

Among the various clones, two are particularly appealing to me: 'Maxima Lutea,' in clear, deep yellow, and the variegated 'Aureomarginata,' with dark orange red flowers and cleanly marked gold and green leaves.

Related plants The dark-hued *Fritillaria persica* has much smaller blooms than its Imperial relative, no more than ½in (1–2cm) long and borne in long racemes of up to thirty pendent, conical flowers. Some forms are disappointing, but the vigorous form known as 'Adiyaman' (6A–8B) from southern Turkey, with its distinctive, deep plum-purple blooms carried on stems 3ft (90cm) or more tall, is a fine garden plant.

Easy to grow and an excellent alpine garden plant, *Fritillaria pyrenaica* is usually only 12 to 15in (30–38cm) tall with slender glaucous leaves and one,

Fritillaria imperialis (see p.145)

occasionally two, rather "squared" bells, usually purple-brown and tessellated without and a glistening greenish-yellow marked purple-red within. *F. pyrenaica*, which flowers in mid- to late spring in cultivation, is also well worth trying in light woodland and in short grassland where it may self-seed.

Narcissus obvallaris (Amaryllidaceae) (3A–9A)

Among a genus that contains such a plethora of good garden plants, *Narcissus obvallaris*, the Tenby Daffodil, so-called because of its occurrence, wild or naturalized, near Tenby in South Wales, is an admirable species for general cultivation in grassland or in light woodland. Apart from its upright, sturdy stance (no flopping of foliage or stems) it has, in my view, the neatest and most uniform blooms of any trumpet daffodil. The flowers, 2 to 2½in (5–6cm) long and of pure gold, often facing slightly upwards rather than horizontally deflexed, display a six-lobed, only marginally frilled trumpet with broad, patent, evenly matched, overlapping perianth segments. These give a roundness and neatness to the individual flower, which has a grace lacking in some of the more gross modern clones that look so top-heavy when in bloom.

In all probability the Tenby Daffodil is not a garden hybrid, as is sometimes claimed, but an Iberian species that was early imported to Britain and became established in various sites. As a population very similar to the cultivated plant has now been located in the province of Ciudad Real in Spain, this may clear up the mystery of its original birthplace.

Whatever its origins, *N. obvallaris* (sometimes incorrectly grown as *N. lobularis*) is an undemanding and very fine daffodil for general cultivation; its only minor fault, if fault it be, is that it clumps up so quickly that it needs division and replanting very regularly.

Tulipa 'Keizerskroon'

Tulipa 'Keizerskroon' (Liliaceae) (5A–8B)

I have chosen this remarkably resilient late-eighteenth-century tulip to do duty for the vast range of cultivars, mainly of Dutch origin, that provide so much pleasure and colorful beauty during mid- to late spring. 'Keizerskroon,' is a single early tulip just over 12in (30cm) in height, with scarlet flowers, deeply edged yellow. Another successful bedding tulip is the crimson-scarlet 'Couleur Cardinal,' with the exterior of the blooms a darker plum-red.

Bedding tulips, to use a term to cover the majority of the different classification divisions, have a reputation for flowering only for one season unless they are allowed to mature *in situ* in fertile ground. Provided blooms are deadheaded as soon as the petals fall and the plants are fed with a foliar fertilizer, some cultivars will develop a large enough replacement bulb to flower reasonably well the following season. When dormant, they can be lifted, cleaned, stored dry, and then planted in their new quarters in mid- to late autumn. The display, however, is seldom as good as that provided by commercially produced bulbs in their first year. Most gardeners prefer to purchase fresh bulbs each year to ensure good-quality blooms and to avoid the trouble of lifting bulbs and providing the carefully controlled storage conditions required to maintain "home-grown" stock – commercial growers store dormant bulbs at 68°F (20°C) and in a relative humidity of 75 percent.

In my present garden, both 'Keizerskroon' and 'Couleur Cardinal' are in their fourth year of flowering without being disturbed. Encouraged by this, I am now treating various "standard" cultivars in the same way in the hope that their somewhat smaller flowers may fit more naturally with their neighbors.

SUMMER

Bulbs can play a starring role in the summer border: the magnificent *Cardiocrunum giganteum* and the large alliums are effective as vertical punctuation marks, while *Lilium candidum*, the Madonna Lily, brandishes tall, white, highly scented flower-spikes.

Somehow one does not expect exotic-looking lilies to thrive without humus-rich, dappled woodland, or constant cossetting in a more open site. In fact, gardeners can now choose from a range of easily grown hybrids in a range of colors and color combinations, as well as variations in habit and flower shape.

DWARF FLOWERING BULBS

Arisaema candidissimum (Araceae) (6B–9A)

A devotee of this large genus of aroids, to which adjectives such as sinister, weird, and interesting are often applied, I feel that even the most unadventurous of gardeners might be won over by *Arisaema candidissimum*, which has an unexpectedly pleasant perfume.

In general appearance the inflorescence is not unlike that of a slightly compressed *Arum creticum* but in gleaming white, often with a pink- and green-veined throat. In early summer the hooded spathes, in shape like the foghorns of a ship but only 3 to 4in (7.5–10cm) long, with sharply pointed, taillike apices, push rapidly through the soil on slender stems 5 or 6in (12–15cm) in length. As the attractive inflorescences reach their maximum height the foliage unfurls, revealing the very handsome three-lobed leaves, which on vigorous plants may be up to 12in (30cm) across, eventually forming dense clumps that provide surprisingly good ground cover.

Arisaema candidissimum appears to be hardy in areas with mild winters. Prolific in its production of tubers, it is very easy to maintain good stocks and will thrive in almost any site provided with reasonable moisture in the growing season. I find that it flowers and increases best in humus-rich, partially shaded positions. Mark the site well as growth does not start until late spring.

Seed is occasionally set, the bright red fruiting spikes producing it in quantity. Remove the squashy flesh and sow seed as soon as possible.

Although collected by George Forrest in China in 1914 and apparently introduced on a later expedition, *A. candidissimum*, which occurs wild both in open sites and woodland in northwest Yunnan and southwest Sichuan, has never become widely available. It acquired a First Class Certificate from The Royal Horticultural Society in 1970 and is undoubtedly the best species for gardens, deserving to be more widely grown.

Calochortus vestae (Liliaceae) (8A–9B*)

One of the most exciting, if not always tractable, genera of bulbs to grow is *Calochortus*, known colloquially as Cat's Ears, Fairy Lanterns and Mariposa or Globe Tulips, although their relationship with garden tulips is fairly remote. Well over half of the sixty or so species grow wild in California, where most occur in grassland or open, dry, summer-baked sites. In the uncertain climate of Britain virtually all *Calochortus* are best grown as pot plants or in bulb frames that may be closed against summer and early autumn rains. Under such conditions and with a reasonably fertile sharply drained soil-based potting mix, they often come into growth in early to late winter and flower between midspring and midsummer, depending on species. By way of exception, *C. barbatus* (8B–9B*) and its close relations are summer-growing and -flowering, and winter dormant.

Propagation from seed, sown as soon as possible, is not difficult. The seedlings, once germinated, should be kept growing as long as possible until they begin to die down naturally. In the following growing season fertilize occasionally with weak liquid manure, and in their third season plant out seedlings in a bulb frame. Plants may well flower the following year. Some *Calochortus* produce bulbils in the leaf axils and also at bulb-level; the bulblets are dealt with as seedlings.

Most beautiful of the *Calochortus* to me are those of the Mariposa group, with sumptuous, erect, bowllike blooms, often up to 2in (5cm) or more across and borne on slender wiry stems sparsely set with long, narrow leaves. The delightful *C. vestae* (8A–9B*), in the forms I have grown white or very pale lavender with central reddish-purple and yellow markings in the hairy throat, flowered well for me over five or six years unprotected outdoors in a raised bed, reaching 1½ to 2ft (45–60cm) in height. In the same site, although for lesser periods, the similar white-flowered, yellow-centered, purple-marked *C. superbus* (8B–9B*) and the gorgeous deep yellow, brown-red-marked *C. luteus* (8B–9B*), both Californians like *C. vestae*, grew successfully, all three shedding bulbils that "germinated" *in situ*.

Roscoea purpurea

Roscoea purpurea (Zingiberaceae) (6B–7A; 9A*)

Some seventeen species of *Roscoea* from the Himalaya and China make up a group of unusual summer-flowering plants. The six or seven in cultivation have proved hardy, but it is sensible in cold regions to plant them with the crown of the fleshy tubers 4 to 6in (10–15cm) deep. Although they prefer a moist, leaf-rich soil, it is important that the drainage is fairly sharp, because in nature most of the species have a dormant period of dry cold, often with snow cover. They are easy enough to grow in cool woodland or peat garden conditions, and one or two species, such as the yellow- or purple-flowered *R. cautleoides* (6B–7A; 9A*), will grow well in the herbaceous border. Young growths develop late in spring, and may be damaged by careless cultivation earlier in the season.

Roscoea purpurea (also known as *R. procera*), from Bhutan and Nepal, is the finest of the species. Its stems, 12in (30cm) or so high and clothed with sheathing, broadly lance-shaped leaves up to 6in (15cm) long, bear large, usually deep purple, long-tubed, orchidlike flowers amid the leaf clusters in continuous succession from midsummer until early autumn. The individual flowers are up to 2in (5cm) long, sometimes longer, hooded, with two lateral perianth segments and a broad, protruding lip, which may be longer than 2in (5cm). Flower color varies from deep to pale purple and, in one form grown at Wisley as *R. procera*, beautiful blooms of bicolored white and purple.

The stockier *R. humeana* (6B–7A;9A*), with similar blooms, begins the season, flowering profusely in early summer; the flower color is usually purple, sometimes yellow or white. It is hardy and easy to grow and propagates well from division or from seed, which is freely provided but is the devil to collect because it is held deep within the bracts at the base of the flower tubes.

Scilla peruviana

Scilla peruviana (Liliaceae) (7A–9A)

In spite of its specific name, this beautiful Cuban Lily is native to the western Mediterranean region, occurring in Italy, Sicily, the Iberian Peninsula, Algeria, and Morocco, Linnaeus, who described it originally, having been misled as to its original home. An extremely variable plant in flower and leaf characters, with twenty or so names given to different forms, *Scilla peruviana* in its best clothes is an extremely attractive plant, the large bulbs producing rosettes of long, dark green, strap-shaped leaves in late autumn or early winter, well before the flowers appear. In early summer the great pyramid-shaped inflorescences rise from the centers of the rosettes, often containing up to a hundred of the deep violet-blue, starry flowers densely set on a stem 9 to 10in (23–25cm) high. There is an equally attractive white-flowered form, but some of the color variants in paler lilac-purple or brownish-purple are less desirable plants. Bulb increase is fairly rapid, and I have raised seedlings from a deep-hued clone that after four years produced offspring similar in color to their parent.

Opinions differ as to the most favored site in which to grow *S. peruviana*. In the wild it is recorded in damp meadows, woodland, and dry rocky areas at fairly low altitudes. In cultivation it seems to be hardy and to grow well in dry sunny positions and in damper conditions in full sun, whether in acidic or alkaline soils. Flowering capacity is unaffected by severe winter weather, but foliage can become rather tattered. Grown between low herbaceous plants that spread their young foliage in spring to partially cover the elderly scilla leaves – *Geranium renardii*, *G. himalayense*, or *Alchemilla mollis* are ideal – it will bloom well in early summer and, by the time fresh foliage from the bulbs appears in late autumn, the companion plants will have gone to rest.

LARGER FLOWERING BULBS

Allium 'Globemaster' (Liliaceae/Alliaceae) (4A–9B)

Until this relatively new hybrid onion appeared on the horticultural scene, the spectacular *Allium giganteum* held pride of place, with its globular, lilac-purple flower heads, 5 or 6in (12–15cm) across, held aloft on stems 4 to 5ft (1.2–1.5m) high in early summer. Although of slightly lesser stature, a mere 3 to 4ft (90–120cm) in my garden, 'Globemaster' effortlessly produces globelike inflorescences 9 to 10in (23–25cm) across, consisting of hundreds of small but vivid violet-purple blooms (see p.150). These remain in color for several weeks in early summer, after which the perianth segments slowly harden and change to light brown, when they may be cut and fully dried for winter decoration. A magnificent flowering plant for any sunny border in well-drained soil, 'Globemaster' increases well from bulb offsets, but has not set seed for me as yet. Seedlings, in any case, would not be entitled to the clonal name 'Globemaster.' Modern techniques of twin scaling the bulbs or micropropagation have been successfully used for *Allium* species and hybrids, so it should not be long before this superb plant is as readily available as many other ornamental onions.

A hybrid between *A. macleanii* (*A. elatum*) (4A–9B), a close relative of *A. giganteum* and *A. christophii* (*A. albopilosum*) (4A–9B), 'Globemaster' would appear to derive its huge flower heads from the latter species and its stature and the character of its recurving, fresh, and shining green leaves, which are strap-shaped and marginally ciliate, from *A. macleanii*. Both its parents are excellent garden plants, *A. christophii*, in particular, providing pleasure not only when its ball of starry, purplish-blue flowers with a curiously metallic sheen is displayed in early summer, but also from the dried flower heads that remain on the plant for months, opening to reveal black seeds that contrast with the sear brown of the rigid, almost spiny perianth segments.

Related plants Clearly allied to, and possibly a clone of, *Allium aflatunense*, 'Purple Sensation' (4A–9B) bears glowing violet-purple globes 4in (10cm) across on stems 3 to 4ft (90–120cm) high in early summer, more intense in color but complementing those of 'Globemaster,' *A. giganteum* and their ilk. It increases well from offset bulbs and promises to be as easy to maintain as its close relatives. I have it growing among low herbaceous plants and deciduous shrubs, which obscure its slightly passé leaves at flowering time.

Allium 'Globemaster' (see p.149)

SOUTH AFRICAN BULBS

The richness of South Africa's flora has given us an outstanding range of bulbous plants, many of them hardy in the various North American climates. Many red-hot pokers, *Kniphofia* species (strictly rhizomatous or clump-forming rather than true bulbs) grow happily unprotected in many parts of North America. Crimson Flags, *Schizostylis*, with their wiry rhizomes and lovely spikes of red, pink, or white cup-shaped blooms, appear unperturbed by cold winters, as do *Amaryllis belladonna*, *Nerine*, *bowdenii*, the deciduous *Agapanthus*, and a few *Crinum* species, such as *C. bulbispermum* and its hybrid *C.* x *powellii* ('Album' is shown; see p. 152). South Africa is a happy hunting ground for bulb-lovers, with a plethora of genera still to be introduced.

Cardiocrinum giganteum (Liliaceae) (7A–9A)

Most magnificent of all lilies and perhaps of all bulbous plants, the Himalayan *Cardiocrinum giganteum* (*Lilium giganteum*) fully lives up to its specific name both in the wild and in cultivation, where it will often reach 10ft (3m) when in full flower in midsummer. It occurs naturally from Nepal across to southeastern Tibet, between 5,000 and 10,000ft (1,000–3,300m).

It has taken readily to cultivation, its massive stems arising from a rosette of shining dark green, broadly ovate, basal leaves, often over 18in (45cm) long and wide in early spring and thrusting skywards to 8ft (2.4m) or more by early to midsummer. The bold, handsome leaves, similar to those of the basal rosette, are spaced alternately on the stem, which terminates with up to twenty or more huge, slightly down-pointing, trumpet flowers with flared reflexed segments, 6in (15cm) or more long, in midsummer. The deliciously fragrant white blooms are tinted green on the outside and internally marked with reddish-purple. Seed is freely set, and the spikes of upright capsules are most decorative, particularly when the seed has been shed.

An ideal woodland plant, *C. giganteum* will thrive in humus-rich soil, associating well with rhododendrons and *Meconopsis*, but there are also records of it being grown and flowered in lime-rich soils. In areas prone to early spring frosts other woodland plants may afford the young foliage some protection.

Cardiocrinum giganteum

A gross feeder, *C. giganteum* appreciates heavy mulching with leaf-mold, as well as dressings of well-rotted manure, particularly when bulbs are nearing flowering size – usually in their sixth or seventh year from seed (if well treated) or in the fourth year of growing on offset bulbs. The old bulb passes on after flowering, leaving a number of offsets to continue the life cycle. These should be replanted in fresh rich soil so that they will build up strength to bloom as soon as possible. Ideally, plant offset bulbs, and seedlings each year to maintain a succession of flowering-sized bulbs.

Crinum bulbispermum (Liliaceae) (7B–10B)

Two species of this beautiful genus, *Crinum bulbispermum* and *C. moorei* (7B–10B), both inhabitants of marshy areas and riversides in various provinces of South Africa, have proved hardy in the southern and western states and, given some winter protection, could well be tried in colder gardens.

In cultivation they do not demand constant moisture if provided with a fertile deep soil and an annual mulch to maintain good growth, preferably in full sun. It is advisable to grow small plants for a year or two under glass, before planting out established clumps in late spring, making sure that the top of the "neck" of the bulb is at or near soil level. As a precaution one or two offsets may be grown as pot plants free from frost. Offsets provide the simplest means of propagation,

although the large, fleshy seeds will germinate readily.

In Natal, I have seen *C. bulbispermum* producing flowering stems almost 5ft (1.5m) tall, bearing huge umbels of ten or twelve curving, long-tubed trumpets, white with a red stripe and sweetly scented. The handsome, curved, glaucous green leaves, which have no noticeable midrib, are 2 to 3ft (60–90cm) long, sheathed at the base to form a false "stem" about 12in (30cm) high. The flower stems form at the side of this, developing from the large, long-necked bulbs 5 to 6in (12–15cm) in diameter (see p.152). Curiously, in many *Crinum* species, including this one, the previous season's leaves, having died back in winter, grow again in spring, the truncate tips differentiating them from the new foliage with its long apices.

Normally, *C. bulbispermum* reaches no more than 3 to 4ft (90–120cm), slightly taller than the equally attractive pink- or white-flowered *C. moorei*, which has a somewhat larger bulb, characterized by its stemlike "neck" up to 2ft (60cm) long. Unlike those of most other species, the leaves mature in one year, frequently reaching 5ft (1.5m) in length and having, unusually in South African species, a thickened central midrib. Its cup shape flowers are often 5 to 6in (12–15cm) across.

Both species are worth a place in any warm border. They can be protected by growing as pot plants, and will often bloom profusely in containers, congestion of the bulbs seeming to enhance flowering potential.

Crinum bulbispermum (see p.151)

Crocosmia 'Lucifer'

Related plants The hardiness of *Crinum* x *powellii* (6B–10B), the beautiful hybrid between *C. bulbispermum* and *C. moorei*, is unquestioned, and the various named clones are reliable late summer bulbs. The bright-green leaves, which can be untidy by flowering time, are best masked by the foliage of surrounding plants. The flowers, of open trumpet shape and deliciously scented, vary from deep pink to paler hues. 'Album,' with large umbels of pure white blooms, 5in (12cm) across, is outstanding, quickly forming large clumps of the long-necked bulbs that may, with some difficulty, be divided in spring to increase stock.

Crocosmia 'Lucifer' (Iridaceae) (5B–9A)

The common montbretia, *Crocosmia* x *crocosmiiflora* (5B–9A), with its gay sprays of bright orange and a propensity for spreading somewhat too widely by means of its rapidly increasing corms, is an unassuming and well-known plant both in gardens and naturalized in waste places in Britain, particularly near the sea, where it blooms freely for many weeks from mid- to late summer. Pleasant though it is, in garden value it is far surpassed by many of the hybrids raised in East Anglia early this century, most rescued by the plantsman Graham Thomas and now freely offered by nurserymen as a result of his diligence and persistence. In addition, the popularization of the very fine, brilliant orange-red *C. masonorum* (6B–9A) from South Africa and its subsequent use, partnered by *C. paniculata* (6B–9A) (colloquially known as "Aunt Elisa" from its former inclusion in the genus *Antholyza*) as a parent for some very fine offspring, has raised interest in these delightful, easy, and free-flowering plants to a high level.

Outstanding among the taller hybrids is 'Lucifer,' with its tremendous vigor, stalwart hardiness, and startling color. In midspring the pleated, swordlike leaves appear from dense clusters of corms, quickly forming vertical shafts of dark green, from which, in mid- to late summer, long, branched sprays of vivid bright red, curved, trumpet flowers are produced on 4 to 5ft (1.2–1.5m) stems.

'Lucifer' can survive in areas with mild winter months. It increases rapidly, and is readily propagated by splitting the congested, vertically developed corm masses in midspring.

Related plants There is now plenty of choice among *Crocosmia* clones, with more than fifty available. Although they prefer fairly moisture-retentive soils, they are tolerant of most well-drained sites and, in addition to their fine late summer display, make excellent cut flowers.

Clones of lesser stature include the delightful 'Emily McKenzie' (5B–9A), usually reaching only 2ft (60cm) or so in height. It is free-flowering, and the large, open, slightly nodding flowers are dark orange, splashed centrally with a deep red star. It is easily grown and hardy.

Dierama pulcherrimum (Iridaceae) (7A–9B)

Known by a range of evocative common names, including Fairy Wand, Angel's Fishing Rod, Wand Flower and in its native Africa, Hairbell, *Dierama pulcherrimum* is one of the most graceful and beautiful of all bulbous plants and is not difficult to grow even if it is not always easy to establish.

Like all of the forty or so species now recognized it is evergreen, although the foliage is often browned by cold winter weather and so may appear deciduous. In late spring fresh grasslike leaves 2 to 3ft (60–90cm) long, but only ⅓in (8mm) or so in width, develop from the fiber-covered corms to be followed by elegant, arching inflorescences that reach a height of some 5 to 6ft (1.5–1.8m) by the time the blooms open in mid- to late summer. Each of the wiry stems bears at its tip a number of shorter secondary sprays of four or five tubular, straight-sided, bell-shaped flowers. These are 2 to 3in (5–8cm) long and sway attractively in the slightest breeze. The basal bracts are silvered brown, but the flower color varies from the palest rose to dark red-purple, and all variants are worth growing.

Dieramas should be transplanted with great care to avoid damaging the thick and brittle, contractile, fleshy roots that develop from the uppermost corm. Spring transplanting in cold areas is usually successful, but in more clement climates division of the corms soon after flowering, before the new roots develop, works well. Seed is also freely produced: sown in spring, it will normally germinate rapidly, and the corms will often reach flowering size within two or three years.

In gardens *D. pulcherrimum* thrives in moisture-retentive soils mirroring the conditions of the summer rainfall areas of South Africa from which it originates – it grows in open grassland up to an altitude of 5,500ft (1,700m) in the mountains of the eastern Cape and the Transkei. The hot, dry conditions often recommended for South African plants are unsuitable, although I have known it seed freely on the dry Bagshot sands, near Wisley. *D. pulcherrimum* and several other species appear to be hardier than some garden books allow.

Dierama pulcherrimum

Eremurus robustus (Liliaceae) (5B–9B)

Among the most magnificent of all bulbous plants are the foxtail lilies, species of the genus *Eremurus*, given their common name from the similarity in shape of their tall inflorescences to the erect "bush" of a fox. The majority of the forty or so species occur wild in central Asia, often forming large colonies on mountainous slopes, where they are apparently unpalatable to grazing animals.

The growth pattern for all the species is very similar. The rootstock consists of a mass of fleshy roots that radiate starlike from the central crown, which, in spring, develops a dense rosette of linear or lanceolate leaves, triangular in cross-section and rather succulent in texture. In early or midsummer, sometimes later, the strong, upright flower spikes are produced, densely set with hundreds of small, cup- or star-shaped flowers, which give way to marble-sized (and shaped) seed pods. In the case of *Eremurus robustus* the huge stems extend to 8 or 10ft (2.4–3m), the upper 2 to 3ft (60–90cm) providing an aerial display in pink or, occasionally, white.

This species naturalizes readily from the freely produced seed. If sown in autumn, seed usually germinates freely the following spring, and one-year seedlings will normally flower two or three seasons later. Careful division of the fleshy roots in early spring provides an alternative method of increase, the crowns being planted, roots spread out, just below soil level.

The dying foliage, which is somewhat unsightly, can be effectively hidden by midsummer if *Eremurus* are grown among roses, shrubs, or herbaceous perennials. Full sun and a well-drained, fertile soil provide the ideal conditions for most foxtail lilies, but they tolerate a range of soils from clays to sharply drained highly calcareous ones.

If garden space is limited, try the clear yellow *E. stenophyllus* (*E. bungei*) (5B–9B) which is 3 to 5ft (90–150cm) tall, or named hybrids such as the orange 'Cleopatra.' Make sure, however, that you obtain freshly lifted crowns with fat, succulent-looking roots.

Gladiolus papilio (Iridaceae) (7A–9B)

A few of the South African species of *Gladiolus* have, perhaps surprisingly, proved hardy with no or minimal protection out of doors in Britain. Among these *G. papilio* (*G. purpureo-auratus*), a common plant from the Transkei area to Natal, where it occurs in damp grassland, has become well established. This is probably due to its extraordinarily rapid increase by stolons, because the charm of its curved, hooded flowers is muted; they are of smoky lilac-purple, lightened by a greenish-yellow throat and with prominent purplish-mauve markings on the lower segments. Six to ten blooms to a stem, which is 3ft (90cm) high and slightly arching, are borne in late summer and early autumn.

I first came across G. *papilio* under the name G. *purpureo-auratus,* and, in due course, received corms, which spread alarmingly in my Wisley garden, producing only a few flower-spikes until they had settled. Restricting the root-run of this plant would be worth trying to encourage a more profuse display. In sun or partial shade and given good drainage, it is easily cultivated. This distinctive species is variable in nature, and other color forms could be worth introducing.

The very showy and extremely variable G. *natalensis* (8A–9B) (possibly correctly entitled G. *dalenii* and often known as G. *psittacinus*) might well be established, at least in the milder areas with some winter cover – I have seen it flowering as a garden escape in the Scilly Isles. It produces a host of cormlets ("spawn") around the main corm, but also runs by means of stolons. The flowers, 3in (7.5cm) long, hooded, and upward looking, are borne in late summer and autumn on stems that are 3 to 4ft (90–120cm) high. They are yellow to orange or red, sometimes heavily speckled or streaked, sometimes plain colored. The most commonly available variant, apparently originating from the cooler parts of its range, has bright red flowers, with yellow, red-edged lower segments. Probably from the same range comes the plant known as G. *primulinus* (8A–9B), with clear yellow flowers. Both are worth growing for the garden and for cutting.

Lilium candidum (Liliaceae) (4A–9A*)

The myth that all lilies require constant attention has, happily, been dispelled – all the lily species listed here needing only a period of winter cold. One species that is not too demanding and highly desirable is *Lilium candidum,* the Madonna or White Lily. Grown by the Ancients, its reputation as a cure-all and its religious symbolism led to its wide distribution in Europe. In Britain it used to be common in cottage gardens, often thriving with no special care.

There is some uncertainty over its distribution, but I have found colonies that I judged to be wild in northern Greece and in southwestern Anatolia in Turkey. In one site they were growing at the edges of beechwoods in heavy, leaf-rich soil; elsewhere I have found them flowering freely in hot dry conditions among limestone rocks. The bulbs in all cases were very close to the soil surface, frequently with the tips of the bulb scales showing. In cultivation, unusually for lilies, the bulbs

Lilium candidum

are best planted very shallowly, if possible in late summer, by which time the top growth will be dying down. Fresh leaf rosettes appear from the bulbs in autumn, overwintering to send up flower-spikes 3 to 5ft (90–150cm) high, which are clothed in numerous lanceolate, fresh green leaves below the racemes of up to fifteen, sometimes more, dazzling white, outward-facing blooms. Green-tipped in bud, the deliciously scented flowers, which open in early or midsummer, are 4in (10cm) long, trumpet-shaped, with gently recurving tips and bright yellow anthers.

Most cultivated plants are, unfortunately, sterile, but more recent introductions from wild stock may form abundant seed. Sown in autumn, it will usually produce flowering-sized bulbs in four or five years. Scaling bulbs is the usual method of propagation.

Lilium candidum can be infuriating, thriving in one garden but sulking or failing in a neighboring garden given apparently identical treatment. Although succeeding in a range of soil types and conditions, probably the most suitable site is on a well-drained, fertile, alkaline soil with its feet in shade and its top in sun. Apart from mild fertilizing when in full growth, the best advice is to leave flourishing plants alone! Botrytis and virus are sometimes problems, the latter usually carried by aphids. It is a wise precaution with all lilies to use control methods as routine.

Related plants The magnificent *Lilium regale* (3A–9A*), introduced by E. H. Wilson from western

Sichuan, China, in 1905, is vigorous and easy to grow, prolific in seed production, and a most useful parent for breeding. Despite a natural habitat that is rocky, with intense cold in winter and blistering summer heat, it appears indifferent to soil type in cultivation, although perhaps most at home in free-draining alkaline conditions. Plant the bulbs where precocious growth will be protected by other plants and 6 to 8in (15–20cm) or more deep to allow for stem roots to form. In midsummer the strong 3–4ft (occasionally 6ft) stems, often bear more than ten sweetly perfumed trumpets, 4 to 5in (12–15cm) long, vinous red-purple without, glistening white and yellow-throated within. Seed-raised plants will often flower within two years from sowing.

Lilium monadelphum (Liliaceae) (3B–9B*)
It is now generally accepted that the two lilies formerly grown as distinct species, *Lilium monadelphum* and *L. szovitsianum*, are best united under the older name, because the slight differences in characteristics are known to vary within natural populations.

A plant of meadows and woodland edges up to 8,000ft (2,400m) altitude in the Caucasus and adjacent regions as well as in northern Turkey, *L. monadelphum* is an extremely handsome and stately lily, often reaching 5ft (1.5m) or more in height. The strong stems are densely set with numerous, glossy green, broadly lance-shaped leaves, the stems terminating in four to ten (in well-grown specimens more than twenty) large, pendulous or semi-nodding trumpets. These are of a beautiful clear yellow, sometimes crimson-spotted, 3 to 4in (8–10cm) long, with the tips of the perianth segments strongly recurved. Variation from a soft pale yellow to a much stronger hue with the buds often crimson-purple at the base and apex and the pollen varying from deep yellow to orange may also occur.

Altogether a very satisfactory and most attractive garden plant, *L. monadelphum* grows well in deep, humus-rich and well-drained soils, but may flourish also in heavier soils and does not object to lime, although not a plant for dry highly calcereous or very acidic conditions. At Wisley earlier this century a large colony of *L. monadelphum* (then grown as *L. szovitsianum*) was established in the Wild Garden, together with the pink-flowered Japanese *L. rubellum* (3B–9B*). Reduced maintenance during World War II meant that the deep ditches draining the area became clogged. When I joined Wisley only a few bulbs remained, owing to the waterlogged soil, and these passed on a year or two later. Ample moisture in the growing season but free drainage is essential for this group of lilies.

LILIES OF THE CAUCASUS

Among the many Caucasian plants that grace our gardens is the superb Turk's-cap lily, *Lilium monadelphum* (illustrated below; plant entry, left), which has a number of close relatives, some now established in cultivation. *L. kesselringianum* has cream or straw-colored flowers and much narrower perianth segments than *L. monadelphum*, while the attractive *L. ledebourii* has fragrant, pale creamy Turk's-cap flowers, heavily purple-spotted at the base.

Nearer to the well-known *L. pyrenaicum* botanically is *L. ponticum*, which has deep yellow, tight Turk's-caps, somewhat wider leaves and hairy filaments, and grew well in woodland at Wisley. *L. ciliatum*, often confused with *L. ponticum*, has ivory or sulphur-colored flowers and distinctively ciliate leaf edges. Regrettably, few of these lilies have yet penetrated the general garden market, handsome and amenable though they are.

From seed *L. monadelphum* takes six or more years to produce flowering sized bulbs; increased from healthy bulb scales, plants will still take several years to bloom. It is worth the wait though, for the species is long-lived and one of the finest members of an outstanding genus.

Related plants *Lilium chalcedonicum* (3B–9B*), the "Red Martagon of Constantinople" as it was called by Parkinson, has been cultivated for nearly four centuries, not surprisingly in view of the brilliant sealing-wax red coloration of its Turk's-cap flowers. Similar in general aspect and height to *L. pyrenaicum*, *L. chalcedonicum* is less tractable as a garden plant, being susceptible to Botrytis and virus infection, and also because it is not always given the sharp drainage and full sun that suit its constitution. It is native to Greece, and where I have found it growing wild, in the Mount Olympus region, it occurred in low scrub, the racemes of up to ten bright scarlet blooms a startling sight in early summer, swaying above the gray-green of the low maquis vegetation.

Tigridia pavonia

Tigridia pavonia (Liliaceae) (8B–10B)

Well named as the Tiger Flower or Mexican shell-flower, *Tigridia pavonia* is found wild in Mexico and Guatemala but, because it is widely cultivated and produces ample seed, it has also become naturalized in many frost-free areas of the world. It has an extraordinary flower color range in reds, orange, yellow, white, and violet-mauve, some unmarked but usually with the three short inner segments heavily striped and spotted in contrasting patterns. Initially the blooms are cup-shaped, but the three long outer segments soon spread horizontally to 4in (10cm), gradually reflexing as they age. Borne on stems about 18in to 2ft (45–60cm) high, the flowers are developed in succession from the long green spathes, with up to six of the short-lived but exotic blooms in each.

Nowadays most of the corms offered are seed-raised and available in mixed colors rather than in selected color variants. *T. pavonia* is particularly prone to virus problems, and raising from seed has the advantage of providing virus-free corms. Corms of flowering size may be produced within a year, and will sometimes flower the same season as sown.

If the corms are planted 3 or 4 in (7.5–10cm) deep in midspring in a free-draining site, they will bloom during the summer months, a continuous succession of bloom being achieved by planting corms in batches between midspring and midsummer.

Some gardeners have found *T. pavonia* to be hardy in more clement areas of Britain but, although occurring at heights of 6,000ft (1,800m) in the Sierra Madre and other mountainous areas of Mexico, it seldom over-wintered with me at Wisley. Corms should be lifted in autumn and stored dry in frost-free conditions.

AUTUMN

After the hectic palette of summer, the appearance of exquisite late-flowering bulbs is greatly appealing. Massed together, their effect can be hypnotic, in the garden and, on a larger scale, in the wild. From my travels in the Mani in Greece I will never forget the sight of *Crocus goulimyi* spreading a lavender carpet in a fig tree's shade.

The selection here includes *Amaryllis belladonna*: I have yet to see a form that I would not grow, but my favorite is the superlative clone 'Hathor'. It flowers before the leaves appear, the foliage overwintering and eventually dying away in the early summer – a growth pattern adopted by related bulbs such as some *Nerine* and certain *Colchicum* species.

DWARF FLOWERING BULBS

Colchicum speciosum 'Album' (Liliaceae) (4B–9B)

A widespread species in the Caucasus and north and east Anatolia and probably other parts of Asia Minor, *Colchicum speciosum* opens its rich lilac-purple, goblet-shaped blooms in early autumn. Each of the large corms produces several flowers, which emerge from the soil leafless, a growth habit that has given rise to the common name Naked Ladies.

In the wild *C. speciosum* occurs in vast numbers on mountain meadows, often coloring the turf purple and frequently mixed with the white-flowered *Crocus vallicola*. An equally fine display can easily be achieved in gardens, since *C. speciosum* has taken readily to cultivation and soon forms great drifts of color, either planted among shrubs or naturalized in orchards or other grassy areas. There is considerable variation in flower color, from the deepest purple-red to pale lilac, the long flower tube also varying in the same manner and in one form, erroneously known as var. *bornmuelleri*, being greenish-white.

But finest of all is the exquisite 'Album,' with large, glistening white goblets, 3 to 4in (7.5–10cm) high, consisting of six overlapping, broad perianth segments of great substance. In spite of the vagaries of the seasonal weather and its chaste appearance, *C. speciosum* 'Album' remains upstanding into midautumn, unlike some of its cousins, whose flower tubes collapse after a period of wet or windy weather, leaving their flowers at the mercy of slugs and snails. I rate this clone, which increases rapidly from offset corms, as top or very close to top of the autumn bulb league table for the longevity and quality of its flowers and for the immense pleasure it provides before one is plunged into winter proper.

Like all its autumn-blooming relatives, _C. speciosum_ produces its foliage in late winter or spring. The bold clusters of glossy rich green leaves are handsome in their own right, although sometimes reviled as "too large and untidy." Before they fade in early summer, quietly remove withered leaves to the compost heap.

Related plants The small-flowered _Colchicum atropurpureum_ (4B–9B), whose origins are mysterious, provides pools of deep magenta-red blooms in midautumn, usually rather later than _C. autumnale_, to which it is sometimes assigned, although it is closer to the Balkan _C. turcicum_, which often has flowers of a similar hue. The small corms each produce two or three blooms, which are 2in (5cm) high and emerge from the soil white or pale rose before changing quickly to their mature coloration. The neat, dark green leaves are produced in late spring and disappear by midsummer. Although uncommon in gardens, _C. atropurpureum_ is not difficult to grow in any freely drained, fertile soil and is well worth obtaining for its autumn brilliance.

Crocus goulimyi (Iridaceae) (4A–8A)

Among the true autumn-flowering crocuses (not to be confused with colchicums, which are frequently, but misleadingly, referred to as "autumn crocuses") are several Greek species of great beauty. The delightful _Crocus goulimyi_ has deservedly become very popular and available commercially at a very reasonable price. Known only in the Peloponnese, where it was first seen in flower in November 1954, it occurs abundantly on limestone formations in olive groves, often by stone walls, and in rocky open areas in the rich terra rossa soil in the Máni Peninsula.

Less than twenty years after its discovery, while in Greece studying and mapping the autumn-flowering _Crocus_ and _Colchicum_ species close to Areopolis on the Máni Peninsula, we came across large populations of _C. goulimyi_. The marvelous drifts of this graceful species, especially one colony forming a carpet of bright lavender in the shade of a great fig tree, remain vivid in my memory.

Crocus goulimyi increases rapidly by seed and by proliferation of the hazelnutlike corms. Each of these produces one or two honey-fragrant flowers, which are

distinctively globular and lavender-blue, the three inner segments of paler coloring than the outer. The blooms have tubes 4 to 5in (10–12cm) long, and the clusters of four to five leaves are often well developed at flowering. Grown in a bulb frame or as a pot plant, its qualities may be savored in spite of adverse weather in mid- to late autumn, when it is in bloom, but it seems quite hardy outdoors in a warm, open site. In my Wisley garden it increased happily in a south-facing border and in South Carolina it thrives happily in a fully shaded location with an organic-rich, moist soil.

Although remarkably constant in flower color in all the populations we saw on the Máni, white flowered selections have now been found, and one, named 'Máni White,' is a beautiful clone which should soon be available to complement the normal lavender-blue form.

Related plants One evening in November 1973, returning, somewhat wearily, to our base in Kalamata after a day's work mapping _Crocus_ sites in the Peloponnese, we saw the pale ghosts of hundreds of crocuses briefly lit by our car's headlights. In an old olive orchard we had discovered one of our goals, the superb but poorly known _Crocus niveus_ (4A–9B). Later collections on the Máni Peninsula showed that _C. niveus_ often occurs with _C. goulimyi_, in the Peloponnese flowering at the same period. It produces huge, yellow-throated, white flowers, sometimes with pale lavender outer segments, borne on long tubes that may reach 5 or 6in (12–15cm) or more in length, the bowls of the flowers often exceeding 2in (5cm).

Crocus niveus is a robust plant, increasing freely from offset corms and also from seed. It seems perfectly hardy outdoors in sites similar to those recommended for _C. goulimyi_ and is at home in a bulb frame.

Crocus goulimyi

Sternbergia lutea (Amaryllidaceae) (6A–9B)

The late-flowering members of this small genus of daffodil-relatives from the Mediterranean region are among the most pleasing of autumn bulbs, their cheerful yellow flowers often appearing in early autumn and continuing until midautumn. Superficially they resemble yellow crocuses, but *Sternbergia* species have daffodillike bulbs and their flowers have six stamens, not the three of crocuses.

The commonest species in cultivation, *Sternbergia lutea*, widespread from the Iberian Peninsula across to Greece, grows particularly well in sharply drained, alkaline soils, thrusting its goblet-shaped flowers, bright golden and 2in (5cm) tall, through the soil in late summer and early autumn, the clusters of strap-shaped, glossy, green leaves appearing with or shortly after the blooms open.

Sternbergia lutea has a reputation for being shy-flowering in gardens but, if grown in a warm, sunny position where little summer rain penetrates, it will usually bloom abundantly and soon develops into large clumps of bulbs that appear to flower particularly freely when congested. Clonal variation may play a part in the regularity of flowering, but no comparative data to support this appears to have been produced. The best course for a good display is to beg a bulb or two from a friend's garden where it grows well and to give it comparable treatment in your own garden.

The closely related *S. sicula* (*S. lutea* subsp. *sicula*) differs in having narrower, dark green foliage with a grayish central stripe and smaller flowers. In very well-drained conditions it will bloom freely in midautumn. In its natural habitat it is often a mountain plant, frequently found in soil pockets in limestone rock crevices in Crete and Greece, sometimes finding a comfortable home in archeological sites like Dodona in northwest Greece, where it has colonized gaps in the steps of the amphitheater.

Both *S. lutea* and *S. sicula* are easily grown and, if correctly sited, free-flowering. Apart from poor drainage, their one real enemy is the narcissus fly, which, unfortunately, attacks daffodil-relatives as well as daffodils.

Zephyranthes candida (Amaryllidaceae) (7A–9B)

While most members of this genus of attractive daffodil-relatives are unsuited to cold temperate regions and require frost-free conditions to grow well, *Zephyranthes candida* (*Argyropsis candida*) – slightly surprisingly in view of its marshland habitat in Argentina and Uruguay – is relatively hardy. It may be seen flowering freely at the Royal Botanic Gardens, Kew, positioned in sunny, sheltered borders where, in early to midautumn, the white, sometimes green-tinted, crocuslike flowers, with lightly veined perianth segments, appear above the rushlike foliage on stems that are 4 to 6in (10–15cm) long. The foliage is usually persistent so that a small tuft of the very narrow, linear, dark green leaves, 6in (15cm) or so long, remains throughout the year. Vegetative increase from daughter bulbs is fairly rapid although seed is, apparently, rarely produced in British gardens.

I grew this species at Wisley, and in the free-draining soil of my garden it remained unharmed for over twenty years, providing a very welcome succession of its delicate blooms over a long period of the autumn.

OTHER PLANTS

Allium beesianum (Liliaceae/Alliaceae) (5A–10B)

During two autumn expeditions to the Lijiang range in northwest Yunnan, China, where it was originally collected by George Forrest in 1910, I have seen this dwarf onion sparkling among the grassy slopes and screes at 11,000 to 12,000ft (3,000m) or more, the clusters of eight to twelve pendent, bright blue, 1in (2.5cm) long, tubular flowers carried on stems 6 to 10in (15–25cm) high. The depth of its blue coloring varied slightly, and scattered white-flowered plants occurred occasionally in the populations.

This delightful plant is not difficult to grow in well-drained humus-rich soil, forming neat clumps of fiber-coated bulbs, which may be gently teased apart in spring. My plants, from a wild source, flower in early autumn, earlier than in their mountainous home, and produce seed freely.

Cyclamen hederifolium forma *album* (Primulaceae) (5A–9B)

Widely distributed in the Mediterranean region, *Cyclamen hederifolium* (also known as *C. neapolitanum*) varies greatly in the size, shape and markings of the often silver-patterned foliage, which remains in beauty from autumn to spring. The large tubers root mainly from the top and sides and, between late summer and midautumn, produce a constant succession of blooms with reflexed petals, usually before the foliage appears. In the wild and in cultivation flowers are rich to pale pink or white, and some individuals are fragrant. The characteristic dark purple-magenta mark at the mouth of the flowers is usually lacking in forma *album*. Although I willingly grow all variations, those with pure white blooms provide the greatest pleasure.

Zephyranthes candida

This superb garden plant is easy to grow in open positions, in shrub borders, or in woodland, where, particularly in leaf-rich soils, it will rapidly form large drifts from self-sown seed.

Eucomis bicolor (Liliaceae) (7B–10B)

The genus *Eucomis* is a somewhat neglected and homogeneous group of mainly South African bulbous plants, most of which have proved remarkably hardy. The bulbs produce basal rosettes of strap-shaped, fleshy leaves in spring to be followed in late summer and autumn by strong flowering stems with dense racemes of starry, broad-segmented flowers, topped by a rosette of small leaves (hence the common name, Pineapple Flower). I have grown several species of these handsome plants successfully outdoors without protection, my favorite being the wavy-leaved *Eucomis bicolor*, from Natal. It blooms in early autumn or later, the stem, 12in (30cm) high, bearing a conspicuous top-knot of leaves and pale greeny-cream flowers, edged purple and about 1in (2–3cm) across. It is a most attractive and distinctive plant for a sunny border.

LARGER FLOWERING BULBS

Amaryllis belladonna 'Hathor' (Amaryllidaceae) (7B–10B)

The Cape Belladonna (sometimes known botanically as *Brunsvigia rosea*) is an outstanding, autumn-flowering South African bulb that produces large umbels of up to twenty, sometimes more, funnel-shaped, sweetly scented blooms that are 4 to 5in (10–12cm) long. These are usually in shades of pink, often being white toward the base, with a yellow throat. In the very fine clone 'Hathor' they are ivory-white in bud, opening to pure white. All forms are superb for garden decoration and as long-lasting cut flowers.

Amaryllis belladonna flowers before the leaves develop, the strong stems, bronze-purple or purple-flushed green and 1½ to 3ft (45–90cm) tall, emerging from the soil in early autumn. It blooms for six to eight weeks, often into late autumn. The strap-shaped, bright green leaves overwinter, dying down in early summer.

In the wild *A. belladonna* grows in grassland, on light hilly woodland, and among scrub. The bulbs are resistant to rapid burn-overs, and I have seen them, together with *Watsonia, Haemanthus,* and other bulbous plants, flowering abundantly after bush fires. This behavior provides a clue to its successful cultivation in temperate regions, where it does not always bloom as freely as might be desired.

It seems essential to provide an open site in a very sunny position. A south-facing house or greenhouse wall where reflected heat helps warm the soil is ideal; an abundance of water in late summer combined with warm summer weather should trigger abundant flowering. At Wisley there was an astonishing flowering in the autumn of 1949, attributed to a providential leak in the laboratory water supply after the hot summer. Watering in 1–2oz (30–60g) of a high-potash fertilizer around the bulbs during the spring when they are in full growth should aid flower initiation. To allow summer ripening, plant with the necks at soil level, not deep, as is sometimes recommended. In congested clumps bulbs often become partially exposed, and this seems to enhance flowering. It is wise to surround the developing foliage and bulbs with protective cover in very severe weather.

Propagate by separating bulb offsets, which are freely produced, soon after or as the foliage dies down. The fleshy seeds are only occasionally produced in Britain, but sown immediately and protected during the winter germinate readily. A wait of four or five years is to be expected before flowers are produced.

Nerine bowdenii 'Fenwick's Variety'

Nerine bowdenii 'Fenwick's Variety' (Amaryllidaceae) (7A–10B)

Between early and late autumn, established clumps of *Nerine bowdenii* produce a succession of somewhat succulent flowering stems, each bearing a terminal spray of six or seven rose-pink (occasionally white), lilylike flowers with narrow segments that are reflexed at the tips and have wavy edges. Strap-shaped leaves are produced as the flowers fade, remaining until early to midsummer, when they die back, leaving the upper parts of the bulbs exposed to the warmth of the sun.

Native to the Drakensberg area of Natal and to the southwest Cape, *N. bowdenii* occurs in similar grassy or scrub-covered habitats to *Amaryllis belladonna*. In cultivation a position that suits the Cape Belladonna is ideal for *N. bowdenii*, but it will also perform well in more open sites.

Even in the severest British winters I have never lost bulbs through cold, even though they were partially above the soil surface and unprotected, but those living in cold and wet areas might need to provide some protection, just in case.

The increase by offset bulbs is almost too great on occasion. Young side bulbs are readily detached when the bulbs are dormant and may be grown on in pots or planted in a sunny site. Congested clumps may need to be divided if flowering declines but, with only an occasional feed of a balanced general or potash-rich fertilizer, will often continue to flourish for many years. In most seasons *N. bowdenii* will also set seed, clusters of "green peas" that, sown fresh, will germinate rapidly.

In my view the finest selection to date is the vigorous and elegant 'Fenwick's Variety' (incorrectly renamed 'Mark Fenwick'), with flowers over 3in (7.5cm) in length, borne on stems that are often well over 2ft (60cm) tall. It is as prolific in bulb and flower production as other variants and a superb cut flower.

WINTER

In my garden *Eranthis hyemalis*, the Winter Aconite, spills drifts of gold beneath a yew hedge, where very little else will grow, often coinciding with the numerous snowdrops, both species and hybrids, that bloom in rpofusion from midwinter to early spring ('April Fool' occasionally sneaking over into midspring to justify its name).

Equally valuable are two clones of *Iris unguicularis*, 'Walter Butt' and 'Mary Barnard', to me both greatly preferable to other named forms (particularly 'Variegata', a dissolute plant, almost certainly virused, fit only for the bonfire).

DWARF FLOWERING BULBS

Eranthis hyemalis (Ranunculaceae) (4A–9A)

The Winter Aconite, *Eranthis hyemalis*, may be relied upon to expand its bright, glossy yellow, cup-shaped blooms by mid- to late winter and some years, in my garden, admittedly at the foot of a sheltering yew hedge, is showing color by Christmas. Tucked in among the rooty base of the hedge, it seeds around, appearing perfectly happy where very little else will grow. By midspring the seed is shed and the leaves die back to the knobbly little tubers, which then remain dormant until the following winter. Each tuber may produce several shoots 3 to 5in (8–12cm) high with a single flower, ½in (1–2cm) across, nestling in a tuft of leaflike dissected bracts, giving a "Jack-in-the-Green" effect above the palmately divided basal foliage.

Eranthis hyemalis is a woodland plant in Europe, but in cultivation thrives in sun or shade. In alkaline clays it will often naturalize freely under deciduous trees and in grass, but in acidic conditions is less effective. In the very acidic soil of my Wisley garden it was never particularly vigorous. Propagation by division is best carried out soon after flowering, but established colonies should normally be left undisturbed and only replanted if they are diminishing.

The fine hybrid between *E. hyemalis* (4A–9A) and the closely related (if not conspecific) *E. cilicicus* (4A–9A) is also an easy plant to accomodate. Named *E. x tubergenii*, after the raisers, the famous Dutch bulb

Eranthis hyemalis

bulb firm Van Tubergen, it thrives in the open and in semi-shade and, in my experience, is perfectly at home in acidic or alkaline soils. The very vigorous, easily grown clone 'Guinea Gold' produces gorgeous bunches of glistening gold cups about 1in (2–3cm) wide, set in ruffs of bronze-purple, in late winter and early spring. It is apparently sterile, but Sir Frederick Stern recorded that in his famous limestone garden, Highdown, by the southeast coast of Britain, seedlings of the hybrid occurred, appearing virtually indistinguishable from the parent plants, and he stated that this had also occurred in Holland. This may account for disputes among some gardeners as to whose stock is the "true" 'Guinea

Gold.' However, all variants are lovely, a joyous prelude to the multitude of spring bulbs to come.

Galanthus 'S. Arnott' (Amaryllidaceae) (3A–9B)

I have particular difficulties in selecting snowdrops from the plethora now available, but there is little doubt that, for general garden purposes, 'S. Arnott' is the finest all-rounder. It is a remarkably vigorous hybrid, with large flowers of great substance and a strong, honey scent. The outer perianth segments are over 1in (2–3cm) long and beautifully formed and rounded, the inner segments decorated around the notch with an inverted dark green, V-shaped mark.

Among other tributes, it has received a Royal Horticultural Society Award of Garden Merit, only given to plants of outstanding garden value.

The very fine 'John Gray' (3A–9B), which increases well in my garden, is usually the first of the hybrids to appear with me and is occasionally out by Christmas. It is particularly noteworthy for the most attractive X-shaped marking, a mix of dark and brighter green, suffusing the outer surface of much of the inner segments. The flowers are borne on long pedicels, and always remind me of the way in which *Dierama* blooms are displayed, although on a much reduced scale.

Some regard double snowdrops as inelegant and lumpy, but several have beautifully formed rosettes and the additional merit of lasting long in flower (they rarely waste energy producing seed). One of the best is 'Hill Poe' (3A–9B), a rapidly increasing, late-season clone with noticeably glaucous foliage and neat double blooms, which have five or six broad outer perianth segments, while the inner segments of the rosettes are strongly marked dark green.

My favorite among the many variations of the Common Snowdrop, *G. nivalis* (3A–9B), is the very beautiful 'Lutescens' (possibly correctly known as 'Sandersii' but also occasionally grown as 'Flavescens' or 'Howick Yellow'), which differs in having yellow rather than green markings on the inner segments, complemented by yellow ovaries. It is often said to be difficult to establish and maintain, but one stock of six bulbs planted in peat banks in my Wisley garden increased rapidly to several hundred, despite frequent "losses" to fellow snowdrop enthusiasts.

At one time considered a subspecies of *G. nivalis*, the winter-flowering *G. reginae-olgae* (4A–9B) differs particularly in its precocious flowering, often blooming in early autumn, and also by the dark green leaves, silver-lined in the center and with the edges slightly turned back. The foliage, when mature, is notably recurved and can be almost flat on the ground. The species is, however, very variable in flowering time, from early autumn to early spring. The spring-flowering variants having been separated as subsp. *vernalis*.

After the Common Snowdrop, the most frequently grown species is *G. elwesii* (4A–9B) (almost certainly encompassing plants grown as *G. caucasicus*), in the wild widely distributed from Bulgaria and northeastern Greece and the adjacent islands to western Turkey. It has wide, glaucous leaves folded one within another (supervolute), and usually large flowers, with the inner segments having both apical and basal markings, sometimes joined to form a solid patch of green. However, this handsome and prolific snowdrop is very variable in

Galanthus 'S. Arnott'

the wild and in cultivation. Its various clones give a season from early winter to early spring.

Many other selected clones and several species, including *G. ikariae* (5A–9B) and *G. plicatus* (4A–9B), are excellent garden plants for the early part of the year, and most are of easy culture, remaining happy for years on a well-drained, fertile, and preferably humus-rich soil in open or deciduous woodland conditions with plenty of winter light. They often seed around, providing the hybrid offspring from which most named clones are derived.

Measures may need to be taken to control the two species of narcissus flies whose grubs turn the insides of the bulbs into a smelly mess. Another enemy is the dreaded snowdrop disease (*Botrytis galanthina*). This can cause serious losses if not spotted and controlled quickly. All new acquisitions to my collection, however reliable the source, are subjected to immediate fungicide dusting and if the wilting leaves or gray mold on the foliage that signifies an attack of *Botrytis* are seen, the clump is dug up, any damaged foliage burnt, fungicide applied and the bulbs isolated from other snowdrops. In my experience, *G. nivalis* suffers from the disease less than other snowdrops.

"Lifting in the green" is often recommended as appropriate when transplanting. However, it is better to avoid lifting bulbs when in flower (although I frequently do to give away!) because there is an inevitable loss in bulb weight when the plants are in full leaf, the transplanted bulbs seldom achieving their flowering potential in the first season. Although most snowdrops are very equable plants, it is better to lift once the foliage has yellowed completely and before late summer, when new roots often develop. In all cases replant the bulbs as soon as possible, desiccation often leading to losses.

Iris unguicularis (I. stylosa) **(Iridaceae) (6B–9B)**
Extolled for the beauty of its winter-produced blooms, the Algerian Iris (widespread also in the eastern Mediterranean countries) may flower right through the winter, from late autumn to early spring, and is justly regarded as indispensable at this season.

In nature it occurs in dry rocky sites at relatively low altitudes, but in spite of its origins is very hardy and, given a sharply drained, sunny position at the base of a wall, will flower freely if the slender branching rhizomes have had a summer baking. In the southeastern states it also does well in light to medium shade and a moisture-retentive, organic soil. Growth and flowering potential are also encouraged by occasional dressings of bonemeal and a high-potash fertilizer, as well as the

removal of the older foliage as it browns so that the rhizomes are exposed to summer sun. The narrow, evergreen leaves become leathery when senescent and need to be cut out individually.

The long-tubed flowers are usually 2 to 3in (5–8cm) across, the perianth tube acting as a false flower stem and pushing the flower 6in (15cm) or more above the rhizomes. The beautifully scented blooms may vary in color from lavender to deep purple (and occasionally white), attractively veined with a central yellow band along the falls, and are produced in long succession through the winter. They also make fine, if fairly short-lived, cut flowers and as the buds reach full height should be slowly and gently pulled, not cut, so that the short stem is detached as well. At the top of my league table of named clones are the very large-flowered, richly fragrant, and free-flowering 'Walter Butt,' in silvered lavender, closely followed by 'Mary Barnard,' with smaller blooms of deep violet-purple.

Propagation is usually by rhizome division, either soon after flowering or in early autumn. The divided pieces must be kept well watered until thoroughly reestablished. Seed, produced in capsules deep down in the leaf tufts, is formed in some years and may produce worthwhile variants if you grow several different clones close to one another.

Iris unguicularis

ALPINES

Any list of my most memorable plant-collecting experiences would have to include the thrill of discovering a roadside colony of *Lewisia tweedyi*, now uncommon in the wild, sporting their peach-pink blooms in granite shale in the mountains of southern British Columbia. Indeed, so excited was I that, most unprofessionally, I forgot to record very much about the surrounding vegetation. Alpines play a large part in my plans for future botanical forays, too, since I have yet to see the rich red summer haze of *Dianthus alpinus* in bloom on the mountain slopes of Austria or Italy, even though the habitat is within easy reach of home.

Alpines are the jewels of the garden – often small, beautifully colored, and exquisitely detailed. Whether they are grown in a formal raised bed, a sink or a trough, a dry-stone wall, a rock or scree garden, a peat bed, or a pot in an alpine house or frame, depends partly on taste, but also on the plants' requirements. Whatever site you choose for them, try to bring them near to eye-level so that their delights can be fully savored, and remember that plantings in containers or raised beds facilitate sharp drainage and make it possible to accommodate special soils.

In general, alpines have a reputation for being difficult, and some are, but I have found by careful experiment that many will adapt to a wide range of sites. The dwarf shrub *Euryops acraeus*, for example, known in the wild only at 9,800ft (300m) in the Drakensburg Mountains of southern Africa, has done well for me on my Sussex peat bank.

SPRING

My selection from among the spring-flowering *Dodecatheon* is *D. hendersonii*, but given more space I would also have listed *D. meadia*, grown in Britain since the eighteenth century. Another genus with excellent spring-flowering alpines is the gentians: I once climbed Mount Olympus and saw, high on the home of the Greek gods, superb mats of *Gentiana verna* spattering the turf. Dwarf shrubs may also be suitable for the alpine garden; one of the finest introduced in the last fifty years is *Euryops acraeus*, which, unusually, was grown in gardens before being described botanically.

FLOWERS

Anchusa cespitosa (Boraginaceae) (5B–7B*)

The mountains of Crete are home to many beautiful alpine plants worthy of cultivation, none more so than the exquisite *Anchusa cespitosa* (often misspelt *caespitosa*), an endemic species known to occur wild only in the White Mountains (Lefka Ori) at an altitude of 4,000 to 7,250ft (1,200–2,200m).

An account of his plant-collecting exploits in Crete by the botanist Dr Peter Davis, published in 1937, provided the stimulus for me to grow this superb alpine and to see it in its natural habitat. He had described *A. cespitosa* growing on Agion Pneuma, the Holy Ghost Mountain, running down cracks, flowing over screes and, even in bare earth, lying "like a sapphire carpet." Some twenty years after first reading his account, I found that plants in the wild fully bore out his evocative word picture. The rosettes of linear, bristly, dark evergreen leaves, 2in (5cm) or so long, form dense mats and congested hummocks, beset during mid- and late spring with large clusters of almost stemless, brilliant blue flowers, which are star-shaped with white centers. There is sometimes a further display later in the year. At one time *A. cespitosa* was confused with the Turkish *A. leptophylla* subsp. *incana* (3B–8A) (also known as *A. angustissima*), a delightful and easily grown alpine garden plant, which also has striking, dark blue flowers, borne in spikes 12in (30cm) or so long.

Anchusa cespitosa is much more tractable in cultivation than some accounts allow. In the alpine garden it may be used as a crevice plant or grown in open sites in free-draining near-scree conditions. It is also an excellent pot plant for the alpine house or cold greenhouse if given a well-drained, fairly rich potting mix and a deep pot that allows a free root run. In a trough or tufa it forms tight, neat rosettes that mirror its growth habit in the wild.

Seed rarely seems to be produced in cultivation, but *A. cespitosa* is readily incubated from rosette cuttings, taken usually in late spring or early summer.

Anemone trullifolia (Ranunculaceae) (4A–7B*)

In 1981 a Sino-British Himalayan expedition visited Yunnan and, from the Cangshan Mountains near Dali, brought back one of the most delightful wind flowers yet available to gardeners. My first sight of *Anemone trullifolia* was sizeable clumps awash with blue or white buttercup-shaped blooms in spring, with the display still continuing in midsummer. Although this attractive plant has received scant attention until the last ten years, now it is readily available because it may be increased quickly from seed and presents few difficulties in cultivation when grown in a leafy, neutral to acidic soil in open conditions. These conditions mirror those found in the high, yak-grazed pastures in which I saw it in Yunnan. Alas, it was not then in flower.

The stout, almost woody, rootstock bears basal clusters of silky leaves, broadly obovate to oblong-elliptic, up to 2½in (6cm) long and three-lobed at the apex, with each lobe sometimes toothed as well. The flowering scapes are up to 8in (20cm) or more tall, each bearing up to three (occasionally more) blooms about ½in (1–2cm) across. In cultivation the foliage is often much larger, but this change is matched by the profusion of flowering stems produced over a period of two to three months from midspring to early summer.

Anemone trullifolia occurs wild in the eastern Himalaya from Nepal to Bhutan as well as in southern Tibet and western China at altitudes of 11,500 to nearly 16,400ft (3,500–5,000m), and is hardy in Europe. In Sikkim and Bhutan it is recorded as having golden-yellow blooms, which are sometimes purplish on the reverse. *A. trullifolia* is far easier to grow and an excellent substitute for its close relative, the much-vaunted *A. obtusiloba* (5A–7B*), the so-called "blue buttercup," which also produces variants with white and yellow flowers.

Dodecatheon hendersonii (Primulaceae) (4A–9B*)

The attractive pendent flowers of the shooting stars, with their swept-back petals and projecting styles and stamens that have given rise to their common name, have always fascinated me. Almost all of these primula-relatives come from North America, with the greatest concentration of species in California and the adjacent states. Of these, *Dodecatheon hendersonii* is a common and somewhat variable plant occurring from central California northward to Vancouver Island, from near sea level to about 3,300ft (1,000m) and, with related taxa, occasionally at higher altitudes in a spread southward that reaches just into Mexico. I have seen it in California in sparse grassland, where the flowers, carried on stems that are 8 to 12in (20–30cm) high, stand out clearly with their crimson-pink petals and yellow, white, and black zoning at the mouth.

For the most part, the species take to cultivation admirably. All are deciduous perennials with a short, fleshy rootstock or caudex and a basal leaf rosette, which appears rapidly in spring, before the flowers. As summer progresses, seed capsules form and the foliage dies down. During the growing period new plants develop from the fleshy roots, eventually forming large clumps. In the case of *D. hendersonii* and a few other species, fleshy "bulblets" or "rice grains" are also pro-

Dodecatheon hendersonii

duced in quantity at the base of the leaf rosette. They provide a pain-free method of propagation and normally reach flowering size in their third year. The shooting stars are also easily raised from seed.

Alpine growers often cultivate *D. hendersonii* as a pot plant or in a bulb frame, where a period of summer rest can be provided, but in my Sussex garden it has proved amenable out of doors annually producing 3 to 6 flowered umbels in early to midspring in well-drained soil on a raised bed. It prefers an open position and can produce inflorescences with up to twelve flowers each.

Lewisia tweedyi (Portulacaceae) (5A–8A*)

Most growers of alpines would ascribe star status to *Lewisia tweedyi*, much cherished as a show plant and with a reputation, not fully deserved, for being "difficult" to grow. This species has a very restricted natural distribution in Washington State and southern British Columbia in the Cascade, Wenatchee, and Walathian mountain ranges at an altitude of 2,000 to 6,500ft (600–2,000m). Sadly, it is now uncommon in the wild. Where I have been fortunate enough to see it in Canada, plants were growing in the unstable granite detritus it seems to prefer and flowering profusely in light shade and also in more open situations.

L. tweedyi has long, fleshy, deep-penetrating roots emanating from a tough, swollen rootstock or caudex, which is surmounted by a rosette of fleshy, obovate, often purple-tinged, evergreen leaves. In cultivation the sumptuous peachy-pink flowers, each 2 to 2¾in (5–7cm) across, with eight or nine (sometimes more) petals, often open in mid- to late spring, but in the wild plants may still be in bloom in midsummer at the higher altitudes of the range. Well-grown plants may produce several flowering scapes, each with three or four (occasionally up to eight) blooms, forming an exotic dome of color 4 to 6in (10–15cm) high. Color variations, including clear pinks, ivory, and white, are known both in the wild and in cultivation.

Although *L. tweedyi* is hardy to −30°F (−34.5°C), excess moisture around the crown and collar in winter leads to rotting of the rootstock. In North America it is most successfully grown in a pot or trough or in a scree bed, and protected from excessive winter moisture. It thrives in a sharply drained, neutral to slightly acidic, reasonably rich potting mix, with a watering regime providing ample moisture in spring and minimal amounts in winter. Outdoors, it is best planted on its side near the top of a dry wall, so that roots can plunge deeply while the collars of the rosettes are protected from excess rain by an overhang. The evergreen *L.*

Lewisia tweedyi

Ramonda myconi

cotyledon (5B–9A*) is more tractable, and its numerous selections and hybrids, in a wide color range, are readily grown as pot or trough plants.

Fresh seed, sown in early or midautumn and subjected to a period of cold, provides a ready means of increasing *Lewisia* species. Rosette cuttings, taken from the side crowns that form around the main crown after flowering, root easily in a sandy potting mix, and their removal may improve air circulation around the main crown, reducing the risk of crown rot.

Ramonda myconi (Gesneriaceae) (6B–7B*)

Ramonda myconi, sometimes still listed as *R. pyrenaica*, is one of the most tractable of alpines, as well as the most beautiful. It was recorded by Parkinson in the seventeenth century and has remained a favorite of gardeners ever since. It has a restricted natural distribution in the French Pyrenees and the adjacent mountains of northeast Spain, where it particularly favors shady crevices in moist limestone rocks. I have seen it filling, like so many purple starfish, every available crevice in the almost vertical, wet rock walls above a fast-flowing river near Cap de Long. *R. myconi* is also found in light woodland in damp places.

In cultivation it prefers shaded rock crevices with ample moisture at the roots. *R. myconi* is, however, very tolerant, exhibiting remarkable resistance to drought, and can readily be grown as a pot plant, in a shaded position in the alpine garden or on a peat bank. The rock-hugging rosettes, 6in (15cm) or more across, are composed of dark green, crinkled, and corrugated leaves, hairy all over. In late spring and early summer the deep violet to lavender-purple blooms, set off by the bright yellow cone of anthers in the center, appear in sprays of two to six flowers on stems 4 to 6in (10–15cm) high. The best selections have broad, overlapping petals in deep violet or mauve, forming rounded, flattish blooms about 1in (2–3cm) across.

The seed of *Ramonda* species is very fine and dust-like and is best surface-sown (not covered) on a peat-based seed potting mix in small pots or pans in early autumn and given a period of cold before being brought into gentle heat, about 45°F (7°C), in midwinter. All species can be raised from leaf cuttings taken in early to midsummer. Firm, undamaged leaves should be selected and pulled with the base of the petiole that clasps the central stem still intact. This method and division of clumps of rosettes in early spring are ideal for increasing selected clones of high quality.

Soldanella alpina (Primulaceae) (4B–8A*)

A plant of rocky areas and wet pastures that is widespread in mountain regions of Europe, *Soldanella alpina* is one of the most beautiful of alpine plants, often found blooming in company with *Crocus vernus* as the snows melt. Its pendent, fringed, violet bells hang in clusters of three or four on stems 3 to 4in (8–10cm) high that stand above the neat, rosetted carpets of rounded, dark evergreen leaves. Cultivation is not difficult, given slight shade and moist but well-drained soil, but its flower buds may fall prey to slugs if unprotected. I have grown it as a trough plant, positioned by a rock for partial shade, and on a peat bank, where it grew well although flowering was sparse. The flowers usually appear in spring in cultivation, as do those of the equally fine but taller *S. montana* (4B–8A*). Both may be divided into clumps after flowering and, so long as they do not dry out in summer, will usually transplant satisfactorily. The very fine seed loses viability quickly and should be sown soon after it is ripe.

OTHER PLANTS

Erinacea anthyllis (Leguminosae) (6B–9A*)
This hummock-forming, spiny shrub is found on limestone soils above the tree line in the mountain ranges of Spain. In cultivation it is seldom more than 12in (30cm) across and rather less high, the silver-green spines and distinctive habit being attractive all year. In late spring or early summer it is covered with lavender-blue peaflowers about 1in (2–3cm) long. It is quite hardy in a sunny, well-drained site, and is suitable for containers.

Gentiana verna (Gentianaceae) (6B–9A*)
The Spring Gentian is a native of the mountains of Europe, flowering soon after the snows melt, its glorious deep blue stars standing about 3in (8cm) high, sparkling in the grazed turf or scree like sapphires.

It is easily managed in the open alpine garden in well-drained but humus-rich soil, flowering freely in late spring or early summer. It will also thrive and flower well in a trough if provided with a deep root run.

Oxalis purpurea 'Ken Aslet' (Oxalidaceae) (8B–9B*)
The genus *Oxalis* has a dubious reputation, as a number of species, attractive at first sight, have on further acquaintance proved to be pernicious weeds. This stigma cannot be applied to *O. purpurea* or its selected clones, all of which are delightful, noninvasive, tuberous alpine-house plants, not totally hardy. Widespread in Cape Province, South Africa, it flowers there between midspring and early autumn and in the northern hemisphere during early and midautumn. The clone 'Ken Aslet,' named after the great plantsman who was alpine garden Superintendent when I first went to Wisley and grew this plant there as *O. speciosa*, makes a pleasant color combination, the cup-shaped, lemon-yellow flowers, about 1½in (3–5cm) across, being borne freely just above the gray mound of softly hairy foliage, about 2¾in (7cm) high. It requires protection in severe winters for its tubers to survive. Grown as a pot plant in a standard well-drained potting mix, it blooms abundantly if allowed to become almost pot bound.

FLOWERS AND ORNAMENTAL FOLIAGE

Euryops acraeus (Compositae) (7B 9B*)
Undoubtedly one of the outstanding dwarf shrubs suitable for the alpine garden introduced in the last fifty years, *Euryops acraeus* is among the relatively few plants that, recently at least, have been grown in gardens before being described botanically.

It rapidly became one of the "standard" alpines after being exhibited at Chelsea Flower Show in 1952, but was initially confused with *E. evansii* (7B–9B*), a much taller, more open-growing species that resembles it in leaf and which occurs in the Drakensberg Mountains on the border of Lesotho (Basutoland) and Natal. It is from this region that the original material of *E.acraeus* is believed to have been obtained. It was not described as a new species until 1961, eight years after fresh material was collected from the Drakensberg range at 9,800ft (3,000m). It is still apparently known only from two sites in the range, where it occurs in the alpine belt among *Helichrysum* and *Erica* species. The confusion between the two species (in gardens at least) was not unraveled until 1970, after material was sent to me at Wisley for investigation.

Euryops acraeus

It forms a neatly rounded, compactly branched shrub, usually under 18in (45cm) high and less than 2ft (60cm) across. The silvered, linear leaves, conspicuously veined, are not much more than 1in (2–3cm) long. They contrast beautifully with the rich yellow daisy flowers, each about 1in (3cm) across, which are borne in abundance in late spring and often continue into early summer. In an open, sunny position on the alpine garden or raised bed *E. acraeus* has proved perfectly hardy in most parts of Britain. It has also performed well for me when grown experimentally on a peat bank.

Propagation from the short basal runners, produced freely around the main stem, or from half-ripe cuttings of the young shoots, presents no problem. Viable seed is also sometimes produced and is best sown in autumn or early spring.

Jeffersonia dubia (Berberidaceae) (5A–8A)

I have a particular affection for the herbaceous members of the *Berberis* family, typified by the well-known *Epimedium* species and hybrids. Almost all are attractive woodland plants with delicate, unusual leaf forms and relatively fleeting blooms. *Jeffersonia dubia* (sometimes relegated to the genus *Plagiorhegma*) was discovered by the Russian botanist Maximowicz in the Amur region of Manchuria in 1855, and possesses in full measure the almost ethereal beauty characteristic of these plants. The genus itself was named in honor of Thomas Jefferson – the noted and revered US President (1801–1809), who was also a patron of botany.

In early spring mounds of the delicate flowers, each about 1in (2–3cm) across and borne on stems 5 to 6in (12–15cm) high, unfold from rounded buds to reveal the five to eight cool lavender or lavender-purple petals that mimic wood anemones in their form. The foliage soon pushes through the falling petals, unfolding to show the very attractive metallic purple, rounded, kidney-shaped leaf blades, which slowly change to green as the season advances. Even the curiously lidded seed pods are, to me, attractive.

Jeffersonia dubia is quite hardy and not difficult to grow in any leaf-rich soil, thriving in acidic and alkaline conditions, provided there is light shade and shelter from winds to protect the delicate petals. It is best planted in autumn.

Propagation from seed, preferably sown in autumn and subjected to winter cold, provides the most reliable means of increase. The seedlings usually will not flower until they are three or more years old, but it is worth growing on as many youngsters as possible to pick out

those with the finest flower and foliage color. I have found no difficulty in increasing *J. dubia* by dividing plants only a few years old in late winter, before new growth appears, but with old clumps, considerable aftercare may be needed.

Related plants Only one other species in the genus is known to exist: the white-flowered *J. diphylla* (5A–8A), the Twinleaf or Rheumatism Root, a woodlander found from Ontario as far south as Tennessee; it is as easy to grow as *J. dubia* and flowers in late spring. After *J. dubia*, however, my second choice of herbaceous berberis would be not this but *Ranzania japonica* (5A–8A), a rhizomatous perennial from mountain woodlands in Japan, which in mid- and late spring bears clusters of pendent, lavender-purple, six-petaled flowers of open-cup shape. It is now rare in cultivation but should be relatively easy to grow if obtainable.

Pulsatilla vulgaris (Ranunculaceae) (5A–9A)

It was probably the herbalist John Gerard who gave *P. vulgaris* its common names. In his *Herball* of 1597 he says: "They flower for the most part about Easter, which has moved me to name it Pasque flower, or Easter flower; and often again they flower in September." Another possible explanation is that a green dye from the roots was used to stain eggs at Easter.

The beautiful, slightly nodding flowers of open-bell shape, each 3in (8cm) or more across and borne on stems about 6in (15cm) long, appear in early and mid-spring. In the wild they are deepest purple to palest lavender; in cultivation there are variants in red, pink, and white, all with central tufts of yellow anthers. Secondary, if less abundant, flowering may occur also in late summer or early autumn, and further benefits are long-lasting, silvery seed heads and filigree-like foliage. The Struwwelpeterlike heads of long-styled feathery seeds and nectar-secreting structures of the flowers characteristic of all species of *Pulsatilla* distinguish this genus from the closely related *Anemone*.

Pulsatilla vulgaris occurs on open chalk downs or limestone pastures in many parts of central Europe. Although very tolerant in its soil requirements, growing equally well in acidic and alkaline soils in sunny positions, its diet should be relatively spartan.

Seed sown fresh in late summer or early autumn germinates readily, and some seed selections provide relatively uniform plants. As Pasque Flowers do not take kindly to division, propagation from root cuttings is the only sure way of maintaining a particular clone. In this technique, root sections at least 1 to 1½in (3–4cm) long and ⅒in (3mm) or more in diameter are

Pulsatilla vulgaris

taken in midsummer and inserted upright (and right way up!) in pots of sandy potting mix.

Related plants Equally attractive and easy to grow are *Pulsatilla halleri* (5A–9A) and its subspecies *grandis*, with blooms from violet-purple to lavender and with less divided leaves. The taller *P. alpina* (5A–7B*), white with a blue-purple flush, and its yellow subspecies *apiifolia*, which prefers acidic soils in the wild but is less fussy in a garden, are beautiful alpine meadow plants.

OTHER PLANTS

Euphorbia myrsinites (Euphorbiaceae) (6A–8B)
Widespread from the Balearic Islands eastward to Turkey and on to Turkestan, this is one of the easiest and most ornamental perennial spurges for the garden. The radiating stems, 8 to 12in (20–30cm) long, are clothed with spirals of blue-gray, fleshy leaves that provide year-round interest and beauty. In early to midspring, sometimes earlier, the neat terminal flower clusters are bright greenish-yellow for several weeks. It is easily propagated from seed or basal cuttings.

Ranunculus ficaria 'Cupreus' (Ranunculaceae) (4A–8A)
Most appealing to me of the many beautiful variants of the lesser celandine that flower in early spring and thrive almost anywhere are 'Cupreus' (or 'Aurantiacus') with rosettes of bronzed leaves and single copper orange flowers; and 'Collarette,' which makes a tight ground-hugging dome, with small double, anemone-centered blooms and leaves with a dark blotch at the center.

Saxifraga grisebachii 'Wisley' (Saxifragaceae) (5B–8B*)
The species belongs to the Engleria subsection of the genus. 'Wisley' was raised at The RHS's garden there, seed coming from around Mount Tsukala, Albania. The silver-encrusted leaves form symmetrical rosettes, from which, in early spring, brilliant crimson flower-spikes emerge. Although the plant is hardy, free-draining potting mix is vital, and it is best grown as an alpine house plant or in tufa on a raised bed.

Saxifraga 'Tumbling Waters' (Saxifragaceae) (6B–8B*)
The monocarpic Pyrenean *Saxifraga longifolia* is the dominant parent of 'Tumbling Waters.' A natural hybrid found wild in 1913, it produces side rosettes used for propagation. In late spring or early summer plumes of white flowers, 2ft (60cm) long, arch out from the large, silvery rosettes. It is best as a crevice plant.

SUMMER

For me any summer selection has to include at least one bellflower. I finally settled upon *Campanula chamissonis*, which needs none of the attention demanded by its cousin *C. zoyzii*, so pampered and cooed over by the alpine cognoscenti.

Among the blue-flowered *Cyananthus*, *C. lobatus* is deservedly popular. Untested as yet is the recently introduced *C. spathulatus*, with yellow flowers, found in 1990 on a China expedition of which I was a member.

Other choices include, for flowers, *Dianthus alpinus*, *Phlox* 'Chattahoochee,' and *Viola* 'Huntercombe Purple;' and, for flowers with ornamental foliage, *Convolvulus althaeoides* and *Verbascum* 'Letitia.'

FLOWERS

Campanula chamissonis (**Campanulaceae**) (**4B–8A***)

There are many fine alpine garden plants among the 300 or so species and many hybrids in this marvelous genus, including some of the most reliable alpines, *Campanula cochleariifolia* (*C. pusilla*), and *C. pulla*, "the imperial glory of the alpine section" of Campanulas. *C. chamissonis*, which is better known and often still listed as *C. pilosa*, I rate very highly. It is one of the most beautiful of alpines and deserves much wider cultivation, as it is by no means difficult to grow.

A sound perennial, *C. chamissonis* runs gently to form neat mats of rosetted, virtually evergreen, spoon-shaped or lanceolate, glossy leaves, ½ to 1½in (2–4cm) long, from which the upright bellflowers appear in early and midsummer. In the form known as 'Superba,' also sold as var. *dasyantha*, the sky-blue flowers are funnel-shaped, 1 to 1½in (3–4cm) long, white-haired on the edges and within the bell, and borne singly in the leaf axils on stems that elongate to 4in (10cm).

The species is widespread, occurring wild in the mountains of northern Japan, the Aleutian Islands, parts of Siberia, and Alaska. It grows in gravelly or sandy soils or in scree conditions, requiring similarly well-drained soils in cultivation.

Campanula chamissonis produces seed freely, which germinates well if sown fresh, but the offspring, variable in flower shape as well as color, may range from pale to deep blue, with some white-flowered plants occasionally. It is better to propagate variants like 'Superba' (which may or may not be a single clone) by removing short runners and treating them as cuttings.

It is difficult to leave this marvelous genus without returning to the virtues of *C. cochleariifolia*. Hardy, free-flowering, long-lived, easily propagated from division and seed, and providing a massed display of its blue, sometimes white, "fairy thimbles" in the summer in the garden, this is undoubtedly one of the most reliable of alpines.

Cyananthus lobatus (**Campanulaceae**) (**5A–8B***)

One of the great pleasures for me of visiting gardens and nurseries in Scotland in summer and early autumn is the sight of *Cyananthus* species growing happily in moist conditions similar to those of their mountain homes in the Himalaya and western China. I have been fortunate enough to have seen a number of species growing wild in northwest Yunnan toward the end of their flowering period. In a range of habitats from river banks to much drier high moorland I came across a very fine form of *Cyananthus lobatus*, the deep blue chalices, 1½ to 2in (4–5cm) across, peering through the branches of *Rhododendron fastigiatum*, probably the only place safe from grazing yaks.

Cyananthus lobatus is the most frequently seen species in gardens, the periwinklelike flowers varying from deep blue or purple to pale lavender and white. Given cool, peaty soils and dappled shade, plants develop into robust clumps, with radiating flowering shoots. They will also thrive in open sunny sites, provided the soil or potting mix is moisture retentive.

All *Cyananthus* may be readily propagated from seed, which is often produced in abundance, and is best sown immediately it is ripe or in early spring. The seed is tiny and should be covered only very lightly. Cuttings of short shoots taken in spring or in late summer root well and allow color variants to be maintained.

Dianthus alpinus (**Caryophyllaceae**) (**4A–8A***)

One of the most beautiful and indispensable of all alpine garden plants, *Dianthus alpinus* is undervalued by many alpine enthusiasts, as it has become a garden center standard. However, it fully deserves its popularity, even within a genus that provides so many outstanding plants among its more than 300 species and in excess of 30,000 named cultivars.

It occurs wild in the eastern Alps of Austria, Slovenia and Italy, inhabiting calcareous rocks and moorland limestones above 3,300ft (1,000m), where the mountainsides are covered in summer with a crimson haze from the abundant blooms. Although not perhaps a true cushion plant, the alpine pink is more or less ground-hugging, forming relatively tight, matted hummocks of bright green, blunt, linear, evergreen leaves that are ornamental in themselves. Add to that the profusion of five-petaled, typical "pink," solitary blooms, 1 to 2in (3–5cm) across, borne on stems 2 to 4in (5–10cm) high, that appear throughout summer and sometimes earlier, sometimes later. The color range varies from rose-crimson and cerise to salmon-pink, often with central markings that are pleasantly speckled white or purple. Some pure (and no doubt a few dirty) albinos occur in natural populations.

As is so often the case, the natural habitat indicates the preferred soil conditions – calcareous, well-drained and endowed only with limited nutrients – but *D. alpinus* is very tolerant of all but heavy, poorly drained soils. I have even grown it experimentally in a peat block, and in spite of the absence of lime it remained healthy and flowered freely for several years.

It is easily propagated from seed, which is freely produced, but selected forms should be maintained from soft wood cuttings. The most brilliant of these, and possibly a hybrid, is 'Joan's Blood;' it is characterized by bronze-tinted, neatly packed leaves and glowing blood-red single flowers which have black centers and bluish-gray pollen.

Related plants To avoid the annual or biennial propagation required to maintain some cultivars in good condition, perenniality and freedom of flowering should be major considerations when choosing pinks from the multitude of fine plants available. Most pleasing are some of the laced pinks, particularly two that are delightfully scented. The vigorous, strong-growing 'Dad's Favourite' (5B–7B), probably an eighteenth-century selection, is a semidouble white, laced ruby red, with purple zoning. 'Becky Robinson' (5B–7B) has semidouble, warm pink flowers that are beautifully laced ruby red with an "eye" of the same color.

Oenothera missouriensis (**Onagraceae**) (4B–8A)

The large genus *Oenothera* contains more than 120 species that are widely distributed in North and South America, with some, like the Common Evening Primrose, *O. biennis*, established firmly, apparently as natives, in many parts of Europe. Most people's idea of an evening primrose is of a tall, somewhat gangling plant, with a sparse showing of yellow blooms that open late in the day and have little garden value. Happily, that image is not fully justified, for a number of fine species have proved to be garden plants of high quality.

One of these is *O. missouriensis* (sometimes disputedly known as *O. macrocarpa*), from the southwestern United States, where it was found not far from the city of St Louis during the early years of the last century. This sound perennial has now become a very popular

Oenothera missouriensis

alpine garden plant. When grown in full sun, where its long, decumbent, red-suffused stems, amply clothed with narrowly ovate, fresh green, silky leaves, can flow over rocks to display the huge, citron-yellow flowers from early summer until the first frosts, it is a magnificent sight. The long-tubed, cup-shaped blooms, often 4 to 5in (10–12cm) across, are borne singly in the axils of the leaves, and the long flower buds, protected by red-flecked calyces, develop slowly during the mornings to open fully soon after noon, usually fading by nightfall. In hot summers, flowers are followed by the distinctive, strongly winged capsules. Propagation is by autumn-sown seed or division after flowering. Spring cuttings may also be rooted successfully after the young shoots emerge from the woody rootstock.

Oenothera missouriensis requires no more than a well-drained soil in an open, sunny site to thrive happily for years: providing each season the very long succession of beautiful flowers that make this plant so attractive in the alpine garden, or even the front of a perennial border where my own plants currently reside.

Origanum dictamnus (Labiatae) (7B–9B)

Evocative of the world of the Ancients, the Dittany of Crete is, to my mind, the loveliest member of a genus that provides many attractive garden plants, including Common Marjoram or Oregano, *Origanum vulgare* (4B–8B).

Origanum dictamnus is a Cretan endemic, known locally as *diktamos*. The dried leaves and inflorescences are much used to make an infusion valued for its medicinal properties. It is now regarded as an endangered species, but is well established in gardens and is also cultivated in Crete. A plant of shady calcareous cliff faces, *O. dictamnus* is to be found from sea level to 6,250ft (1,900m) in the mountains and gorges of the island. I have seen the walls of gorges plastered with this and another superb Cretan endemic, the yellow-flowered *Linum arboreum*, the two species sometimes even colonizing the rock rubble at the base of cliffs.

Origanum dictamnus is a very distinctive, evergreen subshrub, some 6 to 8in (15–20cm) high, producing numerous, slightly woody stems that are densely clad with rounded leaves, about ½ to 1in (1–2.5cm) long. The stems are covered with white hairs and the leaves with white felt. Between early summer and midautumn long-lasting pendent, hoplike inflorescences appear above the gray leaves, the small, long-tubed, pink flowers peeping out between the overlapping, rose-purple bracts. The whole plant emits a warm, fragrance.

The felted leaves of the Cretan Dittany deeply resent winter wet. In Britain it is difficult to ensure the plant's well-being without the protection of an alpine house or cool greenhouse, although it has been grown successfully outside in tufa and in crevices in a sunny wall where the foliage could be protected. It readily takes to pot culture in sharply drained potting mix and can even be grown as a window plant. Seed is seldom available in cultivation, but *O. dictamnus* may be increased without difficulty from cuttings of the young shoots taken in mid- or late spring or from nonflowering shoots in summer.

Related plants In contrast to *Origanum dictamnus*, the Turkish *Origanum laevigatum* (5B–8B) (which also occurs in Cyprus and Syria) has proved to be perfectly hardy and is a first-rate alpine garden and border plant.

It forms dense stands of slender, purplish stems 12in (30cm) high, neatly clothed with narrow, gray-green leaves and with terminal, branched inflorescences bearing masses of small purplish flowers all summer. In the cultivar 'Hopleys' the flowers are deep pink and the leaves green; 'Herrenhausen' is taller, with purplish young shoots and pale lilac flowers set off by purple bracts.

'Kent Beauty' fully lives up to its name, combining the hoplike flower heads and rounded foliage of *Origanum rotundifolium* (4B–8B) with the deep purple-pink coloring of *O. scabrum* (5B–8B). Like other members of the genus, this delightful plant thrives in any well-drained, alkaline soil.

Phlox 'Chattahoochee' (Polemoniaceae) (4A–9B)

The alpine *Phlox*, particularly the numerous named clones and hybrids that derive from *P. subulata* and *P. douglasii*, are among the stalwarts of the alpine garden, flowing over rocks and down screes to provide foaming mats of color during late spring and early summer. The choice of colors is legion, individual taste dictating which are given room in the alpine garden or raised bed, where they bask in open, sunny, well-drained positions and flower regularly and profusely.

Although I admire, grow, and have grown many of these floriferous beauties, there are several named clones that have particular appeal, all preferring light shade and more humus in the soil than is either required or liked by *P. subulata* and its brethren. Chief among these is 'Chattahoochee,' a derivative of *P. divaricata* subsp. *laphamii*, which gains its name from the river valley in which it was found in northern Florida by Mrs. Norman Henry, probably in the 1940's. It has proved to be a remarkably free-flowering selection, notable for its large, rounded flowers, over 1in (2cm) across, of a bright lavender-violet, centrally marked with a contrasting crimson eye. At one time it was thought to be difficult to grow, because it was treated as a sun-lover, but once planted in a cool position in moisture-retentive soil, it flourishes, sending out from a central rootstock spreading shoots, 6in (15cm) or more in length, with linear, hairy leaves that terminate in large heads of twenty or more flowers. When grown on a peat bank or in dappled shade, it has few rivals for freedom or longevity of bloom.

Its more or less continuous production of flowering shoots from late spring to late summer makes propagation difficult, since few sterile shoots are available for cuttings. These will, however, root readily if taken early in the growing season, before flower buds develop.

Related plants Requiring similar growing conditions to 'Chattahoochee,' *Phlox adsurgens* (6A–8B*), the periwinkle phlox, from Oregon and northern California, has provided a number of fine garden cultivars. 'Wagon Wheel' (sometimes misspelt 'Waggon Wheel'), originat-

Phlox 'Chattahoochee'

ing from the famous Siskiyou Rare Plant Nursery in Oregon, probably stands supreme. Easier to grow than most forms, it is distinguished by the spokelike, narrow-petaled, salmon-pink flowers, cream on the reverse, which are borne freely in clusters of six or more at the tips of the semi-decumbent shoots.

'Bill Baker,' reputedly a selection of the variable *P. carolina* (4B–9A) from the eastern United States, is of the same easy-growing persuasion, having a more spreading habit than is usual for *P. carolina* but still achieving 12 to 15in (30–40cm) in height. Early summer is the main flowering period, it continues to display its large heads of pink, pale-eyed blooms, offset by glossy, bright green leaves and dark stems, until autumn.

Viola 'Huntercombe Purple' (Violaceae) (6A–8B)

Apart from the many lovely spring-flowering violets and their larger cousins, the winter pansies, there is a host of very attractive long-flowering perennial violas for the summer garden. Whether used at the front of the herbaceous border, in the alpine garden, or even for bedding purposes, they flower continuously and abundantly over several months, requiring little attention apart from deadheading to maintain continuity of bloom.

Many are derived from *Viola cornuta* (6A–8B*), the Horned Violet, which is to be seen coloring Pyrenean meadows in violet, blue, or white during the summer months. Some cultivars prove very vigorous, spreading by means of threadlike underground shoots to form dense mats of evergreen foliage and producing an apparently endless supply of bloom from early summer to the frosts. Others, usually those which show signs of *V. x wittrockiana*, the pansy, in their flower characters, prove less perennial and need to be propagated regularly from cuttings to maintain them in good health.

'Huntercombe Purple,' in deepest purple-violet, with a diminutive white center, belongs to the first group. I have known it for over forty years, encountering it first when I worked at Carlile's Hardy Plants, where it was always a feature in the alpine frameyard. Having grown it then and several times since in other gardens, I still rate it very highly indeed. It is easily grown, reliably perennial, readily propagated by cuttings or division, and in constant flower during most of the summer. What more could one ask?

Related plants Indispensable *Viola* cultivars include the compact 'Molly Sanderson,' which has masses of velvet-black blooms with tiny yellow eyes, 'Jackanapes,' named after the English plantswoman, Gertrude Jekyll's pet monkey and cheerfully bizarre in bright yellow and deep red-brown, and 'Irish Molly,' curiously hued in khaki, yellow, and bronze. All need regular propagation to ensure health and continuity.

Two firm perennials are 'Nellie Britten' ('Haslemere'), lavender-pink and of neat habit, and *V. cornuta* 'Minor,' which forms compact hummocks with miniature blooms of pale lilac-blue and self-seeds freely true to type.

OTHER PLANTS

Hypericum olympicum (Guttiferae) (6A–9A)

This subshrub (*Hypericum polyphyllum* of gardens), native to the Balkans and western Turkey, has been divided into several botanical forms, of which forma *minus* and forma *uniflorum* provide the best alpine garden plants, although all variations are worth growing for their abundant yellow blooms produced throughout summer, and attractive gray-green foliage. They thrive in all but poorly drained soils.

My favorites are 'Grandiflorum,' with large, golden, red-budded flowers, over 2in (5cm) across, and 'Citrinum,' with smaller, lemon-yellow blooms, both referred to as f. *uniflorum* botanically, erect in habit and 8 to 9in (20–23cm) high. Equally valuable is the pale yellow 'Sulphureum,' with prostrate stems, making it ideal for the top of a wall or for tumbling over rocks. All these named clones need to be raised from cuttings.

FLOWERS AND ORNAMENTAL FOLIAGE

Convolvulus althaeoides (Convolvulaceae) (7A–9B)

The thought of cultivating bindweeds fills most gardeners with horror, and an entry for *Convolvulus althaeoides* should, perhaps, be accompanied by a minor health warning, because there are reports that it may be invasive. Its garden value, however, is considerable, and for me it is nostalgically associated with Greece. It is a familiar plant there in spring, trailing over rocks and among the archeological ruins, displaying its beautiful pink or purple-pink flowers in abundance during mid- and late spring. In cultivation in Britain it flowers later, in June and July, and, although hardy in the milder regions (succumbing only to the severest winters), it is less happy where winters are always very cold.

In its typical form *C. althaeoides* produces long, trailing stems with alternately disposed, handsome, gray-green, lobed, and heart-shaped leaves, resembling those of the hollyhock (*Althaea* or *Alcea*) in miniature. Although naturally evergreen, in cold climates plants die back to the rootstock in winter. Clusters of one to three (occasionally up to five) open, trumpet-shaped flowers of purple-pink, occasionally with darker central zoning and each up to 2in (5cm) across, are produced in the leaf axils for much of the summer. Even more beautiful, however, is *C. althaeoides* subsp. *tenuissimus*, often given specific rank as *C. elegantissimus* (7A–9B), a name that I much prefer. The intensely silvered foliage is much more deeply and finely lobed, and the flowers are usually of a clear, silvery pink, mirroring the outstanding elegance of the leaves.

Seed is seldom produced in cultivation, but pieces of the fleshy roots, about 2in (5cm) long, may be potted up in spring. In cold areas plants should be grown on in pots for a season and planted out the following spring.
Related plants *Convolvulus sabatius* (7B–9B), often grown as *C. mauritanicus*, is slightly less hardy than *C. althaeoides*. Native to north-west Africa and Sicily, this mat-forming perennial has woody-based stems and softly hairy, small leaves which die back in winter after a long summer display of the showy, funnel-shaped flowers, ½ to 1½ in (2–4cm) across. Color variation to purple-blue and, rarely, pink is known, but none is more beautiful than the clear blue form commonly available today. The plant grows well tucked into a sunny wall or in paving where some protection from severe cold is provided. More unusually, it makes a fine hanging basket plant.

Verbascum 'Letitia' (Scrophulariaceae) (6B–10A)

In any one year very few alpine or rock garden plants are awarded a Royal Horticultural Society First Class Certificate. *Verbascum* 'Letitia' received this distinction in July 1965, remarkable only five years after it occurred as a chance seedling at Wisley.

It was spotted by the keen-eyed and erudite Ken Aslet, then Superintendent of the Wisley alpine garden, growing in the shingle of the alpine house bench adjacent to plants of the dwarf *V. dumulosum* (6B–10A) from western Turkey and the Cretan *V. spinosum* (6B–10A). It was clearly intermediate in character between them, combining the woody, intricately branched growth and small, lobed leaves of *V. spinosum* with the racemose inflorescence (not solitary as in this latter species), velvety texture, and blue-gray leaf coloring of *V. dumulosum*.

The parents are not always amenable to general garden cultivation, yet *V.* 'Letitia' (named after Ken's wife) has proved hardy in the open garden in a sunny, freely drained site and has also proved an ideal trough and raised-bed plant, as well as being a popular show plant.

A small, densely but finely branched shrub, 8 to 12in (20–30cm) in height and as much across, *V.* 'Letitia' produces its profusion of bright yellow blooms of shallow cup shape during early and midsummer, often with further flushes later in the season. The flowers, each about 1in (3cm) across, have orange anthers and are marked red-brown at the base (in the manner of *V. dumulosum*). Easily propagated from root cuttings or by heel cuttings of the young shoots, it is small wonder that within a few years of its introduction *V.* 'Letitia' had become a standard of the nursery catalogs, and is undoubtedly one of the finest alpine garden plants introduced during the last fifty years.

OTHER PLANTS

Geranium cinereum subsp. *subcaulescens* (Geraniaceae) (5A–8A)

The real quality of this plant (sometimes known as *Geranium subcaulescens*) only dawned on me when, with excitement, I saw it on Mount Olympus in northern Greece nestling among rocks at about 6,500ft (2,000m), the startling, bright magenta, saucerlike flowers, black centered and black veined, about 1in (3cm) across, standing proud of the rosettes of rounded, deeply cut, dark green, canescent leaves. A number of selected clones are cultivated, all of them untemperamental, fine garden plants, easily raised from seed or propagated by division or from cuttings.

AUTUMN

In autumn the foliage of many spring-flowering alpines remains unchanged in hues of green, gray or silver, but some alpines take on attractive hints of autumn color. Others mark the season's passage with decorative fruits – such as *Nertera granadensis*, with its orange globes, *Coprosma* 'Blue Pearls,' and *Myrtus nummularia* with its edible berrylike fruits in red or pink.

I place the gentians high on any list of autumn-flowering alpines, and my selection here is the vigorous and prolific *Gentiana sino-ornata*, whose deep blue trumpetlike blooms have a serene beauty.

Both my other autumn-flowering selections provide hotter color accents – the vivid red of *Zauschneria cana*, foremost among the shrubby Californian fuchsias, and the strong yellow of *Ranunculus bullatus*, an apparent anachronism to any one used to the buttercup-carpeted meadows of late spring and early summer.

Gentiana sino-ornata (see also p.178)

FLOWERS

Gentiana sino-ornata (Gentianaceae) (5A–9A*)

This superb autumn-flowering gentian is undoubtedly one of the finest introductions of the remarkable Scottish plant collector George Forrest (1873–1932), who brought back so many outstanding plants from his explorations in China. Unlike so many alpine plants, it has settled down admirably in cultivation, adapting to low altitudes and drier climates than the clear, moist mountain air of its native habitat. Originally discovered by Forrest in northwest Yunnan in 1904, it was not introduced until 1910, when he re-collected it at 14,000 to 15,000ft (4,250–4,500m) in the Lichiang range.

A strong perennial, *Gentiana sino-ornata* forms overwintering, tufted rosettes of narrowly lance-shaped, deep green leaves that are sharp-pointed and about 1in (3cm) long. In spring and summer, slender shoots, 4 to 5in (10–12cm) long, spread from these rosettes like starfish tentacles across the ground.

During early and midautumn (and sometimes on into late autumn) funnel-shaped flowers, each about 3in (7–8cm) long, appear singly at the ends of the shoots. They are of a vibrant and deep royal blue, banded vertically with yellow-green.

Unlike so many alpine plants, *G. sino-ornata* has settled down admirably in cultivation. It will grow very happily in full sun if the soil is fairly rich, leafy, and moist, provided it is lime-free, but in drier conditions is best sited in dappled shade if it is to thrive. Given similar, moisture retentive soil in a deep trough it may also be grown very successfully provided the root run is cool and is not allowed to dry out.

The spreading shoots will often root at the nodes, where further leaf rosettes form in the axils of the paired leaves, providing a ready means of increase. After flowering the spreading stems die away, and the overwintering rosettes may be lifted in the spring, separated, and replanted individually to form further colonies, or given away to deserving friends.

Zauschneria cana (Onagraceae) (7A–10B*)

It is unlikely that most gardeners will pander to the current botanical view that the genus *Zauschneria*, a beautiful and (horticulturally at least) distinct group of garden-worthy plants that flower in late summer and autumn, should be relegated to the obscurity of the mainly weedy genus *Epilobium*. Zauschnerias, sometimes known as Californian fuchsias, are readily distinguished by the brilliant red, fuchsialike flowers with narrow, funnel-shaped tubes about 1in (3cm) long.

Opinions differ as to the number of species in the genus *Zauschneria*, because of the extraordinary variability within populations. For garden purposes the two most distinctive are *Z. cana*, a subshrub of 12in (30cm) or more, with very narrow, almost filiform, hairy, gray leaves, and *Z. californica* (7A–10B*), sometimes merged with *Z. cana* but with rather wider leaves, particularly in the entity known as *Z. californica* subsp. *latifolia*, in which they may be up to ¾in (1.5cm) wide. All grow naturally in dry, rocky, or sandy places. In California I have seen the flowers spraying out from cliff faces, as well as plants colonizing roadside detritus. Sharply drained sites in full sun provide ideal conditions in the garden. It is somewhat surprising that these plants, which occur in the wild at relatively low altitudes, are fairly hardy in Britain, although in very severe and prolonged winters they may be killed. At Wisley *Z. cana* has grown and flowered well as a crevice plant in a dry wall for over forty years, the brilliant vermilion flowers in late summer and autumn providing a delightful contrast to the silver-gray, narrow foliage.

The flowered shoots of *Zauschneria* species are best cut back to the base in early spring, fresh growth quickly springing from the woody rootstock to reach a height of 8 to 12in (20–30cm) or more before the terminal flower-spikes appear in late summer. Seed is not readily available, but basal cuttings of young growths taken in late spring or early summer root readily.

Related plants *Zauschneria californica* is most frequently seen in its broad-leaved form, subsp. *latifolia*, distinguished by its green or gray-green leaves, which are often tomentose and sometimes glandular. Although very variable in leaf characters, all forms are well worth growing, especially the shell-pink 'Solidarity Pink,' a free-flowering clone found in a population growing by the Solidarity Mine in California. Add to this the vigorous, greener-foliaged and white-flowered 'Alba,' and the vivid orange-red 'Dublin,' and you have a trio of superb alpine garden plants for late summer.

OTHER PLANTS

Ranunculus bullatus (Ranunculaceae) (7A–9A*)

An autumn-flowering buttercup may appear to be an anachronism. However, the flowering period for *Ranunculus bullatus* is from autumn to very early spring. In many Mediterranean countries, it occurs prolifically in dry rocky areas and in olive orchards. I vividly remember seeing sheets of it in Crete one November twenty years ago. The rosettes of midgreen and noticeably corrugated (bullate) leaves emerge from the tuberous root cluster with the autumn rains. The bright yellow, glossy, and violet-scented buttercups soon follow, carried on stems 1 to 2in (3–5cm) high, although the stems later elongate in fruit. *R. bullatus*, like many Mediterranean species, needs a summer resting period and is best grown in an alpine house or bulb frame.

GENTIAN-HUNTING IN CHINA

In the autumns of 1987 and 1990 I was able to visit the Lichiang area and the Zhongdian plateau in Yunnan, southwest China. It was from the Lichiang range of mountains that in 1910 the Scottish plant collector George Forrest sent back to the West the first seed of *Gentiana sino-ornata* (see p.177).

It was therefore with excitement that I saw swathes of *G. sino-ornata* in full bloom. Knowing how well *G. sino-ornata* grows in soils that are moist but by no means wet, it was a surprise to find it nearly always growing in waterlogged, marshy grassland. A second surprise was the variation in flower color: seed-raised plants from Forrest's original stocks have produced only marginal variation in cultivation. Most of these gentians were the familiar deep, bright blue, but occasionally there were white variants with either green- or pink-flushed blooms (illustrated); others were bicolored, with alternating "panels" of very dark blue and pale blue. I collected a little seed, scarcely ripe, and should this germinate I hope it will produce plants with some of the color variations I found in China.

FRUIT

Nertera granadensis (Rubiaceae) (9B–10B)

Nertera granadensis, from South America, parts of Southeast Asia, Australia and New Zealand, has striking ornamental fruit in late summer and autumn, when the dense mats of tiny ovate leaves are almost smothered by the bright orange, globose berries, which last for several months. It thrives in moist, humus-rich soil, over which the creeping shoots spread rapidly to form low hummocks of foliage. It is not hardy, but is often grown as an alpine house or cool greenhouse pot plant. Under glass keep it cool and humid to encourage fruit set. Increase by division or from spring-sown seed.

Nertera granadensis

OTHER PLANTS

Coprosma 'Blue Pearls' (Rubiaceae) (7B–9B*)

Most *Coprosma* species are native to New Zealand; many of them are valued for their evergreen foliage and very fine fruits. This female hybrid between *C. acerosa* f. *brunnea* and *C. petriei* (both 7B–9B) forms a prostrate, evergreen shrub with stiff, spreading branches, which, in summer and autumn, carry translucent sky-blue berries about ⅓in (8mm) across. It is frost-hardy in sharply drained but moisture-retentive soils. For fruiting, grow near by a male plant of its parents, or a male hybrid, like 'Bruno,' of the same parentage.

Myrtus (Myrteola) nummularia (Myrtaceae) (9A–10B*)

This wiry-stemmed shrublet from New Zealand has tiny, evergreen leaves, bronze-tinted in autumn and winter spangled with red or pink, berrylike fruits, deriving from creamy white flowers in early summer. Cool, humus-rich, acidic conditions are preferred.

TWO OR MORE SEASONS

All the shrubby plants selected here are worthy of inclusion for their handsome, long-lasting, silver or gray foliage alone. Indeed one of my favorites, *Stachys candida*, has foliage that engagingly responds to very hot or wet weather by adopting different colorations. Altogether a very satisfactory garden plant, its year-round beauty and hardy, vigorous growth thoroughly commend it.

As well as their undoubted foliage interest, each of my selections is also brightened by flowers at midsummer, although some gardeners cut off the yellow buttons of *Tanacetum haradjanii* to preserve the silvered foliage. *Chrysanthemum hosmariense* has a longer flowering season (through spring and summer), its white, daisy flowers having a charming simplicity. Lastly, although it is fairly unassuming in flower or foliage, I would not willingly be without the *Nepeta phyllochlamys*, although quite why it has this attraction for me it is difficult to say.

FOLIAGE

Chrysanthemum hosmariense (Compositae) (7A–10A*)

The banishment of this delightful plant from the genus *Chrysanthemum* (in which it was originally placed in 1877) to *Leucanthemum* or *Pyrethropsis* on botanical grounds in no respect diminishes its horticultural quality. Its synonymy is formidable (*Chrysanthemum maresii* var. *hosmariense*, *Leucanthemum hosmariense*, and *Pyrethropsis hosmariense*), and because juggling with its generic status may well continue in the future I have opted to use the name by which it is most commonly known to gardeners.

Chrysanthemum hosmariense, which occurs wild in the Lesser Atlas Mountains in Morocco at altitudes over 3,300ft (1,000m), is a mound forming subshrub, reaching a height of 6 to 12in (15–30cm) under garden conditions. It has elegant, rich silver, tripartite leaves, with each section further divided into three linear lobes. If grown in soils lacking in nutrients, it tends to develop a tighter, more compact, almost mat-forming habit than it does in well-endowed soils. The growth produced in the latter conditions is softer and more liable to frost damage and prone to diseases than that of harder-grown specimens.

Many gray-foliaged and silver-foliaged plants have flowers that are of limited horticultural significance, but the yellow-centered, white-rayed, solitary flower heads of *Chrysanthemum hosmariense*, often over 2in (5cm) across and borne on stems 2 to 4in (5–10cm) tall, are very attractive and, particularly in hard-grown plants, are produced in abundance during the spring and summer months. In spartan conditions it has proved relatively hardy in open, sunny sites, where its silveriness is intensified.

The ease with which this plant may be propagated from softwood cuttings in early summer and its overall garden value have ensured that *C. hosmariense* has become a favorite with the horticultural trade and with gardeners.

Stachys candida (Labiatae) (7A–9B*)

An evergreen subshrub that is beautiful at all times of the year, *S. candida* is among my favorite alpine garden plants and one that I have grown continuously during the last twenty-five years or more. I first saw it (and collected seed) in Greece, where it is common in the Taygetos (Taiyetos) Mountains, growing in rocky areas and somewhat shaded cliff faces. The rounded, ovate leaves are about ½in (1–2cm) long, densely hairy and velvety gray. Turning them over reveals that they are strongly three-veined and that the light gray surface is deeply impressed and netted with cross veins.

Intriguing, too, is the way the foliage assumes different coloration according to the weather. In wet weather the basic silvered gray of the upper leaf surfaces changes to a soft, fresh green, and in very hot conditions a creamy sheen overlays the hairs that normally give the foliage its gray coloring. In midsummer the upright leafy inflorescences produce their pleasant haze of tiny, white, strongly pink-veined, deadnettle flowers, which are encased in woolly calyces.

Although often recommended as a pot plant for the alpine house, it is bone hardy. In my present garden, an

Stachys candida

eight-year-old plant on a sunny, well-drained low wall has formed a 9in (23cm) high mound of silver-gray over 2ft (60cm) across, and its cascading growth threatens to spill across a brick path. It provides a meeting place for most of the snails in Christendom – which do it no harm at all. Luckily, *S. candida* is very tolerant of pruning, which I normally carry out after flowering. A haircut, preferably not too neat, will induce fresh growth to appear rapidly and cover any bare spots that may develop as a result of cutting vigorous shoots hard back.

Seed is freely produced and germinates readily. In my garden self-sown seedlings appear every year among the crevices in the brick paths, and some have spread into leaf mold under nearby shrubs, where they grow perfectly happily. Cuttings of the young growths may be rooted in spring or after flowering without difficulty.

Tanacetum haradjanii (Compositae) (6A–9B*)

One of the best of all dwarf foliage plants, the hardy *Tanacetum (Chrysanthemum) haradjanii* was introduced by Dr Peter Davis from Turkey in 1949 and very rapidly became a popular and readily available alpine garden plant. Unfortunately it is often confused in gardens and nurseries with the similar, but quite distinct, *T. densum*, which usually has the epithet *amani* added.

An aromatic subshrub of some 8 to 10in (20–25cm), *T. haradjanii* is densely covered with a silvery white tomentum. The leaves are ovate-lanceolate in outline, 2 to 4in (5–10cm) long and dissected primarily into four to five pairs of leaflets, with each leaflet then being further subdivided twice to provide an attractive feather-like effect. Although loose corymbs of the bright yellow flower heads (which lack marginal female ray florets) are produced in midsummer, they are sometimes removed by foliage enthusiasts as they develop, so that they do not distract the eye from the silvered mound of foliage, which is the plant's major asset.

As with most silver-foliaged plants, *T. haradjanii* requires a well-drained, sunny site, and conditions akin to those of its rocky limestone home in the Amanus Mountains, its only known location. It is best grown "hard" in poor soil, when it becomes almost matlike in habit, with smaller leaves of a more intense silver. It is an ideal plant for paving, a raised bed, or a trough. Propagation is easy from soft or half-ripe cuttings.

Related plants The lovely *Tanacetum densum* (6A–9B*), occurs in limestone rocks in Anatolia, Lebanon and Syria. Dr Peter Davis, who introduced *T. haradjanii*, with which it is confused, is credited with the introduction of subspecies *amani*, which differs only in marginal botanical characters from other forms of the species. The silvery white foliage is as attractive as that of *T. haradjanii*, but the leaves are smaller, more rounded, and with more finely divided and more closely set segments. The yellow ray flowers surrounding the central disk flowers also separate it from *T. haradjanii*. Both species require similar cultural conditions and may be used for the same purposes.

OTHER PLANTS

Nepeta phyllochlamys (Labiatae) (7A–9A)

Unspectacular though it is, I rate this diminutive catmint from southwest Anatolia very highly, although I cannot quite explain its appeal. A demure, neatly spreading, evergreen shrublet with tomentose, gray-white, triangular leaves, at most ⅓in (8mm) long, it is grown mainly for its slightly waved, gray foliage, although the inflorescences of relatively large white, pink-suffused, catmintlike, blooms also feature pleasingly in midsummer.

It is suitable for trough cultivation, but is also happy on the alpine garden in sharply drained soil, particularly if the plant is positioned to allow the decumbent shoots to spread over adjacent rocks.

Tanacetum haradjanii

SHORT-LIVED PLANTS

For most gardeners the beauty and versatility of short-lived plants amply reward the challenge of growing them. Some are very labor-intensive because they have to be replanted annually or biennially. Among those treated as annuals are a number of perennials too tender to survive winters in cool temperate regions, but capable of flowering in their first season. I have also taken short-lived plants to include free-flowering perennials and shrubs whose energies are exhausted after a few years.

In a new garden as short-term fillers, or for those who content themselves with containers by choice or necessity, or as a way of filling in gaps among more permanent planting, annuals and biennials offer valuable solutions: so runs the familiar orthodoxy of modern garden design. However, quite apart from such utilitarian thinking, many short-lived plants are beautiful in form and color, as well as providing a welcome chance for the gardener to change the planting frequently and to experiment.

In this chapter I single out my favorites – not only annuals and biennials, but also short-lived perennials – in a range of genera including *Delphinium*, *Lathyrus*, *Lobelia*, *Nemesia*, *Nicotiana*, *Osteospermum*, *Pelargonium*, *Salvia* and – an increasingly popular genus – *Diascia*.

SUMMER

Growing annuals from seed is an appealing way of filling gaps or creating splashes of color in the summer border. In addition to well-tried standards there are delightful plants such as *Collinsia heterophylla* that have, to my mind, been unduly neglected.

Certain *Delphinium* clones such as 'Loch Leven' can be long-lived if well treated, although others have a limited lifespan. My selection also includes the delightful *Cosmos atrosanguineus*, introduced into Britain in 1835 from seeds from Mexico; I first came across it some fifteen years ago, and a request for cuttings to grow at Wisley led by stages to its wider distribution.

For flowers and ornamental foliage, I list *Eryngium giganteum*, a majestic sea holly, from the Caucasus and Turkey; my second *Lotus berthelotii*, both handsome plants, the latter effective for hanging baskets.

FLOWERS

Collinsia heterophylla (Scrophulariaceae)

The attractive, western North American genus *Collinsia* provides a number of delightful, long-flowering hardy annuals, the most commonly seen of which, *Collinsia heterophylla*, was long known as *C. bicolor*, and given the curious common name Chinese Houses in the United States. It is widespread in California in shaded sites and moist, fairly rich soils, although it is usually grown in open, sunny positions in annual borders or as a filler between herbaceous plants or shrubs.

An erect annual, *C. heterophylla* produces slender, willowy 2ft (60cm) high stems clothed with opposite pairs of lanceolate, toothed, or sometimes lobed, leaves 2 to 3in (5–8cm) long and terminating in extended, whorled inflorescences of showy, bicolored, usually violet and white, 1in (2.5cm) long, antirrhinum-like blooms. Considerable variation in flower color occurs both in the wild and in gardens: the upper lip may be white or lavender with darker tips, while the lower lip varies from pale to deep violet or rosy purple. Occasionally pure white or totally violet-purple forms are also found.

Seed sown in open ground in early spring usually germinates in about fourteen days and is best sown very thinly in rows about 6in (15cm) apart, and the seedlings thinned gradually until they are 3 to 4in (8–10cm) apart within the rows. As with all annuals, it is important to thin the seedlings, because they may develop elongated, weak stems if not given ample room to spread sideways. Early use of thin twigs for support is sensible on windy sites. Successive sowings, if required, can be made at four- to six-week intervals to give a flowering season from midsummer through autumn, and an autumn sowing in pots under cold or cool glass will provide useful color in a sunroom in spring. *Collinsia* also provides long-lasting, charming cut flowers, an added bonus if the freely produced seed is not required for the following year's display.

Collinsia is typical of a number of genera of annuals like *Nemophila* and *Phacelia* that, although well known in the past, have lost favor with seedsmen. In my eyes, these less intensively bred genera blend much more readily into mixed plantings than Petunias, Impatiens, and Ageratums, and it is encouraging to see them returning to the fold.

Cosmos atrosanguineus (Compositae) (6B–9B)

Sadly, this superb Mexican dahlia-relative is now almost certainly extinct in the wild, but it has remained in cultivation in a few gardens, and thanks to recent vegetative and micropropagation it is now widely available and may soon be reintroduced into its habitat.

In general aspect, the flower heads are similar to those of the well-known annual *Cosmos*, but much neater, with a constant supply of the cupped, solitary, dark maroon, 2–2½in (5–6cm) blooms with yellow central florets, produced from early summer until late autumn on slender stems above 1½–2ft (45–60cm) mounds of finely cut, bronze-tinted foliage. The sun shining through the flower heads makes them glow like dark Venetian glass, and they give off a delicious scent that reminds me strongly of chocolate.

Cosmos atrosanguineus has a tuberous root from which strong shoots, set with finely dissected, pinnate, dark green leaves up to 6in (15cm) or so long, arise in late spring. If the tubers are overwintered and then potted up and brought into growth early in the year, like dahlia tubers, they will soon produce vigorous young shoots which, taken as basal cuttings about 2in (5–6cm) long with a short sliver of the tuber, quickly root. Potted on, they will produce sturdy plants that are

Cosmos atrosanguineus

ready for planting out as soon as danger of frost is past.

At Wisley and in Sussex, I have grown *C. atrosanguineus* outside in a sunny, sharply drained border for several years without lifting the tubers, which are mulch-protected in winter. The young plants were planted with the top of the tuber 4 to 6in (10–15cm) below soil level in a hollow. During the first season, soil was gradually added to fill the hollow, and by the end of summer the tuber was sitting comfortably several inches below soil level protected from all but the most severe weather, although unfortunately not from the soil-dwelling black slugs that need control on occasion. This technique may be used for a number of plants that are on the borderline of hardiness, particularly fuchsias and the lavender-flowered *Dahlia merckii* (8A–9B).

A beautiful plant of character and great quality that, even if it were as common as a daisy, I would endeavor never to be without.

Delphinium 'Loch Leven' (Ranunculaceae) (3B–9B)

To include the stately and much-loved delphiniums of our borders in this category of short-lived plants may produce frowns of disapproval from delphinium enthusiasts. In many cases, however, they prove less reliably perennial than one would like, although there are fine clones that, with care, will provide great joy in summer for many years. One of the factors that affected the longevity of many clones introduced during the middle of this century was the use in breeding in California of the short-lived Pacific Giants, which produced very fine delphinium seed races for annual or biennial flowering, but unfortunately passed on their lack of perenniality to many clones bred in Britain.

Few of the named clones that I recall from the late 1940's still exist. In their place is a host of other excellent clones such as a series named after Scottish lochs, of which 'Loch Leven,' with strong spikes and evenly spaced, large, light blue, white-eyed florets was probably the best, although close run by the somewhat similar, but taller, 'Loch Nevis.' Both are still available commercially, as is lovely 'Spindrift,' a confection of turquoise and soft blues of medium height. Personal preference inevitably comes into choice of color and form, but it would be unfair to exclude such superb plants as the bright midblue 'Blue Nile;' the very late-flowering, deep lavender 'Mighty Atom,' relatively short in stature as its name indicates; the tall, black-eyed 'Sandpiper' in pristine white; and the amazing 'Chelsea Star,' rich velvet-purple with a contrasting clean white eye.

All are, to me, outstanding plants of great quality that will grace any border during the summer months and, if cut back to ground level after the main flowering is over and given ample fertilizer and water, may well produce good spikes of lesser stature to extend the season into autumn. Provided the clones being grown are normally robust, reasonably long-lived, and well fertilized, a second flowering may often be achieved without exhausting the plants unduly, and lessening the following season's pleasure. Delphiniums, however, are generally intolerant of hot and humid summers.

Related plants   The Belladonna group of Delphiniums (3A–7B)– derived it is thought from *Delphinium elatum* (parent of the tall border clones) and *D. grandiflorum*, a shorter east Asian species with spreading, branched racemes – has provided some of the best herbaceous plants both for garden decoration and for cut flowers. They also exhibit more heat tolerance than many other strains. They range from 2 to 4ft (60–120 cm) in height and provide a succession of their delicate, butterflylike blooms from midsummer until the autumn, remaining soundly perennial if well treated and increasing readily from division as well as from basal cuttings in spring.

This group of delphiniums includes my personal favorite, the bright gentian-blue 'Wendy,' a vigorous, strongly branched, 4ft (1.2m) plant ideal as a cut flower. All, except perhaps the slightly dirty-white 'Moerheimii,' are worth a place in any garden.

Isotoma axillaris (Campanulaceae)

It is curious how plants that have been cultivated for many years, like this delightful bellflower-relative from Australia, suddenly become extremely widely grown after years of virtual obscurity. *Isotoma axillaris* (now sometimes called *Solenopsis axillaris*), is one of these, a perennial herb 12in (30cm) or so high that occurs wild in Victoria, New South Wales, and Queensland, preferring open, sunny, well-drained sites to retain its rounded, tight habit. The leaves are dark green, narrow, very deeply cut, and up to 3in (7.5cm) long, forming dense mounds of foliage and, from the leaf axils, a continuous succession of the elegant, long-tubed, bright blue, starry, 1in (2.5cm) flowers that appear from late spring to early autumn.

Isotoma axillaris has regained its popularity in the last five or so years and is now frequently seen as a pot plant in commercial outlets. Because it is frost-tender it is best grown as an annual, either from seed or from autumn-struck cuttings of soft shoots, overwintered under glass and planted out after the danger of frosts is over. In cooler frost-free areas of California it is perennial. Its neat but spreading habit and continuum of very attractive flowers over a long period make it an ideal container plant as well as providing a beautiful center for a hanging basket, bordered by pendent companions such as the floriferous *Lobelia richardsonii* and *Scaevola aemula* (annual or 9A–10B) to provide a long-lasting symphony of blue throughout the summer and the early autumn.

The sap of *I. axillaris* may cause skin irritation, so it is advisable to use gloves when handling plants if there is a chance you may be affected.

Lathyrus odoratus Jet Set Group (Leguminosae)

Gardeners owe much to the good Father Cupani from Sicily who, in 1699, sent to a Dr Uvedale in England seed of the wild sweet pea, *Lathyrus odoratus*. Although of restricted distribution in Sicily and southern Italy and reasonably stable in flower color (as is the relatively uniform *Primula auricula* in the wild), *L. odoratus* had the latent generic potential to vary.

Once no longer subject to the pressures of natural selection in the wild, some variants no doubt appeared in cultivation among generations derived from the original seed and were swooped on by sharp-eyed gardeners who continued the selection process. From the Grandiflora and Spencer races, they developed the pre-

Lathyrus odoratus Jet Set Group

sent-day range, providing a galaxy of colors and flower forms, usually blessed with a delicious fragrance, without which such intense breeding and selection would probably not have occurred.

Most sweet peas available are the familiar cultivars that clamber by tendrils over and through twigs or trained against a framework of bamboo stakes, but there are now many nonclimbing selections that are grouped for convenience under var. *nanellus*. Some twenty years ago, various color selections of the Jet Set Group were sent for trial at Wisley from America. This range of compact, 2 to 3ft (60–90cm) high, free-flowering and very fragrant, often frilled sweet peas flowered for a long period of the summer and were easier to manage than those requiring some support. They rapidly gained in popularity, because they could be grown as group plantings in borders either sown direct or more usually raised under glass in late winter. Planted out in mid-spring they then provided masses of long-stemmed flower sprays both for cutting and garden decoration during the summer months.

Initially, individual color selections in scarlet, pink, cerise, mauve, blue, and cream were available, but now only mixed color ranges are normally offered, a result no doubt of the introduction of several other dwarf races, Bijou, Cupid, Snoopea, and Little Sweetheart among them. The distinctions between these selections are not particularly obvious, but they all provide the advantages of the taller sweet peas without the work of training them.

Rehmannia elata (Scrophulariaceae) (8A–10B)

The foxglovelike Chinese genus *Rehmannia*, although long known in cultivation, has had little attention, even though it contains several attractive herbaceous perennials with large, brightly colored flowers borne more or less continuously through the summer and autumn.

Finest of the species is the robust *Rehmannia elata* from central China, which has become somewhat confused in cultivation with *R. angulata*. It may reach 4 or 5ft (1.2–1.5m) in height, forming a large bushy plant with handsome dark green, 6–8in (15–20cm), lobed leaves often slightly glistening from their covering of glandlike hairs. In early summer the lax, leafy flower stems appear, producing long-stalked, bright purple-pink, yellow-throated, tubular blooms up to 4in (10cm) long, with ridged calyces and two flipped-back, rounded upper lobes, the three remaining lobes forming a spreading lip 1in (2.5cm) or more long and nearly 2in (5cm) across. As the flower stems extend, further pairs of leafy shoots develop in the axils of the older leaves,

and in turn produce flowering shoots. Unfortunately, *R. elata* is not fully hardy, although it will withstand some frost, as will the other currently cultivated species, *R. glutinosa* (annual or 10A–11), which has smaller, red-brown and yellow blooms and seldom exceeds 12in (30cm) or so in height.

Because *R. elata* readily produces seed, it is sometimes grown as a biennial, although I have found it is strongly perennial when grown as a tub plant, brought into a cold greenhouse in late autumn, rested with limited watering, and, after re-potting, returned outdoors in late spring. The fleshy roots may develop fresh shoots and, having filled their container, often push out leafy growths from the drainage holes, which has caused me problems during re-potting. Broken-off pieces, however, may be used to build up stocks of young plants, since they establish readily and will flower later in the season.

In nature, it is said to inhabit cliff faces and rocky places, but is clearly less fussy as a garden plant, and with its ebullient growth habit and ability to spread from its fleshy roots, *R. elata* might thrive as a hanging-basket plant, given good drainage, a fertile potting mix and ample water when in full growth.

Rehmannia elata

OTHER PLANTS

Cynoglossum amabile (Boraginaceae)

Fully living up to its epithet *amabile* ("beautiful"), this annual or biennial from China and other areas in eastern Asia provides a mass of brilliant sky-blue forget-me-nots on stems 1½ to 2ft (45–60cm) high for long periods of the summer. Like all species of "Hound's tongue," it has coarse, hairy, dark green leaves, but these are scarcely noticed once the showers of one-sided racemes of scented blooms develop in midsummer from early spring sowings. Autumn-sown plants may be overwintered to flower outside in early summer, but then need to be grown in light, well-drained soil. On heavy soils, they are best treated as annuals and sown in spring.

Various selections have been made, including a very good white, 'Avalanche,' but none can surpass the startling coloring of the sky-blue cultivars such as 'Firmament' and the somewhat taller, 2ft (60cm), azure 'Blue Showers,' a recent introduction bred for the cut-flower trade but equally valuable in the garden.

Limnanthes douglasii (Limnanthaceae)

One of the finest springtime sights in the marshy grassland meadows of the western United States is the Meadow Foam, *Limnanthes douglasii*, known in Britain as the Poached Egg Flower, a reference to the yellow, white-tipped 1in (2.5cm) blooms produced in abundance above the greeny yellow, finely cut foliage. I have seen it in Californian meadows, where it covered all the low, damp depressions with 6in (15cm) mounds of yellow and white, together with a few colonies of the uncommon, pure yellow subsp. *sulphurea* in some areas. An attractive annual for late spring or early summer flowering, seeding around happily and usually self-supporting for many years, *L. douglasii* is also pleasantly fragrant and a useful early bee flower. Try it also from autumn sowing as a pot plant for late winter and spring flowering. It germinates within three weeks and seldom fails to delight.

Nemophila menziesii (Hydrophyllaceae)

Selection from *Nemophila menziesii*, a Californian annual known as Baby Blue Eyes, has resulted in a number of fine variants, including the startling 'Pennie Black,' with deep purple-black, white-edged blooms, and the contrasting 'Snowstorm,' white and speckled centrally with tiny purple-black spots. Neither perhaps has quite the same charm as the bright sky-blue, white-centered variant simply offered as *N. menziesii*, with its abundance of cup-shaped, 1½in (4cm) blooms borne over 4in (10cm) mounds of pale green, deeply cut leaves in late spring and summer. Slightly taller, with equally attractive white flowers with purple apices to each petal, is *N. maculata*; also Californian and known as Fivespot.

Sown under glass in early autumn and planted out in early spring, both species will be in flower during early summer; sown in the open ground in late spring they bloom by midsummer, providing massed color for several months in a moist site. Many Californian annuals are adapted to growing with ample spring moisture, then seeding and disappearing rapidly as the ground dries out. Their behavior in gardens mirrors this, and in dry spells they will quickly die down, but self-sown seedlings will usually appear the following season.

Phacelia campanularia (Hydrophyllaceae)

Closely related to *Nemophila* is the large genus *Phacelia*, although *P. campanularia*, the most commonly grown species, prefers drier, well-drained soil. It may be distinguished from *Nemophila menziesii* by its short racemes of bell-shaped, brilliant, dark gentian-blue, upright flowers over 9in (23cm) mounds of oval, toothed, dark green, pleasantly scented leaves. An outstanding, easily grown annual, *P. campanularia* is an excellent pot plant for early spring flowering if sown in autumn under glass. Outdoors, it will bloom from mid- to late summer if the first flush of flowers is cut back as they fade, and gentle fertilizing and watering provided to stimulate fresh growth.

Scaevola aemula (Goodeniaceae) (Annual or 9A–10B)

A species from coastal dunes and semiarid areas of Australia, *Scaevola aemula* has only recently come into prominence as a garden plant in frost-free areas or as summer bedding elsewhere. I recall seeing it occasionally in nurseries in California some years ago, where it was grown as a ground cover, for which its spreading habit and ability to root down from procumbent shoots are ideally suited.

Full sun, sharp drainage, and a mildly fertile soil are its main requirements. Given too rich a diet, its slightly fleshy foliage spreads far and wide without providing many of its 1½in (3–4cm) wide, pale to deep blue-mauve flowers. Grown harder, it will flower profusely all summer, and is particularly attractive as a hanging-basket plant with the shoots, some spreading, some more upright, showing off the fan-shaped blooms very well. Its recent popularity has resulted in two clonal selections, 'Blue Fan' and 'Blue Wonder,' propagated from cuttings, becoming widely distributed.

FLOWERS AND ORNAMENTAL FOLIAGE

Eryngium giganteum (Umbelliferae) (5B–8B)

Much lauded for its qualities as a floral arrangers' plant, this stately monocarpic sea holly from the Caucasus and Turkey, where it occurs in dry mountain valleys, is a most handsome plant for garden decoration. It is particularly valued for the effect of its 4in (10cm) flower heads, the broad, glaucous, spiny bracts being a silvered pewter shade, with a cone of tiny, soft blue-green flowers in their center. They are borne on 3 or 4ft (90cm–1.2m) stems arising from basal clusters of large, green, undivided leaves that have disappeared by flowering time in high summer.

Commonly known as Miss Willmott's Ghost, *Eryngium giganteum* does not appear to be directly connected with that remarkable gardener Ellen Willmott, although it was originally introduced around 1820 and it is likely that she and the equally formidable Gertrude Jekyll used it in their planting plans.

Easily raised from the abundantly produced seed, *E. giganteum* should be grown in relatively poor, dryish soil to give of its best and, when suited, will produce an abundance of self-sown seedlings that may often take two or three years to reach flowering size. Having produced seed, the plants will die, but the stems remain like brown sentries unless removed to dry for winter decoration in the house.

It is unwise to rely entirely on self-sown seedlings, and to maintain a continuous supply of flowering-sized plants fresh seed should be sown in pots in autumn and plunged outdoors to freeze over winter. Since the seedlings quickly develop strong tap roots, they should be planted out when young where they are to flower to allow them to develop to their full potential height. Larger pot-grown plants may often be stunted, because the root system has been unable to develop naturally.

Recently, a new stock of *E. giganteum* that produces huge, branched inflorescences with very long-lasting, larger-bracted flower heads has been introduced from northern Turkey. This promises to be an outstanding variant, clearly distinct from the garden viewpoint and as easy to grow as the more usually seen form. Its cultivar name 'Silver Ghost' aptly describes its beautiful grayed-white bracts and small, silvery white, pale blue-touched flower cones.

Eryngium giganteum

Lotus berthelotii

Lotus berthelotii (Leguminosae) (4A–10B)

Thought now to be virtually extinct in the wild in its native Tenerife, *Lotus berthelotii* is widespread in cultivation in Europe and is even said to be naturalized in the United States in some frost-free areas. Its undoubted attractions as an ornamental, particularly for containers and hanging baskets, will ensure that, should it die out in its natural habitat, it will not be lost entirely and could be reinstated.

A woody shrublet with long, mounding, eventually pendulous branchlets, densely set with alternate, silvered, palmate leaves each with linear, ½in (1–2cm) leaflets, *L. berthelotii* is given the common names Coral Gem or Parrot's Beak, references to the scarlet, long-beaked keel of the flowers, which are like miniature editions of those of the well-known wall shrub Parrot Beak, *Clianthus puniceus*. The 1in (2–3cm) long blooms, mainly borne in axillary clusters at the ends of the branchlets, may vary a little in color from orange-scar-

let to deep red, but the most commonly seen clone, offered under the invalid clonal name "Kew form," has bright red flowers and intensely silvered leaves. It flowers in midsummer with further flushes of bloom later in the year.

As might be expected from its natural habitat of cliff crevices, *L. berthelotii* enjoys sharply drained, relatively nutrient-poor soils, but it will also grow surprisingly well in humus-rich potting mixes, although the foliage lacks the sparkle of specimens grown under harder conditions.

It is readily propagated from cuttings of side shoots which, taken in late summer and overwintered at 45 to 50°F (7–10°C), will form fine plants by early summer, when they may be planted out to bloom. Grown over the edge of sunny raised beds, in containers, or hanging baskets, *L. berthelotii* remains attractive throughout summer and early autumn but, because it is tender, must be brought into frost-free conditions for the winter months. Cut back gently each spring, it may be maintained for several years in a container, but in my experience old plants are less floriferous and the foliage lacks the lustre of vigorous, freshly propagated youngsters. So I have reverted to annual renewal from cuttings to be sure of enjoying to the full the dense silver curtains of foliage emblazoned for several weeks of summer with the vivid scarlet of the beautiful blooms.

OTHER PLANTS

Verbascum bombyciferum (Scrophulariaceae)

One of my early horticultural memories is of this striking mullein growing at Carlile's Nursery, where I was working in 1949; it has large, silvery rosettes of broadly ovate, 15in (38cm) leaves covered by a thick indumentum of long, snow-white hairs extending over the 6ft (2m) stem and inflorescence. Its magnificent spires of tightly packed, bright lemon-yellow blooms embedded in white wool appear in midsummer. A biennial, or occasional monocarpic if the rosettes take two years to develop fully, it is to my mind the finest of its breed, readily raised from seed and thriving in dry, sunny positions, a magnificent border plant both for foliage and flowers, particularly since the latter lack the harsh coloring of some other yellow mulleins and are enhanced by brick-red anthers.

Introduced from the Bithynian Mount Olympus Ulu Dag in western Turkey in 1930, named selections – notably 'Silver Spire,' 'Silver Lining,' and 'Polarsummer' ('Arctic Summer') – are now available, but so far I have seen nothing that offers an improvement on the original stock.

TWO OR MORE SEASONS

Among short-lived perennials with double-season interest, *Erysimum* 'Bowles' Mauve,' flowering abundantly from spring for many months, is outstanding. Apparently self-sterile, it is reputed to produce "good" seed pods occasionally, but I have yet to see any offspring that could be attributed definitely to it. If it could be used as a parent to pass on its incredibly long flowering period to other perennial wallflowers, it might be possible to create a fine range of new clones of different flower colors for our enjoyment.

Also indispensable to me is the subshrub *Lavatera* 'Barnsley'. Judging by the numbers sold at RHS shows (at Hampton Court Show in July the car park turns into a waving forest of pink and white mallows as visitors carry away their spoils), it must be one of the most popular plants to have been marketed for many a year, and well deserves it success.

SPRING TO SUMMER FLOWERS

Erysimum 'Bowles' Mauve' (Cruciferae) (7A–9B)

Botanically boxed and coxed between the genera *Erysimum* and *Cheiranthus*, Mr Bowles' superb, perennial, evergreen wallflower is, to me, indispensable in the garden. A rounded subshrub with densely packed, dark gray-green, linear, 2in (5cm) leaves forming a mound more than 3ft (90cm) across and almost as much high, even in winter it provides a few of its deep lilac-purple flower-spikes. From early spring onward, the mature shoots produce large clusters of dark purple buds that open a warm lilac-purple and deepen to bright purple as the flower stem elongates. These often reach 12in (30cm) in length and produce well over fifty blooms on each raceme before being replaced by side shoots that continue producing flowers for months on end. Regrettably, the slight scent does not compare with the delicious perfume of bedding wallflowers.

Since 'Bowles' Mauve' is so floriferous, it is some-times difficult to find suitable cutting material, but unflowered side shoots, 3 to 4in (8–10cm) long, taken with a heel, will root readily during most of the growing period to replace older plants that after three or four years usually die of exhaustion. 'Bowles' Mauve' is apparently self-sterile, and although I have been told that occasionally "good" seed pods do form I have yet to see any offspring that could be attributed to it.

Apparently unaffected by any but poorly drained sites, 'Bowles' Mauve' should be placed where it is not likely to be subject to wind-rock, which may result in the main stem keeling over and the plant becoming lop-sided, a fate suffered by several perennial wallflowers in my present garden. They still grow and flower perfectly well, but lose their looks to some extent. If you are raising your own plants from cuttings, make sure that you pinch out any developing flower-spikes (which appear even on very young plants) until a bushy habit and strong main stem form, because this will help to maintain the stability and attractive mounded habit to spite all but the most ferocious of winds.

Related plants In growth *E.* 'Bredon' (8A–10B) is similar to 'Bowles' Mauve,' forming a rounded, but less densely clothed, woody, evergreen subshrub usually no more than 1 to 1½ft (30–45cm) high, with slightly blue-green foliage and racemes of bright, clear yellow flowers. The flower-spikes are rather broader and shorter than those of 'Bowles' Mauve' with slightly larger individual blooms, purple-brown in bud. The display is not

Erysimum 'Bowles' Mauve'

so prolonged, although it blooms profusely during mid- to late spring and occasionally again later in the season. I particularly like 'Bredon' for its clean-cut appearance, which I prefer to the rather messy, dull purple and cream of several modern cultivars derived from *E. semperflorens* and perhaps *E. bicolor*, both of which have bicolored and sometimes striped flowers in shades of lilac, white, and cream.

Erysimum 'Harpur-Crewe,' a most attractive, bushy, evergreen double wallflower, is sometimes reputed to be a chance relic from the age of Elizabeth I. It flourished for many years in the garden of Lady Crewe in Hampshire and was brought into prominence by a noted gardening relative, the Reverend Henry Harpur-Crewe, in the midnineteenth century. It is still with us today, propagated vegetatively from side shoots that appear below the inflorescence as the small, sweetly scented, neatly double, deep yellow, bronze-touched flowers fade. Only reaching 12in (30cm) or so in height, 'Harpur-Crewe' should be propagated regularly, because, although perennial, it deteriorates within a few years. Although usually attributed to *Erysimum* (*Cheiranthus*) *cheiri*, our common wallflower, 'Harpur-Crewe' is probably of hybrid origin, with one of the subshrubby Canary Island or Iberian species in its parentage as well.

OTHER PLANTS

Erysimum x *allionii* (Cruciferae)
It is doubtful that we shall ever know the exact origin of the Siberian Wallflower, currently called *Erysimum* x *allionii* but also referred to as *E. asperum* (from North America), *E. hieraciifolium* (from Europe), and *E. perofskianum* (from Afghanistan and Pakistan) – a bewildering array of possible parents for one of the brightest and best of spring bedding plants. How its common name became attached to it is now a mystery!

Although marginally perennial, it is usually grown as a biennial, raised from summer-sown seed for early autumn planting to bloom the following spring. Its remarkably vivid orange, sweetly scented, four-petaled flowers appear in abundance on 12in (30cm) high, bushy plants with neat wallflower foliage. Obligingly, it will seed around if plants are not tidied away too quickly; those who find the brilliance of its blooms overwhelming can substitute an equally good but more demure yellow-flowered form.

SUMMER TO AUTUMN FLOWERS

Alonsoa warscewiczii (Scrophulariaceae) (Annual or 10A–11)

A sound perennial in its native Peru and sometimes subshrubby in habit, *Alonsoa warscewiczii* is almost always grown as an annual, although it is easily maintained over winter under glass. Since it is readily propagated from cuttings of the soft young growths, seedling variants that differ from the usual bright red species may be perpetuated vegetatively as clones. One of these, with most attractive apricot-rose flowers, has recently been selected and is distributed under the name 'Peachy Keen.'

Alonsoa warscewiczii is a vigorous species, usually 1 to 2ft (30–60cm) tall, with ovate, toothed, fresh green

Alonsoa warscewiczii

leaves. Whether seed-raised or grown from cuttings, the growing points of the young shoots should be pinched out when 2 to 3in (5–8cm) high to encourage a bushy habit. Left unpruned, the shoots will quickly produce their long, terminal racemes of brilliant scarlet, 1in (2.5cm) wide, open-faced blooms, but tend to be rather spindly in growth. A little delay in flowering as a result of pinching out is amply repaid by the production of more shoots and a constant supply of blooms from midsummer until the frosts. A more compact selection is sometimes available, but differs only marginally in height in my experience.

Seed sown under glass at a temperature of 55 to 60°F (13–16°C) in late winter germinates rapidly and the seedlings should be grown on in pots before planting out in well-drained, fertile soil once all danger of frost has passed and when they will normally just be coming into flower. In the open, early spring-sown seed will bloom somewhat later, and at the end of the season the old plants can be lifted, cut back, and potted into 4–6in (10–15cm) pots to grow on at 60°F (16°C) for winter flowering. Alternatively, early summer-sown seed will produce plants for a fine winter display in a greenhouse or warm sunroom. Such versatility and longevity of flowering is rare, and it is well worth a little trouble not only for *A. marscewiczii* and its variants but also for other species like the deep red, orange, or white-flowered *A. acutifolia* which, after years of neglect, is once again appearing in a few seed catalogs.

Argyranthemum 'Jamaica Primrose' (Compositae) (9B–11*)

During the last ten or so years, there has been an upsurge in interest in many tender perennials that were formerly often considered "too much trouble" to grow because they needed annual propagation to maintain stocks. Most, in fact, are less difficult to grow than dahlias and early-flowering chrysanthemums, and many have the great virtues of being easily established and flowering from early summer until late autumn. Among the most versatile are the shrubby marguerites, formerly included in the genus *Chrysanthemum* and now considered to deserve a genus of their own, *Argyranthemum*. Most species occur in the Canary Islands and Madeira, varying in the color of the daisy like ray florets from white (the majority) to yellow or pink, with the central-disk flowers yellow, pink, or purplish-red.

This diversity of coloring has allowed chance meetings of various garden species and semi-intentional breeding to produce well over fifty cultivars in a range of colors with single, double, or anemone-centered flower heads. All are shrubs varying in height from 2½ to 4ft (75–120cm) or so with gray or green, coarsely or finely dissected leaves. The fine-textured, almost filiform foliage of *A. foeniculaceum* and *A. gracile* with its clone 'Chelsea Girl,' all with white, yellow-centered flower heads, are particularly attractive as specimen plants, but my personal choice, given only one selection, would be 'Jamaica Primrose.' It was introduced

to Wisley over forty years ago and was the first *Argyranthemum* to receive a Royal Horticultural Society award, well-deserved recognition of its all-round garden qualities. A vigorous, bushy shrub of some 3ft (90cm) or more in height and as much across with large, broad-lobed, divided, gray-green leaves and bright, well-formed primrose-colored 3in (7.5cm) flower heads with darker yellow centers, 'Jamaica Primrose' provides a continuous succession of bloom from the time it is planted out in early summer until early autumn, a flowering period difficult to equal even among this genus of prolific and long-flowering daisies.

Bidens ferulifolia (Compositae) (9B–11)

In this genus of largely weedy plants a few species stand out for their ornamental qualities and among them is *Bidens ferulifolia* from Mexico and the southern United States. A tender, short-lived perennial raised

Bidens ferulifolia

annually from autumn-struck cuttings to flower the following year, *B. ferulifolia* has long, questing shoots and much-divided ferny leaves with linear segments similar to those of fennel. It will spread to 2ft (60cm) or more in a season, producing a profusion of its bright yellow, dark-centered flower heads continuously through summer and well into autumn. The individual flower heads are over 1in (2.5cm) across and borne in

Cobaea scandens

terminal sprays of three or more and, although not noticeably scented, are a continual attraction to bees.

Initially, the growth is more or less upright, soon becoming spreading and semipendulous at the tips, an ideal habit for a hanging basket or wall pot, where *B. ferulifolia* will display its golden blooms to perfection, particularly if complemented by *Lobelia richardsonii*, with its constant flow of pale blue during the same period. Use a well-drained but moisture-retentive potting mix and a deep container or hanging basket, because *B. ferulifolia* quickly fills the available soil space with its dense fibrous roots and is then sensitive to dry conditions, drooping rapidly if bereft of a reasonable water supply as I know to my cost.

The cultivar name 'Golden Goddess' is sometimes found attached to the botanical name, presumably for commercial purposes, since the plant differs, in no way that I can see, from the plant that is cultivated simply as *B. ferulifolia*.

Cobaea scandens (Cobaeaceae/Polemoniaceae) (9A–11)

Among the most attractive of all climbers, *Cobaea scandens*, strictly a perennial in frost-free conditions, is normally grown as an annual in North America, planted out in late spring in a position where it can spread without overwhelming neighboring plants.

Seed sown under glass in late winter at 60 to 70°F (16–21°C) germinates after three weeks or more, sometimes rather irregularly. The resultant seedlings need support from the start, because they quickly develop the distinctive pinnate leaves, with two to three pairs of oval leaflets, terminating in long, flexible tendrils. These are finely branched, ending in tiny sharp hooks that attach themselves firmly to any nearby object around which the tendrils can coil.

Planted out in a well-drained site against a sun-drenched wall or on an arbor, they will rapidly extend to 15 or 20ft (5–6m) by late summer, producing flower buds from midsummer onwards.

The flowers are borne singly on long stalks often 8 to 10in (20–25cm) long and at first are upright and protected by the earlike calyx segments before the flower stalks bend over to reveal the greeny white, 2in (5cm), musk-scented, tubular bells that develop a pleasant honeylike scent and turn to violet-purple. In a warm summer there will be a constant succession of bloom until early autumn and the early flowers will usually develop large capsules containing winged seeds.

Cuttings of young side shoots may be rooted in late summer, particularly in order to retain any deeper color

FASHIONABLE PLANTS

Plants undergo changes in fashion, and recent years have seen great interest in the selection, breeding and naming of new cultivars. *Diascia*, for example, has gained favor, with more than forty species and hybrids now available – including *Diascia anastrepta* (below; see page 196), 'Salmon Supreme', 'Lilac Belle', 'Jack Elliott' and 'Rupert Lambert' – when fifteen years ago there were only two. There has been a similar explosion of *Argyranthemum* and *Osteospermum* hybrids.

The vogue for half-hardy or borderline hardy plants that give summer color for many months, are easily propagated, and require minimum heat to be overwintered under glass is history repeating itself – as one has only to look back at the vast lists of named cultivars of violas, sweet peas, pinks and hyacinths in 19th-century catalogues to realize.

variants that may occasionally arise from seed. A white-flowered form is also available and comes true from seed, the seedlings being readily identified by their pale green foliage.

Frost will cut *C. scandens* to the ground, and although I have been told by some gardeners that, by protecting the rootstock, they have succeeded in retaining plants to flower the following season, my attempts to do so have so far failed. Since seed is readily available, however, it is no hardship to raise plants annually for the great pleasure provided by the color changes of the upturned Canterbury bells that characterize this most beautiful climber.

Diascia fetcaniensis (Scrophulariaceae) (8A–9B)

There has been an astonishing rise in popularity of this South African genus of annuals and herbaceous perennials in the last fifteen years. Many of the species have proved to be excellent garden plants, and gardeners have been quick to select seedlings and hybridize the

Diascia fetcaniensis

newly introduced species so that now over twenty-five named clones, in addition to the species, are available.

For me, the most satisfactory of the species as a garden plant is *Diascia fetcaniensis*, a perennial of compact growth and bushy habit with ovate, 1in (2.5cm), deep green leaves clothing the freely branching stems that mound to about 9in (23cm) in height. Flowering begins in early summer, the elegant 8–9in (20–23cm) spikes densely but evenly set with rose-pink, shallowly cup-shaped, short-spurred, open flowers ½in (1–2cm) across. Subsidiary racemes appear in a continual succession of bloom into early autumn, with a spattering of flowers continuing into late autumn in mild weather.

Diascia fetcaniensis, which can be distinguished from most other species except *D. stachyoides* by the sticky glandular hairs that cover the plant, often occurs wild in damp areas by streams or in slight shade in the eastern Cape, where it grows at altitudes up to around 10,000ft (3,000m).

In cultivation, it is happy with an open, sunny site, preferring a well-drained but humus-rich soil, although it appears to be very tolerant of a wide range of conditions. So far, it has proved hardy in my Sussex garden, as has *D. vigilis* from the high Drakensberg Mountains, similar in many ways but with softer pink blooms, touched maroon and yellow within and with somewhat paler green foliage. However, a few cuttings rooted each summer and overwintered under glass should always be taken as a wise insurance. Young plants maintained under glass start blooming immediately they are planted out in early summer, while mature

plants growing outside since the previous season do not usually flower again until midsummer.

Related plants *Diascia anastrepta* (see p.195) is a mat-forming species from the Drakensberg Mountains that occurs in damp, often shaded places, where it forms long-spreading stems with dark green, ovate leaves, terminating in 12in (30cm) long sprays of well-separated, rich pink flowers, spotted purple within. It has a long flowering period through summer and autumn, and is easily propagated by dividing the matted clumps into small portions in spring. To date, it has proved hardy with me and with its more prostrate habit is most useful for its contrast with more upright species like *D. vigilis*.

Diascia barberae (6B–8B) is also a mat-forming species, most commonly cultivated in the form 'Ruby Field.' It is frequently sold as an alpine-garden plant and, as such, is grown as a sun-lover in sharply drained soil. It grows wild in seepage areas in the Drakensberg Mountains and lives longer in humus-rich, moisture-retentive soil in open or slightly shaded sites, where it produces a continuous summer supply of deep rose-pink flowers marked internally yellow and maroon. In recent years, I have grown a sport, 'Blackthorn Apricot,' which has proved very vigorous, a 3in (8cm) pot-sized plant spreading to form a patch 12in (30cm) across in one season and covered all summer in warm apricot blooms.

Lavatera 'Barnsley'

Lavatera 'Barnsley' (Malvaceae) (7A–10A)

Among the most prolific of summer-flowering sub-shrubs, *Lavatera* 'Barnsley' has been widely publicized and propagated in recent years.

A subshrub of some 6ft (1.8m) or more when mature, with handsome, dark green, shallowly lobed, alternate leaves, 'Barnsley' appears to be a hybrid between *L. olbia* and *L. thuringiaca* from southern Europe, and was found only ten or so years ago. Its popularity is well deserved, as from summer until late autumn it produces spike after spike of mallowlike, 3 to 4in (8–10cm) blooms that open pale pink with a crimson eye and turn white as they mature, so that, at any one time, there are blooms at different stages of changing color.

It is extremely fast-growing, and a small plant can, in fertile soil, reach almost full size in a season, so should be allowed ample space to develop. The one fault of 'Barnsley' and its relatives is their tendency to become top-heavy and partly keel over on windy sites, particularly if they have been purchased as fairly large plants in relatively small pots, where they have not been able to exercise their natural tendency to send out their thick main roots far and wide. Rooted cuttings produced from side shoots in a plant incubator, or from slightly woodier material simply pushed into the soil, tend to produce their anchor roots quickly and often remain upright because of this. Even so, it is sensible to prune out, in the flowering period if necessary, shoots that are altering the overall balance of the plant.

While 'Barnsley' may thrive for a number of years, it is probable that, after a few seasons, splits will appear in the woody but soft centered shoots at the base of the stem. This is a sign that cuttings need to be rooted if you are to continue to enjoy the undoubted charms of this astonishingly floriferous and beautiful plant.

Related plants Some purists dismiss the brightly colored selections of the widespread Mediterranean hardy annual *L. trimestris* as too garish, but, as a lover of all mallows, I remain unrepentant in regarding it highly. The older, taller selections like the deep rose 'Loveliness,' have been largely superseded by some fine cultivars, including the 2–3ft (60–90cm) 'Silver Cup,' with 3–4in (8–10cm) open trumpets of glowing, bright pink with slightly darker veins; 'Pink Beauty,' with dark-veined, very pale pink blooms; and the equally compact, white-flowered 'Mont Blanc.'

All are readily raised from seed sown *in situ* from late spring to early summer and, from successive sowings, will flower in profusion from early summer until early autumn.

Maurandya erubescens

Maurandya erubescens (Scrophulariaceae) (10A–11)

If you prefer (although I do not), this is also known as *Asarina erubescens*. Until recent years, this mainly Mexican genus has been neglected in gardens, perhaps due to the tender nature of all the species that inhabit dry, frost-free areas in the wild. All are perennial herbaceous plants with twining or scandent stems, but may readily be grown as half-hardy annuals from the abundantly produced seed, which is best sown under glass at 65 to 70°F (18–21°C) in late winter, when germination usually takes about two weeks. Young plants gradually hardened off in early spring may be planted out once danger of frost is over in a sunny, open, well-drained site. Given a support their twining stems will rapidly clamber by means of their twisting leaf-stalks to 6 or 7ft (2m) or more, producing a constant succession of snapdragonlike flowers all summer.

All species are well worth garden space for their freely borne, brightly colored blooms, and even if wall or fence space is not available may be used in borders or among shrubs grown on wigwams of bamboo stakes where, once they reach the top, the stems will cascade downward and continue blooming until the frosts. The sinuous nature of the stems also makes maurandyas useful for clothing banks in summer and for large hanging baskets. For those able to provide greenhouse space at 60 to 65°F (16–18°C), Maurandyas from early summer-sown seed may be used to provide welcome color for much of the winter, preferably placed against netting, where their soft shoots can ramble at will.

Supreme among the species is the delightful *M.*

erubescens, with densely soft-downy, pale green, more or less triangular, toothed, 2–3in (5–8cm) long leaves, bearing in their axils long-stalked, tubular open-faced blooms, each some 2½ to 3in (6–8cm) long, of a beautiful rose-pink, discreetly marked white and lined with golden hairs in the throat.

Happily, after years of relative obscurity, seed of *M. erubescens*, the somewhat smaller-flowered *M. scandens* in white, purple, and pink, and the 2ft (60cm) high, red-purple *M. purpusii*, is now readily available (listed under the genus *Asarina* in some cases). All are plants deserving much wider cultivation for their most attractive, colorful flowers and versatility in the garden.

Mimulus aurantiacus (Scrophulariaceae) (8A–10B)

Known to many gardeners as *Mimulus* (or *Diplacus*) *glutinosus*, this delightful shrubby monkey flower from California can be as a half-hardy biennial, although in favored gardens it may be maintained for a number of years against a south wall. A bushy, evergreen shrub of some 4 to 5ft (1.2–1.5m) in height with pale brown, woody stems, *M. aurantiacus* is well clothed with slightly aromatic, opposite pairs of handsome, glossy, elliptic, toothed, noticeably veined, 2–3in (5–8cm) leaves that are somewhat sticky. The trumpet-shaped, lobed, more or less two-lipped flowers, 1½in (3–5cm) or so long and about half as much across, vary from the dark brick-red or deep orange-red of var. *puniceus* to shades of apricot, orange, yellow, and buff in *M. aurantiacus*. They are produced in opposite pairs in the leaf axils of the slender young shoots continuously through summer and autumn and, in mild seasons, sometimes until Christmas.

It is readily raised from summer-struck cuttings of young, nonflowering side shoots, the young plants being overwintered in frost-free conditions, pinched back in early spring to encourage bushy growth and then planted out in late spring.

In the wild, I have seen it growing in rocky banks in open positions near the Californian redwood forests in very sharply drained soil, and, although it appreciates rather more fertile and moisture-retentive sites in gardens, ample light and free drainage are essential if it is to give of its best.

Mimulus aurantiacus and its allies are all well worth growing as garden plants, particularly *M. longiflorus* and its lovely cool yellow clone 'Santa Barbara' and the orange-yellow to buff *M. bifidus*. New clones such as the ivory-white 'Popacatapetl' and the Verity Hybrids, varying from purplish-red to lemon-yellow, have been introduced and, while they are unlikely to displace the better known red and orange variants of *M. aurantiacus*, they are as easy to grow and provide a most useful extension to the color range of these very desirable small garden shrubs.

Nemesia fruticans (Scrophulariaceae) (7B–9B*)

This lovely perennial *Nemesia* is widely spread in southern Africa, where it grows in sandy or rocky sites from near sea level to over 6,000ft (2,000m) altitude. In the wild, it is extremely variable, from sprawling to erect in habit and sometimes subshrubby rather than herbaceous.

The color ranges from violet-purple to pink or white, and in view of its variability and distribution spread in nature it is not surprising that it has acquired a number of specific names in the past, including *N. capensis, N. foetens,* and *N. thunbergii,* all currently subsumed under *N. fruticans.*

The forms now in cultivation are herbaceous perennials that have survived several years outdoors in my garden in a well-drained site (as well as in a stone container) without damage. Caution dictates annual propagation – from unflowered, short shoots in late summer – because it may disappear in very hard winters and is therefore best treated as a short-lived plant.

The clone 'Joan Wilder' is proving to be one of the most attractive plants available for the alpine garden, front of the border, or for container cultivation. Forming a compact, 8–10in (20–25cm) mound of opposite, lanceolate, toothed, midgreen leaves about 1in (2.5cm) or so long, covered in terminal, dense spikes of 1in (2.5cm) long, bright violet-blue snapdragon flowers with creamy white palates, it will bloom from spring until the frosts without ceasing, an astonishing display by any standards.

As the season advances the inflorescences elongate several inches, and by the end of the season may each have produced over fifty flowers. By midsummer, the plants have often lost some of their neatness but, cut back to within a few inches of the base and given a little liquid nourishment, will usually be rejuvenated and soon come into bloom again.

Seed is freely set and some variation in flower color and habit occurs, as might be expected.

At least one further clone, 'Jack Elliot,' has been selected with flowers of a bright lavender-pink and a contrasting central yellow crest. Regrettably, the two clones have already become confused in commerce, in spite of the distinct color differences. Obtain either (or both), however, and they will prove an unfailing delight in the garden for over six months, year after year.

Nicotiana 'Lime Green' (Solanaceae)

Among the many ornamental and often sweetly scented cultivars of flowering tobacco available, none is so pleasing to me as *Nicotiana* 'Lime Green,' an offspring of the South American *Nicotiana alata*, which has been the main parent of this invaluable race of garden plants. *N. alata* is a perennial that may reach 5ft (1.5m) or more in height, but is not fully hardy, even though in mild winters it may be overwintered, particularly in well-drained soils.

Its derivatives are almost always grown as half-hardy annuals, readily raised from seed sown under glass in early to midspring at 65 to 70°F (18–21°C) and planted out in late spring or early summer to bloom throughout summer and into autumn. Germination normally occurs in ten to fifteen days, and the seedlings should be pricked out into individual pots once they are large enough to be handled without damaging the soft young growth.

The main aim of breeders has been to produce very compact plants, ideal for mass bedding, like the colorful Domino and Nicki Series, which are seldom more than 12in (30cm) or so high, but in the process they have lost much of the grace of the species, with its looser growth. The 2ft (60cm) tall 'Lime Green' has a more spreading, open growth habit and salver shaped, long-tubed, 1in (2.5cm) blooms of bright yellowish-green borne in profusion, and remains my favorite because its subtle color allows it to blend successfully in mixed plantings with herbaceous plants and small shrubs.

Equally good in this respect is the similarly colored, 3 to 4ft (90cm-1.2m) tall, *N. langsdorffii* (annual or 9A–11), distinctive in its pendent, waisted bells of apple-green with contrasting bluish stamens, well spaced in long-lasting terminal panicles above the rounded, ovate, fresh green leaves. Again perennial, it is just as easy to raise from freshly produced seed and will flower continuously all summer and autumn.

Osteospermum jucundum (Compositae) (9A–10B*)

What would we do without these daisylike flowers produced in their thousands from cuttings each year to provide summer color as bedding plants, in containers, or in borders? Most require annual renewal from late summer cuttings that root readily and overwinter well in a cool greenhouse. Planted out in late spring in well-drained, open sites, they will flourish with little attention other than deadheading to promote a summer and autumn display of large, colorful flower heads.

Well over fifty clones are now available, but hardiest of its kind is *Osteospermum jucundum*, very widespread in South Africa. I have seen this in flower in the Drakensberg foothills, growing in open, short grassland and among rocks, where it formed dense, evergreen mats of neat lanceolate to ovate, entire or slightly toothed, aromatic leaves, and produced an abundance of magenta-purple, buff-backed flower heads, 1½in (3–5cm) across, borne on 4–6in (10–15cm) stems. The center of the flower heads is dark blue, opening to reveal yellow, black-tipped disk flowers, and ray flowers that vary from magenta purple to bright purplish-pink. This population matched closely with plants grown in Britain as *O. jucundum* 'Compactum,' often offered mistakenly as *O. barberiae* 'Compactum.'

Osteospermum jucundum, fairly variable in stature and habit, may sometimes reach 1 to 1¼ft (30–38cm) high with more or less upright shoots or form spreading mats with long-stemmed flower heads (the latter sometimes referred to as 'Prostratum.' All are excellent garden plants, free-flowering and hardy, although it is sensible to renew them every few years, or in cold climates annually, from cuttings.

For those whose garden space is limited, there are two clones that form neat, tight mats, flower freely, and do not spread too much: 'Blackthorn' (or 'Blackthorn Seedling') has flower heads of the darkest magenta-crimson on stems 5 or 6in (12–15cm) long; 'Weetwood,' similar in stature, is white-flowered with the backs of the ray flowers a greenish-buff, tinted pink at the base.

Much taller than these is the robust, woody-based *O. ecklonis* from the Cape, which will easily reach 2ft (60cm) in height, with the branched stems well clothed in 2–3in (5–8cm) leaves. Ample supplies of the large 2–3in (5–8cm) flower heads, the white ray flowers with

Nicotiana 'Lime Green'

blue or blue-gray backs and bright blue disk florets, are produced all through summer and autumn. It is less hardy than *O. jucundum*, but is equally easy to maintain from cuttings.

'Buttermilk' is upright in habit and reaches about 2ft (60cm) in height, the often reddish-brown stems closely set with obovate, 2in (5cm), deeply toothed, almost lobed leaves. Very free-flowering throughout the summer and autumn, its mahogany-backed buds open to reveal 2–3in (5–8cm) wide flower heads of cool lemon-yellow that become pale as they age. It has received the Award of Garden Merit from The RHS, one of the few selections of this extremely garden-worthy genus to achieve this distinction to date.

Pelargonium 'Splendide' (Geraniaceae) (8A–9B*)

Among the profusion available, it is an unenviable task to pick out only one or two representatives of this fascinating, beautiful, mainly South African genus, but undoubtedly one of my selections would be *Pelargonium* 'Splendide.' Long grown in Europe, it is a woody based subshrub, 6 to 9in (15–23cm) or more in height, with semierect and spreading branchlets clothed with broadly ovate, regularly toothed, long-stalked, silver-gray leaves, 1in (2.5cm) or so long, very similar to those of one of its parents, *P. ovale* from the Cape. In its flower characters, 'Splendide' resembles *P. tricolor* (*P. violareum*), also from the Cape, producing two- to three-flowered clusters of striking, 1in (2.5cm) wide, five-petaled flowers, the lower three petals white, the upper two dark red with blackish-red bases and dark purple stamens. These are borne in abundance from spring to late summer.

While 'Splendide' may readily be raised from cuttings of nonflowering shoots taken in late summer, it is important not to overwater the young plants during winter because, like the adult plants, they require sharply drained potting mix to thrive. Frequently grown as a cool greenhouse pot plant, 'Splendide' is also useful for summer display outdoors in a sunny position and, particularly if several plants are grown together in a large container, is effective both for its silvered foliage and contrasting bicolored deep red and white blooms.

Penstemon 'Hidcote Pink' (Scrophulariaceae) (7A–9B)

This huge genus of perennial herbs and subshrubs, most of which come from North and Central America, provides many fine garden plants both for the alpine garden and for herbaceous plantings.

Many modern cultivars are available both as clones propagated from cuttings and as seed-raised stock, which vary considerably in flower color. Their long, terminal, elegantly held sprays of tubular, bell-shaped, more or less two-lipped flowers in mauve, purple, red, pink, or white and their handsome, lush green foliage borne on strong stems 2 to 3ft (60–90cm) high make a magnificent display throughout summer and autumn.

Most are treated as short-lived plants, raised as half-hardy annuals from late summer tip-cuttings and overwintered in a cool greenhouse or frame before being planted out in spring to flower all summer and well into late autumn in many gardens. Many are, in fact, hardy in all but the severest weather, flowering well if cut back almost to the woody base each spring.

There are very few of the named clones that I would not grow, if I had room. 'Hidcote Pink' I find particularly satisfying, with its bright rose-pink, open-mouthed bells, crimson-streaked on the lower three petals and down into the throat. With me, it reaches 3ft (90cm) in height when in full flower, unlike the equally attractive 'Evelyn' (6A–9B), which is seldom half as tall and has spikes of many slender, curved, tubular, ½ to ¾in (1–2cm) long, rose-pink flowers set off by narrow foliage on stems 15 to 18in (38–45cm) high at most.

More rumbustious is 'Schoenholzeri' (Annual or

Rhodochiton volubile

8B–9B) (also known as 'Firebird'), often over 3ft (90cm) tall with blooms of the brightest scarlet.

Rhodochiton volubile (Scrophulariaceae)

Also known as *Rhodochiton atrosanguineum*, this superb and very graceful climber, which occurs in the mountains of southern Mexico in rainforests at altitudes of 7,000 to 8,000ft (2,000–2,500m), is not hardy in North America but is readily raised from seed and will flower abundantly the same year.

Grown as a cool greenhouse plant with minimum temperatures of 45 to 50°F (7–10°C), *R. volubile* will bloom for much of the year, given adequate support, but it is most frequently grown as a half-hardy annual from seed sown in late winter at 55 to 60°F (13–16°C), the seedlings being pricked out individually and trained up stakes initially. Planted out in late spring against a south wall or allowed to thread its sinuous stems through netting around a framework of stakes it will climb to 6 or 8ft (1.8–2.4m), producing, in the axils of the well-spaced, heart-shaped, angularly toothed, pale green leaves, pendent, long-stalked flowers, that immediately attract attention for their beauty and unusual coloration. The 2in (5cm) long, narrowly tubular corollas are deepest maroon-purple with five spreading lobes and contrasting white anthers, subtended by a deep rosy-pink, bell-shaped calyx that sits, umbrellalike, at the base of the pendulous corollas.

After fertilization, the corolla drops, leaving the developing seed pod under the cover of the persistent calyx that gradually loses its pink coloring, but remains ornamental for several weeks. The flat, paperlike seeds are produced in large numbers in the rounded capsules, and should be stored in cool, dry conditions until late winter when the annual cycle begins again.

I have grown this versatile and decorative climber for a number of years both as a tub plant and against a wall and, apart from guiding its questing shoots where I would like them to go, have found it trouble-free and undemanding. Ordinary well-drained garden soil or a loam-based potting mix suit it equally well, and it seems tolerant of both open and somewhat shaded sites, blooming constantly from early summer to autumn before succumbing to hard frost in early winter. *R. volubile* is still relatively unknown, and deserves much wider cultivation for the beauty of its striking flowers.

Salvia fulgens (Labiatae) (8B–10B)

Although the brilliantly colored, woody based *Salvia fulgens* is not hardy in most areas of North America, it is very readily raised from cuttings in late summer, the

Salvia fulgens

young plants being overwintered in a cool greenhouse to plant out in early summer.

In its native Mexico, it is a forest-dweller growing to 3 or 4ft (90–120cm) in height with angled, ovate, 2 to 3in (5–8cm) long, aromatic leaves, dark green in color with strongly netted veins, often grayish beneath. In late summer, and on into autumn, *S. fulgens* produces 6–9in (15–23cm) spikes of whorled, fiery, deep scarlet, 1½in (4cm) long flowers with noticeably hairy upper lips, immediately distinguishing it from other shrubby, red-flowered sages such as *S. microphylla* and its allies.

Salvia fulgens has several relatives that are of equal value in the garden. The plant long grown under the name *S. rutilans* gives off a very strong pineapple fragrance when the foliage is gently rubbed. It is valued much more for its aromatic leaves than for its flowers, which seldom appear until very late autumn, by which time frosts may have intervened as it is very tender. Grown under glass it makes an excellent pot plant, providing a display of scarlet, tubular blooms in midwinter as well as its scented, handsomely veined, dark green, ovate leaves. Almost certainly, it is a variant of the Mexican *S. elegans,* which, in the clone I grow at least, has rather smaller foliage that is somewhat less aromatic, although still pineapple-scented. Both clones (if such they be) are readily raised from late-summer cuttings and need greenhouse protection in winter.

Salvia patens (Labiatae) (8A–9B)

One of my prime favorites, *Salvia patens* is an outstanding species in a genus which contains many fine garden plants. Half-hardy in many parts of North America, the

SUMMER TO AUTUMN FLOWERS/ORNAMENTAL FOLIAGE

Salvia patens

sight of its glorious royal-blue, typically sagelike blooms through the summer and autumn is always uplifting, particularly when it is planted with cool yellows.

A tuberous-rooted perennial, *S. patens* occurs wild in central Mexico in open short grassland, producing strong, erect stems, 3 to 4ft (90–120cm) high, covered with 3–4in (8–10cm) long, hastate, sparsely hairy leaves. The shoots terminate in 12in (30cm) long, sometimes branched, racemes bearing opposite pairs of 2in (5cm) long, hooded and broad-lipped flowers that vary in color from deep, bright blue to white.

Among the selections available are the pale-hued 'Cambridge Blue,' the lilac 'Chilcombe,' and an astonishing new introduction from Mexico, named 'Guanajuato' from the area in which it was discovered, which produces very large flowers, 3in (8cm) or more long, on plants over 5ft (1.5m) tall. It is, in effect, a giant form of the most commonly grown form of *S. patens*, with similarly colored deep blue flowers and the attribute of coming true to type from the freely produced seed.

The fleshy tuberous roots of *S. patens* will be killed by temperatures of 23°F (-5°C) if left in the ground over winter, but for those with the facilities, it may be stored like a dahlia. If this is not possible, it is best treated as a half-hardy annual, because it is easily grown from seed sown under glass in spring. The young plants should be planted out in early summer in fertile, well-drained but moisture-retentive soil, where they will give much pleasure until late autumn when the seed for next year's plants should be collected and, if required, the tubers dug up and stored. This is an exquisitely colored plant of the greatest garden merit.

Agastache mexicana (Labiatae)

Agastache mexicana (also known as *Brittonastrum mexicanum*) is an aromatic perennial with a creeping rootstock from which the 2–3ft (60–90cm) erect, angled stems with pairs of gray-green, ovate-lanceolate, pointed, 2in (5cm) leaves are produced in spring. The terminal 8in (20cm) spires of whorled, rose-crimson flowers, each over 1in (2.5cm) long, appear in June and provide continuous color until the frost. This longevity combined with the pleasant minty smell of the whole plant provide ample reason to grow *A. mexicana*, although, sadly, it is not long-lived and will succumb to cold, damp conditions in winter in many areas.

A well-drained, sunny site on sandy soil is preferable for *A. mexicana* and its relatives, although they will still thrive on rather heavier soils. *A. mexicana* raised from the generously produced seed will flower within a few months, but it is probably best raised annually to ensure continuity of stocks. It may also be propagated readily from soft tip cuttings and it is always worth overwintering a few young plants raised in this manner.

Dahlia merckii (Compositae) (8B–10B)

Although few of our garden dahlias, mainly developed from two Mexican species, *Dahlia coccinea* and *D. pinnata*, are hardy, one or two may be grown successfully in the open for a number of years with minimum protection. However, they are unlikely to survive very severe winters.

Dahlia merckii will withstand considerable cold and is a very attractive species to use in a border among the tougher herbaceous plants. Its elegant, divided foliage and the continuous supply of single, lilac-pink flower heads, each 2in (5cm) across with a central base of bright yellow disk flowers, from midsummer until late autumn, make it a most useful and long-flowering border plant.

Like all dahlias, it has tuberous roots, and these may be lifted each autumn and stored in frost-free conditions before being brought into growth again in early spring, when basal cuttings may be taken to increase stock. Planted out in early summer, it will rapidly develop to some 4 or 5ft (1.2–1.5m) in height, with slender, burnished-reddish stems and dark green, opposite, pinnate leaves, which produce the slightly

Two or More Seasons/*Winter to Spring Flowers* 203

nodding, long-stemmed blooms from the leaf axils of the upper shoots. Seed is freely set, and seedlings show some variation in leaf characters and flower color as well as in eventual height. One of my seed raised plants grows to no more than 2ft (60cm) and has much paler foliage and somewhat deeper lilac blooms than its siblings. So far, *D. merckii* has withstood five winters quite unharmed in the open garden with no protection, having been deep-planted initially so that the top of each tuber is 4 to 5in (10–12cm) below soil level.

Similar treatment worked well in my garden for two or three seasons with 'Bishop of Llandaff,' which received a Royal Horticultural Society Award of Merit in 1928 after trial at Wisley. Growing to 3½ft (1m) in height and producing semidouble blooms of rich, deep scarlet, 3½in (9cm) across that contrast well with the coppery purple foliage, 'Bishop of Llandaff' clearly remains a favorite with many gardeners. Having first grown it myself in 1950, I hope to continue to do so for many years for its sumptuous flowers and foliage, despite the constant battle with snails.

Lobelia 'Dark Crusader' (Campanulaceae) (3B–9B)

The Cardinal Flower, *Lobelia cardinalis*, and the similar but more tender *L. fulgens* have long been cultivated and are fine garden plants in moist soils, although fairly frequently requiring division or propagation from seed to maintain them in good condition.

In 1967, we received at Wisley six selected *Lobelia* clones produced from a breeding program carried out by Dr Wray Bowden at the Plant Research Institute at Ottawa, Canada, and, having grown them on for several years and found them to be hardy and prolific in Britain, we obtained permission to name and distribute them. They were all tetraploids resulting from crosses between the blue *L. siphilitica* and forms of the red-flowered *L. cardinalis*, and varied, considerably in flower and foliage characters, as might be expected.

'Dark Crusader' proved to be extremely attractive, a sturdy plant between 2 and 3ft (60–90cm) high, with deep maroon stems and broad, lanceolate leaves of similar coloring, but occasionally suffused deep green. The 6–8in (15–20cm) terminal inflorescences are densely set with deep ruby red flowers, the calyces mirroring the maroon of the foliage. Like the other clones, it was easily increased by division of the rosetted rootstock and has remained in commercial cultivation, along with three other of Dr Bowden's clones: the taller, green-foliaged, blood-red-flowered 'Brightness'; 'Cherry Ripe,' with green and maroon leaves and cherry-red blooms; and 'Will Scarlet,' blood-red in flower and with the foliage a mix of green and maroon. All, like 'Dark Crusader,' thrive in moist soils, preferring open sites rather than shaded positions to give of their best.

Sadly the two other clones, 'Greensleeves' and 'Red Plush,' are no longer offered commercially, but perhaps still exist in some gardens in Britain or in Canada, where stock of all six clones was returned in 1979, because none had been retained at Ottawa when the material had been generously sent to Wisley some twelve years previously.

WINTER TO SPRING FLOWERS

Viola, Universal Series (Violaceae) (Annual or 6A–9B)

Although there are now garden pansies available for bedding, borders, and containers at almost any season, to me their main value is in winter, when very few plants are available to provide color and brightness in the garden. While they may also be used for summer bedding, the F1 hybrids in the Universal Series have been specifically bred to withstand cold winters, and although they stand still in snowy or frosty conditions, they continue flowering as soon as the weather mellows. Frequently blooming from autumn or early winter until late spring, they may be obtained in mixed or separate colors and, like most pansies, vary greatly in the color range and the extent of the marking of the "faces."

Seed sown in midsummer, and preferably kept cool and moist, should germinate within two weeks, and if the seedlings are pricked out into individual containers or strips they will develop steadily and be ready to plant out in early autumn to replace the faded summer bedding. If established early in autumn in well-drained, fertile soil or, if in containers, in a loam-based potting mix, they will quickly come into bloom and continue to provide flowers all through winter and spring unless checked by very cold conditions.

I use them in containers underplanted with various *greigii* and *kaufmanniana* hybrid tulips, particularly those with attractively mottled or striped foliage which, even without flower, complement the patterned, rounded blooms of the Universal Series. Seed of F1 hybrids, however, is expensive, and for those looking for cheaper seed, the Floral Dance Series gives neat, free-flowering and cold-hardy pansies. Ubiquitous they may be, but on a dull winter morning the smiling faces of these pansies lift the spirits for the rest of the day.

WARM-CLIMATE & GREENHOUSE PLANTS

Whilst the pleasures of gardening using plants that will flourish in frost-prone, cold climates are great, there is as much enjoyment in "messing about in a greenhouse", particularly when the weather is inhospitable in the garden.

Whether a greenhouse or conservatory is extensive or a mere 6 by 8 feet (2 by 2.5m), cold, just frost-free or sufficiently warm to grow bananas is not important – there are numerous plants that can be very successfully grown and enjoyed in all these circumstances.

Space restriction prevents the inclusion of many plants that, had I the appropriate glasshouse accommodation, would find a place in my garden, but the selection provides, I hope, a useful cross-section of plants suitable for such a protected and controlled environment.

Among the climbers are the gorgeous red passion flower *Passiflora racemosa* and the fiery *Pyrostegia venusta* contrasting with the cool blue *Plumbago auriculata* and the great trumpets of *Brugmansia* (*Datura*) 'Grand Marnier'. Less statuesque and ideal for small greenhouses are the strongly fragrant *Boronia megastigma* and the winter-flowering bulbs *Lachenalia rubida* and *Veltheimia bracteata*, while for hanging baskets the succulent Kalanchoe uniflora is delightful over a long period in winter and spring.

SPRING

Species of the genus *Agapetes* are seldom grown as greenhouse plants, but some of them are very colorful in bloom and not at all problematic to grow. The most familiar in cultivation is *A. serpens*, first in my selection of flowering climbers; it has occasionally been cultivated successfully without protection in mild regions, but will flower elsewhere if given the protection of glass

Lapageria rosea, similarly, has been grown outdoors in sheltered conditions, but gives its best under glass. It may be a challenge to obtain and to please, but such is the quality of its blooms that it is worth every effort.

The genus *Hoya* offers the magnificent *H. imperialis*, as well as species that are less vigorous and less demanding such as *H. carnosa*.

Lastly, I suggest a flowering succulent, *Kalanchoe uniflora*, for hanging baskets. Related to the ubiquitous houseplant *K. blossfeldiana*, it will provide pleasure for several months with minimal care and attention.

FLOWERING CLIMBERS

Agapetes serpens (Ericaceae) (9B–11)

The genus *Agapetes* (now held to include *Pentapterygium*) contains a number of extremely attractive species that are not difficult to grow, yet only *Agapetes serpens* has made much impact. It is a scandent, evergreen shrub with long, arching, bristly stems and neat, spirally arranged, slightly fleshy, oblong-ovate leaves. The beautiful, waxy, pendulous flowers are borne singly, or occasionally in twos or threes, in the leaf axils, providing a winter and early spring display of often 6–9in (15–23cm) sprays at the ends of the branches. Each bright red flower is about 1in (2.5cm) long, tubular, and slightly inflated with reflexed lobes, and neatly patterned with darker, V-shaped markings.

In Sikkim some years ago, I saw what looked like red streamers beneath the canopy of the subtropical forest. The fallen flowers appeared to be those of *A. serpens*, later confirmed when we found a plant that had tumbled from a tree. It was exciting to find it in its

Agapetes serpens

natural habitat and to see how it had adapted to an epiphytic life on the branches.

At its best as a hanging-basket plant, *A. serpens* forms red curtains of bloom, akin to those of the many *Columnea* species and hybrids grown in this manner. If wall-trained, it will slowly reach a height of 5 to 6ft (1.5–1.8m), but should not be rigidly supported, or the effect of its elegant pendulous growth will be lost. It requires an acidic, leaf-rich soil and, although worth trying outside in the milder zones, it will also grow and flower elsewhere under glass.

Increase by cuttings of the ripe growths is the usual method of propagation. White, purple-flushed berries from which seed can be extracted may occasionally be produced in cultivation, although hand-pollination is required for a good crop.

Sometimes the equally beautiful 'Ludgvan Cross' (9B–11), a hybrid of *A. serpens* and *A. incurvata* (9B–11) (*Pentapterygium rugosum*), may be offered. This is somewhat more shrubby in habit, with much longer leaves and pink, attractively patterned flowers more densely produced than in *A. serpens* and possibly slightly hardier. It is worth trying any members of this delightful genus, particularly *A. variegata* var. *macrantha* (9B–11), with large bells of waxy pink, and *A. smithiana* var. *major* (9B–11), with clusters of puffed-out, yellow blooms, an excellent hanging-basket plant for the warm greenhouse.

Distictis buccinatoria (Bignoniaceae) (9B–11)

Mexico has provided gardeners with many plants of great merit but none more so than the Blood-red Trumpet Vine, often known as *Phaedranthus buccinatorius*, a vigorous and very beautiful evergreen climber. Each handsome evergreen leaf consists of two large, 4in

(10cm) stalked, ovate leaflets with three long-branched tendrils with adhesive pads by which it attaches itself to any available support. Its superb racemes of large, deep coral-red or rosy crimson, yellow-tubed, 5in (12cm) trumpets provide a long-lasting display throughout the year when the weather warms.

Distictis buccinatoria thrives without protection in gardens in South Africa, southern California, and similar climes. In the interior valleys of California, a protected site is recommended. Nevertheless, if conditions are remotely suitable, it is well worth attempting to achieve a replica of the magnificent display to be seen at the Hanbury Botanic Gardens at La Mortola in northern Italy. There, it luxuriates on terrace walls below the *palazzo*, a sight of great beauty through spring and summer, untroubled by the occasional winter frost that it has withstood for many years.

In the garden, it is best given a high, south-facing wall or a strong arbor over which to climb, but it is also effective trained to form a hedge over a fence or given free rein to wander through a tree. *D. buccinatoria* may also be successfully cultivated under glass if room is available, but as it is capable of achieving 30ft (10m) or more in height it must be kept firmly under control by pruning back the shoots hard to a woody framework after flowering. This will encourage fresh young growth from which the following year's display will be produced. It thrives in fertile, well-drained soil and full sun; preferably let it clamber along supports 1ft (30cm) below the glass, where the pendent, exotic sprays of blooms may readily be admired. Propagation from greenwood or semiripe cuttings in early summer or seed, if available, usually presents no problems.

Hoya imperialis (Asclepiadaceae) (10A–11)

The Wax Plant, *Hoya carnosa* (9A–11), widely distributed from southern China to northern Australia, has long been a favorite, valued for its ability to withstand temperatures down to 25°F (−4°C) in winter and for its beautiful, rounded umbels of up to fifty, pink, crimson-eyed, starry flowers, deliciously scented late in the day and at night.

Hoya is, however, a large genus, and many little-known species of great horticultural value are now available from specialist nurseries. One of these I saw in Australia for the first time some years ago: *Hoya macgillivrayi* (9A–11) has dark red, white-centered flowers, each 3in (7.5cm) across, in umbels of between four and ten. But perhaps the most spectacular is the Malaysian and Indonesian *Hoya imperialis*, a robust evergreen climber to 20ft (6m) or so with opposite pairs of fleshy, leathery, elliptic leaves, 6 to 8in (15–20cm) long and 8in (20cm) umbels of dark red-brown or magenta flowers with prominent creamy white centers.

Like all hoyas, *H. imperialis* should not be subjected to direct sunlight. Strong, filtered light, fairly high humidity, and temperatures of 55 to 65°F (13–18°C) are ideal. An acidic, humus-rich soil is required for cultivation in a greenhouse border or as a pot plant, with a liquid fertilizer when plants are in full growth, and less water when active growth has finished. It flowers when the temperature and light conditions are most suitable during the summer months, but, as with a number of the species, not always at any set season.

Semiripe stem cuttings inserted in a peaty potting mix at 60 to 70°F (16–21°C) root well, but, before insertion, allow the milky sap from the cut shoots to dry off – as with most asclepiads, latex exudes from damaged parts.

Few gardeners in temperate regions have the space to allow these superb climbers to grow naturally, but gently training the succulent growths around a pillar or similar structure, or horizontally around wire hoops, is often very successful, providing a great ball of dark foliage against which the beautiful, pendent inflorescences with their glistening, nectar-rich, scented flowers can be fully appreciated.

Should species such as *H. imperialis* and *H. macgillivrayi* prove too vigorous, *H. carnosa* and *H. lanceolata* subsp. *bella* (9A–11) are among the easiest of this delightful genus to grow, ideal both as pot plants and as hanging-basket plants.

Lapageria rosea (Liliaceae/Philesiaceae) (10A–11)

Among the most beautiful members of the lily family, *Lapageria rosea* is remarkable in having a twining, woody stem – unusual in this predominantly bulbous group. It is, for this reason, usually included in the small family Philesiaceae, and is the only species in its genus. It is the national flower of Chile, where it twines through vegetation to a height of 12 to 15ft (3.5–4.5m).

In cultivation, it requires shade, ample water during the growing season and porous but humus-rich acidic soil. It is best cultivated under glass in temperate climates, but has been grown successfully in sheltered gardens, where it may withstand a few degrees of frost. If reasonably shaded and draught free, it will grow well in the angle between two walls, where it can benefit from any retained heat.

Given the support of a trellis or plastic-covered wire mesh, the wiry stems, clothed in dark green, leathery, narrowly heart-shaped, alternate leaves, 3 to 4in

Lapageria rosea

FLOWERING SUCCULENTS

Kalanchoe uniflora

(7.5–10cm) long, will produce their superb, pendent flowers singly or in clusters of two or three from the leaf axils. Each exquisite and often long-lasting bloom is 3in (7.5cm) long and shaped like a slender trumpet, with the six, waxy, fleshy-textured segments ranging in color from deep crimson to a glistening white. The first flowers appear during summer, sometimes earlier under glass, at the tips of the old wood and, as the season extends into autumn, are also produced from the current season's growth.

Most commonly seen are forms with rich crimson, paler-flecked bells; variations in flower color, from rich pink to the white var. *albiflora*, are available only infrequently, because they increase but slowly by vegetative means. Serpentine layering can be successful, and occasionally cuttings of mature shoots may be rooted to increase named forms. Seed produced in fleshy berries provides a more ready means of propagation, but must be sown fresh and kept at about 50 to 54°F (10–12°C), germinating then in about five to six weeks, although several years will elapse before the seedlings reach flowering size.

Slugs and snails may be troublesome, so regular control is needed. Apart from this, only routine care and careful removal of any spent stems are necessary for established plants which, with the right conditions, should grow happily for many years.

Kalanchoe uniflora (Crassulaceae) (10A–11)

Among the most satisfying plants for greenhouse and house cultivation are the many species of *Kalanchoe*, many of which occur wild in Madagascar and southern Africa. The numerous, vastly popular cultivars of *K. blossfeldiana*, massed with starlike blooms in shades of red, pink, orange, and yellow, are all excellent, easily grown and maintained plants for home decoration.

Distinctive in growth habit and flower form is *Kalanchoe uniflora* (10A–11) (also known as *Kitchingia uniflora* or *Bryophyllum uniflorum*), an epiphytic Madagascan species best planted in a hanging basket to accommodate its trailing, pendent 2ft (60cm) stems, densely set with fleshy, sparingly crenate, rounded leaves no more than ½in (1cm) long that form a curtain around the rim of the basket. In winter and spring, they develop an abundance of coral-red, urn-shaped, 1in (2.5cm) blooms that continue for many weeks.

Easily propagated from stem cuttings, *K. uniflora* will also layer itself, the creeping stems rooting down quickly if gently pinned on to a flat of potting mix or the equivalent.

A well-drained, but reasonably moisture-retentive, not too rich potting mix is suitable to grow *K. uniflora* and other related species which will thrive in a greenhouse or as house plants in a light, sunny (but not hot) position with a minimum temperature of 45°F (7°C).

SUMMER

My recommendations for this section are broken down into two categories: Flowering Climates and Flowering Shrubs/Perennials.

Combining as it does a long display of bright and attractive flowers, handsome foliage, and an equable temperament, *Begonia sutherlandii* remains a firm favorite of mine, giving me pleasure year after year with little trouble or care. In cool temperate regions, with climates comparable to that of Britain, it requires only a cool greenhouse for winter protection.

Other choices here include *Brugmansia* 'Grand Marnier'. The *Brugmansia* species and hybrids known as Angels' Trumpets provide some of the most satisfying of tropical plants, creating a magnificent display at the Hanbury Gardens near La Mortola in northern Italy and other gardens in the south of France. In cooler climates they may thrive in favored spots.

FLOWERING CLIMBERS

Plumbago auriculata (Plumbaginaceae) (9B–11)

Among the most versatile of summer-flowering climbers, the South African *Plumbago auriculata* (often known also as *P. capensis*) is indispensable in frost-free climates, and one of the most attractive and easily cultivated cool greenhouse plants.

A scrambler rather than a true climber, it will reach 12 to 15ft (3.5–4.5m) in height if given appropriate support and training, but may be grown in a small greenhouse, because it withstands hard pruning and will rapidly regenerate to produce vigorous young shoots clothed in fresh green, oblong-ovate, 2–3in (5–8cm) long, wavy-edged leaves.

In some areas, it will flower all year producing, on the current season's shoots, a profusion of beautiful, clear, sky-blue, 1in (2.5cm) wide flowers, rather similar to those of a phlox in shape, and borne in loose clusters at the ends of the slender, arching shoots. If the plant begins to look a little tired, shearing it over will very soon stimulate a further flush of bloom to continue the display. In winter, when flower production is usually diminishing under glass, cut back the growths hard to the main branch framework to encourage the development of further shoots at a lower level and provide an even coverage of bloom from the following spring.

In warm climates, it makes an excellent informal hedging plant, around a fence or simply planted in a line and shaped as required. *P. auriculata* can also be used as a sentinel plant, forming a great mound of evergreen foliage almost always in bloom, tumbling over or planted on a steep bank, where it forms very effective ground cover, making undulating mounds that only require occasional pruning with hedge shears.

Indifferent to all but poorly drained, heavy soils, *P. auriculata* requires little attention other than occasional fertilizing to maintain strong growth. If greenhouse grown, either planted out or in a pot, it needs ample ventilation and a spray over with water daily in hot weather to keep the humidity reasonably high and deter red spider mite which, together with whitefly, may need to be controlled.

Soft or half-ripe cuttings of the young growths root readily, producing plants for friends wishing to enjoy its virtually nonstop display of delicate beauty.

Plumbago auriculata

Pyrostegia venusta (Bignoniaceae) (9B–11)

Aptly called the Flame Vine or Cracker Vine, the South American *Pyrostegia venusta* (sometimes known as *P. ignea*) is one of the most beautiful climbers in cultivation. A robust, evergreen twiner, it will readily climb by means of its leaf tendrils to 30ft (10m) or more, through trees or over some other support. *P. venusta* is particularly effective trained against a wall or on a strong arbor where it produces spectacular festoons of brilliant,

Pyrostegia venusta

glowing orange, tubular, 2in (5cm) flowers between autumn and spring in frost-free climates. It will bloom equally well when allowed to trail across a bank, the smooth, dark green leaves providing dense ground cover when the explosion of blooms has diminished.

Although it is not hardy in many areas, it is still possible to enjoy its colorful display in a warm greenhouse or sunroom where the temperature does not drop below 50 to 55°F (10–13°C). Grow it either as a pot plant or planted out in fertile, well-drained soil and provide reasonably humid conditions, particularly during its main growth period. Even in a relatively small greenhouse it is possible to grow *P. venusta* by training it somewhat like a grape vine "rod." A young plant should be pruned so that a single stem (two or three if room allows) is trained vertically and then extended along the length of the greenhouse ridge, about 1ft (30cm) below the glass. Each spring after flowering, the lateral shoots are all cut back to two or three buds and fresh side shoots soon appear. These are guided onto wires where they will form a dense canopy of foliage from which the large flower panicles appear later in the year. Spring is also the time to prune back any wayward shoots or reduce the size of the plant if required. It is easily propagated from semiripe cuttings in summer.

Thunbergia grandiflora (Acanthaceae) (9B–11)

Odd though it may appear, this glorious genus of climbers and shrubs is classified in the same family as Bear's Breeches, *Acanthus*. The Indian *Thunbergia grandiflora* is greatly valued in many tropical and subtropical countries for its cascades of large, trumpetlike, usually blue-violet flowers produced over a long period. The individual blooms are about 3in (7.5cm) across, with five spreading petallobes, narrowing to a long, yellow-throated tube that complements the blue-violet, lavender, or occasionally white petals of the different color forms. The opposite pairs of rough-textured, ovate, evergreen leaves, up to 6 or 8in (15–20cm) long, are also most handsome and provide pleasant curtains of dark green, even when *T. grandiflora* is out of bloom.

I have seen it in Indonesia and Singapore, twining through trees, where the abundant blooms, borne singly or in short racemes, peered down from 20 or 30ft (6–10m) above, and I have also seen it planted against an arbor where the beauty of the flowers could be appreciated at close quarters.

Its vigor may need to be curbed when the twining shoots spread too far, and in colder areas, where it mainly blooms in summer under glass, it should be treated much as *Pyrostegia*, having very similar cultiva-

Thunbergia grandiflora

tion and propagation requirements. *T. grandiflora*, known by many common names, including Sky Flower and Blue Trumpet Vine, deserves wider cultivation as a greenhouse plant where room allows.

OTHER PLANTS
Passiflora antioquiensis (Passifloraceae) (10A–11)
In a genus almost overendowed with beautiful flowering climbers, *Passiflora antioquiensis* is one of the loveliest of all passion flowers, with huge, 5in (12cm), long-tubed blooms of deep rose-red with a jewellike, central purple ring from which the long-exserted stamens and green stigmas protrude. A hummingbird pollinated species from the mountains of Colombia, the Red Banana Passion Fruit, so called because of the banana-shaped, golden-yellow fruit, is very vigorous, climbing to 15ft (4.5m) or more, but it may readily be grown in a sunroom or greenhouse at temperatures above 45°F (7°C). It is also an excellent houseplant, flowering freely over many months during summer if given adequate support, ample light and ventilation with a fairly humid atmosphere, although such conditions are, admittedly, not always easy to achieve in modern houses. So spectacular are the flowers, however, it is worth any effort to grow successfully.

FLOWERING SHRUBS/
PERENNIALS

Begonia sutherlandii (Begoniaceae) (8B–11)
The race of begonias contains a bewildering variety of species and hybrids. If I had to choose only one, it would be *Begonia sutherlandii*, one of the most attractive and amenable greenhouse or houseplants one can grow.

In the wild, it occurs on moss-covered rocks in shaded forest areas in dappled light on the Natal Drakensberg and adjacent mountains, where it forms gentle mounds of light green, unequal-sided, toothed, ovate leaves, lobed at the base and up to 5in (12cm) long, with reddish veins and edges. The delicate, orange, red-shaded, 1in (2.5cm) flowers are borne in pendent, terminal, and axillary clusters in profusion from late spring, and look lovely in hanging baskets.

Begonia sutherlandii is a tuberous species, and once the foliage dies away in autumn, water should be withheld until signs of growth are seen again in spring, although the tubers must not be allowed to dry out or they may shrivel. It is better, most years, to repot the tubers as soon as the young shoots appear in spring, using a well-drained, leaf-rich potting mix that will retain moisture, because, once in growth, they should not become too dry since this may encourage mildew.

Begonia sutherlandii is one of the few species that is almost hardy in mild temperate regions so only requires overwintering in a cool greenhouse. Propagation is easily effected by collecting the bulbils that develop in the axils of basal leaves in late summer, and storing them over winter in frost-free conditions before "sowing" them in spring.

Begonia sutherlandii

Brugmansia 'Grand Marnier'

***Brugmansia* 'Grand Marnier' (Solanaceae) (9A–11)**
Among the most rewarding of subtropical plants are the Angels' Trumpets, species and hybrids of *Brugmansia* often still included in *Datura*. All are shrubs or small trees with large, velvet-soft leaves and magnificent, pendulous, trumpetlike flowers up to 12in (30cm) long and almost all delightfully scented. In gardens where frost is very rare, they provide an almost continuous supply of graceful blooms in white, yellow, pink, peach, or orange-red from spring until early winter.

In areas where they are not generally hardy, they may be grown in very favored spots but in severe winters will usually be killed unless it is well protected. Brugmansias can also be grown as pot plants or as rather over-sized bedding plants, lifted in autumn, cut back slightly, and potted up to overwinter in frost-free conditions. They drop most of their leaves at this period, but once cut back to within 12in (30cm) or less of the base in late winter or early spring, brought into a light, airy greenhouse at 50°F (10°C), watered and fertilized, they soon revive, and by planting out time, in late spring, should be bursting with flowers. Increase from semiripe heel cuttings in summer presents no problems.

Most species occur wild in the Chilean, Colombian, and Ecuadorian Andes and some very fine hybrids have been produced, of which *B.* x *candida* (9A–11) is most commonly seen. Both single and double variants of *B.* x *candida* produce 12in (30cm) long, scented, flared trumpets, cream in bud and opening to pure white. Equally as good is *B. sanguinea* (9A–11) with more tubular, vermilion or orange-red flowers, but outstanding in my view is 'Grand Marnier,' which produces 8–10in (20–25cm) flowers of a delicate, peachy apricot.

TWO OR MORE SEASONS

The exotic *Beschorneria yuccoides*, combining evergreen, fleshy foliage with giant flowers in summer, performed spectacularly in my garden in the hot British summer of 1976, and hopefully it will repeat its performance in my present garden, as it does in the gardens of the most southern parts of Britain.

Many warm-climate and greenhouse plants provide dual-season beauty by flowering for long periods, and this is particularly valuable in autumn and winter, with bulbous plants such as *Lachenalia* and *Veltheimia*. Also included here are some excellent foliage plants (including the Polka Dot plant, *Hypoestes phyllostachya*, surprisingly tolerant as a house plant) and some prolifically flowering climbers such as *Jasminum polyanthum*.

SPRING OR SUMMER FLOWERS/ EVERGREEN FOLIAGE

***Beschorneria yuccoides* (Agavaceae) (8B–11)**
Even if it did not flower, this Mexican relative of the agaves would be worth growing for its handsome foliage. It has large rosettes of glaucous, lanceolate, fleshy leaves often 2½ft (75cm) long, radiating from a very short caudex or rootstock, elegantly poised and with slightly curving tips like a refined, less stiff *Yucca*, as the species name suggests. My first acquaintance with it was one spring, when I was given a small plant by a friend with the warning that I must keep it in a frost-free greenhouse, which at the time I did not have. A sheltered corner against a south-facing wall was the nearest I could manage so, with the promise of some winter protection, I planted it in the well-drained sand that passes for soil at Wisley and hoped for the best.

The protection was forgotten, but in spite of some severe winters the young plant thrived, produced several offset rosettes and four years later, in the baking summer of 1976, rapidly produced three gigantic, green-red inflorescences arching to over 7ft (2m), branching in the upper third to produce a great panicle of tubular, fuchsialike, 2in (5cm), green, yellow-suffused, pendulous flowers. These were borne in bunches of two to five and contrasted attractively with the conspicuous rhubarb-red bracts, flower stalks, and branchlets of the inflorescence, providing a marvelous sight during midsummer. They did not, however, meet with approval from the family, who likened them to plantlike monsters peering in the windows waiting to pounce! In spite of this, *B. yuccoides* has a place in my present garden, where, I hope, it will repeat its star performance.

A sharply drained, reasonably fertile soil and full sun in a sheltered site fulfil its main needs, either as a tub plant or planted in the garden where, even if it cannot be persuaded to flower, *B. yuccoides* is strikingly attractive, well deserving of cultivation under glass should climatic conditions be unfavorable outdoors. And if it becomes too large for the site you have to offer, detached rosettes usually provide welcome gifts to friends who admire its glaucous elegance.

MEXICAN PLANTS

Central America might seem an unlikely source of plants likely to be hardy or near-hardy in cool temperate zones, but it has provided a surprising number of ornamentals that may be grown outdoors for at least part of the year. All our garden dahlias originate from Mexico, as do *Cosmos atrosanguineus*, *Beschorneria yuccoides* (illustrated below) and *Rhodochiton volubile*, all valuable garden plants. Probably the greatest contribution, apart perhaps from the genus *Dahlia*, comes from the sages, of which over 250 species have been described. Among the shrubby species the brilliant blue *Salvia chamaedryoides* has proved hardy unprotected at Wisley for well over forty years, as has the red-flowered *S. microphylla* (*S. grahamii*). *S. fulgens* is somewhat less hardy, with the brilliant blue, tuberous-rooted *S. patens* and the herbaceous *S. farinacea* in dark or pale blue both being grown as half-hardy annuals.

Hypoestes phyllostachya (Acanthaceae) (10B–11)

Although subshrubby in habit, the Pink Polka-dot or Flamingo Plant, *Hypoestes phyllostachya*, from Madagascar, is usually raised from cuttings or seed annually and has become an extremely popular greenhouse and houseplant. If grown naturally, it will develop into a small, rounded, evergreen subshrub 2 to 3ft (60–90cm) high, with most attractive, dark green, 2in (5cm), ovate leaves heavily splashed and freckled pink or lavender-rose, an arresting combination with individual leaves on a plant exhibiting some variation in the variegation pattern (see p.214).

An amenable houseplant if offered a temperature of 55 to 60°F (13–16°C), draft-free conditions, and well-drained but humus-rich potting mix, *H. phyllostachya* provides delightful foliage color year-round and a modicum of its two-lipped, lavender and white flowers peeping from the leaf axils during winter and spring if unpruned and allowed to develop naturally. Normally, however, it is gently pruned back once it becomes a little untidy, to encourage production of fresh, young leaves of heightened color which quickly hide any signs of the minor surgery. This can be achieved by regularly pinching or cutting out the soft, young shoots, very useful to root if increased stock is needed, so that it develops into a sturdy, rounded plant that may easily be maintained for several years. Because it is so easily grown from cuttings, many gardeners prefer to propagate *H. phyllostachya* annually and use it as a window plant rather than allowing it to develop into a large specimen.

Considerable variation in leaf markings occurs with seed-raised plants, and a number of selected clones can now be obtained. In 'Purpuriana,' the leaves are plum-red with relatively few markings, 'Splash' has very large, bright pink spots, while the leaves of 'Wit' are strongly marbled white, and 'Carmina' has rather brighter red foliage than the other selections. All are delightful for house decoration as well as in the greenhouse; if you are unable to make up your mind which to grow, put one or more of each in a large container, as I have done, and allow them to meld into a very decorative mélange of carmine, pink, white, and green.

OTHER PLANTS
Puya alpestris (Bromeliaceae) (9B–11)
A remarkable genus of bromeliads from the High Andes, the many species of *Puya*, varying from the giant 30ft (10m) *P. raimondii* (9B–11) to cushionlike pygmies only 4 or 5in (10–12cm) high, produce some of the most spectacular flowers in the plant kingdom.

Hypoestes phyllostachya (see p.213)

Several are readily raised from seed and are not difficult to grow under cool-house conditions in well-drained soil, among them the closely related *P. alpestris* and *P. berteroniana* (9B–11), both from Chile and forming rosettes of spiny-edged, rigid leaves, arching at the tips, bright green above with white-dusted undersurfaces. *P. alpestris*, seldom more than 4ft (1.2m) in height when in flower, is probably more easily accommodated in the average greenhouse than *P. berteroniana,* which is twice as high or more in bloom. Both have branched inflorescences packed with open, three-petaled, fleshy bells of an astonishing blue-green.

Although they take many years to flower, the wait for their sumptuous blooms is very worthwhile; while waiting, there is much to admire in the handsome spiny rosettes that are the equal of many cacti in the quality of foliage texture and form.

AUTUMN AND WINTER FLOWERING BULBS

Cyrtanthus elatus (Amaryllidaceae) (8B–11)

This is an unfamiliar name for one of the most beautiful and easiest bulbous plants for cultivation in a cool greenhouse or in areas with only light or infrequent frosts, the Scarborough or George Lily, known for many years as *Vallota speciosa* (or *V. purpurea*).

My first acquaintance with it was on the windowsill of the Botany department at Wisley, when I first joined the staff as an assistant there in 1958: a pot full of bulbs bursting at the seams with "pups" falling over the rim. In late summer or early autumn, stem after stem of the superb, salmon-pink, open-funnel-shaped flowers were produced from the massed bulbs. This color variant, 'Delicata,' had been sent originally from South Africa and is seldom available from nurseries. The scarlet, white-eyed form is better known, having first reached the Yorkshire coast, so it is said, from a wrecked Dutch ship some time before 1800, and been grown as a cottage-window plant in the Scarborough area, from where it became widely dispersed in cultivation.

It often remains more or less evergreen in cultivation, producing a fan of straplike, linear, dark green leaves often up to 1½ft (45cm) long, with the strong flower stems, usually emanating from near the edge of the bulb, terminating in a magnificent umbel of open trumpets, each 4in (10cm) or so across when fully expanded, and carried on 1in (2.5cm) long pedicels.

Occurring wild in moist, shaded sites, *Cyrtanthus elatus* should be planted with the bulb tips slightly proud of the potting mix, and preferably divided in early or midsummer before the fleshy roots become active prior to flowering in late summer. Any well-drained but reasonably fertile potting mix is suitable, and while the foliage is in full growth ample water should be given with regular liquid fertilizing with a high-potassium, tomato-type fertilizer, with a reduction as the leaves begin to yellow and the bulbs go into semidormancy. The more crowded the bulbs in the pot, the freer the flowering, although there comes a point when re-potting and removing the abundantly produced offsets for growing on becomes essential.

Lachenalia rubida (Liliaceae) (10A–11*)

Among the most ornamental and useful cool greenhouse plants, members of the South African genus *Lachenalia* have long been appreciated for their winter and early spring flowering display. They are by no means difficult to grow, but since they are frost-tender, conditions of not less than 41°F (5°C) are needed. Dormant bulbs should be obtained in mid- to late summer and potted into a sharply drained potting mix. They should be kept reasonably cool and the potting mix moist initially; when the foliage tips push through the soil, a more liberal watering regime should be instituted, with a feed with a balanced liquid fertilizer two or three times during the growing period. Once the leaves begin to turn yellow, reduce watering and then eliminate totally; store the dormant bulbs in a cool, dry place, then repot in late summer.

The lovely *Lachenalia rubida* from Cape Province often comes into bloom by late autumn in cool temperate regions. The strap-shaped, succulent-looking, rich green, often dark-spotted leaves, borne in pairs or occasionally singly, appear at the same time as the developing flower buds. The 5–10in (12–25cm) flower-spikes, with their beautiful, pendent cylindrical, deep red, usually white-flecked blooms, 1in (2.5cm) or so long, open as the red-mottled flower stems extend.

The very popular *L. aloides* (10A–11) (*L. tricolor*) is particularly fine in var. *quadricolor*, with distinctive tubular blooms, orange-red at the base with yellow, green-tipped, short outer perianth segments and maroon-red tipped, long inner segments.

Lachenalias increase prolifically from offsets as well as being propagated from leaf cuttings. Fresh, mature leaves are inserted vertically with the base about 1½in (3–5cm) below the surface of the potting mix and in a month or so should have developed roots and small bulblets, which may reach flowering size a season later.

Veltheimia bracteata (Liliaceae) (9B–11)

Soon after I joined the staff at Wisley, I was offered some of the curious, three-winged fruits of *Veltheimia bracteata*. I warmly accepted them, extracted seeds, germinated them in a home-made plant incubator and grew them on to flowering size, three years later. The seedlings rapidly produced rounded, fleshy, scaly bulbs with basal rosettes of shiny, bright green, gently undulating leaves, over 12in (30cm) long and 2 to 3in (5–8cm) wide on mature bulbs.

As with a number of South African bulbs, the flowering season is reversed in America. The bulbs start active growth in autumn, developing their 1½ft (45cm) red-mottled, flowering spikes topped by dense, *Kniphofia*-like inflorescences of pendulous, 1½–2in (3–5cm), tubular, deep rosy-pink flowers, with darker pink flecks, in mid- to late winter.

In spite of, or perhaps because of, relative neglect,

my potbound plants have always flowered regularly and freely, with no more than a feed with a liquid fertilizer in early autumn to maintain their vitality. *V. bracteata* requires no real rest period, so no attempt should be made to dry it off artificially. As the old leaves begin to fade in late summer, they are soon replaced by a fresh rosette.

This attractive winter-flowering plant has for many years masqueraded under a false identity: the plant correctly entitled to the name *V. capensis* has glaucous, markedly undulate foliage and long, narrow bulbs with papery tunics. It also requires a rest period of several months. The name now legitimately applied to the bulb described above is *V. bracteata*. As *V. bracteata* has also been known as *V. viridifolia*, some gardeners have become confused as to which one they have.

As a cool greenhouse or houseplant at a minimum of 40°F (5°C) and grown in a well-drained but reasonably fertile potting mix, *V. bracteata* is an ideal plant to brighten the early weeks of the year, flowering for almost two months and, in some seasons, developing large, winged, often red-suffused seed pods.

Veltheimia bracteata

WINTER AND SPRING FLOWERS/ EVERGREEN FOLIAGE

Acacia baileyana

Acacia baileyana (Leguminosae) (10A–11)

Of all the ornamental wattles that the Australian flora provides, my favorite is *Acacia baileyana*, with its mass of silvered, blue-gray, neatly divided fernlike foliage all year round and a profusion of rich gold, small, fluffy pompon flower heads in late winter and spring.

A small tree, some 20 to 30ft (6–10m) tall, *A. baileyana* will occasionally survive in very sheltered gardens with wall protection in marginally hardy areas, but is better grown as a cool greenhouse plant. It is preferable to plant it out and prune the plant hard after flowering, which occasionally stimulates a second flowering as well as providing further vibrant young foliage. As a pot plant, it seldom attains its full potential.

Seed, preferably scarified, is the simplest means of propagation, but since *Acacia* species produce strong tap roots it is important to plant out seedlings when they are no more than 2 to 3ft (60–90cm) tall. If grown in containers for very long, the tap roots curl around the inside of the pots and, once planted out, seldom act as effective anchors for the mature plants.

Most acacias will grow in any well-drained soil or potting mix and if *A. baileyana* proves too vigorous, several smaller species take well to pot culture. Try the Queensland silver wattle, *A. podalyriifolia* (10A–11); the very free-flowering, *A. pulchella* (10A–11); and the near-hardy *A. paradoxa* (*A. armata*) (10A–11). All flower abundantly in early spring and, if pot grown, may be summered outdoors in light, open positions.

Boronia megastigma (Rutaceae) (10B–11*)

At one time very popular as pot plants, few species of the Australian genus *Boronia* are grown in our greenhouses today. They are relatively undemanding to cultivate, free drainage, a humus-rich acidic to neutral soil and a growing temperature of 50°F (10°C) being their main requirements. In the wild, most species occur in sandy, heathland areas and shaded gullies among deep leaf litter and, like many *Clematis*, require a cool root run with their heads in the sun.

Since most are small shrubs, seldom more than 3ft (1m) high, and respond well to pruning after their spring flowering period, they are ideal sunroom plants, providing attractive, frequently fragrant, four-petaled flowers in a range of colors from blue, mauve, red, and pink to white, yellow, and chocolate brown and, in most species, aromatic foliage as well. All species may be propagated from seed or semiripe heel cuttings in midsummer and, with occasional pinching back to maintain a bushy habit should bloom, within two seasons.

The sight of row after row of the Brown Boronia, *Boronia megastigma*, in a nursery on a visit to Western Australia remains in my memory not only for the neat, trifoliate leaves with scented, narrow leaflets and the freely borne ½in (1–2cm), cup-shaped flowers, purple-brown externally and contrastingly yellow within, but also for the very strong and pleasant fragrance of the blooms that wafted across the field. Interspersed with it was an equally attractive lime-yellow variant, and both provide delightful sprays of cut flowers.

Boronia megastigma and its variants, as well as several other species such as the deep carmine *B. molloyae*

Boronia megastigma

(*B. elatior*) (10B–11) and the lemon-scented *B. citriodora* (10B–11) with starlike, soft pink blooms, make attractive pot plants for a sunroom or greenhouse in late winter and spring. With their tolerance of pruning and freedom of flowering, they should be given a warm welcome if the opportunity arises to obtain plants or propagating material of this neglected genus.

Tradescantia sillamontana (Commelinaceae) (10B–11)

A plant I first encountered on the windowsill of the Botany Department at Wisley, a rooted cutting derived from a specimen sent for naming, was the attractive *Tradescantia sillamontana*, which, unlike its often untidy relations *T. zebrina* (10B–11), and *T. fluminensis* (10B–11), maintains a neat, demure habit of growth.

Now known to be native to northeast Mexico, *T. sillamontana* has had the misfortune to be saddled with five or six names both in the genera *Cyanotis* and *Tradescantia*, despite appearing on the garden scene only in the mid-1950's. Among its synonyms are *T. pexata*, *T.* 'White Velvet,' and *T.* 'White Gossamer,' this last particularly apt, because the leaves are clothed in a matted covering of soft, white, cottony hairs.

Grown in any well-drained, but not rich, potting mix, *T. sillamontana* produces in spring a number of wool-covered rosetted stems, 6in (15cm) or more long, usually ascending initially and then curving and spreading more laxly as summer advances. The leaves are ovate, 2 to 2½in (5–6cm) long when mature, with gently recurving tips. Produced in succession from the upper leaf axils in summer and autumn are the very pretty, bright magenta-rose, three-petaled flowers, ¾in (2cm) across, with yellow anthers, contrasting with the silvery white foliage.

It is important to grow *T. sillamontana* in full light to maintain compact growth because, in shade, the tightly packed internodes elongate so that the cushion-like habit of the plant in its early stages of growth is lost. In late autumn, it is best to withhold water for a period, inducing a state of semidormancy, when the current season's growths may be removed to be replaced by short shoots that appear from the basal leaf nodes. It increases easily from cuttings.

Like many gray-foliaged plants, *T. sillamontana* should not be kept too wet: overwatering may rot it. It is an ideal windowsill plant, its densely cobwebbed rosettes and shoots giving pleasure all year, punctuated irregularly by the neat, brightly colored blooms.

PLANTS WITH EXTENDED FLOWERING PERIOD

Jasminum polyanthum (Oleaceae) (8B–11)

The Common White Jasmine, *Jasminum officinale* (8B–11), from the Himalaya and western China, is a familiar sight in many temperate areas of the world, its profusely borne blooms scenting the garden in summer. Attractive though it is, I find much more desirable the closely related winter- and spring-flowering *Jasminum polyanthum* from Yunnan in China, where it grows at altitudes below 8,000ft (2,000m). Although it normally requires greenhouse conditions with a minimum temperature of 45°F (7°C), it has been grown on sunny walls outdoors in the more clement areas of North America and has also been developed as a pot plant for the Christmas trade.

It will climb rapidly from 12 to 20ft (3.5–6m) or more, with pinnate, fresh green leaves, composed of five to seven ovate-lanceolate, evergreen leaflets, and a profusion of deliciously scented, white, pink-budded, five-petaled flowers ¾in (2cm) across.

An ideal sunroom plant, *J. polyanthum* looks particularly fine trained against a pillar and across the roof, where an abundance of large, loose sprays, each with thirty or forty blooms, will trail down from late winter to early spring.

Its vigorous growth needs to be curtailed after flowering by severe pruning, but thereafter, unless it threatens to outgrow its space, pruning should be kept to a minimum to allow its graceful shoots to develop and

Jasminum polyanthum

hang down preparatory to flowering again the following winter. It is possible to grow *J. polyanthum* as a houseplant in a large pot, restricting its growth by training around a frame. Remove the spent sprays and train the young growths around the supports; prune out any wayward or unwanted shoots, and use the young sideshoots as heel cuttings if fresh stock is required. Once the danger of severe frost is over, the pots may be plunged outdoors in a light, open (but not hot) position to spend the summer and returned inside in autumn. Occasional, training and pruning shoots should be carried out to keep the plant within bounds in summer, together with two or three applications of high-potassium fertilizer to initiate the winter flower display, which is assisted by cool, airy conditions indoors.

An open, loam-based potting mix is preferable to the peat-based ones in which it is usually sold if this delightful jasmine is to be maintained for more than one season. It is worth taking a little trouble to wean the plants from their peat addiction and encourage their roots to adapt to loam.

Justicia brandegeana 'Yellow Queen' (Acanthaceae) (9B–11)

Better known to many gardeners as *Beloperone guttata* or the Shrimp Plant, this most attractive Mexican shrub has rightly proved to be one of the most popular plants for greenhouse or sunroom cultivation, flowering almost constantly through the year and tolerant of relatively low temperatures and fairly low humidity.

In frost-free climates, it makes a slightly lax but well-clothed shrub of some 3 or 4ft (1–1.2m) in height

Justicia brandegeana 'Yellow Queen'

and as much or more across, with soft, ovate, noticeably veined, evergreen leaves, 2 or 3in (5–7.5cm) long, producing an apparently endless supply of terminal, arching inflorescences up to 6in (15cm) long. The beauty of the plant lies mainly in the shrimplike spikes of overlapping, more or less heart-shaped bracts, which usually vary from pinkish brown to brick-red, but in the cultivar 'Yellow Queen' are very distinctive, a combination of lime-green and chartreuse-yellow.

While all forms of *Justicia brandegeana* are well worth growing, 'Yellow Queen' is particularly attractive, providing a positive, bright contrast if planted in association with darker-hued neighbors. The small, tubular flowers come almost as a surprise, virtually concealed within the bracts, where they stick out their white, red-lipped tongues to announce their presence.

Justicia brandegeana is a most accommodating plant, and is readily propagated from soft tip or semiripe cuttings, but it normally flowers so abundantly it is sometimes difficult to find unflowered shoots for propagation. It may be cut back without sulking, so a mature specimen can be pruned hard to encourage the production of young shoots for this purpose.

Grow on the rooted cuttings in a loam-based potting mix at 45 to 50°F (7–10°C) and pinch back the tips of the young shoots regularly so that a bushy, compact framework is established. Although young plants will quickly develop flower-spikes, it is best to remove the first flush of bloom to ensure that the desired habit is developed.

Ample water and application of a balanced fertilizer every two or three weeks is enough to keep Shrimp Plants in flower, although a hard haircut and repotting into a fairly rich potting mix in early spring is sometimes required to keep them in peak condition.

Justicia brandegeana needs winter protection in most of Zone 9, and is dependably perennial only in Zones 10–11. Prune in late winter, early spring. It responds to several hours' sunlight daily – preferably in the early morning.

Passiflora racemosa (Passifloraceae) (11)

My first acquaintance with this superb passion flower was one summer, many years ago, where it was a magnificent and memorable sight in full flower with its streamers of bright red blooms carried in profusion.

Native to Brazil, in regions near Rio de Janeiro, *Passiflora racemosa* is unusual in cultivated species in producing 12in (30cm) long racemes rather than solitary or clustered flowers. It requires temperatures of 60°F (15°C) or more to bloom freely and, although it

Passiflora racemosa

will withstand cooler conditions, it seldom thrives at less than 50°F (10°C). It is, a plant for the warm greenhouse, and few climbers can be so effective covering a wall or pillar, where it blooms through summer and autumn with some racemes still being produced in winter and occasionally into spring.

A vigorous climber that can grow to 30ft (10m) or more in nature, with three-lobed (sometimes entire), leathery, deep green leaves, it produces up to forty bright scarlet, white-centered flowers, 4in (10cm) or more across, on each raceme. With such an abundance of bloom there is a very long display with often three or four blooms open at any one time on the individual racemes and the sharply angled, five-winged, bright red buds promising further beauty in the weeks to come.

Like most passion flowers, *P. racemosa* should be given a well-drained, open, soil-based potting mix – water-saturated, peat-based mixtures often bring about their decline – and if grown as a pot plant it will require a regular feed with liquid fertilizer in summer to maintain strong growth. If practicable, train the long, wandering shoots against wires or trellis close to the greenhouse wall and then below the ridge, so that the showy racemes are seen to best effect.

Pruning will almost certainly be needed in view of its vigor, and unwanted shoots (useful for providing cuttings) may be removed in late winter or spring.

Streptocarpus saxorum (Gesneriaceae) (10B–11)

Although the very colorful *Streptocarpus* hybrids, available in a wide color range, are among the most desirable greenhouse and houseplants, I have a particular affection for *Streptocarpus saxorum*, which occurs wild in Tanzania and Kenya, growing on exposed cliffs and rock faces. Unlike the well-known hybrids, it is a caulescent (stemmed) species, and almost succulent in habit, producing mounded, spreading, 6–12in (15–30cm) stems clothed in fleshy, usually opposite pairs of evergreen, hairy, ½–¾in (1–2cm) leaves. The axillary inflorescences produce only one or two of the lavender-violet, lobed, open-mouthed, 1½in (4cm) white-tubed flowers on long elegant stems, but they appear regularly and freely over many months during summer and autumn and often at other seasons too.

As the plants age, the lower parts of the older stems gradually lose their leaves, becoming prostrate and almost pendulous in growth, and fresh shoots often appear near the center of the plant. This growth habit makes *S. saxorum* ideal as a hanging-basket plant, and, given a well-drained but humus-rich potting mix, it will grow and flower well in lightly shaded conditions at 45 to 50°F (7–10°C) without difficulty. Old, untidy plants may be discarded after a few years and replaced by youngsters propagated from the young shoots that root readily in a sandy cutting mix at any time of year.

Related plants Somewhat more flamboyant than *Streptocarpus saxorum* are the numerous hybrids deriving from a number of the large-leaved, rosetted species, chiefly the white or lavender-mauve South African *S. rexii* (10A–11), which, crossed with other species such as the red *S. dunnii* (10A–11), produced a range of flower colors and sizes, including the very popular, deep purplish-blue 'Constant Nymph.' Since then, further breeding has resulted in a magnificent range of large- and small-flowered clones, flowering profusely over long periods both as greenhouse and houseplants. All are readily grown in well-drained, humus-rich soil, providing long displays of tubular, two-lipped, open-faced flowers in a variety of colors.

The large-flowered 'Albatross,' with spray after spray of pure white, yellow-throated blooms, and the dark, velvet-purple 'Elsi,' are particular favorites in this group while 'Falling Stars,' with silky-blue flowers like a cloud of butterflies, is outstanding among those with more abundant, smaller blooms.

Streptosolen jamesonii

Streptosolen jamesonii (Solanaceae) (9B–11)

It is not surprising that one of the common names for this long-cultivated Peruvian and Colombian shrub is the Marmalade Bush as the color of its flowers, a mix of bright and paler orange, is very reminiscent of home-made bitter orange marmalade.

Widely grown in frost-free gardens throughout the world as a specimen shrub or informal hedge for its abundantly produced flowers, *Streptosolen jamesonii* is also frequently seen as a cool greenhouse or sunroom plant in North America, sometimes free-standing or as a pot plant, but also trained on a greenhouse wall or trellis, to which its lax, scandent growth is well suited.

Easily raised from cuttings of young shoots in spring or summer, it may be grown as an annual, since it blooms freely in the first year, but if it is not to be replaced each year it is important to pinch out the shoot tips of rooted cuttings to develop a strong, bushy plant. As rooted cuttings may sometimes flower when very young, the developing inflorescences should be removed as soon as seen to ensure that a sturdy, strongly branched plant is produced. Thereafter, gently pinching and pruning to achieve the required shape is all that is needed, apart from an occasional feed with liquid fertilizer every three weeks or so to supplement the nutrients in the well-drained, fairly rich, loam-based potting mix in which it should be grown.

Streptosolen jamesonii is a most obliging plant, because although frost-tender, it makes an admirable patio container plant, producing a continuous supply of its loose terminal clusters of salver-shaped, burnt-orange to yellow, 1in (2.5cm) blooms from midspring to midautumn, where hardy, with occasional blooms at other times. It is also readily trained as a standard, and I have seen it grown as a hanging-basket plant. My own preference is to train it against a white-washed, lean-to greenhouse wall, where its 2in (5cm) long, wrinkled, ovate, deep green leaves and brilliant, long-lasting flower sprays show to best effect, particularly if it is gently and informally trimmed and trained to maintain it within its allotted space.

Tibouchina urvilleana (Melastomataceae) (10A–11)

The common name Glorybush or Princess Flower is most appropriate for *Tibouchina urvilleana*, which provides a glorious display of blooms from late spring to autumn when grown as a sunroom or greenhouse shrub. Often grown as *T. semidecandra*, a related but rarely cultivated species, *T. urvilleana* occurs wild in Brazil and has taken admirably to cultivation, but requires a minimum of 45 to 50°F (7–10°C).

Although it may reach 15ft (4.5m) or more in height, *T. urvilleana* is readily maintained as a shrub of no more than 6ft (1.8m) or so by careful pruning. The flowered shoots are then cut back in winter or early spring to two or three buds, leaving short spurs from which the following season's flowering shoots will develop. As these develop, they may be pinched back to provide additional flowering branchlets. Care should be taken not to lose the elegant growth by over-pruning, however, because the natural inclination of *T. urvilleana* is to spread gracefully to display its velvety, rich green, opposite pairs of evenly spaced, 4–6in (10–15cm) long, ovate, beautifully veined leaves.

A more-or-less continuous supply of the 4in (10cm) wide, five-petaled, open flowers, reddish in bud and opening to sumptuous blooms of satiny, rich purple will appear from the terminal, forking branchlets from late spring onward, declining only with the onset of winter. Judicious removal of exhausted flowered shoots often extends the season further.

Tibouchina urvilleana requires a well-drained, neutral to acidic, loam-based, moisture-retentive potting mix to thrive. A monthly boost from a high-potassium fertilizer during the growing season and cool, airy growing conditions are all that are needed to maintain it in robust health. Propagation from spring or summer-

Tibouchina urvilleana

produced sideshoots is uncomplicated.

In areas of North America where it is not hardy, *T. urvilleana* can be grown in the open bedded out or in tubs in the summer but is well worth the effort of over-wintering in frost-free conditions for the exuberant showers of blooms for over half the year. Where hardy, grow with shaded roots, sunny tops. Protect from wind.

Tweedia caerulea (Asclepiadaceae) (10B–11)

This beautiful, marginally scandent, 3ft (1m) subshrub from Uruguay and southern Brazil continues to suffer the indignity of periodic generic switches and, while currently resting in the genus *Tweedia*, may well also be offered as a species of *Oxypetalum* or *Amblyopetalum*. Its quality as a greenhouse plant has been recognized recently by the Award of Garden Merit of The RHS, and it is one of the most easily cultivated greenhouse plants either planted out or in pots, valuable both for its foliage and its continuous supply of distinctive and attractive summer blooms.

Readily raised from seed, *Tweedia caerulea* flowers in its first season if sown in early spring at 50 to 55°F (10–13°C), but it may also be propagated easily from late spring or summer cuttings of sideshoots from established plants. Grown in a well-drained, moisture-retentive and preferably loam-based potting mix, plants will rapidly produce lax, twining shoots, bearing opposite pairs of oblong, cordate-based, 4in (10cm), grey-green leaves, the whole plant being white-pubescent.

The starry, upright, 1in (2.5cm) flowers are produced abundantly in sprays from the leaf axils of the upper third of the stems, opening from pinkish buds to reveal green-tinted, sky-blue petals, changing with age to blue-purple and finally to lilac.

Although writers seldom mention the seed pods, they are freely produced and provide an extra reason for growing *T. caerulea*. Shaped like narrow, slightly curved cigars, they open, when ripe, to reveal neatly packed rows of brown seeds, each with long tufts of white hairs that expand when dry to form "parachutes."

After flowering has finished in autumn, less water is required and the plants can be rested (but not dried out) until early spring, when all the shoots should be cut back to 2in (5cm) or so from the base.

Apart from requiring a little support for its gently wandering stems, *T. caerulea* is not difficult to grow in a cool greenhouse or sunroom. When coming into flower it may be transferred to a light, airy position in the house, or alternatively the stems may be cut and used for floral decoration, as the flowers are long-lasting in water.

USEFUL ADDRESSES

Retail Mail-Order Nurseries

This list of North American plant and seed suppliers lists specialities where they are not apparent from the company's name. When no speciality is given, the company supplies a wide range of plants. For further information, a selection of North American plants finders is included at the end of this section.

Alpenflora Gardens
17985–40th Avenue,

Surrey, BC, Canada V3S 4N8
Rock garden and alpine plants.

Kurt Blumel, Inc.
2740 Greene Lane,
Baldwin, MD 21013–9523
Ornamental grasses, sedges, and rushes, bamboos and perennials.

The Bovees Nursery
1737 S.W. Coronado,
Portland, OR 97219
Hybrid and species rhododendrons, shrubs, and alpines.

Borbeleta Gardens
15980 Canby Avenue,
Faribault,
MN 55021
Lilies, day lilies, Siberian and bearded iris.

Canyon Creek Nursery
3527 Dry Creek Road,
Oroville, CA 95965
Wide range of perennials.

Colorado Alpines, Inc.
P.O. Box 2708,

Hardiness Zones

The zone listings (1–11) used throughout this book in brackets after plant names refer to internationally recognized hardiness zones, as shown on the map below (courtesy of USDA). "A" refers to the north of a zone, "B" to the south.

An asterisk next to a zone listing indicates that the plant is grown only on the West Coast.

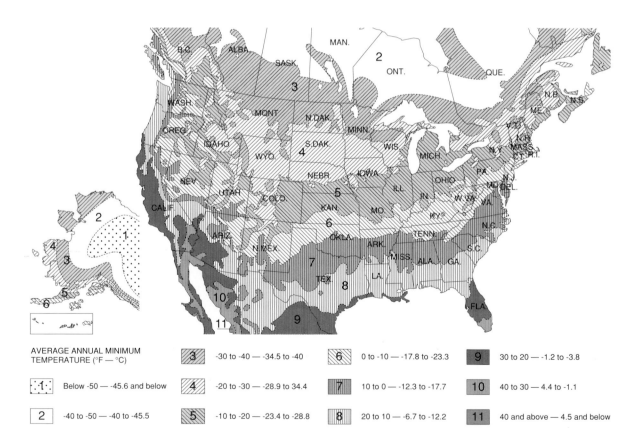

AVERAGE ANNUAL MINIMUM TEMPERATURE (°F — °C)			
1 Below -50 — -45.6 and below	**3** -30 to -40 — -34.5 to -40	**6** 0 to -10 — -17.8 to -23.3	**9** 30 to 20 — -1.2 to -3.8
2 -40 to -50 — -40 to -45.5	**4** -20 to -30 — -28.9 to 34.4	**7** 10 to 0 — -12.3 to -17.7	**10** 40 to 30 — 4.4 to -1.1
	5 -10 to -20 — -23.4 to -28.8	**8** 20 to 10 — -6.7 to -12.2	**11** 40 and above — 4.5 and below

Avon, CO 81620
Alpine and rock garden plants.

Dominion Seed House
115 Guelph Street,
Guelph Street and Maple Avenue,
Georgetown, ON, Canada L7G 4A2
Wide range of seeds.

Fancy Fronds
1911–4th Avenue West,
Seattle, WA 98119
Wide range of hardy ferns – worldwide.

Gardenimport Inc.
P.O. Box 760,
Unit 5, 2 Essex Avenue,
Thornhill, ON, Canada L3T 4A5
Annuals, perennials, and bulbs.

Glasshouse Works
P.O. Box 97,
10, Church Street,
Stewart, OH 45778–0097
Exotic, tropical, and variegated plants.

Gossler Farm Nursery
1200 Weaver Road,
Springfield, OR 97478–9663
Magnolias, daphnes, stewartias, and other unusual trees and shrubs.

Heronswood Nursery
7530–288th Street N.E.,
Kingston, WA 98346
Wide range of unusual woody and perennial plants.

Holbrook Farm and Nursery
Route 2, Box 223B,
Fletcher, NC 28732
Perennials, native species – broad selection.

Klehm Nursery
Route #5, Box 197,
Penny Road,
South Barrington, IL 60010–9555
Hostas, day lilies, herbaceous and tree peonies, and perennials.

Kline Nursery Co.
17401 S.W. Bryant Road,
Lake Oswego, OR 97035
Perennials, hardy cyclamen, ferns, and species lilies. Alpines.

Lamb Nurseries
E. 101 Sharp Avenue,

Spokane, WA 99202
Perennials, rock garden plants, and violets.

Lilypons Water Gardens
P.O. Box 10,
6800 Lilypons Road,
Lilypons, MD 21717–0010
Water lilies, lotus and bog plants.

Logee's Greenhouses
141 North Street,
Danielson, CT 06239
Begonias and other greenhouse exotics.

Grant Mitch Novelty Daffodils
P.O. Box 218,
Hubbard, OR 97032
Choice hybrid daffodils.

Oregon Trail Daffodils
3207 S.E. Mannthey Road,
Corbett, OR 97019
Choice hybrid daffodils.

Park Seed Co., Inc.
P.O. Box 46,
Highway 254 North,
Greenwood, SC 29648 0046
Wide range of flower and vegetable seed. Plants and bulbs.

Plant Delights Nursery
9241 Sauls Road,
Raleigh, NC 27603
Hostas and many unusual shrubs and perennials.

Prairie Nursery
P.O. Box 306,
Westfield, WI 53964
Native prairie plants.

Rice Creek Gardens
1315–66th Avenue N.E.,
Minneapolis, MN 55432
Alpine and rock garden plants.

Roses of Yesterday and Today
802 Brown's Valley Road,
Watsonville, CA 95076 0398
"Old Garden" roses – wide range.

Schriner's Gardens
3625 Quinaby Road N.E.,
Salem, OR 97303
Fine modern iris hybrids.

Siskiyou Rare Plant Nursery
2825 Cummings Road,
Medford, OR 97501
Wide range of alpine and rock garden plants.

Anthony Skittone
1415 Eucalyptus,
San Francisco, CA 94132
Spring and summer bulbs worldwide.

Thompson and Morgan
P.O. Box 1308,
Farraday and Gramme Avenues,
Jackson, NJ 08527
Wide selection of seeds – all types of plants.

Andre Viette Farm and Nursery
Route 1, Box 16,
State Route 608,
Fisherville, VA 22939
Broad selection of perennials.

Wayside Gardens
1 Garden Lane,
Hodges, SC 29695–0001
Wide selection of trees, shrubs, perennials, and bulbs. Roses.

We-Du Nurseries
Route 5, Box 724,
Marion, NC 28752
Rock garden, woodland plants. Unusual Asiatic selections.

Woodlanders, Inc.
1128 Colleton Avenue,
Aiken, SC 29801
Southern U.S. natives and hard to find exotics.

Yucca Do Nursery
P.O. Box 655,
Waller, TX 77484
Unusual trees, shrubs, and perennials for Zones 8 and 9. Native Texan plants and their Mexican and Asiatic counterparts.

SPECIALIST SOCIETIES

Alpine Garden Club of British Columbia
13751, 56A Avenue,
Surrey, B.C., Canada V3W 1S4

American Conifer Society
P.O. Box 242,

Severna Park,
MD 21146

American Daffodil Society, Inc.
1686 Grey Fox Trails,
Milford, OH 45150

American Fern Society, Inc.
Dept. of Botany,
University of Tennessee,
Knoxville, TN 37996–1100

American Herb Association
P.O. Box 353,
Rescue, CA 95672

American Hosta Society
5300 Whiting Ave.,
Edina, MN 55435

American Iris Society
7414 E. 60th Street,
Tulsa, OK 74145

American Peony Society
250 Interlachen Road,
Hopkins, MN 55343

American Plant Life Society
P.O. Box 985,
National City, CA 92050

American Rhododendron Society
P.O. Box 1380
Gloucester, VA 23061

American Rock Garden Society
15 Fairmead Road,
Darien, CT 06820

California Horticultural Society
1847–34th Avenue,
San Francisco, CA 94122

California Native Plant Society
909–12th Street #116,
Sacramento, CA 95814

The Magnolia Society, Inc.
907 S. Chestnut Street,
Hammond, LA 70403–5102

New England Wild Flower Society
Hemenway Road,
Framingham, MA 01701

North American Heather Society
62 Elma-Monte Road,
Elma, WA 985541

North American Lily Society, Inc.
P.O. Box 272,
Owatonna, MN 55060

Rhododendron Species Foundation
P.O. Box 3798,
Federal Way, WA 980603–3798

The Perennial Plant Association
Dept. of Horticulture,
Ohio State University,
2001 Fyffe Court,
Columbus, OH 43210

PLANT FINDERS

*The Andersen Horticultural Library's
Source List of Plants and Seeds*
Compiled by Richard Isaacson (1993).
Andersen Horticultural Society,
Minnesota Landscape Arboretum,
3675 Arboretum Drive,
P. O. Box 39,
Chanhassen,
MN 55317
*Approx. 47,000 plants and seeds from 400
retail and wholesale outlets in the United*

*States and Canada. All are prepared to ship
interstate. Does not include orchids, cacti
and succulents.*

The Canadian Plant Source Book
Anne and Peter Ashley (1992).
93 Fentiman Avenue, Ottawa,
ON Canada K1S OT7
*14,000 hardy plants available at retail and
wholesale nurseries across Canada, including
those who ship to the United States. English
names and English and French cross-indexes.*

Garden Seed Inventory
Edited by Kent Whealy (1992).
Seed Saver Publications,
3076 North Winn Road,
Decorah, Iowa 52101
*Lists every non-hybrid vegetable variety
available from 223 mail-order seed
companies in the United States and Canada,
with descriptions and sources for each.*

Hortus Source List (1992)
Baily Hortorium, 462 Mann Library,
Cornell University,
Ithaca, NY 14853
*More than 22,000 plant entries from 63
nurseries, most in New York State.*

Northwest Native Plant Directory
Edited by Dale Shank (4th issue, 1993).
Hortus Northwest, P.O. Box 955,
Canby, OR 97013
*126 native plant nurseries in Oregon,
Washington, British Columbia, and north-
ern California.*

SELECT BIBLIOGRAPHY

GENERAL

The New Plantsman, published regularly by The Royal Horticultural Society, Vincent Square, London SW1P 2PE. (Also *The Plantsman*, 15 Vols 1979-94.)

Beckett, K. A. 1987. *The RHS Encyclopaedia of House Plants*. Century Hutchinson, London.

Brickell, C. D. (ed.) et al. 1980. *International Code of Nomenclature for Cultivated Plants*. Utrecht. (New edition due 1995.)

Brickell, C. D. (ed.) 1989. *Gardeners' Encyclopaedia of Plants and Flowers*. Dorling Kindersley Inc., New York.

Chittenden, F. J. (ed.) 1965. *The Royal Horticultural Society Dictionary of Gardening* (2nd edn). Oxford University Press.

Heath, R. E. 1981. *Collectors Alpines*. Collingridge, Twickenham.

Hillier Manual of Trees and Shrubs (6th edn). 1991. David & Charles, Newton Abbot.

Huxley, A. (ed.). 1992. *The New Royal Horticultural Society Dictionary of Gardening*. Stockton Press Inc., New York.

Innes, C. F. 1985. *The World of Iridaceae*. Holy Gate International, Ashington, Sussex.

Jacobsen, H. 1973. *Lexicon of Succulent Plants*. Blandford, London.

Jellitto, L. & Schacht, W. *Hardy Herbaceous Perennials* (3rd edn edited by W. Schacht & A. Fessler). Timber Press, Portland, Oregon, USA.

Krussmann, G. (English edn trans. M. E. Epp) 1984-1986. *Manual of Cultivated Broadleaved Trees & Shrubs* (vols I-III). Batsford, London.

Mabberley, D. J. 1987. *The Plant-Book*. Cambridge University Press.

Phillips, R. & Rix, E. M. *Shrubs*. 1989. Pan Books, London.

Phillips, R. & Rix, E. M. 1991/2. *Perennials*. Pan Books, London.

Stearn, Prof. W. T. 1992. *Stearn's Dictionary of Plant Names for Gardeners*. Cassell, London.

Thomas, G. S. 1990. *Perennial Garden Plants* (3rd edn). J. M. Dent & Sons, London.

Walters, S. M. (ed.) et al. 1984, 1986 & 1989. *The European Garden Flora* (vols. I-III). Cambridge University Press.

Willis, J. C. 1973. *A Dictionary of the Flowering Plants and Ferns* (8th edn) revised H. K. Airy Shaw. Cambridge University Press.

GENERA

Acer De Jong, P.C. et al. *International Dendrology Society Year Book*, 1991. London.
van Gelderen, D.M., De Jong, P.C. & Oterdoom, H.J. 1994. *Maples of the World*, Timber Press, Oregon, USA

Allium Davies, C. G. 1992. *Alliums*. Batsford, London.

Bulbs Bryan, J.E. 1989. *Bulbs* (2 vols.), Timber Press, Oregon, USA.
Duplessis, N. & Duncan, G. 1989. *Bulbous Plans of Southern Africa*. Tafelberg, Cape Town, South Africa
Grey-Wilson, C. & Matthew, B. 1981. *Bulbs*. Collins, London.
Rix, M. & Phillips, R. 1981. *The Bulb Book*. Pan Books, London.

Clematis Lloyd, C. & Bennett, T. H. 1989. *Clematis*. Viking, London.

Conifers Krussmann, G. (English trans. M. E. Epp). 1985. *Manual of Cultivated Conifers*. Batsford, London.

Crocus B. Mathew. 1982. *The Crocus, a revision of the Genus Crocus, Iridaceae*. Batsford, London.

Cyclamen Grey-Wilson, C. 1988. *The Genus Cyclamen*. Christopher Helm, Bromley, Kent.

Daphne Brickell, C. D. & Mathew, B. 1976. *Daphne*. Alpine Garden Society.

Ferns Mickel, J. 1994. *Ferns for American Gardens*. Macmillan, New York, USA.

Geranium Yeo, P. F. 1985. *Hardy Geraniums*. Croom Helm, London.

Hebe Chalk, D. 1988. *Hebes and Parahebes*. Christopher Helm, London.

Hedera Rose, P. Q. 1980. *Ivies*. Blandford Press, Dorset, UK.

Helleborus Mathew, B. *Helleborus*. Batsford, London.

Hosta Grenfell, D. 1990. *Hosta*. Batsford, London.
Schmid, W. G. 1991, *The Genus Hosta*. Timber Press, Oregon.

Hydrangea Haworth-Booth, M. 1975. *The Hydrangeas*. Garden Book Club, London.

Iris Mathew, B. 1981. *The Iris*. Batsford, London.

Lewisia Mathew, B. 1989. *The Genus Lewisia*. Christopher Helm, Bromley, Kent.

Magnolia Callaway, D.J. 1994. *The World of Magnolias*. Timber Press, Oregon, USA.
Gardiner, J. M. 1989. *Magnolias, their care and cultivation*. Cassell, London
Treseder, N. G. 1978. *Magnolias*. Faber & Faber, London.

Meconopsis Cobb, J. L. S. 1989. *Meconopsis*. Christopher Helm, Bromley, Kent.

Narcissus Blanchard, J. W. 1990. *Narcissus*. Alpine Garden Society, Woking, Surrey.
Wells, J. *Modern miniature daffodils: species and hybrids*. 1989. Batsford, London

Paeonia Harding, A. & Klehm, R. G. 1993. *The Peony*. Batsford, London.

Papaveraceae Grey-Wilson, C. 1993. *Poppies*. Batsford, London.

Rosa Beales, P. 1992. *Roses*. Harvill, London.
Phillips, R. & Rix, M. 1988. *Roses*. Macmillan, London.
Thomas, G. S. 1994. *The Graham Stuart Thomas Rose Book*. Saga Press/Timber Press, Oregon, USA.

Saxifraga Kohlein, F. 1984. *Saxifrages and Related Genera*. Batsford, London.
Webb, D. A. & Cornell, R. J. 1989. *Saxifrages of Europe*. Christopher Helm, Bromley, Kent.

Syringa Fiala, Fr J. L. 1988. *Lilacs*. Christopher Helm, Bromley, Kent.

A TO Z OF TERMS
AND TECHNIQUES

Words in *italics* have a separate entry giving further information. Techniques are introduced with **CAPITAL** letters.

acute *see page 228.*

alternate leaves borne singly at intervals on alternate sides of the stem.

anther the pollen-producing part of a *stamen.*

awn a whisker-like projection on the end of a leaf, petal or seed, particularly grass seed.

axil the angle between the point of attachment of a leaf or *bract* to a stem.

axillary situated in or arising from an *axil.*

bipinnate a compound *pinnate* leaf, where the segments are also pinnately divided.

biternate a leaf divided into three, each subdivision divided into three leaflets.

bract a leaf, often modified or reduced, at the base of a flower or *inflorescence.*

breastwood shoots growing forwards from wall-trained trees and shrubs.

budding *see* grafting.

bulb a storage organ, usually underground, consisting of fleshy leaf bases on a short stem.

bulb frame a glass frame used to create an entirely dry environment for *bulbs* during their resting period.

bulbil a small *bulb* or *tuber* developing on a plant above ground level.

bulblet a small *bulb* produced at the base of a mature one.

bullate having a corrugated or puckered surface.

calyx (pl. calyces) the collective name for the *sepals*, the outermost ring of modified leaves that protect the flower in bud.

campanulate bell-shaped.

canescent white or greyish due to the presence of numerous short white hairs.

carpel the female part of a flower, consisting of a *stigma*, a *style* and an ovary.

caudex (pl. caudices) a thickened persistent stem base.

cauline relating to or growing from a stem.

chimera a plant in which there are two genetically different sorts of cell, as a result of *mutation* or *grafting.*

chlorosis fading of the green color (chlorophyll) in plants, caused by mineral deficiency, inadequate light or infection.

ciliate having a fringe of hairs.

clone a group of genetically identical plants vegetatively propagated from a single parent.

colchicine an alkaloid derived from the autumn crocus, used to produce mutations to increase the number of chromosomes in plant breeding.

corm an underground storage organ formed from a swollen stem base.

corolla the part of the flower formed from the petals or floral leaves.

corona an outgrowth sometimes developed on the *corolla*, such as the trumpet of a daffodil.

corymb a flat-topped flower cluster.

cotyledon embryo leaf or leaves contained within a seed. Flowering plants are divided into those with one seed leaf (monocotyledons) and those with two seed leaves (dicotyledons).

crenate a leaf with rounded teeth around its edge.

crown the part of a plant at or just below soil level, from which shoots grow. Also the upper, branching part of a tree.

cruciferous having four petals arranged in a cross shape.

cultivar short for "cultivated variety", a horticulturally selected plant with characteristics that distinguish it from others of the same species, and that are retained when the plant is propagated. Indicated by placing the name in single quotation marks.

CUTTING part of a plant (stem, root, leaf or bud) separated from its parent and induced to produce roots and, in time, a new plant.

Stem cuttings are the most commonly used. The method employed varies slightly according to the maturity of the stem. The use of rooting hormone powders is most beneficial with semiripe and hardwood cuttings.

Softwood cuttings are fast-growing but immature shoots taken from plants outdoors in spring. They have a high capacity to produce roots but they wilt easily and are vulnerable to fungal attack. **Greenwood cuttings**, like softwood cuttings sometimes referred to as **tip cuttings**, are taken a little later, when the stem is slightly harder. Softwood and greenwood cuttings, taken early in the morning, while leaves are turgid, should be trimmed to a length of about 4in (10cm), a sharp, clean blade being used to cut them just below a *node*. Leaves are stripped from the bottom half or third of stems before they are inserted in a free-draining, sterile rooting medium. A moist atmosphere will help to keep leaves from wilting and bottom heat encourages the rapid development of a root system. Professionals usually place these cuttings in mist propagation units.

Reasonably good results can be achieved by placing pots of cuttings in a clear polythene bag, which is then sealed and placed in a warm position but out of direct sunlight.

Semiripe (semihardwood) cuttings, used to propagate a wide range of shrubs, are taken in the second half of summer. They are normally trimmed to 4–6in (10–15cm), the bottom half stripped of leaves and the tip removed if it is soft, before cuttings are inserted in a free-draining rooting medium. A cold frame provides suitable conditions in which to keep semiripe cuttings while they root; it should be insulated with matting while there is danger of frost.

Hardwood cuttings provide an easy means of propagating many deciduous trees and shrubs. Mature stems of the current season's growth give the best results, and if they are taken in autumn can be inserted in a sheltered position in the open garden. The cuttings, 6–15in (15–38cm) long, should be inserted to a depth equal to between half and one-third their length and left in position for a full growing season.

Heel cuttings are often used for plants that are slow to root. Softwood, greenwood, semiripe and hardwood cuttings can all be taken as heel cuttings: that is a stem pulled away with part of the parent stem still attached. The heel must be trimmed with a sharp, clean instrument before the cutting is inserted in the rooting medium.

Root cuttings are mainly used to propagate thick-rooted perennials and shrubs. The cuttings, 2–4in (5–10cm) long, are taken when plants are dormant. To avoid the risk of confusing top and bottom it is usual to make the top cut horizontal and the bottom cut sloping. After being dusted with a fungicide, the cuttings are inserted vertically in a container filled with potting compost, best stood in a cold frame.

Leaf cuttings offer a way of propagating a number of plants with thick, fleshy leaves, most of which are greenhouse plants in temperate regions of the world. The main difficulty is the risk of rot, and very high standards of hygiene must be maintained. The simplest method with those that are of manageable size is to select healthy leaves complete with stalks and insert them in a compost of equal parts of sand and peat. A propagator with bottom heat provides ideal conditions for rapid rooting. Large leaves of suitable plants can be cut crossways into several sections, each section being treated as a separate cutting and inserted vertically.

cyme an inflorescence in which the central or terminal flower opens first.

deadheading the removal of faded flowers to prevent seed setting, encourage further flowering and improve appearance.

decumbent lying flat with the tip growing upwards.

decurrent extending down the stem.

dicotyledon see cotyledon.

digitate *see page 228.*

disc one of the small, usually tubular florets that comprise the central part of daisylike flowerheads.

dissected in the form of narrow lobes or segments.

distichous organs arranged in two vertical rows on opposite sides of a stem.

DIVISION the simplest method of vegetatively propagating most perennials, often combined with rejuvenating the *crowns* of established plants with fibrous roots. When old plants are lifted and split, the tough center should be discarded and only well-rooted outer portions used for new plants. When perennials are rhizomatous, the young outer sections used should be about 3in (8cm) long, each showing strong growths. Divisions of plants with naturally tough, woody crowns, such as delphiniums, should include a proportion of roots and growth buds.

Natural division occurs in many bulbs and corms with the formation of *offsets*. Certain bulbs can be increased by scaling, carried out during the dormant season. Scales, separated from the parent bulb as close to the basal plate as possible, are treated with a fungicide and then mixed in a polythene bag with a damp, sterile medium such as vermiculite. The bag is then closed and stored in a warm place. When bulblets form at the base of the scale leaf, usually within 6 to 8 weeks, the scale leaves should be taken out and planted in a potting compost so that

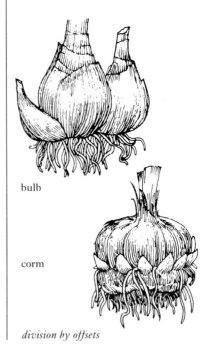

bulb

corm

division by offsets

heel cutting

the tip of the leaf is just visible. At the end of the growing season, the bulblets should be lifted and separated from the leaf scale before being replanted.

dormancy a period of inactivity in plants.

elliptic *see* below.

ericaceous shrubs, trees and other plants in the heather family, including azaleas and rhododendrons.

exserted protruding.

fall the outer *perianth segments* of an iris which project outward or downward.

family the primary category of plant classification, comprising one or more *genera*.

farina a powdery white deposit occurring on some leaves and flowers.

filiform threadlike.

floccose covered with woolly tufts or hairs.

floriferous bearing or capable of bearing many flowers.

forcing the artificial acceleration of plant growth, usually by raising the temperature.

forma a variant within a *species*, usually with only minor distinguishing characteristics.

genus (pl. genera) a category in plant classification that comprises one or more species.

germination the beginning of growth in a seed.

glabrous without hair, smooth.

gland a secretory organ such as the stinging gland, or glandular hair, of a nettle.

glaucous with a bluish-green, gray or white bloom.

globose spherical.

GRAFTING a method of propagation by artificially uniting the scion of one plant onto the (root)stock of another, so that the tissues unite and function as one plant. When the scion material is a bud, the technique is often referred to as **budding**. **Chip-budding** is a relatively simple grafting technique in which the material from the scion consists of a piece of bark and wood with a bud. This is used to replace a piece cut out of the rootstock, the chip being tied in place with polythene tape until the union is made. The rootstock is cut back to just above the bud in winter.

greensand a type of sandstone.

half-hardy a plant that in a given climatic zone needs protection against frost.

hardy a plant capable of growing outside throughout the year without any protection.

hastate arrowhead-shaped, with narrow basal *lobes* pointing outwards.

herbaceous plants that are fleshy rather than woody, and that die down at the end of the growing season.

hispid covered with stiff hairs.

hybrid the offspring of genetically dissimilar parents; a plant resulting from cross-breeding between two different *species* or *genera*.

incised a deeply and sharply cut edge, usually applied to leaves.

indumentum a thick covering of hairs or down.

inflorescence the flowering part of a plant, often made up of a number of flowers grouped together.

internode the part of a stem between two *nodes*.

lanceolate *see page 228*.

lateral a side growth that arises from a shoot or root.

LAYERING a method of *propagation* in which a shoot is induced to form roots while still attached to the parent plant. The rooted stem is then separated from the parent plant and grown on.

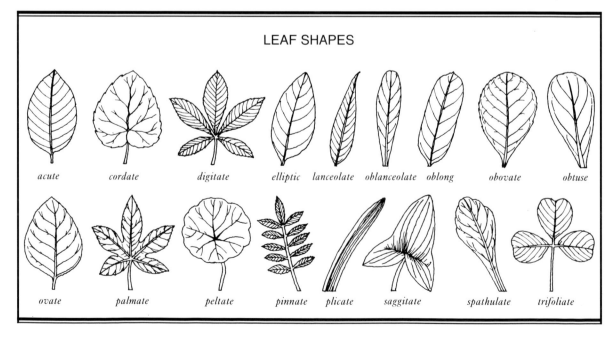

LEAF SHAPES

acute   *cordate*   *digitate*   *elliptic*   *lanceolate*   *oblanceolate*   *oblong*   *obovate*   *obtuse*

ovate   *palmate*   *peltate*   *pinnate*   *plicate*   *saggitate*   *spathulate*   *trifoliate*

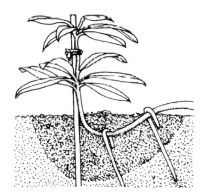

layering

Simple layering is a technique in which the parent plant is pruned the previous season to produce vigorous stems that can be lowered to ground level. In late winter or early spring a trench is dug 9–12in (23–30cm) back from the tip of a selected stem. The underside of the stem is nicked about 9in (23cm) from its tip, set in the trench and then bent to a near vertical position and tied to a supporting cane. The layer can usually be separated from the parent plant by the following autumn.

Serpentine layering is a modification used on plants with long, pliable stems. The stem is pegged down at intervals with buds that can develop into shoots left exposed.

Air layering requires the rooting medium to be taken to the shoot. In spring or summer a slit is made on the underside of a vigorous stem. Moist sphagnum moss is packed into and around the slit and covered with a plastic sleeve, which is then sealed and kept in place until roots develop. This may take 18 months or more.

linear a long narrow leaf.

lobe a rounded projection forming part of a larger structure.

micropropagation *see box, page 92.*

monocarpic a plant that flowers and fruits only once before dying, usually applied to plants that take several years to reach flowering size.

monocotyledon *see cotyledon.*

MULCHING the application to the surface of the soil of a layer of organic matter or other material as a means of conserving moisture, suppressing weeds and maintaining an even soil temperature. Although organic materials such as garden compost and bark are the most commonly used mulches, inorganic materials such as gravel and plastic can be highly effective.

mutation an induced or spontaneous genetic change that gives rise to a new form, a mutant or sport.

naturalize to establish a plant in conditions where it reproduces itself freely, as in the wild.

nectary a *gland* producing a sugar solution known as nectar.

node the point on a stem from which a leaf or leaves arise.

offset, offshoot a young plant produced asexually next to its parent, and easily detached from it.

orbicular flat, with a circular outline.

oblanceolate *see page 228.*

oblong *see page 228.*

obovate *see page 228.*

obtuse *see page 228.*

opposite describes leaves borne in pairs, on exactly opposite sides of a stem.

ovate *see page 228.*

palmate *see page 228.*

panicle a branched *inflorescence*.

pedicel the stalk on which a single flower is borne.

peltate *see page 228.*

perennial a plant that lives for more than two years.

perianth the collective term for the *calyx* and the *corolla*, particularly when they are very similar in form, as in many bulb flowers.

perianth segment one portion of a *perianth*, resembling a petal and sometimes known as a *tepal*.

petal a single part of the *corolla*.

petiole the stalk of a leaf.

phyllode a flattened leaf stalk, which functions as and resembles a leaf.

pinnate *see page 228.*

pinnule one of the lobes or divisions of a pinnate leaf.

plicate *see page 228.*

plunge to sink potted plants into a bed of soil or other material to protect them from extremes of temperature.

pot-bound describes a pot-grown plant whose roots have entirely filled its container.

propagation the methods by which plants are increased or reproduced fall into one of two main categories. Sexual propagation is by *seed* and the plants produced may differ from their parents. Vegetative propagation, for example by **cuttings**, **division**, **grafting** or **layering**, is asexual and the plants produced are genetically identical to their parents.

PRUNING the removal of stems or branches of a tree or shrub in order to alter plant shape, increase vigour or remove damaged parts. When in doubt about the advisability of pruning, the best course is to limit the operation to the removal of dead, diseased and damaged wood and weak growth. These simple steps should be the first when any pruning is undertaken.

raceme a simple (unbranched) flower cluster with several or many short-stalked flowers borne on a single stem.

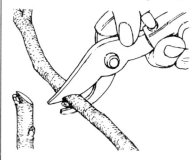

basic pruning cut

radicle the first root to appear as the seed germinates.

ray one of the florets, usually with strap-shaped petals, that together form the outer ring of daisylike flowerheads

recurved curved backward or downward.

reflexed bent sharply backward.

remontant flowering more than once in the growing season.

rhizome a rootlike, often horizontal, usually underground stem that acts as a storage organ and bears leafy shoots.

rogue a plant with characteristics that deviate from those desired. Roguing is the culling of such plants.

rootstock an underground stem from which leaf- and flower-bearing shoots and roots arise. More specifically, the part of a plant used to provide the root system for a grafted plant.

rosette a cluster of leaves radiating from approximately the same point. Also, a circular arrangement of petals.

rugose wrinkled.

saggitate see page 228.

scandent climbing by means of long stems that grow over supports or other plants, without tendrils, suckering pads or aerial roots.

scape a flower stem, usually leafless, that grows directly from the base of a plant, such as a daffodil.

scarification abrasion or chemical treatment of seeds before sowing to allow them to take up water and induce germination.

scion a shoot or bud from one plant to be grafted on to another.

SEED, GROWING FROM increasing plants from seed is in many instances a very simple procedure. The major difficulties are presented by seeds that require special conditions to germinate. When the needs of a seed are not known it is worth dividing the supply so that more than one method of sowing is used. The patient gardener is often rewarded, some seed taking three or more years to germinate.

Some seeds will not germinate readily if sown fresh. In fact it is probably the general rule rather than the exception that seed requires a period of after-ripening. However, the seeds of some plants remain viable for a relatively short period only.

The majority of plants germinate best in dark conditions. Some, however, do require light, and this is espe-cially true of plants with small seeds.

Some seed must undergo a chilling process after first having taken up water. The easiest method of **vernal-ization**, the exposure of seed to cold treatment, is to sow seed in pots in autumn and to leave them outdoors all winter. The process can be simulated by placing seed mixed with moist peat in the refrigerator, but the chilling period required depends on the plant.

To break dormancy of many seeds with a tough or fleshy covering, the technique of **stratification** is used. In autumn ripe seed is sown in pots con-taining a mixture of peat and sand and stored outdoors. During the following summer the compost needs to be kept moist. Seeds may germinate then, but in many cases germination will only occur 18 months or more after sowing.

Some plants, peonies particularly, have double dormancy. They require chilling followed by a warm period, when roots grow, but it is only after a further period of chilling that shoots will develop.

sepal one of the modified leaves forming the *calyx*.

soil a simple soil-testing kit can deter-mine the acidity or alkalinity of soil, which is measured on a pH scale of values from 0 to 14: neutral soil has a pH value of 7, acidic soil less than 7 and alkaline soil more than 7.

spadix a fleshy, spikelike *inflorescence* bearing numerous tiny stalkless flow-ers, usually surrounded by a *spathe*, as in the arum family.

spathe a large *bract* that surrounds a *spadix* or an individual flower bud.

spathulate see page 228.

species a category of plant classifica-tion, into a which a genus is divided, containing closely related individuals. It may be further subdivided into sub-species, varietas and forma.

sport a naturally occurring or induced *mutation*.

stamen the structure within the flower that bears pollen, comprising an anther and a filament (stalk).

stigma (pl. stigmata) the part of the *carpel* that receives pollen, usually at the tip of a style.

stipule a leaf or scalelike growth, usu-ally one of a pair, borne at a node or below leaf-stalk.

stolon a horizontally spreading or arching stem, usually above ground, that forms roots and new growth at the tip.

style the part of the flower bearing the *stigma*.

ssp. subspecies.

subtended situated immediately below.

sucker a shoot arising from a plant's roots or underground stem.

tap root the main, downward-grow-ing root of a plant.

tepal a segment of a *perianth* that can-not be distinguished either as a *sepal* or a petal.

tetraploid having four (instead of two) sets of chromosomes.

tomentum a feltlike covering of downy hairs.

trifoliate see page 228.

trilobed having three lobes.

tripartite consisting of three parts formed by divisions extending almost to the base.

truncate having a blunt, square end, as if cut off.

tuber a swollen, underground root or stem, used as a storage organ.

umbel a flat-topped or rounded *inflo-rescence* in which the individual flower stalks are all the same length and arise from the same point on the main stem.

undulate having a wavy or rippled appearance.

var. varietas, a naturally occurring variant of a **species**, between the rank of subspecies and forma.

whorl a group of three or more leaves or flowers arising from the same point.

INDEX

How to join The Royal Horticultural Society

If you love gardening, there are so many good reasons for joining The RHS. Members enjoy a number of valuable privileges, including:

A copy of the Society's journal, *The Garden*, every month

Privileged tickets for the Chelsea Flower Show, the Hampton Court Palace Show, shows at Malvern and Harrogate, among others

Free entry to the Society's gardens at Wisley, Rosemoor and Hyde Hall

Free entry to the monthly Westminster Flower Shows and lectures

Free advice on your gardening projects and problems from RHS experts

To join The Royal Horticultural Society write to the Membership Manager, The Royal Horticultural Society, 80 Vincent Square, London SW1P 2PE, England. Annual subscription costs US$40.

ACKNOWLEDGMENTS

The publisher thanks the following photographers and organizations for their kind permission to reproduce the photographs in this book:

1 S&O Mathews; 2 Eric Crichton; 3 S&O Mathews; 4 *left* and *right* Andrew Lawson; 4 *center* Eric Crichton; 5 *left* Andrew Lawson; 5 *center* Eric Crichton; 5 *right* Biofotos/Heather Angel; 6 S&O Mathews; 7 Andrew Lawson; 8 Eric Crichton; 9 Hugh Palmer; 10–11 Garden Picture Library/Lynne Brotchie; 13 Photos Horticultural; 15 *left* Eric Crichton; 15 *right* Hugh Palmer; 16 Hugh Palmer; 17 Andrew Lawson; 18 Royal Botanic Garden, Edinburgh/Sidney J Clarke; 19 Hugh Palmer; 21 *left* Eric Crichton; 21 *right* Photos Horticultural; 22 Garden Picture Library/J S Sira; 23 Andrew Lawson; 24 Hugh Palmer; 25 *above* Andrew Lawson; 25 *below* Photos Horticultural; 26 Andrew Lawson; 27 Photos Horticultural; 28 Eric Crichton; 29 John Glover; 30–31 Photos Horticultural; 32–33 Eric Crichton; 34 A–Z Botanical Collection; 35 The Harry Smith Collection; 37 *right* Photos Horticultural; 37 *left* Eric Crichton; 38–39 Eric Crichton; 40 Photos Horticultural; 41 *above* Eric Crichton; 41 *below* Photos Horticultural; 43 *above* Lamontagne; 43 *below* Neil Campbell-Sharp; 44 Photos Horticultural; 46 *left* Eric Crichton; 46 *right* Hugh Palmer; 47 HughPalmer; 48 Garden Picture Library/Clive Nichols; 49 Andrew Lawson; 50 Eric Crichton; 51 *right* Photos Horticultural; 51 *left* Eric Crichton; 53 S&O Mathews; 54 Photos Horticultural; 55 Andrew Lawson; 56 Christopher Brickell; 57 John Glover; 58 Lamontagne; 59 *above* Derek Gould; 59 *below* Photos Horticultural; 60 Andrew Lawson; 61 Photos Horticultural; 62 Derek Gould; 63 *above* John Glover; 63 *below* Eric Crichton; 64–65 Hugh Palmer; 67 Garden Picture Library/John Glover; 69 Clive Nichols; 71 Andrew Lawson; 72 Christopher Brickell; 73 Hugh Palmer; 74 *above* Photos Horticultural; 74 *below* Christopher Brickell; 76 *above* Christopher Brickell; 76 *below* John Fielding Slide Library; 77 Photos Horticultural; 78 Eric Crichton; 81 Andrew Lawson; 82 Eric Crichton; 83 Photos Horticultural; 84–85 Andrew Lawson; 86 S&O Mathews; 88–89 Neil Campbell-Sharp; 91 Eric Crichton; 93 Hugh Palmer; 94 Photos Horticultural; 95 Hugh Palmer; 96–101 Photos Horticultural; 102 Garden Picture Library/Marijke Heuff; 103–104 Photos Horticultural; 106 *left* Eric Crichton; 106 *right* Photos Horticultural; 107 Photos Horticultural; 108 A–Z Botanical Collection/Malcolm Richards; 109 Heather Angel/Biofotos; 110 Eric Crichton; 111 Photos Horticult-ural; 113 Andrew Lawson; 114 Photos Horticultural; 115 Eric Crichton; 117 Christopher Brickell; 118–121 Eric Crichton; 121 Hugh Palmer; 122 Photos Horticultural; 123 Clive Nichols; 125 Hugh Palmer; 127 A–Z Botanical Collection/J Malcolm Smith; 128 Clive Nichols; 130 Andrew Lawson; 131 Hugh Palmer; 132 Eric Crichton; 134–135 Hugh Palmer; 137–138 Andrw Lawson; 139 Photos Horticultural; 140 Christopher Grey-Wilson; 141 Clive Nichols; 143–144 Photos Horticultural; 146 Hugh Palmer; 147 Eric Crichton; 148 Christopher Brickell; 149 Photos Horticultural; 150 Andrew Lawson; 151 Eric Crichton; 152 *left* The Harry Smith Collection; 152 *right* Andrew Lawson; 153 Photos Horticultural; 154 Neil Campbell-Sharp; 156 S&O Mathews; 157 Royal Botanical Garden, Edinburgh/Sidney J Clarke; 159 Eric Crichton; 160 The Harry Smith Collection; 161-162 Photos Horticultural; 163 A–Z Botanical Collection; 164–165 Andrew Lawson; 167 Eric Crichton; 168 The Alpine Garden Society/Mike Ireland; 169 Photos Horticultural; 171 The Alpine Garden Society/Mike Ireland; 173 Photos Horticultural; 175 Eric Crichton; 177 Photos Horticultural; 179 Photos Horticultural; 180–181 Harry Smith Collection; 182–183 Clive Nichols; 185–186 Eric Crichton; 187 Photos Horticultural; 189 Clive Nichols; 190 Eric Crichton; 191–193 Andrew Lawson; 194 Eric Crichton; 196 *above* Garden Picture Library/Didier Willery; 196 *below* Andrew Lawson; 197 Derek Gould; 199 Garden Picture Library/Steve Wooster; 200 Andrew Lawson; 201 Eric Crichton; 202 Eric Crichton; 204–205 Andrew Lawson; 206 Christopher Brickell; 208 *left* Royal Botanical Garden, Edinburgh/Sidney J Clarke; 208 *right* The Harry Smith Collection; 209 Photos Horticultural; 210 A–Z Botanical Collection/Andrew Brown; 211 A–Z Botanical Collection; 212 Christopher Brickell; 214 Oxford Scientific Film/Deni Brown; 215 S&O Mathews; 216 *above* Andrew Lawson; 216 *below* A–Z Botanical/Geof Kidd; 217 John Glover; 218 Eric Crichton; 219 Christopher Brickell; 220–221 Photos Horticultural.